Recovering Women's Voices

Recovering Women's Voices: Islam, Citizenship, and Patriarchy in Egypt

BY

REHAM ELMORALLY

American University in Cairo, Egypt

United Kingdom – North America – Japan – India – Malaysia – China

Emerald Publishing Limited
Emerald Publishing, Floor 5, Northspring, 21-23 Wellington Street, Leeds LS1 4DL.

First edition 2024

Copyright © 2024 Reham ElMorally.
Published under exclusive licence by Emerald Publishing Limited.

Reprints and permissions service
Contact: www.copyright.com

No part of this book may be reproduced, stored in a retrieval system, transmitted in any form or by any means electronic, mechanical, photocopying, recording or otherwise without either the prior written permission of the publisher or a licence permitting restricted copying issued in the UK by The Copyright Licensing Agency and in the USA by The Copyright Clearance Center. Any opinions expressed in the chapters are those of the authors. Whilst Emerald makes every effort to ensure the quality and accuracy of its content, Emerald makes no representation implied or otherwise, as to the chapters' suitability and application and disclaims any warranties, express or implied, to their use.

British Library Cataloguing in Publication Data
A catalogue record for this book is available from the British Library

ISBN: 978-1-83608-249-1 (Print)
ISBN: 978-1-83608-248-4 (Online)
ISBN: 978-1-83608-250-7 (Epub)

INVESTOR IN PEOPLE

Contents

Preface	ix
Acknowledgements	xi

Introduction 1
1. Veils of Power: Gender, Citizenship, and the Shadows of Patriarchy in Egypt 4

Chapter 1 History of the Arab Republic of Egypt 9
1. From Province to Kingdom to Republic – A Chronology 9
2. Post-independence Egypt 13
3. Personal Authoritarian Rule – The Machiavellian State 14
4. Authoritarianism in Egypt 15
   4.1. Pan-Arabism, Pan-Islamism, and Feminism – Gamal Abdel Nasser 16
   4.2. Secularisation and Resacralisation – Anwar Sadat 19
   4.3. Suppressing and Oppressing the Opposition – Hosni Mubarak 24
5. Civil Societies in Egypt – What are They? 27
6. The Radicalisation of Political Islam in Egypt – The Case of the MB 30

Chapter 2 Feminism, Identity, and the Status of Women in Egypt (19th–20th Century) 37
1. A Brief Overview of Feminist Activism in Egypt 43
2. The First Feminists in Egypt 44
   2.1. The First Feminist Wave: Public Education and Political Representation 47
   2.2. The Second Feminist Wave: Constitutional and Legal Rights 53
   2.3. The Third Feminist Wave: State Feminism and Civil Society 56

3. The Female Identity: Dehumanisation as an Explanation
for Women's Inferiority 60
   3.1. Rationalising the Dehumanisation of Women Using
   Religion 65

Chapter 3   Codifying the Dehumanisation of Egyptian Women 73
1. State-sponsored Feminism and the Status of Egyptian
Women 73
2. The State and the Crackdown on Women's Movements 80
3. Codifying the Dehumanisation of Egyptian Women 82
4. Conceptual Framework 95
   4.1. Conceptual Diagram and Analytical Elements 97

Chapter 4   Methodology, Methods, and Tools 105
1. Research Methodology: Qualitative Interpretivism/The
Interpretivist Paradigm 105
2. Rationalising the Qualitative Methodology 106
3. Research Method: Auto-ethnography 106
4. Textual Analysis and Selection of Legal and Policy
Documents 112
5. Research Tool: Semi-structured Interviews 115
6. Conducting Culturally Appropriate and Sensitive Research 117

**Chapter 5   The Role of Religion and Class in Setting
Patriarchal Bargains** 123
1. Growing Up in Classes 125
2. Islam: A Culture and a Religion 130
3. Education and Son Preference 142
4. Patriarchal Attitudes and Women's Subordination 146

**Chapter 6   The Role of the Hijab in Navigating the
Patriarchal Bargain in Urban and Rural Egypt** 151
1. Contextualising the Hijab in Contemporary Egypt:
What Does it Represent? 154
2. Rationalising the Dehumanisation of Women Using
Religion in Contemporary Egypt 161
3. Women's Active Collusion in the Reproduction of Their
Own Subordination 164
4. Navigating Patriarchal Bargains: The Strategic Use of
the Hijab in Urban/Rural Areas 168
   4.1. 'Yes, the Hijab Protects ME' 175
   4.2. 'Yes, the Hijab Protects HER' 179

Chapter 7 Sufi Islam Versus Sunni Islam: The Role of Religious Interpretation on Women's Roles and Status in Society   **183**
1. Brief History of Siwa *186*
2. Navigating Patriarchal Bargains: The Strategic Use of the Hijab in Siwa *191*
3. Codifying the Status of Siwian Women *196*

Chapter 8   Conclusion   **207**
1. Summary of Findings *207*
2. Discussion *211*
3. Conclusion *217*

Bibliography *219*

Preface

Gender inequality can be attributed to a myriad of causes. This book seeks to unpack the gender disparity in Egypt, which ranks 129th on the Gender Equality Index (El Feki et al., 2017). This book examines a specific aspect of inequality observed in Egypt: women as second-class citizens. Accordingly, this book sets out to understand how the patriarchal system in Egypt prevented women from realising their strategic gender interests, and by extension perpetuating their second-class citizenship. This book also unpacks how the patriarchal system in Egypt exploited and manipulated women, which served to maintain male domination and preserve the status quo. Conceptually, this book makes use of Sylvia Walby's *Six Structures of Patriarchy* in the Egyptian context to gain a better understanding of how the patriarchal system created a 'system of social structures and practices in which men dominate, oppress and exploit women' (Walby, 1990, p. 20). To do this, secondary data were critically approached to re-examine feminist activism from the perspective of movements to attain and realise women's strategic gender interests. The book recognised the essential role of Islam in cultural understandings, thus the book systematically investigated the role of religion and religious interpretation in solidifying women's subordination. This recognition was significant as personal status laws in Egypt, which are meant to protect women's rights, must adhere to the rules of Sharia Islam, making it most relevant to the investigation of how women's subordination was institutionalised. The book also collected primary data, using the Hijab as a pre-identified measure to sensitively interview 100 ordinary citizens (women $N=51$, men $N=49$), who were randomly selected and volunteered their time, from five different locations in Egypt, and examined how women navigate the patriarchal bargain which is universal throughout Egypt.

The data triangulation served to confirm a positive relationship between women's strategic gender interests and citizenship status by highlighting that the findings of the secondary sources, such as legal texts and written documents, are consistent with the collected primary testimonies from ordinary citizens. Findings suggest that if women are prevented from realising their strategic gender interests, they lack the agency to challenge their citizenship exclusion. Further, if women attained strategic gender interests, then they would have the agency and right to full citizenship status and benefits. The reason women are denied strategic gender interests in Egypt is the institutionalisation of the dehumanisation of women, which reproduces women's social inferiority. Simultaneously, the Sunni interpretation of Islam served to legitimise women's *less than human* status and rationalise

x Preface

their secondary status, evidence of which can be seen in both cultural understandings and the legal framework. Secondary data revealed that these processes were established by the patriarchal system to maintain the patriarchal bargain where women must exchange their agency and autonomy for safety from male violence and financial security. In other words, the patriarchal system sets up the bargain in a way where noncompliance with the concrete rules is socially and institutionally sanctioned, forcing women into a position where they internalise their inferiority and reproduce their subordination. The data suggest that the Hijab is strategically used by women in urban and rural areas of Egypt to navigate the patriarchal bargain; however, the results did not apply to indigenous women. The patriarchal manifestations in urban/rural communities and the indigenous community are attributed to the numerous differences, including the Sufi interpretation of Islam espoused in the Siwian indigenous culture.

The significance and purpose of this book are to update and advance the study of Egyptian women's citizenship status and demonstrate the strategies Egyptian women used to navigate the patriarchal bargains constraining the actualisation and realisation of their strategic gender interests. The findings of this study contribute to existing knowledge and produce new empirical data about the patriarchal structures and bargains present in Egypt today, and how Egyptian women navigate these structures to challenge their social inferiority and second-class citizenship status.

Acknowledgements

To my esteemed mentors, Dr Sarah Cardey and Dr Joanne Davies, my journey under your guidance has been transformative. Your unwavering support and insightful critiques have pushed me to explore realms beyond my imagination, fostering my growth academically and personally. You've been my pillar, providing a safe space for intellectual curiosity and emotional resilience through every high and low.

I want to express my profound gratitude to my editor Daniel Ridge for his foundational expertise and steadfast support. His keen insights and encouragement greatly enhanced this work, making the journey both collaborative and enriching.

To the roots of my being, my parents Mohamed ElMorally and Azza Abou El Ezz, your love and sacrifices have sculpted the essence of my being. Mami, your encouragement opened the world of words to me, laying the foundation of my academic pursuit. Papi, you've been the guiding light, instilling in me the values of logic, critical thinking, and the endless pursuit of knowledge. Together, you've been my sanctuary, my unwavering support system.

My sisters, Ingy and Nouran, your boundless love and support have made the distance between us inconsequential. Your presence has been a constant reminder of strength and unity. To my best friends, Ola Emad and Nour Badrawi, your faith in me has been the wind beneath my wings, reminding me of the power of perseverance and the strength of our bond.

Last, but certainly not least, I would like to express my indebtedness to Dr Samuel Poskitt, Dr Patrick Hassan, Annalyse Mosekland, and Tamisan Latherow, for your generosity of spirit and time. Your friendship, collegiality, and support are what allowed this book to be completed on time. You all have my everlasting respect, admiration, and appreciation.

This acknowledgement is a testament to the collective support and love I've received. Thank you for being my compass, my inspiration, and my strength.

Introduction

In Egypt, women are perceived as second-class citizens and are considered socio-culturally inferior to men (Abbott & Teti, 2017; Chang, 2018; Farouk, 2021; Moghadam, 2004; Rama, 2013). This male domination and women's socio-cultural inferiority are attributed to different primary causes depending on the theoretical perspective adopted. When Islam came to Egypt in 640, it was perceived as a progressive religion which asserts the equal status of both women and men, particularly in terms of obligations and spiritual values (Shaikh, 2009, p. 787). However, due to male-dominant interpretations of the Qur'an and Sharia 'a discourse of competing equalities [arose]: men and women are granted rights by traditional approaches to the Sharia, but men have generally been granted their rights and women have not been allowed theirs' (Shaikh, 2009, p. 787). Yet, there are also verses in the Qur'an which do overtly state that men have a higher value than women, for instance, men inherit twice as much as women, and the legal testimony of men is worth twice as much as a woman's (Adang, 2002; Al-Hakim, 2002; Ibn 'Arabi, 1911, p. 89). The religious scholars of Al-Azhar – the institution responsible for Islamic jurisprudence, scripture interpretation, and the source of religious authority in Egypt – referred to in Arabic as *Ulama* [religious jurist/scholar recognised by the State and accredited by Al-Azhar] and/or *Imams*, 'interpreted Islam to emphasise women's second-class status, while downplaying the message of gender equality. Practices such as female veiling and seclusion became sacrosanct, even though the Qur'an does not require them' (Chang, 2018).

Before the British colonisation of Egypt in 1882, Youssef Rapoport in his book *Marriage, Money and Divorce in Medieval Islamic Society,* highlighted that the social norm of 13th- and 14th-century Muslim women in Egypt was to work as peddlers, hairdressers, midwives, and in the textile industry. Rapoport (2005) said, 'Contrary to the ideas commonly prevailing in Europe, a large portion of the votaries consisted of ladies, who were walking to and from without the slightest restraints, conversing with each other, and mingling freely among the men' (p. 246). What changed in the Egyptian society to transform women's social roles and freedoms? Chang (2018) argued that French and British colonisation 'decimated the cottage industries that had employed women in large numbers', and continued to state, that

> only men were allowed to work in factories that used steam power and to receive training on advanced machinery (…)[which] pushed society in a conservative direction. The customs of veiling and

seclusion were practised more widely, and the codification of family laws stamped out rights that women had enjoyed earlier.

She concluded that due to the simultaneous industrialisation of Egypt and Western colonisation processes 'the vibrant and diverse tradition of women's participation in public life was erased. People assumed that women had always lived under severe constraints (...) [because] Egyptian society is often reflexively conservative' (Chang, 2018).

This book focusses on women's inferiority and second-class citizenship in Egypt from the perspective of *strategic gender interests*. Maxine Molyneux (1985) coined the term *strategic gender interests* to refer to women's emancipation efforts in terms of 'the abolition of the sexual division of labour, the alleviation of the burden of domestic labour and childcare, the removal of institutionalised forms of discrimination, the attainment of political equality, the establishment of freedom of choice over childbearing, and the adoption of adequate measures against male violence and control over women' (p. 233), which are the cornerstones to achieving women's equal status. Respectively, Molyneux (1985) also coined the term *practical gender interests,* to refer to

> interests [which] are given inductively and arise from the concrete conditions of women's positioning within the gender division ... practical interests are usually a response to an immediate perceived need, and they do not generally entail a strategic goal such as women's emancipation or gender equality. (p. 233)

Similarly, Anne-Marie Goetz (1995) expanded on Molyneux's definition, adding that practical gender interests 'respond to immediate, situationally specific needs and which may not challenge prevailing forms of gender subordination' (p. 7), that is, responses to women's practical needs aimed at improving their quality of life, yet do not challenge the existing power imbalances or women's subordination. Goetz (1995) also elaborated on the definition of strategic gender interests, arguing that they 'entail transformative goals such as women's emancipation and gender equality', adding that because strategic interests cannot be assumed, it 'makes it difficult for feminist policy analysis to establish a set of values for evaluating policy measures' (p. 7). Additionally, Goetz stressed the significant role the State plays in promoting/suppressing women's strategic gender interests, explaining that 'the state is still a critical arena for the promotion of women's interests' as the state underwrites the 'asymmetrical distribution of resources and values between women and men and ... improving the quality of the accountability of public institutions to their female constituencies' (Goetz, 1995, p. 1).

Goetz (1995) observed that in patriarchal systems of Bangladesh, Morocco, and Mali, *inter alia*, the 'states have both assumed and construed women's identity for public policy as being conditioned by their social relationships as dependants of men and have made them the objects of family welfare policy' (p. 4). She criticised the patriarchal system for setting 'policies for women [that do] not to provide women with institutional survival bases – such as employment or asset ownership rights – which might be alternatives to dependence on men', that is, criticising the development of policies that meet the practical interests of women, but 'at best, such policies improve women's survival at the margins; at worst, they can reinforce the traditional gender ideologies which contribute to women's disadvantaged position in their efforts to mobilise physical and human capital for their self-development' (Goetz, 1995, p. 4).

In essence, Goetz unpacked how the pursuit of practical interests by a state benefits women's overall welfare. However, as practical interests do not challenge the existing gender structures, women's subordination will continue to be reproduced and perpetuated and the patriarchal system will prevail, preventing women from realising their strategic interests. Similarly, Caroline Moser (1993) argued that 'the state in different political contexts effectively controls women's strategic gender needs through family policy relating to domestic violence, reproductive rights, legal status and welfare policy' (p. 2), an issue which is unpacked in the context of Egypt in Chapter 2.

Throughout this book, the term strategic gender interests thereby refers to efforts and needs required to emancipate women and challenge women's subordination to men, as well as practical gender interests – the needs required to overcome the immediate and situationally specific shortcomings, without challenging the existing gender roles or cultural norms. Moreover, practical gender interests are exploited by the patriarchal system to subjugate women via patriarchal bargains and maintain male domination and control. Therefore, throughout this book, practical gender interests are used to refer to the women's responses to immediate needs, while strategic gender interests are reforms at the structural level which challenge women's subordination. Depending on the theoretical school of thought, patriarchal systems can be defined in a myriad of ways. For instance, from a Marxist Feminist perspective, patriarchal system insinuates 'men's domination over women is a by-product of capital's domination over labour' (Walby, 1990, p. 4). From a radical feminist perspective, men's domination over women is 'not a by-product of capitalism' but consider male violence and domination over women's bodies and sexuality to be the root cause of women's inferiority (Walby, 1990, p. 3). This book uses the term patriarchal system more holistically to refer to 'Different aspects of women's subordination ... to take account of the different gender inequality over time' (Walby, 1990, p. 5). More specifically, Sylvia Walby's (1990) definition of the patriarchal system as a 'system of social structures and practices in which men dominate, oppress and exploit women' (p. 20) is adopted for this project and is used to refer to the systemic suppression of women's equal access, status, opportunities, and rights (strategic gender interests) by the patriarchal socio-political and cultural systems. Furthermore, the term 'patriarchal bargain', a term coined by Deniz Kandiyoti (1998) is used in this book to entail the strategies women living in patriarchal systems employ to gain a greater degree of autonomy and security within the 'concrete constraints ... [that] influence both the potential for and specific forms of women's active or passive resistance in the face of their oppression' (p. 275), that is, efforts to gain Egyptian women strategic gender interests.

1. Veils of Power: Gender, Citizenship, and the Shadows of Patriarchy in Egypt

This book sets out to understand how the patriarchal system in Egypt prevented women from realising their strategic gender interests and, by extension, perpetuating their second-class citizenship. This book also unpacks how the patriarchal system in Egypt focussed on the development of women's practical gender interests, which improved women's welfare but did not challenge women's subordination or advance their strategic needs. Consequentially, the sex-based power structure in Egypt was reproduced and the patriarchal system was maintained. The book considers how the perception of women as inferior is a social construct perpetuated and reproduced by the patriarchal system to consolidate and normalise women's second-class citizenship. This is evidenced by the systematic patriarchal suppression of women's strategic gender interests throughout Egypt's history, starting from the 1919 revolution (discussed in Chapter 1).

The book delineated three pivotal objectives, each accompanied by a series of research questions designed to guide the investigation. The *first objective* was to identify the historical and political instances that have established women's second-class citizenship in Egypt. This inquiry was structured around several critical questions: What role has the State played in either promoting or suppressing the political and social status of Egyptian women? To what extent have political Islam, including Islamist opposition and religious institutions like Al-Azhar, influenced the promotion or suppression of women's strategic gender interests? Furthermore, the book is aimed to understand the rationalisations behind Egyptian women's inferiority and their exclusion from full citizenship rights, offering a comprehensive overview of the systemic challenges faced by women in Egypt.

This was achieved by reframing and re-examining the scholarship around women's movements in Egypt and approaching them as efforts to actualise strategic gender interests for Egyptian women. First Chapter 1 sets the scene by providing a historical account of feminist waves and activism and reviewing how the State operationalised the patriarchal system to suppress feminist demands for strategic gender interests. Second, the chapter introduces the process of dehumanisation as a possible explanation of how women's second-class citizenship and women's inferiority were established.

The *second objective* of the book was to identify and analyse the intersectionality of the patriarchal system and Islam in reproducing women's inferior identities and identifying patriarchal bargains. This analysis was driven by questions aimed at unpacking the complex dynamics at play: What role has political Islam played in the resurgence of traditional conservative practices in Egypt, such as the Hijab, and what consequences has this had on women's status and roles in Egyptian society? Additionally, the book explored the construction of the status of Egyptian women by political Islam and examined to what extent religion informs societal perceptions of women and the rights and liberties protected by the legal framework.

To achieve this, Articles from Egypt's Constitution, Penal Code, and personal status code about women's strategic gender interests were selected and analysed to better outline the extent to which they contributed to the institutionalisation of women's inferiority and second class. This necessitated an unpacking of how religion intersects with politics, as personal status laws are based on the principles of Sharia Islam and therefore required a distinction to be drawn over what is a religious mandate and what is cultural understanding/interpretation.

The first two objectives were designed to provide an analytical account of the different instances where women's strategic gender interests were suppressed and the patriarchal system was prevailed. The purpose of the first two objectives was to use secondary data to re-examine literature and policy documents using strategic gender interests as the analytical lens. The third objective was to use the findings and conclusions of the first two objectives to approach the qualitative data.

The *third objective* was to identify and analyse, through the role of the Hijab, how women negotiate social power in Egypt. This objective was pursued through questions that sought to uncover the strategies employed by women to navigate the patriarchal structures of society: What did the data reveal about the patriarchal bargains women employ in Egypt to gain greater security and autonomy? What is the role of the Hijab in signalling adherence to the rules of the patriarchal system? And, considering that personal status laws are based on the Sharia of Islam, what role does religious interpretation play in challenging or perpetuating patriarchal structures? Through these focussed inquiries, the book endeavours to shed light on the nuanced ways in which women in Egypt navigate and negotiate their identities and social power within a deeply entrenched patriarchal system.

The third objective was sought to collect data about the patriarchal bargains in Egypt and gain insights into what strategies women employed to challenge their citizenship exclusion and realise their strategic gender interests. The data collection was designed to gain insights into what strategies women employ to navigate the patriarchal system of Egypt, which forced them to 'often adhere as far and as long as they possibly can to rules (…) that result in their active collusion in the reproduction of their own subordination' (Kandiyoti, 1988, p. 289). This was analysed in relation to women's 'ability to exercise agency [afforded through the actualisation of strategic gender interests] on their own behalf, including the agency needed to challenge their [citizenship] exclusion' (Kabeer, 2006, p. 100). Similar to Sylvia Walby (1990), this book does not distinguish between 'necessary and contingent structures of social system … since patriarchy is an open social system which can take a variety of forms' (p. 19). Using the *Hijab* as a proxy measure, that is, an indirect measure to collect information about patriarchal bargains and perceptions of women's status and role in society sensitively, 100 ordinary citizens (women $N=51$, men $N=49$), who were randomly selected and volunteered their time, from 5 different locations were interviewed (see Chapter 3 for full methodological approach). It was significant to see how women perceive themselves and how men perceive women to gain a better understanding of why and how women's strategic gender interests have been curtailed by the patriarchal system. As Ruxton (2020) expressed, 'if men are still the prime beneficiaries of gender inequality, then dismantling male privilege is, at least in part, men's work'. Therefore, as most men, willingly or unwillingly, have benefitted from the patriarchal system, it became essential to include men's voices to better understand how women and men can work together to challenge the patriarchal system in Egypt. In other words, if the power resides with 50% of the society, and that 50% do not see an issue with the system they are in, then they are deemed to perpetuate and reproduce it. Effectively, it was rational to interview men and women to gain insights into how the patriarchal system in Egypt succeeded in suppressing women's efforts to realise their strategic gender interests. Furthermore, this book highlights how men's understandings of women's status and rights have historically, and in contemporary Egypt, been curtailed using political Islam as an ideology to justify the subjugation of women. According to Are Knudsen (2003), the problem of trying to define political Islam is ever-changing 'many authors dispense with a definition altogether, leaving it to the reader to infer the many meanings of political Islam', however, in this book, the term is used to denote 'Islam used to a political end' (p. 2).

The significance and purpose of this book are to update and advance the study of Egyptian women's citizenship status and demonstrate the strategies Egyptian women used to navigate the patriarchal system constraining the realisation of their strategic gender interests. To address the objectives, the project was sought to make sense of how and why Egyptian women hold a secondary citizenship status and how the patriarchal system in Egypt prevented women from achieving their strategic gender interests. This involved a re-examination of existing literature about women's and feminist movements in Egypt through the perspective of strategic gender interests (objective 1). It also involved the critical analysis of primary interview data and secondary policy papers and legal texts to unpack the extent to which religion intersects with patriarchal structures to socially perpetuate women's second-class citizenship and the discourse of women's inferiority (objective 2). Finally, 100 ordinary citizens (women $N=51$, men $N=49$), who were randomly selected and volunteered their time, from 5 different geographical and environmental communities in Egypt to investigate the types of patriarchal bargains identified by Egyptian women and what they have done to challenge/perpetuate their inferiority and second-class citizenship (objective 3). The data triangulation, therefore, was served to provide a reliable account using three data sources to understand the relationship between women's strategic gender interests and second-class citizenship.

This book contributes to existing knowledge by producing new empirical data about the patriarchal structures and bargains present in Egypt today, and how Egyptian women navigated these structures to challenge their social inferiority and second-class citizenship status. The book also demonstrates how reframing historical and political events through a strategic gender interests' perspective could provide an alternative reading to these events and reveal dimensions of analysis previously unnoticed. Additionally, the new primary data are valuable given the difficult political context of present-day Egypt and the difficulties of accessing certain communities. Cumulatively, this book fills a gap in the literature and contributes to a new updated study of gender, citizenship, and politics in Egypt. The wider benefit of this book is that it includes local accounts from historically marginalised populations, such as the minority-ethnic Amazigh indigenous population of the Siwa oasis, providing valuable insights into this under-researched community.

Chapter 1

History of the Arab Republic of Egypt

1. From Province to Kingdom to Republic – A Chronology

Egypt's leadership changed multiple times over the 18th till the 20th centuries. From 1517 to 1798, Egypt was a province of the Ottoman Empire (Hess, 1973). From 1798 to 1801, Egypt was conquered by Napoleon Bonaparte and became a French colony (Sigler, 2010). However, this short-lived occupation and Napoleon's unsuccessful attempts to maintain control over Egypt and subdue social outrage led to the French expulsion, and Egypt was once again a province of the Ottoman Empire (Reinach, 1882). Shortly after the expulsion of the French forces, an Ottoman military commander in chief of Egyptian origin named Mohamed Ali Pasha was assigned conservatorship over Egypt from 1805 and until his death in 1848 (Fahmy, 1998). After the death of Mohamed Ali Pasha, the era of the *Khedivates of Egypt* commenced and lasted until the beginning of the World War I in 1914. However, from 1882 till 1914, Egypt was a *de facto* and *de jure* colony ruled by British forces as a 'veiled protectorate', that is, British mandate spearheaded by diplomat Evelyn Baring, First Early of Cromer, who believed that Egyptians need to be mandated until they are taught self-governance (Onley, 2005, p. 35).

World War I marked a historical shift and a radical transformation of Egyptian socio-economic and political course. The end of the war in 1918 left Egypt in economic and political turmoil, ultimately leading to nationalist movements for independence (Ramdani, 2016). Inflation, unemployment, public dissatisfaction, the increased social gap, and above all, the British opposition and rejection of providing a platform for Nationalist opposition leaders Saad Zaghloul, Ali Sharawi, Abd el Fahim, and others from *Hizb al Umma* [the People's Party], to stand in the Paris Peace Conference and advocate for Egypt's independence, culminated to an independence revolution in 1919 (Ramdani, 2016). The 1919 revolution led to multiple events ensuing, ranging from public disorder, to student marches and sit-ins, to the political organisation of Egypt's social classes, fuelled by anti-colonial sentiment and rage over the exile of Zaghloul to Malta by the British high commissioner (Ramdani, 2016). This culminated to Britain's loss of control over Egypt and their subsequent decision declared limited independence for Egypt in 1922, which ended its protectorate status. Following the 'fall' of the British, Ahmed Fouad I, Hussein Kamel's half-brother, declared himself the first Sultan

---

Recovering Women's Voices: Islam, Citizenship, and Patriarchy in Egypt, 9–36
Copyright © 2024 by Reham ElMorally
Published under exclusive licence by Emerald Publishing Limited
doi:10.1108/978-1-83608-248-420241002

and King of Egypt and ruled the newly independent *Kingdom of Egypt* from 1922 to 1936 (Tikkanen, 2014). He was succeeded by his son, King Farouk I in 1936, under whose reign Egypt became a member of the League of Nations, signed the *Anglo-Egyptian Treaty* acknowledging the sovereign status of Egypt, and proclaimed the allowance of British troops in Egypt to protect British and French strategic interest in the Suez Canal (Morsy, 1984). This lasted until King Farouk had to forcefully abdicate his position following the Egyptian revolution in 1952. King Farouk's son, Ahmed Fouad II, succeeded him from 1952 until the abolishment of the Monarchy (Mohamed Ali dynasty) in Egypt and the establishment of the Arab Republic of Egypt in 1953 declared by the *Free Officers* (Gordon, 2016).

Two members of the *Free Officers* were selected to be the first presidents of the Republic, Mohamed Naguib and Gamal Abdel Nasser (Awan, 2017, p. 106). Mohamed Naguib ruled Egypt as the first president from 1953 to 1954. Naguib's views collided with Nasser's as he wanted to open up the presidency for a civilian president to be elected advocating that the military should not be involved in municipal politics (Moore, 1974). Nasser accused him of treason, arguing that abdicating power to civilian old-time politicians is counterrevolutionary as their loyalty still resonates with the British colonisers, and placed Naguib under house arrest (McKenna, 2018). Nasser, the second president of Egypt, assumed power in 1954, followed by a formal election in 1956 that legitimised his position (John, 2021). His popularity grew both in Egypt and in the Arab world by virtue of his Pan-Arabist visions (Awan, 2017). Under his reign, Egypt signed *Al-Gala'a Treaty* (The Evacuation treat), which commanded that all British troop members, soldiers, and commanding officers are to leave Egypt and additionally established the right to collective defence for Arab nations should a foreign aggressor violated the sovereignty of a member of The Arab League (Owen, 1989, p. 364).

In return, the United States (USA) and Britain agreed to provide $70 million in aid to Egypt to assist in the construction of the Aswan Dam. John Foster Dulles, then the US secretary of State, withdrew the offer in 1955, thinking the project would collapse without US aid (Onion et al., 2009). Consequentially, in 1956, Nasser turned to the Soviet Union for aid and arms and nationalised the Suez Canal, triggering the Suez Canal Crisis and the *Tripartite Aggression* – an attack orchestrated by Great Britain, France, and Israel on Egypt under the claim they were protecting the Suez Canal – which ended with the intervention of former US President Eisenhower who imposed sanctions on the colluding states and organised a United Nations Emergency Force to force a ceasefire and evacuated Egypt (Tal, 2009, p. 190). One could argue that Eisenhower's support to Nasser was not entirely because of his pacifistic inclinations but rather in self-interest and fear that the nonaligned Egypt (Singh, 1981, p. 115) would become a client state of the former Union of Soviet Socialist Republics (USSR), thus shifting the power dynamics of the Cold War. Nasser viewed this comparative advantage to extend support to colonised Arab nations, like Algeria, to gain independence from their respective colonial and imperial powers (Paul et al., 2013, p. 77). His Pan-Arabist aspirations culminated in 1958 when he declared the unity of Egypt and Syria as the United Arab Republic (UAR) (dissolved 1962). Although that unity was short-lived, Nasser viewed it as a minor setback in his endeavour to unite the Arab world and create a powerful coalition similar to the European Union (Mansfield, 1971). In 1962 he started undertaking major political and economic changes that oriented Egypt towards a socialist state by establishing the Arab Socialist Union (ASU) with the ambition 'to thwart class conflict, to act as a counterweight to the military, and to mobilise the previously disenfranchised elements of society' (Ryan, 2001, p. 4).

Among many of his reformative endeavours to modernise Egypt and strive for a more egalitarian society, he redistributed land, opened up the public sector, nationalised all private banks, insurance companies, and heavy and basic industries, raised minimum wages, instigated a progressive taxation system, and reserved 50% of parliamentary membership to farmers and manual labourers (Waterbury, 1983). In 1967, Israel launched an allegedly pre-emptive strike against Egypt destroying its air force, crippling the Egyptian military, and giving way for the Sinai Peninsula to be invaded and occupied. In the aftermath, Israel had claimed Sinai, the Golan Heights, and the West Bank as its territory. Following this immense loss, Nasser resigned as president, only to be reinstated shortly after by popular demand. In 1968, he launched his unsuccessful attempt, the War of Attrition, in hopes to regain the occupied territory (Bowen, 2017). In 1970, Nasser died of a heart attack (Ahmed, 2010), which urban myths state was the result of heart break over the 1967 loss.

Egypt's third president, Anwar Sadat, Nasser's Vice President for his two terms in power, succeeded Nasser after the unexpected death left Egypt leaderless (MacManus, 2007). Sadat's presidency started with extreme unpopularity to the point that his portrait hung alongside Nasser in all government buildings (Hinnenbush, 1081, pp. 442–443). He resorted to using religion as a veil to gain popularity by amending the constitution and situating Islam as the national religion (Brownlee, 2011, p. 643). Additionally, he released members of the Muslim Brotherhood (MB), who had been imprisoned and forced to go underground under Nasser's rule, to counterbalance the Naaserites in Egypt and gain him some popularity (Guirguis, 2012, p. 199), a strategy that would later prove fatal to him. Sadat's political and economic policies reflected the international atmosphere of the Cold War, whereby he attempted to reorient Egypt from the Eastern camp to the Western camp (Amin, 1982, p. 303; Weinbaum, 1985, p. 212). He diverged from socialism by reinstituting a multiparty political system under the umbrella of the *Corrective Revolution*. In 1973, Sadat orchestrated an attack on Israel, known as the *Yom Kippur War*, in cooperation with Syria and other Arab states. The perceived Arab success ended with the United Nations Security Council passing ceasefire Resolutions 338 and 339, followed by Resolution 344, *Sinai Separation of Forces Agreement,* dictating immediate withdrawal of Israeli forces from the occupied territory (UNSCR, Res. 344, 1973). The 1973 war gained Sadat popularity and social approval in Egypt. He followed that success by the *Infitah* policy (Open Door Economic Policy), which replaced the USSR as the aid-funder of Egypt with the USA and adopted a capitalist economic and liberal political model, which later proved to have grave social and economic consequences (Baker, 1981, p. 379).

In the aftermath of the War and the new Open Door policy, Sadat initiated peace discussions with Israel's President Menachem Begin and US former

President Jimmy Carter. The discussions ended with the signing of the Camp David Accords in 1978, also known as *A Framework for Peace in the Middle East* (Steding, 2014). The Accords won Sadat the Nobel Peace Prize in the same year (Abdelhadi, 2006). The Accord also paved the way for the Egypt–Israel Peace Treaty of 1979, which included, among other things, a clause that Egypt must officially recognise Israel as a State (Glass, 2019). The peace treaty left Egypt alienated and ostracised from its Arab neighbours and its membership suspended from the Arab League (Cohen & Azar, 1981, p. 110). Sadat grew unpopular by Egyptians and the peak of his unpopularity led to *Al Azhar* and the Coptic Churches' condemnation of Sadat (Moustafa, 2000). This eventually led to his assassination by an Islamist military member Lieutenant Khalis Islambouli, who deemed him a traitor of Islam and the Arab unity (Fetouri, 2018).

Sadat's assassination left Egypt, once more, without a leader. Mohamed Hosni Mubarak, Sadat's Vice President, was thus appointed to the position of Egypt's fourth president (Paciello, 2011, pp. 1–2). Mubarak is the second longest ruler of Egypt, after Mohamed Ali Pasha, whose reign lasted for almost 30 years. After Mubarak's appointment, he realised the major issues Egypt was facing, including the economy's fast deterioration, Egypt's fragile relations with its neighbours, and the Nile–Basin water crisis (Lofgren, 1993, p. 414). First on his agenda was addressing public distress and poverty. In 1977, under Sadat, Bread Riots erupted in most major cities of Egypt, where demonstrators were objecting the 'unbearable' living standards that were believed to have resulted from the *Infitah* (CBS News, 2011). In 1980, Mubarak's administration thus aimed to increase affordable housing, furniture, clothing, medicine, more employment opportunities, and increased subsidies on basic products (Springborg 1989a, b, p. 23). In 1982, he successfully reconciled Egypt with its Arab neighbours and restored its membership in the Arab League by allying Egypt with Saudi Arabia, that is, the two major powers of the region. Concerned for his own safety and security, Mubarak initiated the State Security Investigations Service and Central Security Forces (containment and anti-riot forces) to curb any attempts to oppose his regime, especially the MB whose influence had gained prominence and thus rendered them primary targets of his regime (Hashim, 2011a, 2011b; Springborg 1989a, b).

The economy was performing poorly during Mubarak's era, which encouraged him to ask the International Monetary Fund for loans in 1991, 1993, and 1996 (Selim, 2015, p. 194). Corruption, bribery, an increase in social gaps, decline in living standards, literacy, education, police brutality, increased surveillance, and above all, the personalisation of the government and the attempt to re-establish an autocracy by grooming Mubarak's son for presidency have accumulated to such high social stratification that ceased to be means to control the society (Amin, 2011). Despair and poverty culminated until January 2011 when the Egyptian revolution broke out. The bloody confrontations between state forces attempting to disperse revolutionaries by direct orders from the Mubarak administrations failed to deflate the situation and aggravated the revolution (Aziz, 2014, pp. 9–10). On 11 February 2011, Mubarak officially stepped down as president of Egypt (McGreal & Shenker, 2011). The again leader-less nation entered into a period of transition for six months under the military interim government, which was meant to supervise the transition of the state into a democratic nation (Kingsley, 2015).

In 2012, presidential elections took place and Mohamed Morsi, an MB member, is elected as president (BBC News, 2012). Morsi was the first civilian president in Egypt's history, yet his affiliation with the MB, whose interests were prioritised over those of the general public (BBC News, 2019; Hessler, 2019). His attempt to reformulate the constitutional rights granted to the military, challenging their authority by the acceptance of voluntary retirement of top generals and appointing Abdul Fattah El Sisi as defence minister, condemned him 'unfit to lead' (Middle East Monitor, 2014; Sakr, 2014, p. 76). Yet others, such as Barbra Kelemen (2019), drew parallels between Egypt's first President Gamal Abdel Nasser and Abdel-Fattah El-Sisi, arguing that the post-revolutionary period requires 'pragmatic approaches' and a realisation that there is an 'overreliance on his persona' by the Egyptian population as there is a 'predisposition for a strong leader'. In 2013, the Egyptian society, with support of the military, marched once more onto Tahrir square to call for Morsi's resignation (BBC News, 2013a). Abdel Fattah El Sisi demanded concessions from Morsi and for him to step down (Kingsley, 2015). However, unsurprisingly, he rejected most of their concessions and refused to step down. On 3 July 2013, General Sisi in his address speech to the Egyptian public, after forcefully ousting Morsi in a military coup, stated:

> The armed forces couldn't plug its ears or close its eyes as the movement and demands of the masses calling for them to play a national role, not a political role as the armed forced themselves will be the first to proclaim that they will stay away from politics [*sic*]. (Weaver & McCarthy, 2013)

Later, in 2013, the Supreme Court Chief Justice Adly Mansour was selected by Sisi to step in as interim president until presidential elections can be held (BBC News, 2013b). Early 2014 Egyptians witnessed another round of elections, whose winner was former General, Abdel Fattah El Sisi (BBC News, 2020).

2. Post-independence Egypt

On 23 July 1952, Egypt witnessed its first ever *coup d'état*, which offset the monarchy and changed the country's formal political structure considerably (Ahmed, 2018). The country's political structure moved from populist-socialist single-party system, under Nasser, to a multiparty system, under Sadat and Mubarak, that accommodated and integrated opposition into the political framework (Kassem, 2004a, b,c, d, p. 40). Sadat introduced economic and political reforms, including the *infitah* (open door policy) in 1974, which Mubarak followed by an adopted economic reform and structural adjustment program (ERSAP) in 1991 (Kassem, 2004a, b,c, d, pp. 41–43). The multifaceted changes adopted by the Republic's leaders in the post-1952 era reinforced optimism among scholars and academics, one of whom went as far as to describe the trajectory as 'Egypt's democratization is functioning … [with Egypt being] a maturing rather than a matured democracy'

(Korany et al., 1998, p. 65). However, it has become evident that this is not the case, as Egypt's defining political feature has been a personal authoritarian rule. The personal authoritarian governing system endured six decades to date (Ryan, 2001, p. 6). Despite the symbolic implementation of a multiparty system, governance and polity have not substantively affected the formal structure of the government. In fact, the formal branches have perpetually been subservient to the 'overwhelming domination of the executive, and the development of autonomous groupings and constituencies ...' which remains weak and hindered (Kassem, 2004a, b, c, d, p. 2). Additionally, the overwhelming support from Western countries, particularly the USA, of the regime since the 1970s allowed the adoption of a 'liberal political' guise, that is, political liberal frameworks which are in reality insufficient to encourage transformation of the authoritarian system into a functioning democracy. Each of the country's presidents, Nasser, Sadat, and Mubarak, possessed and exhibited distinct characteristics and approaches to governance, yet the nature of their personal authoritarian rule persisted in all three eras. The purpose of examining the authoritarian rule in contemporary Egypt is motivated by the observation that democratic aspirations have repeatedly failed and the authoritarians' resilience to international, and recently domestic, pressures to liberalise and democratise their governance style. The following section will examine the governance styles of Nasser, Sadat, and Mubarak, specifically, how they managed to personalise the government and remain in office in spite of civil unrest.

3. Personal Authoritarian Rule – The Machiavellian State

Middle Eastern governance has been characterised by the majority of its constituencies being governed by authoritarian regimes. Lisa Anderson (2001) noted that there is a 'uniform hostility to democracy' within the region and attributed this, partly, to the contradictory US foreign policy, which helped these governments subsist by 'supporting autocratic but compliant friends' (p. 54). Additionally, she accused the West, in general, and the USA, in particular, of continuously 'colluded with regimes in power, permitting fixed elections and human rights fakery ... that allow it and its client regimes to continue in the game' (Anderson, 2001, p. 54). The implication of such collusion has led to pseudo-political liberalisation and a systematic disregard for human rights abuses by the regime, the global hegemons, and the international community, in exchange for a pledge of allegiance and clientele.

Political liberalisation was never on the agenda for the Egyptian government. Rather, political liberalisation was meant to veil the self-preserving strategies adopted by the presidencies in internal political dynamics (Baaklini et al., 1999a, b; Hudson, 1996; Salamé, 1994; Springborg 1989a, b, 2003). Moreover, if democracy were to result of political liberalisation, it is doubtful liberalisation would positively influence polity because 'even though there are international and societal pressured for reducing authoritarian controls, the process of political liberalization [is] state-induced, and the state retains a considerable degree of management over the process' (Monshipouri, 1995, p. 14). The process, therefore, is well-enough constructed and executed as to signal, at least, an effort of liberalisation for the public but poses no threat to the survival and resilience of the regime.

To signal such liberalisation and effectively manipulate the public but remain unaffected, an authoritarian regime employs 'an arbitrary and usually personal government [using] law and the coercive instruments of the state to expedite its own purposes of monopolizing power and denies the political rights and opportunities of all other groups for that power' (Jackson & Roseber, 1982, p. 23). Therefore, for an authoritarian regime to persist, as is the case in Egypt, the government must depend on a 'balanced use of patronage and skillful co-optation, the adoption of exclusionary laws, and the coercive apparatus of the State' (Kassem, 2004a, b, c, d, p. 3). These measures allow the governing regime to adopt an image of liberalisation without conceding to any measures to actualise it. The stability of an authoritarian regime usually resides in the distribution of patronage and erecting a system of 'clientelism'. Clientelism is

> a system of patron-client ties that binds leaders and followers in relationships not only of mutual assistance and support but also of recognized and accepted inequality between the big man and lesser men. The ties usually extend from the center of the regime [and extends through] extensive chains [of command] of patron-client ties. (Kassem, 2004a, b, c, d, p. 39)

This system ensures the containment of opposition and the regime's monopoly over power. Additionally, exclusionary laws, which virtually provide the regime with unlimited execution power over the internal and external structure of the government, that is, 'a license of unrestrictive commands', are ubiquitous and embedded within the governing apparatuses (Kassem, 2004a, b, c, d, p. 24). The use of such means as well as legal–constitutional framework provides the system with sufficient flexibility to suspend or restructure the electoral and parliamentary system without their legitimacy being challenged. The following sections review how Egyptian leaders have personalised authoritarianism to solidify their socio-political and economical hegemony, and critically evaluate how Gamal Abdel Nasser, Anwar Sadat, and Hosni Mubarak, respectively, have appropriated and co-opted social movements for political gain. This will assist the reader in better understanding the dialectical relationship between the state, the society, and the individual.

4. Authoritarianism in Egypt

Governance in Egypt is marked by the rulers' ability to provide legally sound reasoning for executive control by ensuring that 'the balance of power between executive and legislative branches, which has always favored the former over the latter' is maintained and legitimised (Baaklini et al., 1999a, b, p. 13). Egypt, since 1956, has been rendered the 'most resilient personal authoritarian rule in the world' (Kassem, 2004a, b, c, d, p. 11). This position was captured by Jackson and Rosberg (1982), who concluded that the system in which 'persons take precedence over rules, where the officeholder is not effectively bound by his office and is able to change its authority and powers to suit his own personal and political needs' then 'the state is a government of men and not of laws' (p. 24). This mentality is evident by Nasser's seizure of power from Mohamed Naguib. Naguib believed that the continued rule of the military post-1952 and the dictation of policy by the Revolutionary Command Council is unfavourable and advocated for the transformation of the nation into a constitutional government (Vatikiotis, 1991, p. 254). He was later charged with treason by Nasser and placed under house arrest.

Nasser's confiscation of power marked the first personal authoritarian regime Egypt witnessed as a Republic. The implementation of a variety of laws and regulations created a social contract in which 'a modernization of the economy through the use of a large public sector, bureaucracy, and the mobilization of subordinate classes against the landed elites and private business elites' was facilitated by social submission to the military (Kassem, 2014, p. 13). The domination of the new-elite, co-optation of the politicians, and shrewd and charismatic leadership of Nasser left no doubt that he was the sole source of authority (Bush, 1999, p. 15). One can argue that Nasser's unexpected death in 1970 coincided with the collapse of the pan-Arabist ideals. This ideological break left a void for Sadat to fill. Yet, the presidency and executive, as observed, remained unshaken. Chehabi and Linz (1998) identified this phenomenon as 'Neo-Sultanistic regime', stating that 'loyalty to the ruler is not motivated by his embodying or articulating an ideology, nor a unique personal mission, but by a mixture of feat without restraint, at his own discretion ... unencumbered by rules', and thus without 'any commitment to an ideology or value system' the authoritarian system can self-sustain and be reproduced even when leadership changes (p. 6). Although such systems may be seen as archaic, it could '[in] many ways be modern ... what characterizes them is the weakness of traditional and legal-rational legitimization and the lack of ideological justification' (Chehabi & Linz, 1998, p. 7).

Successive rulers of Egypt have masterfully applied authoritarian rule, which even media outlets have characterised as 'have manipulated the political process with a cunning that would evoke the admiration of Machiavelli' (Menon, 2012). The next chapters will outline and present the different methods and processes contemporary Egyptian regimes have employed to personalise the government, earning them the reputation of Machiavellian State.

4.1. Pan-Arabism, Pan-Islamism, and Feminism – Gamal Abdel Nasser

Following the declaration of the Arab Republic of Egypt, a provisional constitution was formulated and was followed by four other constitutions in 1956 (after the nationalisation of the Suez Canal and the subsequent tripartite attack on Egypt), 1958 (following the declaration of Syria and Egypt as the UAR), 1962 (after the collapse of said union), and 1964 (in which socialist economic and political reform policies were codified). Each of said constitutions was tailored to the president's objectives and visions. This section will selectively comment on the constitutional changes which have assisted in the personalisation of the authoritarian rule.

The most notable changes were observed on an institutional level: the governments' structure and the polity of the state were constitutionally at the president's discretion. The 1956 constitution, for instance, changed the republic from a parliamentary to a presidential system where a 'president appoints and dismisses ministers' (Vatikiotis, 1991, p. 258). As one scholar noted,

> whereas in 1954 Nasser used his closest associates to strengthen his position against Naguib ... now with the consolidation of his position in 1956 and after the elimination of his opponents he brought more civilians into the government ... such alteration of personnel for his retention of power ... was a trademark of Nasser's political style throughout his presidency. (Vatikiotis, 1991, p. 259)

Furthermore, the 1956 constitution replaced the Liberation Rally with the National Union and established a single-party system where representatives are hand-picked by the president. This alteration was used as a political tool to filter and vet nominees for election to the National Assembly (Vatikiotis, 1991, p. 259). This process ensured that members of the parliament are subservient and ideologically in harmony with Nasser's vision for the new independent republic and his personal objectives.

In 1958, when the union with Syria was announced, Nasser decreed an alteration to the constitution. Raymond Hinnebusch noted the enormous funds sent by Nasser for the foundation of a political capital in Syria, which the Syrian military quickly realised was a pretense for bureaucratic rule from Cairo, and staged a military coup to regain political autonomy (Hinnebusch, 1990, p. 42). The failure of the UAR and decline of Arab nationalism and socialism as a legitimate ideology made Nasser wary of social backlash. He decided to further consolidate his power by ending the National Union and replacing it with the ASU. The ASU members, itself a creation of the executive power of the president, were constitutionally the only active members allowed to run as electoral candidates (Baaklini et al., 1999a, b, p. 224). This furthered the selective personalisation of the Nasser regime and ensured his unopposed seizure of power and solidified his position. He followed this by establishing *Mahkamet 'Amn al-Dawla* (Supreme Constitutional Courts – SCC), by Law 81 of 1969, which was designed to 'handle cases of treason and internal subversion, as well as political crimes; of lesser magnitude which are defined as coming under their jurisdiction' (Hill, 1979, p. 35). SCCs, whose members are appointed by the president, formally provided an independent judicial body to supervise the constitutionality of the law issues by the legislative and executive branches. This 'paranoia' reinforced the monopolisation of the government by Nasser.

The personal authoritarian rule of Nasser had far-reaching effects on the Egyptian identity. As the 'founder' of Pan-Arabism and 'liberator of Arabs' (Danielson, 2007, p. 23), Nasser managed to co-opt all social structures to serve his vision of what the Arab world and Egypt ought to look like. Realising the emotional aspect of religion and how it assisted in the nationalist movement and ambition, Nasser co-opted Al-Azhar – the Islamic institution for religious jurisprudence and Islamic scholarship created in under the *Shi'a Fatimid Empire* ('Inān, 1958) and could be perceived as the Islamic equivalent of the Vatican – by making it financially dependent on the state through the process of nationalising its *waqf* (Zeghal, 1999, p. 372). This is significant because Egyptians regard Al-Azhar to be of equal significance as the formal government, so the co-optation of the Azhar did not only make this formerly independent institution part of the formal governing apparatus but also provided the executive branch of government almost total control over religious interpretation and information dissemination. Moreover, scholars such as Zeghal (1999) argued that the creeping control over Al-Azhar was strategically a turning point in Nasser's personalisation of the government; the legitimising power the Azhar has was used to back state-sponsored policies and projects, thereby allowing Nasser to harness its social power. Furthermore, the co-optation of Al-Azhar would force

> Ulama [religious jurist/scholar recognized by the state and accredited by Al-Azhar] from potentially opposing or obstructing his project ... removed of its judicial authority through the State's absorption of civil code, and was reformed through the nationalization and restructuring of its University among other measures. (Zeghal, 1999, p. 373)

This co-optation of a significant institution served as religious backing and resacralisation endeavours, thereby politicising religion, legitimising and guising personal political agendas, and providing the government complete control over the public. Zeghal (1999) additionally argued that

> by creating a state-controlled religious monopoly, the Nasserist regime brough the Ulema to heel and forced them into complete political submission during the 1960s, but gave them, and the same time, the instruments for their political emergence in the 1970s. (p. 372)

With this assertion, Zeghal uncovered how the MB managed to infiltrate the political arena, which now we know, paved the way for their seizure of power in 2012.

The effects of this co-optation and the politicisation of religion are most pronounced in terms of how Egypt responded to female genital mutilation (FGM). The ritualised process was internationally denounced as a violation of human rights in 1951 under the Refugee Convention (NIHRC, 2016). The practice which today affects 9 out of 10 women in Egypt (UNICEF, 2020) is a cultural practice which some scholars believe dates back to the ancient Egyptians (Billet, 2007, p. 19). Under the presidency of Nasser, who pioneered Pan-Arabism and sought to reclaim the Arab and Muslim identity, the practice was supported by the state as a rebellion against colonial powers. The radical state-wide rejection of everything perceived to be 'Western', including women's rights and fashion, reframed FGM as part of the Arab identity. Under Nasser's rule, the Azhar issued numerous *fatwas* in support of FGM, proclaiming it as an Islamic duty and a form of political resistance against Westoxcation. This escalated to the point where the Azhar in 1981 issued a *fatwa* urging women to ignore doctors' medical opinion on FGM and urged men to see that the teachings of Prophet Mohamed are not 'abandoned (...) in favor of the teaching of others, be they doctors, because medical science evolved and does not remain constant' (Aldeeb Abu-Sahlieh, 1994). The ambition to reclaim an Arab identity came at the cost of women's lives and their identities. Not only did the institution not declare that FGM is indeed *not* religiously mandated for women and is only an obligation for men, the governing apparatuses with the co-opted legitimising power of religion actively prescribed the female identity and primed the population to its 'necessity' to further the nationalist cause. The co-opted *Ulama* (religious jurist/scholar recognised by the state and accredited by Al-Azhar) also dismissed scientific findings about the long-term physical effects of FGM on women's bodies in favour of political gains and also encouraged men, under the guise of 'returning to our roots', to adopt pre-Islamic and archaic notions about masculinity and femininity, the role and status of women, and gender roles. This was a major setback for feminists and women's movements. One can even make the logical leap that the effects of the Azhar's political agenda are the main cause for women having a social and cultural inferior status to men. The 'hatred' of the West and rejection of everything the West stood for were a radical move by Nasser. The utter dismissal of women and women's rights, the absorption of civil societies, organisations, and institutions into the state, and the appropriation of the constitution to gain complete executive control did change Egypt. While the change did reorient Egypt's influence and interest towards its regional neighbours, it came at the cost of women's rights, identities, and bodies. It is undeniable that Nasser has had many accomplishments during his tenure, but his vision for the newly independent Egypt, with a unique and rich Egyptian identity based on its 7,000-year heritage, also came at the cost of dismissing the lives of half his population; His vision, perhaps unconsciously, was of a Male Egypt, and the 'women's laws' he implemented, such as providing women with suffrage, were his attempt at silencing voices of dissent.

The prescriptive governing style of Egyptian presidencies was carried on even after Nasser's death and is still observable in Egypt today. The next section will discuss how the Anwar Sadat personalised his government. This genealogical investigation is meant to highlight how gender norms are prescribed by the authoritarian government. Later on in this book, it will become clearer how the prescription of gender norms on the political level ascribes gender identities on the social level, leading to the enforcement of gender interests on a personal level.

4.2. Secularisation and Resacralisation – Anwar Sadat

The sudden death of Nasser left his Vice President Sadat in charge of the nation. His contributions to the formalisation and institutionalisation of authoritarianism were built on the groundwork of Nasser. Sadat launched what is known as the 'corrective revolution', which involved the arrest, dismissal, and purging of any government personnel affiliated with Nasser's government (Ryan, 2001, p. 5). By presidential decree, he declared a new law, Law 38 1972, which gave him the power to nominate members to the People's Assembly, members who he would have vetted and groomed to support his 'new' government (Hamad, 2018). Once 'elected' into office, the president, under the new constitution of 1971, retains the authority to promulgate as well as object to laws (see Article 112 of 1972 Constitution).

This meant that the president has veto power over the legislative branch and executive branch, immortalising and solidifying his position as sole authoritative power. His new constitution also affirmed the president's powers to rule by presidential decree (Article 117), declare a state of emergency (Article 148), and appoint and dismiss the entire cabinet (Article 141). He also has the power to draft the budget of the entire state (Article 115) and formulate the state's general policy (Article 138). This constitution has legally enshrined the preeminent position of the president over the government and state institutions in contemporary Egypt. The 1971 constitution is, up to date, the most overtly authoritative since the establishment of the Republic. The socio-economic and political consequences of this constitution are believed to be the cause of Sadat's assassination in 1981, which will be elaborated further in the upcoming sections. The eruption of the 25 January 2011 Revolution can also be attributed to the erection of these totalitarian laws, as the repercussions of it were a complete suppression of *raison d'état* for personal authoritative interest.

In the 1970s and 1980s, a resurgence of Islamic fundamentalism and feminism found new platforms for expression. Sadat employed a strategy of Islamism in hopes it would foster and groom social support for his government and its objectives. He transformed the state into a promoter of Islamic fundamentalism in hopes it would gain him social support. Guirguis (2012, p. 187) postulated that:

> [Under Nasser] Islamism was eclipsed by Arab nationalism, a secular, socialist ideology of pan-Arab unity and cooperation. Yet the defeat of Nasser's nationalist vision ushered the Islamists back to the forefront of national life. As Muslim fundamentalist movements proliferated and gained broader acceptance in the 1970s, religion became more culturally dominant and increasingly linked to politics, culminating in the assassination of Anwar Sadat in 1981.

Under Sadat's rule, Nasser's anti-Western rhetoric was reoriented and substituted by a pro-Western ideology. This was evidenced by his adoption and implementation of capitalist economic strategies, *Infitah* (Open Door Policy), and political alliance with the USA (Lippman, 1989, p. 99). Simultaneously, a new face for Egyptian feminism emerged: The First Lady Jihan Sadat, wife of Sadat. She was praised for providing a platform for women to voice their opinions and her women's outreach programs. Her mission, coinciding with that of the state, was to contain communism and 'radical' feminism, now associated with Nawal Saadawi (Addison, 2020, p. 6). By sidelining other feminist voices and using her power as the first lady, Jihad Sadat institutionalised a framework of state-tolerated and sponsored feminism (Fowler, 202) and represented the Egyptian delegation at the 1975 International Women's Year Conference in Mexico City. She was credited for the addition of Article 11 to the 1971 constitution, which states:

> the state guarantees a balance and accord between a woman's duties towards her family on the one hand and towards her work in society and equality with man in the political, social and cultural spheres on the other without violating the laws of the Islamic *Shari'ah*.

Under Sadat's presidency and Jihan Sadat's activism, Egypt witnessed a resurgence of the Hijab which many Western-informed feminists had previously advocated against. Specifically, the 1980s witnessed a measurable and significant increase in women wearing the *Hijab* and other types of traditional wear. This could be attributed to the conservative and fundamentalist shift Egypt experienced under Sadat's presidency (see 'From Province to Kingdom to Republic – A Chronology'). Yet, it could also be argued that this is reflective of a new patriarchal bargaining framework, influenced by political Islam and as a product of Nasserism and his political reorientation away from Western ideals. While the increase could be viewed solely as a rejection of the West, for those living and experiencing the framework, it holds a twofold meaning: on the one hand, the Hijab has a utilitarian value where it allows women to access the public sphere and work within the system, and on the other hand, it signals an adherence to the Muslim identity and sexual codes (Ahmed, 1992, p. 224).

For feminists of that era, the Hijab was regarded as a liberating force, meant to counter the imagery of the Western superimposed 'Free women' (Al-Wazni, 2015, p. 326), and propelling the narrative that it 'is a piece of fabric, and, alongside other garments made of fabric, it does not violate rights' (Mancini, 2012, p. 522). The narrative assisted in 'preventing the drawing of clear-cut lines. There is no such thing as a monolithic "Muslim world" in which women are "monstrously oppressed"' (Ahmed, 1982, p. 11). The Hijab particularly worked on changing the discursive notions of the Western Orientalist narrative towards the Muslim woman, that is, the Muslim world being irrational, backwards, and uncivilised which are presented as 'facts'. Leila Ahmed (1982) vehemently argued that 'These are "facts" manufactured in Western culture, by the same men who have also littered the culture with "facts" about Western women and how inferior and irrational they are. And for centuries the Western world has been systematically falsifying and vilifying the Muslim World' (p. 523), and pointed out that

> [the] Western so-called knowledge about the Middle East consists largely of a heritage of malevolently fabricated mythologies, it is also impossible, in an environment already so negatively primed against us, to be freely critical – a task no less urgent for us than for Western feminists – of our own societies. (p. 527)

The supposed 'cultural superiority' of the West and the imperialistic exportation of Western ideals served to radicalise the Egyptian society (Lopez, 2001, p. 282). The frustration of Egyptian and Muslim feminists under Sadat's rule, and their opposition to his Western orientation, allowed for dissident voices to appear. Specifically Islamists and the MB, which by the 1980s had gained access to public university campuses and were supported, funded, and protected by the state (Grömüs, 2016, p. 62), continued to solidify the 'return' of the Muslim identity to counter Western influence. It is thereby unsurprising that the 1980s witnessed a conservative shift in Egyptian youths as 'with the political training and organizational skills they had acquired while working in the student unions ... challenge the regime at every level, including in parliament and in civil society institutions such as the professional syndicates' (Fahmy, 1998, p. 554) the MB was able to resacralise the youth under the guise of anti-imperialism. The resacralisation efforts started by the targeting and recruiting a large number of lower- and middle-class women, and due to the relatively easy access they had to these stakeholders, recruitment was fast and ideological persuasion was effective (Al-Anani, 2020; Gamal, 2019). Taraki (1996) noticed that the MB strongly believed that 'feminism was equated with cultural imperialism', and Ahmed (1992) similarly observed that 'Islamist discourse on women as a discourse of resistance' where women's public dress code and behaviours are propagated 'as proof of the moral bankruptcy of the West and the superiority of Muslims', therefore attempts to 'return to Islam' within this framework could have been attractive to many, particularly those who opposed Westernisation and Sadat's *Infitah* policies.

The recruitment process followed the ideology of the MB which Hassan El-Banna had written back in 1928, in which he called for

> a campaign against ostentation in dress and loose behavior (...) segregation of male and female students (...) a separate curriculum for girls (...) and [for private meetings between women and men] to be counted as a crime unless permitted degree of relationship. (Al-Banna, 1978, p. 126)

Freer (2017) noted that the Muslim Sisters Group, which was established in 1932, was the actualisation of the gender segregation El Banna had envisioned. Freer (2017) posited that the 'primary issues for al-Banna, then, appeared to be the behavior of women in public, their education, and the prevention of gender mixing, which he considered inappropriate'. Other scholars, such as Taraki (1996), who noted that the ideology of the MB is largely based on classical Islamic discourses, in which women's issues are perceived as an 'essence' as opposed to a 'complex and living reality' leading to women's visibility and access to the public sphere receiving 'no more than lip service in the discourse of the Ikhwan [MB]' (p. 141). This later led to her asserting that while the MB had reformed itself over time to keep up with new philosophical and social developments, in hopes to remain relevant, their discourse still maintained that '[women can] work outside the home provided it does not conflict with women's domestic duties or involves contact with men, or the encouragement of female education in "appropriate" fields' (Taraki, 1996, p. 142). Saba Mahmood (2001) argued that the women who were subjected to the MB's discourses on a woman's place in society, and the duties of the 'good Muslim woman', later on discovered that 'their participation is critically structured by, and seeks to uphold the limits of a discursive tradition that holds subordination to a transcendent will (and thus, in many instances, to male authority) as its coveted goal' (p. 204). The systemic recruitment of working- and middle-class women, among other socio-economic and structural variables, has eventually led a deeply embedded inferiority complex, where women perceive of themselves as inferior to men (El Guindi, 1981; Mernissi, 1988b; Radwan, 1982; Williams, 1979).

In 1971, a 'cult book' was disseminated titled *Al tabarruj* (Bodily Display). The author Ni'mat Sidqi, who was a young university student at the time, wrote the book as a manifesto to why women should convert to traditional Islamic dress, adopt traditional gender roles, and remain hidden from the public eye in their quarters to protect their family honour. Studies conducted in the late 1970s on public university students found that 'Veiling, perceived as the symbol of Islamic authenticity, was theorised as a form of protest whether against the secular regime or against cultural dominance by the West' (van Nieuwkerk, 2021, p. 6). Other scholars, such as MacLeod (1991), who conducted similar studies in the 1980s, analysed the discourses around *Hijab* and found evidence of women's internalised inferiority complex, arguing that Egyptian women had accepted the *Hijab* in as much as they accepted the male control over their sexuality, bodies, and behaviours (p. 97). It was unsurprising that with Sadat's presidency and his reliance on the MB for public propaganda and support (Ibrahim, 1992) the Islamic dress spread among the wealthier classes who historically have shied away from it (Sa'id, 1972a, b, 1973). As the *Hijab* was most commonly worn by working women as a 'symbolic action by which they expressed their feelings of conflict and confusion about combining work outside the home with marriage and motherhood' (va Nieuwkerk, 2021, p. 6). This would mean that upper and upper middle-class women, who previously did not work because their financial circumstances did not require them to do so for survival, but now wish to enter the workforce for any reason, may that be economic hardship, interest, or self-actualisation, are adhering to the unspoken socially imposed dress code to avoid social backlash. An alternative perspective is that of MacLeod (1991), who argued that the expressed new wave of women putting on the *Hijab* is an act of political submission, where the Hijab 'takes place not as a remnant of traditional culture or a reactionary return to traditional patterns, but as a form of hegemonic politics in modernizing environment, making its meaning relevant to women' (p. 121).

These observations can mostly be attributed to the resacralisation of the Egyptian society as a whole. Amina Sai'ds, author for a woman's magazine called *Hawa* [Eve], was stunned by what she called, the 'reversal of female emancipation'. She noted that the influence of the MB on Egyptian youth and general discourse led to the decline of women's employment opportunities and criticised the state for having an active role in convincing women to retreat into the private sphere (Zeidan, 2018). It was noted that these actions were not only reactionary but also illegal, as in 'certain practices that are contrary to the constitution and the Egyptian law [were noted] such as advertising in the newspapers for jobs specifying that applicants must be males' (Badran, 1991, p. 224). Unexpectedly, however, the government had enacted a law that ensures women 30 parliamentary seats, and, by presidential decree, Anwar Sadat amended the personal status law, granting women the right to initiate divorce, the right to contest polygamy in court and added protections for women being divorced (Hussein, 1985, p. 231). These amendments later came to be known as 'Jihan's Laws', as the first lady, Jihan Sadat, pushed for these amendments. This upset many in the society, not only fundamentalists who believed it to be un-Islamic for a woman to divorce a man, but others who argued their status in the society is being threatened by the first lady and feminists.

In subsequent years, Nawaal El Saadawi as well as a number of female lawyers, medical doctors, and university professors struggled to obtain permits to establish women-led organisations, such as the Arab Women's Solidarity Association (AWSA). After failing to gain legal status in 1983, the organisation stated 'We knew that the liberation of the people as a whole could not take place without the liberation of women and this could not take place without the liberation of land, economy, culture, and information' (Badran & Cooke, 1990) and registered as a nongovernmental organisation (NGO) with the UN in 1985. Feminists celebrated too early, as in 1985 – tremendous internal tension accumulated due to the peace treaty Sadat signed with Israel alienating the country from the rest of the Arab world – the decree amending the personal status laws was cancelled after turmoil and resistance soared in the society (Graham-Brown, 1985, p. 17). This was followed by a respected and admired Azhar scholar, Shaikh Metwally El Shaarawi, airing on national TV that a 'woman who works while she has a father brother or husband to support her, [is] a sinful woman' (Badran, 1991, p. 226; El Shaarawi, 1987). Additionally, Al Ghazali voiced her disagreement with El Shaarawi stating that a woman seeking an occupation outside the household deserves the dangers awaiting her in the public arena – referring to sexual harassment and assault which skyrocketed during that period and continued to increase up to date – blaming feminists for the encouragement of women to leave their homes and excusing men for their 'nature'. There were some voices of dissent remaining, which asserted that only a 'correct upbringing can protect women, not veiling' (Badran, 1991, p. 227).

As observed, there has been a lot of oscillation with regard to the feminism and women's issues. Throughout the 20th century, the state seems to have favoured the moderate view of an Islamic society without an Islamic state, realising the dangers of an Islamic state after observing the turn events in Iran in the 1970s and 1980s. Radical views, such as those of Al Ghazali and El Saadawi, both lying on opposite sides of the spectrum, were suppressed and shut down by the regimes, regardless of their own political ideologies. At the turn of the century, feminist issues and their respective activists have gone underground with the rise of the Mubarak regime in the 1980s and well into 2011. The 25th January revolution gave some feminists hope for a better future, but this time they became warier of the regimes in place. With the election of the MB member, Mohamed Morsi, into office in 2012, feminists knew that it would not be long until the regime cracks down on them, thus remaining an underground movement. With the impeachment of Morsi and the seizure of power by the military in 2014, embodied in Abdel-Fattah el Sisi, feminists realised the return of the Mubarak regime. To continue living a relatively normal life, one could argue, feminists have chosen to keep their activism hidden for the meantime.

4.3. Suppressing and Oppressing the Opposition – Hosni Mubarak

When Mubarak came to power in 1981, following the assassination of Sadat, he was faced with significant ideological, socio-economic, and political disillusionment. The 1967 war ended the illusion of Arab power, nationalism, and unity. Sadat's peace treaty with Israel reinforced the same idea, while simultaneously creating voices of dissent in the country, and consequentially resulting in isolation of Egypt from the rest of the Arab world. Nasser's socialist experiment with a centrally planned economy left the country in debt. Sadat's attempt at economic restructuring through *infitah* did little to help the problem (Ibrahim, 1995, p. 41). Rather, the *infitah* produced a consumption boom that failed to stimulate investment in productive or export-oriented industries. Mubarak also inherited a newly constructed multiparty arena that could potentially challenge the existence of the personal authoritarian regime. Yet, as the longest reigning authoritarian of the region, Mubarak used these challenges to solidify his tenure.

Mubarak, initially, portrayed himself as an advocate for democracy by stating that it is 'the best guarantee of our future', proclaiming that he 'had no wish to monopolize decision making' (Kassem, 2004a, b, c, d, p. 27). Ironically, Mubarak (2004) who reigned for almost 30 years, stated in 1984, after three years in office, that he does not 'conceal from you [Egyptians] the fact that I believe that the assumption of the office of the president by anyone should not exceed two terms' and pledged 'I will be the first president to whom this rule shall apply' (pp. 27–28).

In 1987, Mubarak stipulated that democracy cannot be achieved 'overnight' stating 'if we cease economic activity and grant freedom ... we consequently place people in an unstable state' (Owen, 1994, p. 189). This emphasised Mubarak's intention to restrict political movements, personalise the government, and maintain the status quo within the society his predecessors neatly paved. He realised the benefit of the state of emergency law and its utility in the maintenance of personal authoritarian rule. The state of emergency law, as Hill aptly summarised, is 'not martial law as is usually understood – the constitution is not suspended and the civil courts have not ceased to function' (Hill, 1979, p. 38), rather, its erection is meant to prominently maintain political control under the guise of 'a state of emergency'. It was enacted in 1958 under Law 162 and was first declared by Nasser during the 1967 war. It can, for example, allow the censorship over political activity and organised movements which the security forces deem 'dangerous'. That can range from monitoring of political activity to the limiting of political expression. This means

> individuals can be arrested solely on the basis of suspicion of political crimes, and the gathering of five or more people or the distribution of any political literature without government authorization gives the government the right to arrest all those involved.
> (Kassem, 1999, p. 58)

More importantly, the state of emergency grants 'the president of the Republic the right to refer to the military judiciary any crime which is punishable under the Penal Code or any other law' (Kassem, 1999, p. 59) thus giving the president a *carte blanche* to 'detain and prosecute civilians in military courts regardless of whether their activity endangers fundamental interests' (Bureau of Democracy, 1997). Noteworthy is that if the military court passes a verdict, there is no appeal, even in the case where a civilian is condemned to capital punishment.

Egypt remained under a 'state of emergency' since the assassination of Sadat in 1981 and until Mubarak's abdication in 2011. Mubarak had requested, and was granted, an extension every three years under the veil of combatting violence and terrorism. He continuously argued that a state of emergency is an 'indispensable deterrent ... and guard ... against the criminal forces who are still intent on seizing all possible opportunities to incite unrest and hit national interests' (Essam al-Din, 2003). This covertly implied the targeting of opposition, specifically organised groups of Islamists and any type of activists, including feminists. Under his reign, Egyptian feminists and activists experienced a new wave of restrictive laws, which continued their descent underground. Sasika Brechenmacher (2017, p. 38) summarised the state of feminist organisations and civil societies under Mubarak, stating:

> Under former president Hosni Mubarak, Egyptian civil society organizations operated in an environment of limited freedom and selective repression. The government had inherited a comprehensive system of state control over civil society established during the 1960s to limit the political and social influence of the Muslim Brotherhood, codified in the law of association (Law 32 of 1964). Mubarak nevertheless tolerated the rapid proliferation of Egyptian civil society organizations during the 1990s, while at the same time closely monitoring and regulating their activities. In a strategy common to autocratic regimes in the region, the government relied on a mix of divide-and-rule tactics, selective enforcement of civil society laws, and unofficial security sector oversight to maintain state control over the sector.

Consequentially, by the early 2000s it became clear that applying emergency rule and trying civilians in military courts substantially increased the government's reliance on the coercive apparatus and solidified the 'rule of terror' (Chiha, 2013, p. 92). This type of political philosophy can be defined as a Machiavellian one. In Machiavelli's (1981) infamous book *The Prince*, he states 'the first opinion which one forms of a prince, and of his understanding, is by observing the men he has around him' (p. 92), which Mubarak and his predecessors appropriated literally and applied to their personalised government schema. Furthermore, he recommended a ruler 'conquer by force or by fraud' (Machiavelli, 1981, p. 32), which Mubarak applied by continuously propagating the supposed 'eminent' threat of the Islamists, or even worse, Egypt's new neighbour, Israel, and the 'enemy from within'. Most importantly, Machiavelli (1981) recommended that a ruler 'be both loved and feared, but, when necessity forces a choice, it is better to be feared, because men love at their convenience but they fear at the convenience of the prince' (p. xvii), which Mubarak employed by constitutional right to defer civilians to be tried in military courts, the vague and inconsistent definition of what constitutes political activity, and above all, the excessive and brutal use of the coercive apparatus. These Machiavellian tactics have been proficiently employed by the successive authoritarian regimes in contemporary Egypt, earning it the title of a Machiavellian State (Benigni, 2018; Soliman, 2012; Trager, 2010).

The next section will dissect the tactics employed to suppress and repress civil societies, civil movements and organisations, and how these tactics have pushed women's and feminist movements further underground. This investigation is meant to showcase why uniting feminist movements became institutionally impossible under the Mubarak regime. The effects of these laws, the crackdowns on civil societies, NGOs, and movements have disallowed the formulation and continuation of an Egyptian female narrative, leading to the solidification of patriarchy.

5. Civil Societies in Egypt – What Are They?

Civil societies are grassroot organisations meant to provide a platform for expression. They are an integral part of a democratic system as they mobilise public support for causes that affect a group within the society, utilising lobbying and campaigning to address local, national, or international concerns. It has been argued that civil societies in the Arab world specifically 'represent the competing ideologies and quest for power of political parties and the idealist concern of society at large through human rights advocacy' (Norton, 1995, p. 7). Therefore, the underlying purpose of such organisations is to provide a platform for the 'peaceful management of difference among individuals and collectivities sharing the same public space – i.e., the polity' (Ibrahim, 1995, p. 28). The following section will analyse the status of civil society under Nasser, Sadat, and Mubarak, as it can be argued that civil societies have been suppressed in favour of personalising the regimes and consolidating power undisputed. The weakness of civil society is arguably in direct correlation with authoritarian regime, especially because they are 'credited for thwarting authoritarian designs and challenging arbitrary rules' (Norton, 1995, p. 7). Therefore, it is crucial for an authoritarian regime to tightly govern and rein over civil society, to avoid them reporting on 'internal corruption and hollow claims for legitimacy' (Al-Sayyid, 1995, p. 282) that could eventually breakdown the regime.

The rulers of Egypt realised the potential threat to their personalised authoritarian regimes and codified their role in the society as to limit their effectiveness and influence. Nasser was the first to realise that. In the 1964 constitution set forth the rule of civil societies, by establishing Law 32 that requires any civil society to seek approval from the Ministry of Social Affairs (MSA) after meeting and agreeing to the prerequisite of not engaging in any 'political activity' (Al-Sayyid, 1995). Political activity, however, is such an obscure and ostensibly defined term, which has allowed the 'ministry to utilize the law to intimidate … societies by threatening to suspend their activity if they continued certain actions or if their elected leaders were not approved by security agencies' (Kassem, 2004a, b, c, d, p. 88). This law also formally prohibited civil societies from gaining a legal status. Additionally, Article 12 provided the government the right to dissolve and reject civil society if its 'founding is not in accordance with security measures or for the unsuitability of the place, health-wise or socially' (Kassem, 2004a, b, c, d). Furthermore, Article 12 stipulated that the foundation of a civil society is to be rejected if 'the environment has no need for the services of other associations' (Kassem, 2004a, b, c, d). This was initially believed to target redundancy, yet the Article in reality provides a legal mechanism for the MSA to exclude unwanted organisations, bearing in mind the MSA is an executive created ministry.

Human Rights Organisations (HROs), most commonly, are rooted in the *Universal Declaration of Human Rights* (UDHR). Where most HROs appropriate and advocate for the necessity of the first 26 Articles of the UNHR, that is, 'notions of equality and nondiscrimination [and consequentially] all human beings deserve to be treated with equal concern and respect' (Gillies, 1996, p. 16), Egypt's HROs emphasise issues of socio-economic and cultural rights of individuals utilising religion. The argument can be made that the more authoritarian a regime is, the weaker HROs and civil societies are, and the less likely they are to function within 'autonomously defined public spaces' (Prezworski, 1986, p. 48). This resulted in HROs and civil societies operating within a 'state constructed arena in which any discussion of issues must be made in codes and terms established by the rulers' (Prezworski, 1986).

The first Egyptian HRO was the *Partisans Association of Human Rights in Cairo* (PAHRC) in 1977. Shortly after its establishment the *Partisans Association of Human Rights in Alexandra* (PAHRA) was established in 1979. The organisation was promising and its members suffered minimal trouble in gaining legal status. It quickly became apparent that the organisations served as 'mouthpieces' for the government. Their main role was to shift local, regional, and international attention from human rights abuses in Egypt by 'conducting' research and producing press releases negating the occurrence of such abuses. Nonetheless, a counter organisation was created to combat the falsification and politically charged guises of the PAHRC/A, the *Egyptian Organization for Human Rights* (EOHR) 1987. Yet, some hope arose when in 2003 Egypt established its *National Council for Human Rights* (NCHR), marking it one of the latest countries in the Middle East to institutionalise human rights. The NCHR generated a sense of optimism within the national and international spheres that human rights abuses, specifically state-sponsored abuses, would not go unnoticed. This optimism was crushed when it failed to report about the targeting of homosexuals under 'debauchery' charges (Kreshaw, 2003) and the use of rape, waterboarding, and other torture techniques as a tool for interrogation in the 'war against terrorism' (Mayer, 2005). The continuous state of emergency Egypt is it made it almost impossible for any organisation or civil society to function conventionally. Also, it has stripped many associations and societies from their right to a legal status, which oftentimes resulted in their persecution and prosecution.

Furthermore, the renewal of state of emergency has allowed minimal politicisation of HROs and civil societies. A senior Egyptian official once explained:

> Human rights means having the right to pray, the right to your religion, the freedom of work, the freedom of movement .... How can [human rights] organizations get involved in politics of the state and say there is freedom or no freedom? This is none of their business. (Kassem, 2004a, b, c, d, p. 119)

Protected by Article 11, the ruling authority has the legal right to 'label the activities of human rights advocates as political and therefore illegitimate' (Kassem, 2004a, b, c, d), which means activists can be persecuted by the state and might be financially penalised or imprisoned under the guise of 'national security'.

An example of such restriction is the police investigation filed by members of a Coptic village in Upper Egypt in 1998 against the government for the unlawful detention, murder, and torture of civilians. An HRO monitoring and reporting about the developments was shortly after prosecuted by the government under suspicion of 'receiving money from a foreign country in order to damage the national interest, spreading rumors which affect the country's interest and violating the decree against collecting donations without obtaining permission from the appropriate authorities' (Aikman, 1999, p. 64). This indicted that reporting on human rights abuses is perceived by the government as a crime 'bordering treason' (Aikman, 1999) adding further restrictions on and relying on state-sponsored interpretations of what constitutes 'treason', 'political activity', and 'abuse'.

Specifically, women's rights organisations, most notably, AWSA (1982–1992) and *Egyptian Center for Women's Rights* (ECWR; 1996–) have been targeted by the legislative and executive apparatuses. In 1992, in the case of *The Arab Republic of Egypt* vs *The AWSA and Dr. Nawal El Saadawi* (the renowned scholar and founder of the organisation), the prosecution erecting the law of association 57(4) in State Council's Administrative Judicial Court to condemn the practice of the organisation as 'violated the rule of law and public order and morality by the practice of political and religious activities through its magazine and publication' (Human Rights Watch, 1997). AWSA and ECWR's objectives were to lobby for an end of violence against women, the deprivation of women from an equal access and legal right to participate in the public sphere, to raise awareness of the harmful practice of FGM, and to end structural and institutional violence (UN, 2005).

Recently, the government started cracking down even more on civil society and women's rights research institutions, most notably *Nazra for Feminist Studies* (shut down by the government in 2016) and *El Nadeem Center for Rehabilitation of Victims of Violence and Torture* (shut down by the government in 2017). *Nazra's* founder and executive director Mozn Hassan, in an interview, explained 'The investigation with Nazra comes within the frame of taking escalating steps to close the public space by conducting a crackdown on independent civil society organizations in different ways', elaborating that civil societies and NGOs in Egypt are directly targeted by the government through the use of coercive means ranging from 'interrogations, to travel bans, summoning of organizations' staff members, and visits of inspection committees to some organizations' (Ford, 2016). Furthermore, *El Nadeem Center*, registered as a medical clinic with the Ministry of Health, had issued a press release articulating their condemnation of 'forced disappearances, arbitrary arrests and illegal detentions' (Raai, 2017), to which the government shortly afterwards responded with foreclosure of the clinic under the accusation it had 'violated the terms of license' (Raai, 2017).

Ever since the erection of Law 32 of 1964, and its revision in 2019 which added more restrictions (Cairo Institute for Human Rights, 2019), civil society organisation have been censored and persecuted by the government. The draconian legal structures (HRW, 2019) and the tyrannical and arbitrary use of the security and coercive apparatuses (Nader, 2019) to suppress civil expression, has been described by some organisations as 'deceptive and superficial (…) and seeks to subordinate them [civil societies and NGOs] to the security apparatus' (Cairo Institute for Human Rights, 2019). The repressive tension in Egypt apexed with the 2011 Revolution, where slogans of *'Esh, Horeya, Adala Egtema'ya* (Bread, Freedom, and Social Equality) rampaged the streets of Cairo. The historically disadvantaged and abused minority groups, especially women, were major proponents and campaigners in the 2011 revolution onwards. However, in 2018, due to the current state of emergency the current Egyptian administration filed and was granted, censorship over social media platforms and media outlets has been used to detain at least 15 women under the guise of 'violating public morals' and 'undermining family values' (HRW, 2020). For example, Amal Fathy, a human rights and women's activist in Egypt, posted a 12-minute video on the social platform, Facebook, detailing her experience with sexual harassment at a bank and the failure of the authorities to protect her. In a span of months, Fathy was arrested and charged with 'belonging to an outlawed group' and 'spreading false news' about the government (Mahfouz & Raghaven, 2018). Najia Bounaim, Amnesty International North Africa campaigns director, responded to the verdict stating '[it is an] outrageous case of injustice ... [and] highlighted the vital issue of women's safety in Egypt ... [describing Fathy as] not a criminal and should not be punished for her bravery' (Mahfouz & Raghaven, 2018). The summer of 2018 also witnessed the charge of a Lebanese tourist to Egypt with eight years in prison for the 'deliberately broadcasting false rumors which aim to undermine society and attack religions' after she posed a video on Facebook detailing her experience with sexual harassment. The authorities justified the charge by claiming 'defaming and insulting the Egyptian people' is a crime punishable by law (Specia, 2018).

The underlying tone of targeting civil societies and HROs is that an 'expression of any form of dissatisfaction in the face of injustice carried out by members of the society or the government is a crime punishable by law'. This sentiment was echoed and supported by government officials as well as the legal structure of the country. The effort to curb and extinguish any efforts carried out by citizens which may 'harm' the personal authoritarian system did not end with the detention and trials of civilians in military courts but carried out on other 'minority groups' in the Egyptian society, specifically the MB. The next section will elaborate on the persecution of the MB and how state-sponsored violence in the post-1952 Egypt has contributed to the radicalisation of political Islam and the conservative shift members of the society witnessed.

6. The Radicalisation of Political Islam in Egypt – The Case of the MB

Opposition groups are oftentimes defined by the political system in which they operate. This has been aptly observed by Lisa Anderson (1997), who stated:

> Opposition, however, has the unusual characteristic of being defined partly by what it opposes; it develops within and in opposition to an ideological and institutional framework and, as such, reveals a great

deal not only about its own adherents, but also about the individuals, policies, regimes, and states in authority. (p. 18)

Accordingly, the absence or weakness of an opposition can be attributed to 'the absence of a reliable, transparent institutional framework for political opposition to work within' (Anderson, 1997, p. 19). This in turn could lead to what she coins 'rejectionist' or 'disloyal parties'. In Egypt, the rejectionists are the Islamists and the MB.

Political Islam as we observe and experience it today emerged as a popular form in 1928. In Egypt, the movement was inspired, and sequentially the MB as an organised group was founded by Hassan al-Banna (1906–1949). Al-Banna's advertised objectives were the 'reform of hearts and minds, to guide Muslims back to the true religion, and away from the corrupt aspirations and conduct created by European dominance' (Zubaida, 1989, p. 48). This idea was influenced by earlier Islamic thinkers, such as Jamal al-Din al-Afaghani, Mohamed Abdu, and Rashid Rida, who questioned and challenged the intellectual and cultural domination of Western colonial powers and called for a recovery from the ignorant, corrupt, and fragmentation of Islamic lifestyle. Their arguments centred around the fact that Islam 'had been subverted by the dynastic empires, and forgotten in the degeneration and corruption of religion in the later centuries' (Zubaida, 1989, p. 45). Nonetheless, the most pronounced difference between the earlier Islamic thinkers and the MB is their attitude towards and critique of the oppressor. For instance, Mohamed Abdu argued that 'Europe, the oppressor, was at the same time the model for progress and strength, for the later [the MB] the West was both oppressive and culturally threatening' (Zubaida, 1989, p. 46). To credit them MB, they quickly acknowledged the social success of their predecessors and chose to adopt their leadership style to maintain social support. Therewith, the establishment of the MB was a step forward for the political opposition in Egypt as they 'spearheaded the shift of Muslim political thought in the contemporary era into the arena of active political participation' (Kassem, 2004a, b, c, d, p. 134).

At the time of its establishment, the MB functioned under the umbrella of charity organisation and sought to introduce 'reform to make [the monarchy] fully Islamic, in both the moral and social sense' (Kramer, 1994, p. 211). Al-Banna's strategy was to play on their charitable cause as a frontier for their efforts to accumulate social support; for instance, by providing education to the remainder of the population as, at the time, it was restricted to a small fraction of the society. His tactics were successful, as their popularity and legitimacy grew through the use of carefully measured and executed tactics. Richard Mitchell summarised the tactics employed by the MB, stating that MB affiliates and members would periodically travel to rural areas and small villages preaching Al-Banna's philosophies in Mosques. As most Muslims go to their local Mosque for Friday prayer, transforming them into hotspots for information dissemination about political Islam provided 'the speakers the legitimacy and respectability they needed. Direct communication with the people in their homes, at their work, and in their places of leisure added to that legitimacy the quality of sincerity and the personal touch' (Mitchell, 1969, p. 9).

Nonetheless, the charitable guise did not prevent the government from perceiving the organisation as threatening. In December 1948, the MB resorted to violent tactics – the assassination of the Prime Minister Nahmoud Naqrashi, who was believed to be a Zionist-sympathiser – as a means to articulate the establishment of the Jewish state, Israel. This resulted in their immediate dissolution and the crackdown of the government on members and affiliates of the MB. However, the Society was not the sole Islamist organisation, 'other extremist organizations of the national-societal variety also appeared in the 1930s and 1940s, which sanctified further violent politics – and political violence' (Vatikiotis, 1991, p. 280). Nonetheless, political violence in Egypt was not an uncommon occurrence as social stratification and distress grew since Egypt's declaration as a British 'veiled protectorate' especially since

> British influence over political affairs in the 1930s, there were serious domestic political, social and economic factors which contributed and facilitated the emergence of new organized groups subscribing to violent ideologies. There were not only opposed to the established order, but also ready to challenge its authority by violent means. (Vatikiotis, 1991, p. 281)

The monarchy in Egypt under the Ministry of Ibrahim Abdel-Hadi, as Mohamed Heikal noted, cracked down on the MB and was 'uncompromising in its suppression … of the Brotherhood', specifically because of the ideological stance of the MB, which opposed the 'secular, liberal constitutional parties, especially the *Wafd* [the main party in Egypt before the Free Officers' revolution in 1952]' (Zubaida, 1989, p. 84).

Since 1952, the successive political leaders of Egypt have routinely targeted Islamists groups and especially the MB. Under the Nasser regime, the government adopted two violent strategies towards the MB: (1) the direct targeting of MV members or suspected affiliated by the security forces, and (2) the criminalisation of their organisation and the penalisation and interrogation of any civilian suspected of having a connection to the outlawed group. From this, the government created a political and social alienation by installing fear of identifying as Muslim (Kassem, 2004a, b, c, d, p. 139). This crackdown has also paved the path for radical Islamic ideologies to emerge whose target was to delegitimise the government, using the plethora of strategies designed by the MB to interact with the society, specifically preaching at mosques. The attempted assassination of Egypt's liberator and former leader, Nasser, in 1954 by members of the MB – the attempted assassination was during a live-radio broadcast in which Nasser was addressing the nation – did not help the organisation's image. Instead, it spurred a public-retaliation movement against the organisation and provided Nasser with 'the opportunity of being done with the Society of the Muslim Brotherhood' (Mitchell, 1969, p. 151). This resulted in a mass-arrest explosion in Egypt, where 'on the following 9 December, six men were hanged; thousands of other Brothers were already imprisoned and the organization has been efficiently crushed'

(Mitchell, 1969, p. 153). In sum, it was argued the relationship of Nasser with the MB was initially based on cooperation towards a common goal, freedom from the British imperial powers, yet some scholars, such as Binder (1988) believe that the ideological clashes between the regime and the MB were not a 'a mere misunderstanding' but were

> the result of an open struggle for power and when Nasser won, he had to decide how to deal with the Ikhwan organization, with Islamic fundamentalism and voluntary Ismaic organizations, and with those classes and groups that had been most responsive to the appeal of the Ikhan. (p. 340)

The Nasser crackdown and the rise of radical political Islam have manifested in Sayyid Qutb, who transformed from

> a very liberal writer in Egypt into the most radical fundamentalist thinker in the Arab world, converting his imprisonment and ferocious torture [under the accusation of being an MB member by the Nasser government] into a radical political theology of violence and isolation. (Moussalli, 1999, p. 96)

Qutb's stance towards the Nasser regime was an offensive one, in which he represented the government as a 'model of *jahiliya*' (Kepel, 1999a, b, p. 47). This roughly means that he perceived the society as one governed by 'an iniquitous prince who made himself an object of worship in God's place and who governed an empire according to his own caprice' rather than the teachings of Islam (Kepel, 1999a, b, p. 48). Qutb, in his literature, called upon the *Umma* to 'undertake *jihad* [armed rebellion] against their leader because they had placed God's Shari'a with their own man-made laws' (Sullivan & Abdel-Kotob, 1999, p. 43). According to the scholars, 'this marked the starting point of the road which the militants of the Islamic movement would travel' (Sullivan & Abdel-Kotob, 1999) as the crackdown handicapped the relatively moderate Brotherhood and generated a vacuum in the political theological trend that contemporary Islamic groups were more than prepared to occupy (Kassem, 2004a, b, c, d, p. 140).

The grave consequences of this became more evident when Sadat assumed power. Sadat's unpopularity made him believe that restoring the MB would gain him a social base to rely on for political support. As Kassem (2004a, b, c, d) noted 'Nasser viewed the Brotherhood as a threat, Sadat perceived the leftists and Nasserists as the main obstacle to both his consolidation of power and efforts to move away from Nasser's ailing socialist experiment' (p. 140). Sadat allowed Islamist groups to participate in the socio-economic and political arenas to establish an organised foundation of social support comprised of the members of underground Islamist movements which emerged to counter Nasser's crackdown. This courtship with Islamist organisations was meant to solidify his position in power by adopting a religious guise; 'I want us to raise Muslim boys and to spend money on them so they can become *rakizitna* [our anchor]' (Sullivan & Abdel-Kotob, 1999, p. 71). Mohamed Heikal, realising Sadat's efforts, commented on the radical turn Egypt has taken, stating:

> Much money was ... going to the universities, where lavish exhibitions of religious literature were frequently staged. Societies were promoted to provide students with what was described as 'Islamic costume', veils for the girls and *galabiyehs* for the boys .... But most energy was devoted to ensuring that the students were correctly represented in their unions. To give just one example: in the elections for the student union in Alexandria University [in 1978] ... candidates from the Islamic association won all 60 places in the Faculties of Medicine, and Engineering, 46 out of 48 in the Faculty of Law, 43 out of 60 in the Faculty of Pharmacy ... knowing that they had the support of higher authority, the Islamic students began to behave as if it was they who were running the universities .... Any students who openly disagreed with the Islamic groups were subject to disciplinary action. Boys and girls seen walking together were beaten up .... It was clear that the religious students were not simply tolerated by the authorities but actively encouraged by them. (p. 133)

Sadat's crackdown followed the 1979 peace treaty with Israel as he started

> realizing that the groups posed an increasing threat, he unleashed a series of responses that signaled the end of the regime's positive involvement with the groups. He withheld subsides from the student unions that were dominated by Islamists ... and deprived the *jama'at* of their legal cover, their organization and their funds. (Heikal, 1983, p. 134)

Yet, that realisation came later as his popularity declined quickly with the *infitah*, leading to an immeasurable gap between the rich and the poor, and the socially condemned peace treaty with Israel. By that point, however, the Islamist organisations in Egypt had already infiltrated and recruited many youths whose frustration with the regime found refuge in said organisations (Kepel, 1999a, b, p. 149). The anti-Sadat atmosphere, consequentially, pinnacled and imploded in 1981 with his assassination, which was well received by the society. The assassinator, Khalid al-Islamboli, justified himself during the interrogation stating 'I did what I did because Shari'a was not applied, because of the peace treaty with the Jews, and because of the arrest of Muslim 'Ulama [religious jurist] without justification' (Heikal, 1983, p. 44). In an interview with another member of the Islamist organisation, the social disparities and distress were reflected. He categorised the regime as 'a corrupt one' elucidating, 'we hear of a member of parliament having been involved in drug traffic system, a minister who is presently being tried for taking advantage of his position, and of individuals becoming millionaires overnight'

(Heikal, 1983, p. 46). These interviews reveal an unfortunate reality in which the majority of the society under the Sadat regime subsisted.

A study carried out by the World Bank emphasised that after Sadat's assassination a 'distributional effects of various policies especially on agriculture' were lobbied for by, mainly, socialists and others to reverse the negative distributional impact of the *infitah* (Gadallah et al., 2014, p. 14). The supposed egalitarian regime, employed by Egypt's socialist leader Nasser, was oftentimes cited as the 'golden ages' of Egyptian social equality. This is not meant to glorify Nasser, especially because after 1952 Egypt was described as 'the half-percent society' (Eshag & Kamal, 1968), that is, 0.5% of the society owned 99% of fertile and agricultural land. Nonetheless, as depicted below, Nasser has contributed a lot to social inequality in Egypt by introducing multiple structural and land reforms which are believed to have dropped the GINI coefficient from 0.889 in 1950 (Radwan, 1977) to 0.46 in 1974–1975, prior to its increase again post-*infitah* (Zaytoun, 1982).

Under Mubarak, the Islamists started to incorporate violence into their policies as to counter the crackdown of the regime and the militarised strategy to silence the movement (Greges, 2002, p. 593). This politically charged environment fell under Mubarak vengeance for Sadat's assassination. One of the 'bloodiest' crackdowns of the century was observed and documented, where '1164 casualties – averaging 291 causalities annually – due to politically motivated violence by Islamist activists' occurred (Ibrahim, 1995, p. 52). This was followed by mass military trials of civilians, which scholars believe to have transformed political Islamism to political fundamental-terrorism (Kassem, 2004a, b, c, d, p. 145). This only aggravated the situation and encouraged militants use their leaders' ideology and implement 'gentle preaching, meeting "bad deeds" with "good deeds" to influence reform in the path of Islam. If this does not succeed [they believed] *jihad* then requires the use of physical force' (Sullivan & Abdel-Kotob, 1999, p. 74). The insurgency of Islamist was forcefully driven underground. With the fall of the Mubarak in 2011, the MB and Islamists saw an opportunity to seize power and regain a position of political and social influence. This was sponsored by how the MB has 'managed to develop a political narrative that was not exclusively ideology-driven, but rather coherent and inclusive in its nature' (Bayat, 2017, p. 177/178). This atmosphere was entrenched by their vocalisation of the discontinuity of the authoritarian leadership, which hinted towards how 'the organization reflected mainstream, liberal, political ideas, which Egypt's authoritarian rulers always voiced but never implemented' (Bayat, 2017, p. 177/178). It can be argued that because of the nature of the organisation as a radical opposition party to authoritarian regimes, upon assuming a political leadership role, an internal conflict arose and was schematised by social demand for secularisation while the organisation's orientation was predominantly conservative. The quick collapse of the MB on 30 June 2013 can therefore be attributed to the organisation's longstanding nonpolitical engagement, and its 'unwillingness to undergo a process of ideological and organizational transformation' ultimately led to their failure (El Sherif, 2014, p. 8).

This chapter chronologically presented how different regimes responded to activism, social movements, and socio-political opposition. It highlighted how Nasser, Sadat, and Mubarak consecutively and periodically personalised their rule in a manner which would monopolise executive and legislative power to the president. The institutional responses to opposition, which include feminist and women's movements, reveal the different levels of state-sponsored oppression inherent to authoritarian rule. The following chapter will build on the literature and focus specifically on how feminists and women's movements in Egypt have operated throughout the 19th- and 20th century. This will include a presentation of Egypt's first feminists, feminist 'waves', and reactionary forces to feminist efforts.

Chapter 2

Feminism, Identity, and the Status of Women in Egypt (19th–20th Century)

The advancement of women's social position, and their move from the private to the public sphere, can be traced back to the mid-19th century. When Mohamed Ali Pasha declared Egypt a sovereign province within the Ottoman Empire, he began to 'wrest women away from the more exclusive control of the family, threatening the authority and domination of men over their women' (Badran, 1991, p. 201). In an attempt to consolidate his power, Mohamed Ali placed the Islamic jurists' institution, Al-Azhar, under the direct control of the State. His reign saw a shift to secular ideologies, specifically in the domains of law and education. Moreover, he spearheaded the ideology of 'state and church' separation, by which he confined religion to the private sphere and personal status law, so as not to upset the Ottoman authorities (Tucker, 1985, p. 112). This ideological shift is believed to have created an awkward atmosphere for women whose roles as members of the religious community (*Umma*) and as citizens of the nation (*Watan*) were compromised, resulting in a split between their obligations and their rights (Mernissi, 1988a, p. 37). On the one hand, women were perceived as a political power necessary to achieve change. On the other hand, as members of the *Umma,* women were perceived as the producers of the next generations of male soldiers, therefore restricted by the social perception of women as mothers, homemakers, and caretakers.

Mohamed Ali Pasha's confinement of religion to the private sphere and personal status laws had grave consequences almost 100 years later. Scholars such as Badran (1991) noted that 'the religious establishment was eroded piecemeal in the drive towards secularisation of education and law. The only exception to this was the sphere of personal status laws' and continued to elaborate that 'in the realm of law there was a secularisation of commercial, civil, and criminal codes leaving only *ahwal shakhsiyah*, or personal status law (also called family law), under the jurisdiction of Islam' (Badran, 1991, p. 201). According to Badran (1991):

> Patriarchal domination remained most entrenched in the family, with modes of control over women varying according to class and circumstances … With the erosion of the instrumental hold of

males inside the patriarchal family over 'their' women as the nineteenth century progressed – a corollary of 'modernisation' of state and society – the personal status laws, or family laws, became a last bastion of control over women. The patriarchal family would not relinquish this control, nor would the State exact it.

One can argue that Badran's observations are still applicable to the Egyptian context in the 21st century, and thus her observations can be used to elaborate on how the patriarchal structure continues to be instrumental in controlling women by ascribing a certain identity to them.

Molyneux (1985, p. 233), which Goetz (1990a, b) expanded on, defined strategic gender interests as

> the abolishment of sexual division of labour, the alleviation of the burdens of domestic labour and childcare, the removal of institutionalised forms of discrimination, the attainment of political equality, the establishment of freedom of choice over childbearing, and the adoption of adequate measures against male violence and control over women.

Walby (1990) conceptually categorised these into six strategic gender interests. The first concept of *Family/Household Production* encompasses 'the abolishment of sexual division of labour' the second concept of *Paid Employment* encompasses the 'alleviation of domestic labour and childcare', the third concept of *Sexuality* encompasses 'the establishment of freedom of choice over childbearing ... and control over women', the fourth concept *Culture* encompasses 'the removal of institutionalised forms of discrimination', the last concepts Violence and the State encompass 'the attainment of political equality and the adoption of adequate measures against male violence and control over women' (Walby, 1990). Each of these is explained in further detail later in this chapter.

Respectively, Kandiyoti (1998) argued that in areas where classic patriarchy is observable, women will often find themselves adhering 'for as far and as long as they possibly can to rules' of the patriarchal bargain (p. 100). The term patriarchal bargain refers to the strategies women employ within concrete constraints or rules set by the sex-based patriarchal system which dictates gender roles. It is essential to note that patriarchy and the patriarchal bargain are experienced differently in different locations, by different classes, religions, and ages of women. In the context of Egypt, Kandiyoti's observation rings true, but only when accompanied by her assertion that some women are complicit in the reproduction and perpetuation of the patriarchal system. The extent to which some women collude with the patriarchal system for their own benefit is explored in Chapter 5, using the Hijab as a tool to collect information about how the collusion is manifested and what purpose and/or benefit it serves these women. This observation is not specific to investigations of gender relations. For instance, between the 16th and 19th centuries scholars observed that 'African traders were willing to supply enslaved Africans to Europeans for the trans-Atlantic trade' (Battle, 2013). Scholars such as Klein (2010, pp. 99–103) argued that the dominant reason African sellers traded in enslaved members of their communities is profit and economic gain. Similarly, Evans and Richardson (1995, p. 678) explained the phenomenon stating that even 'where states went to war for other reasons, the export trade in slaves provided opportunities to realize earnings from captives who might otherwise have been executed on the battlefield'. This example is not meant to insinuate that women's status and roles in Egypt are comparable to the transatlantic slave trade but is used here to highlight that even under extreme circumstances, some groups could still benefit from others' disadvantages. It is also significant to note that the extent to which some women may have colluded with the patriarchal system for personal gain, and women's experiences with patriarchy, and the patriarchal bargain is different depending on location, classes, religion, and age. This is unpacked in Chapters 4 and 5.

Furthermore, Kandiyoti argued that women often employ strategic tactics to gain greater control and security within the patriarchal system (1988, p. 275). However, Kandiyoti (1988) also reported that by complying with the rules of the patriarchal system, some women are in 'active collusion in the production of their own subordination' (p. 289), revealing the significance of recognising the intersectionality and multiplicity of women's lived experiences in a patriarchal system. Similarly, Kabeer (2006) posited that if women are denied or lack the 'ability to exercise agency on their own', which is obtained by having the right to realise their strategic gender interests, then they would also be denied or lack the ability to 'challenge their own [citizenship] exclusion' (p. 100).

In this book, the term strategic gender interests refers to Egyptian women's ability to attain and actualise their 'real interests'. However, Molyneux's definition of what constitutes strategic gender interests is inapplicable to the Egyptian context as the interests Molyneux identified have not been actualised in Egypt and Egyptian women have been prevented from challenging their exclusion. Molyneux stated that one of the key components of women's strategic interests is the liberation from sexual division of labour, which means that some occupations are socially reserved exclusively for one sex. In Egypt, for instance, engineering, law, and medicine, among other high-earning executive positions, are predominantly reserved for Egyptian men, and women were denied access to these degree programmes. While this may not be explicitly stated, women are actively deterred from pursuing occupations which are traditionally occupied by men, particularly when the profession requires the use of critical faculties and/or physical strength. Qualities which were attributed to men exclusively were believed not to possess for women. For instance, when the researcher wanted to apply for a position at the Ministry of Foreign Affairs in Egypt she was informed that, to apply, a woman requires a Grade Point Average (GPA) of 3.8/4 while a man is required to have a GPA of 3.2/4. When the researcher inquired about this, she was informed that the ministry is not keen on hiring women because they require sex-specific accommodations, unlike men; women might request paid maternal leave, which could disrupt ministerial workflow.

Furthermore, Molyneux stated that for women to be emancipated they require domestic burdens, such as domestic labour and childcare, to be alleviated. While in

Egypt, the economic situation since the 2011 Revolution has required more women to enter the workforce to support their husbands. However, the social expectation of women leaving their work still remains, particularly if a woman is perceived to not be able to balance her domestic and employment responsibilities. Article 11 of the Egyptian Constitution (2014) titled 'The Place of Women, Motherhood and Childcare' states that the State supports the empowerment of women, so women could 'reconcile the duties of a woman toward her family and her work requirements'. However, there is no equivalent law titled 'The Place of Men, Fatherhood and Childcare' for Egyptian men, revealing that the social and institutional discourse perceives the rights of women beyond the domestic sphere as a subsidiary and not primary. The primary data also reveal that the dominant social discourse in Egypt is that a woman's place in society is in the domestic sphere, and a woman's primary responsibility is childcare, domestic labour, and motherhood.

Moreover, Molyneux argued that for women to actualise their strategic gender interests, the institutionalised forms of discrimination need to be removed, and the attainment of political equality for women needs to be instated. While Article 11 of the Egyptian constitution does state the State is committed to the equality of men and women, the secondary and primary data revealed that political equality between women and men is an unrealised ambition (see in this chapter). Furthermore, in Egypt, institutionalised forms of discrimination have not been abolished (see in this chapter), though some were made redundant such as Article 291 of the Penal Code (1999), which allowed a rapist to marry their victim and avoid persecution, the legal system structurally allows for laws which have been abolished to still be administered in Customary Courts if requested by the plaintiff.

Finally, Molyneux (1985) states that for women to be emancipated, they should have 'freedom of choice over childbearing and adequate measures against male violence and control over women' (p. 233). While Egyptian women, particularly Muslim women, do have the right to abortion, and Islam does permit the use of contraception, the social and institutional discourses in Egypt do not comply with this, in spite of Article 2 of the Egyptian constitution stating that *Sharia Islam* is the principal source of legislation. Furthermore, while the Egyptian Penal Code does include articles which criminalise various forms of male violence against women, such as sexual harassment and assault, the enforcement of the law is deficient and the law itself is not comprehensive as it does not protect against domestic violence and intermarital rape, *inter alia,* and requires victims of assault and abuse to capture their perpetrator in order to file an official police report.

Molyneux's definition is crucial for this book, yet as the majority of the criteria set have not been met in Egypt, this book uses the term to refer to any effort by women to attain any strategic gender interests. For example, in this chapter, how gender-based legal discrimination has blocked women's emancipatory efforts in contemporary Egypt is unpacked and investigated as a possible mechanism employed by the patriarchal system to prevent women from realising their strategic gender interests. However, whether the abolishment of the sexual division of labour or the desire to reform certain personal status laws are strategic interests Egyptian women desires falls outside of the scope and data collected for this project. Therefore, in this book, the term is used to refer the concept and idea of strategic gender interest but does not identify specific strategic gender interests of Egyptian women. Building on the findings presented in this book, the identification of specific strategic gender interests of Egyptian women ought to be explored and investigated in the future.

To understand how Egyptian women have found themselves in a position where they enjoy practical interests but limited strategic interests, the following chapter reviews feminist movements which promote women's strategic gender interests, equal identity, and citizenship status. First, we need to define what is meant by 'identity'. Defining what is meant by 'identity' is a debateable and complicated task, as sub-disciplines define and contextualise it differently. For this project, works by key gender and development researchers, such as Naila Kabeer, Deniz Kandeyioti, and Margot Badran, are adopted to examine the relationship between identity and citizenship. Two levels of identity have emerged from the literature: personal identity and social identity. According to Erik Erikson (1968), personal identity:

> Employs a process of simultaneous reflection and observation, taking place on all levels of mental functioning, by which the individual judges himself in light of what he perceives to be the way in which others judge him in comparison to themselves and to a typology significant to them; while he judges their way of judging him in light of how he perceives himself in comparison to them and to types that have become relevant to him.

Tajfel (1978) expanded on this definition and articulated how personal identity relates to social identity, stating it is 'that part of an individual's self-concept which derives from his knowledge of his membership of a social group (or groups), together with the value and emotional significance attached to that membership' (p. 63). Hence, one can state that identity is the answer to the question of 'who are you' (Vignoles et al., 2001). As this book focusses on the Egyptian female identity, defining gender identity more specifically is necessary. Judith Butler (1988, p. 520) argued that 'gender identity is a performative accomplishment compelled by social sanction', meaning that gender identity is socially constructed and performed by the subject to avoid social sanction. Vignoles (2017) argued that 'personal identity might be what is leftover from this [social identity]: those parts of the self-concept that are derived from the individual's knowledge of other kinds of self-attribute' (p. 1). Mona Laczo (2003a, b) investigated the relationship between individual identity and citizenship. Laczo (2003a, b) had argued that there is a mutually inclusive relationship between women's individual identities and full citizenship rights, stating that when citizenship is gendered, it leaves women

> vulnerable and without an individual identity [therefore] helping women acquire an individual identity, beyond their roles as wives, sisters, daughter and mothers ... would be an important step in the fight for equal rights of women within the family, the community and the ... State as a whole ... [as] it would enable women to build their own identities and lives. (p. 81)

Comparably, Haywood (1994a, b) argued that if the right to construct one's identity is not protected as a basic human right, particularly in patriarchal contexts where women's citizenship rights are accorded through male relatives, then women 'cannot properly be thought of as "full citizens", even though they may enjoy a range of formal entitlements' (p. 155). These accounts emphasise the interdependency of identity and citizenship, particularly highlighting how patriarchal structures can influence women's self-conception.

Respectively, one can make the argument that personal and social identities are expressions of personhood that 'link rights and agency' to citizenship rights and strategic gender interests (Kabeer, 2006, p. 92). According to Kabeer (2006), the term citizenship can be traced back to traditional understandings of 'the nation-state and taken to refer to membership of the nation-state and the formal duties and rights which membership carries'. Referring to Kabeer (2006), citizenship in the context of this book is used as 'a way to defining the place of the individual in society' which 'serves to reinforce rather than eradicate pre-existing forms of social inequality' by ascribing an inferior citizenship status to women (p. 98). In agreement with Kabeer's (2006) argument that 'how excluded groups view their exclusion. How people define themselves and are defined by others, is likely to be critical to their ability to exercise agency on their own behalf, including the agency needed to challenge their exclusion' (p. 100), this book posits that the Egyptian female identity is socially prescribed, ascribed, and enforced onto women, leading to their socio-political exclusion and their secondary citizenship status in Egypt. Kabeer (2006, p. 92) further argued that the exclusion of historically marginalised groups from full citizenship and group membership ought not to be taken for granted as 'it had to be actively justified through the ascription of various forms of deficiency'. The belief that 'nature has made [women] to be so weak as to require male protection' (Shklar, 1991, p. 49) is the 'deficiency' challenged in this book project, particularly as it is used to justify the exclusion of women from full-citizenship status. Hence, in this book, the extent to which the patriarchal system prevents women from realising their strategic gender interests is examined and explored. Particularly, it explores how women can transport their identities and affiliations out of the private sphere, where it is patriarchally informed, and into the public sphere where they can exercise power and control equally to their male counterparts (Joseph, 1997, p. 79).

In summary, this book identity is used to refer to (a) a socially distinguishing feature that a person takes special pride in and is individually formed, (b) a social category defined by one's group membership and characteristic attributes or expected behaviours. This book uses both understandings of identity to examine Egyptian women's socio-cultural and political inferiority to unearth the patriarchal structures which have led to the perception of women as second-class citizens. The following chapter reviews the historical and political changes in Egypt which set the norm of women's inferiority and second-class citizenship by curtailing women's realisation of their strategic gender interests. The chapter follows the chronological progression of 'feminist waves', movements to reclaim power over women's autonomy, agency, and identity in Egypt. It continues to discuss the concept of dehumanisation and its relationship to the female identity and its effects on power dynamics in Egypt, concluding with a discussion of how the dehumanisation of Egyptian women has been rationalised using religion by the State and solidified as the acceptable social identity. The aim is to set the scene for this book and answer the first research question: what role did the State play in promoting/suppressing the political and social status of women in hopes of better understanding the interplay between the female identity and the perception of women as second-class citizens?

1. A Brief Overview of Feminist Activism in Egypt

Deniz Kandiyoti (1991a, b), in her article 'Women, Islam and the State', investigated the analytical weight Middle Eastern politics bear on women's rights and subordination. Kandiyoti (1991a, b) examined the central role of Islam in gender and politics of the Middle East, stating that conservative leaders used the

> Qur'an, the *Hadith* [the second source of jurisprudence for Islamic Sharia] and the lives of prominent women in the early period of Muslim history as sources ... [to confirm] that existing gender asymmetries are divinely ordained, while feminists discerned possibilities for a more progressive politics of gender-based on the egalitarian ideals of early Islam. (p. 9)

Kandiyoti (1991a, b) argued that this divisive understanding of Islam was oftentimes used by Middle Eastern leaders as means for national consolidation and/or political legitimation (p. 12). Most notable was Gamal Abdel Nasser's authoritarian regime in Egypt. Under Nasser's rule, women's organisations and civil societies which represent women's gender interests were subsumed by the State to solve the dilemma of 'modernising' the country. Kandiyoti (1991a, b) argued that national liberation brought about 'new forms of civic consciousness to liberate all available forces of development, including the labour potential of their female citizens' (p. 11). Egypt gained its independence from the British colonial forces in 1952. As Egypt's first president, Nasser had to consolidate his executive control and did so by granting women suffrage. However, immediately afterwards he outlawed all women's and feminist organisations, instead instigating a programme of 'state-sponsored women's organisations [to act as] docile auxiliaries of the ruling state-party' (Kandiyoti, 1991a, b, p. 12). Yet, what was not accounted for was the radical Islamist backlash which would regard Nasser's actions as a political failure and a 'moral failure, requiring a complete overhaul of the world views underpinning them' (Kandiyoti, 1991a, b, p. 12). Even though Nasser's state-sponsored feminism model advanced women's practical gender interests and did not challenge or reform power structures, the Islamist backlash was over the State sponsoring any interests which would challenge male-domination which they believed is divinely ordained.

Consequentially, a power struggle between politics, Islam, and women's status in the Egyptian context arose. The Islamisation of political endeavours is believed to have been triggered by the struggle to 'forge new notions of citizenship' and national identity for the modern nation-state (Kandiyoti, 1991a, b, p. 10). This struggle included 'women's rights being debated in search for new ideologies to legitimise emerging forms of state power' (Kandiyoti, 1991a, b, p. 10). This identity crisis and the subsequent power struggle between different forces within the country paved the way for the political opposition in Egypt, the Muslim brotherhood, to gain a stronger political following and momentum. In an attempt to reframe Islamic fundamentalism as an effort for national consolidation, Islamic scripture was used to 'reverse what appeared to be the steady expansion of women's rights in the early stages of national consolidation' (Kandiyoti, 1991a, b, p. 12). This reversal was influenced by myriad events in Egypt; most relevant and notable for this book are feminist movements in the years preceding and following Nasser granting women suffrage. Attaining suffrage, in theory, signifies the equal right of men and women to participate in electing officials, which would represent their interests in the government. However, suffrage is only the first step in the struggle for social and political equality. Where women's citizenship rights are 'accorded to women through male relatives, rather than in their own right' (Laczo, 2003a, b, p. 76), suffrage is countermanded. Rubio-Marin (2014a, b), who investigated the gendered construction of citizenship and resistance to female suffrage in the Western context, argued that 'female suffrage (...) was politically contentious because it could undermine family harmony and generate social instability' (Rubio-Marin, 2014a, b, p. 16). She continued to highlight how in Europe's patriarchal systems the male narrative was that 'women's suffrage was unnecessary, because "their men" already represented women's interests' (Rubio-Marin, 2014a, 2014b). The following section unpacks how suffrage and other forms of strategic gender interests were developed and perceived in Egypt, by presenting the historical progression of women's rights in Egypt to contextualise the question: how does the patriarchal system prevented women from achieving their strategic gender interests, perpetuating women's second-class citizenship in Egypt?

2. The First Feminists in Egypt

One of Egypt's first feminist pioneers was Nabawiya Musa,[1] author of *Al Mar'a al 'Amal* (*The Woman and Work*) published in 1920, who argued that more female labourers being employed will result in enhanced economic performance. As Musa predicted and Kandiyoti (1991a, b) recorded, this was indeed executed by the Egyptian Government in 1952. Musa had argued that women's employment would pave the way for a more progressive, inclusive, and egalitarian society, adding that women's visibility in the public sphere would solidify the significant role of women, particularly in the education sector. In her book, she argued that the revolution for independence gave rise to a national idiom that incorporated women's voices. Moreover, Musa and Nasif were among the first women to graduate from the *Saniyya Teachers School* and moved on to become educators themselves. Musa was also the first woman to undertake a baccalaureate in 1907 (Badran, 1988, p. 388) and

---

[1] A founding member of the Egyptian Feminist Union (EFU) and a delegate to the International Woman Suffrage Alliance Conference in Rome in 1923, the first international meeting Egyptian feminists attended.

actively promoted education as a 'national interest' to empower women and liberate Egyptians from colonial powers. Musa was condemned by some Egyptians for stirring up sedition and violating 'social norms' by promoting the intermingling of males and females in educational settings. According to Civantos (2013a, b), Musa was defying 'the social power attached to the typically male privilege of reading and writing', which in turn exposed her to the social backlash, particularly because during this period 'women were taught to read but not necessarily to write, and that poetry was considered a dangerous subject for female pupils' (Civantos, 2013a, b, p. 7). Additionally, Civantos (2013a, b) noted that 'most Egyptians wanted girls to learn only about the domestic sphere, and women's education was tied to the needs of the State. Women were educated to enter healthcare and teaching professions and to be good wives and mothers'. After Musa's controversy, the higher education system was absorbed by British powers, who claimed that 'there was Islamic opposition to women's education' (Civantos, 2013a, b, p. 8), and subsequently refused female admission to universities, and claimed that they aimed to train men for administrative roles and could not, supposedly, accommodate women (Tignor, 1966, pp. 319–320).

Nonetheless, these women continued on their quest for a feminist and gender-conscious Egypt. They collaborated on multiple occasions and gave public lectures designed exclusively for women, lobbied for a more inclusive and representative parliament, and pioneered female activism and roles in the revolution for independence (Yousef, 2011, p. 74). For example, in 1911, Nasif (1962) stood in front of the Egyptian National Congress and demanded subsidisation of women's education and the reform of the Higher Education system to include more women. Furthermore, she advocated opening up the public administrative space for the employment of women. Contrary to the position of their male feminist counterparts, Nasif and Huda Shaarawi, another pioneer, opposed the unveiling of women. They argued that accessibility to the public space should precede taking off traditional garments. This idea resided in fear as 'for women unveiling was a practical matter that they themselves would undertake, with the attendant risks of taunts and assaults on their reputations' (Badran, 1991, p. 26).

The success these feminist pioneers had in raising social consciousness about women's rights, one can argue, was most pronounced with the 16 March 1919 Women's March against British powers, where for the first time Egyptian women fought as equals with their male counterparts towards a common interest, national liberation from the British power. The march marked the first instance in which gender and ideological differences were set aside for the sake of a common goal, national liberation. The march was described by Egyptian poet Ibrahim Hafiz as

> an act of public dissent which led to the death of a woman and many being injured. The violence with which women protesters were met did not bring an end to Egyptian women's organising; on the contrary, it only led to further mobilisation, more organisation and political strategising. (Kamal, 2017, p. 4)

Hala Kamal (2017) documented the similarities between the 1919 women's march and the 2011 Egyptian revolution. Kamal (2017) shed light on how in 1919 and 2011 respectively 'the masses of women [were] violently confronted by the authorities – not only politically but socially as well' (p. 5) highlighting that the intersection between feminist demands and national demands had not changed, and thus neither has the struggle for Egyptian women's rights. This intersection of demands can be investigated using Molyneux's (1985) concepts of 'strategic gender interests' and 'practical gender interests'.

According to Molyneux, *practical gender interests* are 'given inductively and arise from concrete conditions of women's positioning within the gender division of labour' (1985, p. 233), which Goetz (1995) elaborates are interests that directly 'respond to immediate, situationally specific needs and which may not challenge prevailing forms of gender subordination' (p. 7). On the other hand, strategic gender interests are 'what are most frequently considered by feminists as women's "real" interests (...) and are formulated by the women who are themselves within these positions' (Molyneux, 1985, p. 233), which Goetz (1995) elaborated as 'transformative goals such as womeńs emancipation and gender equality' (p. 7). Looking at the involvement of women in the marches of 1919 and 2011, respectively, we can categorise their participation as a response to a *practical* need and not a strategic one. Kamal (2017) noted that while women in both scenarios were received with praise over their 'courageous act of protest' (p. 5), afterwards they were socially confronted with attacks, and sexual violence, and pushed back into the private sphere. One can argue that the national interests which were achieved in both scenarios ended women's practical response to the situational needs, and thereby the condition which justified the temporary suspension of patriarchal gender roles. In a trans-national study by Goetz (1995), she noted that the 'literal domination of decision-making [by men], and the historical embedding of their needs and interests in the structures and practices of public institutions' leave little room for women to occupy a significant presence in the public sphere (p. 4). This observation rings true for the Egyptian context, as Egyptian women's strategic gender interests, including but not limited to

> the abolition of the sexual division of labour, the alleviation of the burden of domestic labour and childcare, the removal of institutionalised forms of discrimination, the attainment of political equality, the establishment of freedom of choice over childbearing, and the adoption of adequate measures against male violence and control over women (Molyneux, 1985, p. 233)

are still central demands for Egyptian women and feminists.

Strategic gender interests can thereby be summarised as the right to agency and autonomy, both critical for the exercise of one's citizenship rights in the public sphere. Hala Kamal (2017) determined that the parallels between the 1919 and the 2011 protests suggest that marginal improvements have been made to advance Egyptian women's strategic gender interests. Philipp (1978) reported that this dynamic led feminists to feel betrayed by their male compatriots, explaining:

> The relationship between the nationalist movement and feminism was by no means as harmonious and positive as it may appear at

first glance. Initially, male nationalists accepted nationalist activism (demonstrations, economic, boycotts, etc). However, after 1919, when nationalist pressures emerged in the wake of promulgation of a constitution for Egypt, women's political rights were not mentioned. Their equality with men was not discussed. (cited in Al-Ali, 2000, p. 62)

Subsequently, the observation that Egyptian women are perceived as inferior to their male counterparts and excluded from full citizenship rights can be attributed to the unrealised strategic gender interests of Egyptian women. To understand how the patriarchal system prevented women from achieving their strategic gender interests, the next section reviews the three waves of Egyptian feminist movements, which demanded equal rights for women. The following sections also highlight the challenges faced by Egyptian feminists to emphasise how the patriarchal system exploited and manipulated women to maintain male domination and preserve the social status quo, elaborating on what Molyneux (1985) called 'mobilisation without emancipation'.

2.1. The First Feminist Wave: Public Education and Political Representation

After the protectorate was ended by the British in 1922,[2] many activists, including revolutionary leader Saad Zaghloul, used this as a path for the establishment of a national constitution. Men and women were initially satisfied with the outcome, as the constitution declared 'All Egyptians are equal before the law. They enjoy equal civil and political rights and equally have a public responsibility without distinction of race, language, or religion' (Egyptian Constitution, 1923). Feminists were positively optimistic about the new constitution, yet their optimism was quickly dispelled. Soon after the declaration, the Electoral Law was established giving suffrage to men exclusively. The following year, the parliament was reopened, and women were only allowed to attend their meetings as wives, not otherwise. The political arena regressed to its original male-catering and male-dominating state.

Huda Shaarawi, a feminist activist and leader, established and led the EFU in 1923 to counter the political climate post-independence and provide a platform for resistance (Salem, 2017, p. 603). The EFU aimed to voice distrust against the governing system and to actively oppose the male domination of every aspect of public and private life. From 1923 onwards, feminist activism in Egypt demanded women's right to achieve *strategic gender interests* in Egypt, in hopes of structurally reforming socio-economic, political, and cultural perceptions of women (Ahmed, 1982; al-Sabaki, 1987; Ghoussoub, 1985; Hatem, 1986; Khalifa, 1973a, b; Philipp, 1978). The organisation sought to renovate and reinvent women's status and

---

[2]It is important to note that while the British declared Egypt as an independent Kingdom in 1922, functioning colonialism still prevailed, and Egypt gained true independence in 1952, after which it became the Arab Republic of Egypt.

identity in Egyptian society. First, the EFU's agenda was to access and subsidise secondary education for women and girls of all social classes (Al-Ali, 2002; Sika 2012; Withcher, 2005). Second, the reform of personal status law to grant women legal protection from respective abuse and control, raise the minimum marriage age of both sexes to prevent forced child marriages, especially in rural communities, and provide women with equal and fair access to the labour force unencumbered and free of harassment or other forms of subjugation (Abu-Lughod, 1988). In 1929, the EFU alongside feminist scholar Ahmed Lutfy Al-Sayyid were successful in lobbying for women's admission into higher education, arguing in parliament its necessity for the Egyptian population (Salmoni, 2005, p. 63). Although higher education was *de jure* open to everyone, women's admission was restricted to the Faculty of Physical Education for Women, Higher Institute for Nursing (Women only), and Women's Faculty (Molek, 1975, p. 14). While women's admission had been allowed at Cairo University since 1908, it was restricted to the aforementioned gender-segregated degrees. Reid (1990) noted that even though this admission system was suspended in 1912 and only reinstated in 1928, it delayed women's equal access to educational services and therefore women's realisation of strategic gender interests. This suspension perpetuated the stereotype of women as caregivers and prevented proximity to their male counterparts in the academic and work environments. As Badran (1991) noted, 'their new work also perpetuated gender segregation in public spaces. However, great numbers of women were also drawn into employment in the expanding textile factories, where they worked more closely with men' (p. 208), revealing that while women were granted constitutional and legal rights, this did not necessarily translate into cultural and societal change.

This highlights that Molyneux's (1985) findings ring true, and mobilisation without emancipation can occur if practical gender interests are pursued over strategic gender interests. From that perspective, constitutional and legal rights afforded to Egyptian women only served a practical interest but lacked the depth to be transformed into the strategic gender interest of equal access and opportunity to public services, such as education. Egyptian women's unrealised strategic needs in the public sphere hindered women's agency development, that is, women's ability 'to define and to make strategic life choices' (Nazir & Ramadan, 2018, p. 155). Lacking the agency and power to make 'strategic life choices' Egyptian women's subordination is reproduced and unequal power structures are maintained. As Kabeer (1999) highlighted '[in] a context where cultural values constrain women's ability to make strategic life choices, structural inequalities cannot be addressed by individuals alone' (p. 457). Kabeer (1999) further stated that

> since women are likely to be given greater respect within their communities for conforming to its norms, and to be penalised if they do not, their own values and behaviour are likely to reflect those of the wider community and to reproduce its injustices.

In another article, Kabeer (1999) further extended the definition of strategic life choices and moved beyond observable action, stating that agency 'encompasses the meaning, motivation and purpose which individuals bring to their activity, their sense of agency, or 'the power within' (p. 438). 'Power within' is also one of the most fundamental aspects of strategic gender interests, as it involves 'an increased critical consciousness and self-respect ... awareness of socially constructed identities and hierarchies ... and the desire for personal and structural change' (O'Neil et al., 2014, p. 4). Kabeer (1999) further argued that without a sense of agency 'the norms and rules governing social behaviour tend to ensure that certain outcomes are reproduced'. Applying these observations to the Egyptian context, one can argue that one's agency is directly related to their perception of their own identity and role in society. Being excluded from exercising their full citizenship rights by being denied admission into university degrees was thereby a declaration of Egyptian women's inferiority and marked the first failed attempt at realising women's strategic gender interests in Egypt. The consequences of this on Egyptian women's identity and status are discussed in more detail in Chapter 4.

The 1930s brought about novel challenges for Egyptian women. The EFU had demanded political reform to allow female representatives, the abolishment of state-sponsored and licenced prostitution, and reform of the personal status law which had not been amended (Yousef, 2011, p. 71). Al-Azhar's Mohamed Abdu Al Fadl at the time wrote to the EFU stating 'we appreciate the value of your honourable association and its diligent effort to spread virtue and combat vice. There are in Egypt now distinguished women whose impact on society is no less important than that of honourable men' (Golley, 2003, p. 36), therewith condoning the practices but also endorsing the establishment of the EFU. Al-Azhar as an institution, nonetheless, proceeded to renounce the legal and political rights of women in the form of *fatwas* (religious decrees), calling the presence of a woman in the public space alongside men un-Islamic, an invitation for promiscuity, and describing it as a form of moral degeneration (Latif, 2002, p. 74). It can be argued that this is an 'old 'Othering' strategy in patriarchal societies, aimed at keeping women outside those civic spaces that offer the possibility of autonomy and independence from male control and dependence' (McFadden, 2001, p. 66).

The EFU's establishment was a celebrated step forward for the advancement of Egyptian women's strategic interests in the public sphere. However, the union had its own structural and ideological incompatibilities, delaying its activism and progress. Although during the 1919 revolution social classes and class differences were overlooked as the common interest and struggle united the stratified society, post-protectorate Egypt was riddled with conflicting ideological movements that appeared to fill the new socio-political void left behind by the British-mandate power (Witcher, 2005, p. 35). Particularly pronounced was the class divide, which the establishment of the EFU emphasised. First, the EFU members were exclusively upper- and upper-middle-class educated women – The founder and leader of the EFU Huda Shaarawi was born and raised in *the Harem*,[3] and while her writings

---

[3]'Although, since 1870, the secular education system introduced by Muhammad Ali was extended to girls, it was not yet popular among the Egyptian elite when Huda Shaarawi was growing up. Rather, young girls from aristocratic families were educated by tutors within the harem' (Russel, 2004, p. 103).

and activism do support women from all social classes, her immediate environment was homogenous, and almost exclusively 'served to push middle-class women to organise themselves in opposition to this socially restrictive goals' (Hatem, 1993, p. 31). Second, the language of the EFU's published journal was French, which was the main spoken language of the elite. When Shaarawi was asked about the use of French as the language of her magazine, *L'Égyptienne,* she stated:

> By founding this review in a language which is not ours, but which in Egypt, as everywhere, is spoken by all the elites, our aim is twofold: communicate abroad about Egyptian women, as they are in our era – with the risk of removing from them all their mystery and charm which their past reclusion gave them in the eyes of Westerners – and to enlighten European public opinion about the real political and social state of Egypt. (Gaden, 2019)

Third, members of the EFU's garment choices depicted Western fashion[4] styles, particularly French and English, foreign to the remainder of the working class, reproving them as un-relatable to other women and setting an invisible barrier of entry to working-class women (Lafranchi-Shaarawi, 2011). These characteristics made the EFU a target for conspiracy theorists and reactionary forces. The organisation was accused of recruiting spies for British powers and depicted them as treacherous women sent to infiltrate the society and extract information from its 'weakest members', that is, women who were believed to be easily manipulated, gullible, and trusting, intentionally defying social tradition to destroy Egyptian identity and cultural heritage (Weber, 2008, p. 88). Furthermore, the national identity of EFU members was often questioned and their loyalty to the Egyptian State was challenged. However, Egyptian men whose fashion choices were Western-influenced and also spoke French and English fluently were rarely attacked or challenged (Jazzar, 2011, p. 163). To further highlight the unequal standards and showcase how women's strategic gender interests in Egypt are denied by the patriarchal system, it is significant to reiterate that, unlike their male counterparts, women were the scapegoats for reactionary forces, and the gender-based symbolic significance of each sex was politically emphasised. It has been noted that 'men could change and retain authenticity (the *tarboosh* or fez),[5] while the burdens of continuity were placed on women' (Badran, 1991, pp. 209–210), highlighting that well into the 1930s, Egyptian women almost exclusively mobilised to respond to the immediate national needs, that is, practical gender interests, yet their subordination was not challenged and the social status quo was maintained.

---

[4]Huda Shaarawi took her veil off on a public train heading towards Cairo. This act was considered against acceptable dress codes for Egyptian women in the public space. She was labelled a 'Westernised' traitor of Islam and the Egyptian culture in the time that followed.

[5]The Ottoman head-dress was forbidden to men by the state following the 1952 revolution.

The apex of this internal conflict was well depicted in the struggle of Zainab Al Ghazali. Al-Azhar educated daughter of a reputed cotton merchant, who joined the EFU shortly after its establishment, showed signs of conflict concerning what Islamic jurists were declaring and the feminist ideology of the EFU. Around the time of her membership, Al-Azhar started a series of educational seminars for women. Al Ghazali's attendance at those seminars, later on, influenced her decision to establish the Muslim Women's Society (MWS) in 1935. Al Ghazali justified her separation from the EFU and the decision to establish her own society by stating 'the EFU wanted to establish the civilisation of the Western woman in Egypt and the rest of the Arab and Islamic World' (Badran, 1991, p. 210). One can argue that in an attempt to promote and achieve strategic gender interests for Egyptian women, Al-Ghazali reoriented her activism to align with the nationalistic narrative dominant at the time, which rejected everything Western (Baron, 1994; Elsadda, 2012; Sobki, 1978a, b). In an interview, Al-Ghazali claimed that Huda Shaarawi, then leader of the EFU, confronted her saying 'you are separating yourself from me intellectually' adding to that 'I ask you not to fight the EFU', which she supposedly responded to saying 'I never fought it' (Interview by Badran,[6] cited in Sharawi-Lanfranchi, 2015a, b, p. 60). The two organisations functioned side by side and successfully co-existed, earning their cooperation the label *Al Shaqiqat* (The Sisters). The harmonious existence lasted until an ideological clash between the two organisations forced them to bifurcate as the EFU's secular ideology conflicted with the MWS's religious one. The most distinguishable feature was how each organisation framed and perceived the role of religion: the EFU perceived Islam as a matter of the private sphere while the MWS saw it as a public lifestyle directed and dictated by Sharia Islam (Badran, 1991, p. 232). Essentially, the EFU extols unconditional equality while the MWS adopts a fundamentalist view in which the sexes are in complementary positions, where male domination of the public sphere and female domination over the private sphere were considered the natural order. This expanded the dichotomies and influenced their understanding of the role of a woman: the EFU advocated for greater access and equality in the private and public domains, while the MWS pioneered the role of women in the household and stressed their duties towards the maintenance of the family and household. The EFU was open to all women of the society irrespective of their religious backgrounds, while the MWS was exclusive to Muslim women.

The contentious debate escalated to *ad hominem* attacks from both sides: the MWS claimed the EFU was an organisation without religion and the EFU claimed the MWS had little understanding of Islam and was not a credible source of information. However, their ideological and personal differences were set aside again when the Palestinian uprisings began. The EFU hosted the first-ever Conference for the Defense of Palestine in 1938. Badran (1991) elicits this event as 'yet another instance when militant nationalism blurred gender lines. The feminists' collective nationalist action in 1938 led to the first pan-Arab feminist conference in 1944 … [which] won the praise of government and Islamic establishment for their nationalist

---

[6]Margot Badran conducted this interview with Zainab Al Ghazali in 1989.

actions' (p. 211). Consequentially, the *Itihad al nisa'I al Arabi* (The Arab Feminist Union – AFU) was established to advance women's political role and advocate for gender equality in the Arab world (Leitz, 2015). In other words, the AFU set out to advocate for another strategic gender interest, namely political representation. This is highlighted in the first issue placed on the AFU's agenda: Personal status laws. The discussion of personal status laws has a systemic issue within Arab countries, developing strategies to challenge these laws and identifying stakeholders and decision-makers qualify the AFU's activities as agency-affirming and strategically motivated initiatives. While many Arab States were slow in adopting the Union's resolutions and reforming their respective personal status laws – believed to be due to Arab regimes not being 'politically strong enough to change family laws significantly and in so doing challenge patriarchal authority in the family as well as threaten the last legal bastion of the religious establishment' (Badran, 1991, p. 210) – gradual changes were introduced. The strive for equal political and legal representation can be considered as another form of strategic gender interests feminists and women's rights activists aspired to realise for Egyptian women. However, the restrictive parameters of personal status laws in Egypt, which are based on Islamic Sharia law, worked to counteract these efforts. Bernard-Maugiron (2010) documented the resistance to personal status laws reformation in Egypt since the early 20th century, arguing that:

> Whenever reformists and women's rights defenders push for reform, conservative groups and individuals resist. The State, caught between these two trends, tries to keep a balance and remains very cautious in interfering in the patriarchal household and in pushing for unpopular women's equal rights within the family. (p. 3)

Bernard-Maugiron (2010) also argued that while some changes have been made to reform personal status laws and progress women's status in Egypt 'discriminatory legal provisions still exist along with biased local practices and traditions which undermine women's status in Egypt' (p. 1). Women's equal political representation remains one of the unactualised strategic interests for Egyptian women and will remain so until the restrictive personal status laws are reformed. The matter is so complex that when the Egyptian Government proposed amendments to personal status laws back in February 2021, the heavy backlash led to the Government withdrawing the draft amendments (Ahmed, 2021). Moreover, evidence from the recent attempt highlighted the Egyptian Government's inability to balance social and religious stability (Ahmed, 2021). It also shows that while feminists and women's activists may fight to realise strategic gender interests for women based on emancipatory ambitions of igniting 'power-within', their efforts will continue to fail if the Government continues to favour a conservative and traditional view of women's status and role in the Egyptian society. This situation could be described as a form of a 'patriarchal bargain' (Kandiyoti, 1998). A patriarchal bargain is a term coined by Deniz Kandiyoti (1998) to entail the strategies women living in patriarchal systems employ to gain a degree of autonomy and security within the 'concrete constraints … [that] influence both the potential for and specific forms of women's active or passive resistance in the face of their oppression' (p. 275). For Egyptian women, the patriarchal bargain appears to be women's acceptance of their second-class citizenship in exchange for the right to initiate divorce and granting mothers' priority over child custody and child guardianship. More on the patriarchal bargain in relation to personal status laws in Egypt is discussed in further detail under the Section *Codifying the Dehumanisation of Egyptian Women* in Chapter 3.

In the early 1940s, the EFU decided to broaden its activities, to elevate the moral and intellectual planes, by publishing in Arabic. Their newspaper, *Al Misriyya*, operated as a communication channel between the union and the society as a whole (Badran, 2005, p. 20). The end of World War II and the weakness of the Egyptian State in its aftermath signalled an opportunity for activists to push for the establishment of political parties to support the EFU and other organisations. The National Feminist Party (NFP), established in 1944, and the Daughter of the Nile Union (DNU), established in 1947 by Doria Shafiq, were the first organisations to form in the new political climate. The EFU, NFP, and the DNU collectively targeted stakeholders for the political advancement of women organised outreach programmes for rural districts and subsidised educational programmes to combat the growing conservative stride of the MB and its *de facto* affiliate committee the MWS (Badran, 1988, p. 376).

In this context, the Muslim Women Society (later referred to as Muslim Sisters (MS)) could be perceived as the equal reactionary force that emerged to balance the EFU. The ideological debates predominantly surrounded the integration and accessibility of Egyptian women into public life, striving for yet another strategic gender interest. At the time the two ideological positions of the EFU and the MWS presented conflicting strategic interest promotions, with the EFU arguing for a Western-informed model of feminist identity premised on the model of the emancipated Western woman, and the MWS for an Islamic-informed one premised on the model of traditional gender roles and identities. The conflict was symbolically manifested in terms of how women dress, which guided the secularist versus conservative nature of the struggle. The *Hijab* was central to this ideological conflict, as it carries a strong symbolic form of signalling identity, where secularists adopted the orientalist framework of it being a symbol of repression, and conservatives adopted the Islamic framework of it being a symbol of freedom with a cost. The following subsection introduces the second wave of feminism in Egypt and presents the reactionary efforts that arose from the first wave's struggle to promote and realise Egyptian women's strategic gender interests. By unpacking the nuances of reactionary organisations and efforts, we can better understand the progression of feminist movements in Egypt and better identify the true causes for women's cultural, political, and socio-economic inferiority.

2.2. The Second Feminist Wave: Constitutional and Legal Rights

The 'second wave' of feminist activism in Egypt was pioneered by the 'educated' generation. Inji Efflatoun, a graduate of the French Lycée in Cairo and the daughter of a middle-class land-owning family, discovered socialism and communism in her early adulthood. Upon admission to the Fuad I University (now

Cairo University), she and her colleague, Latifa Zayyat, established the *League of University and Institute of Young Women*. Their organisation subsidised visits to international conferences, such as the *International Democratic Federation of Women*. In an attempt to mainstream feminist communist ideologies, other organisations, such as the *Provisional National Feminist Association*, started forming with the help of Efflatoun and Zayyat. Efflatoun published two books in which she elaborated and argued on the supposed socialist nature of Islam; *Eighty Million Women With Us*, published in 1948, and *We Egyptian Women*, published in 1949. In these books, she integrated class and gender disparities into her intersectional analysis of women's rights in Egypt from a socialist perspective. Her arguments centred around the compatibility of Islam with women's emancipation, that is, strategic gender interests, and the abolishment of the class society (Botman, 1988; Khater & Nelson, 1988; Younis, 2007). She intensified her arguments by drawing on nationalist sentiments and presenting the oppression of both sexes, but especially women, as a direct result of imperial and colonial occupation and 'contaminated interpretations of Islam' (Efflaton, 2014, p. 247).

Efflaton's struggle coincided with the monarchy's crackdown on the MB. Her fundamentalist counterpart, Zainab Al-Ghazali, responded to the forced dissolvement of the MB by joining forces with its remaining members and changing the name of her organisation, the MWS, to the MS (Uthman, 2011, p. 410). Regardless of the ideological differences, Efflatoun, Al-Ghazali, the EFU, NFP, MB, and DNU joined forces to expel the British troops and political influence in 1952. This coalition formed what came to be known as Harakat Ansar Al-Salam (*The Movement of the Friends of Peace*) in 1950 (Badran, 1996, p. 152). In 1952, when the Free Officer's resistance began to expel the British forces and impeach the monarchy, the coalition corresponded to the efforts of the Free Officers by creating a grassroot organisation, *the Women's Committee for Popular Resistance*. The Committee's activities resonated in politicising rural areas of Egypt and encourage active participation in the rally for true independence (Elsadda & Abu-Ghazi, 2001, pp. 39–41; Kamal, 2016, p. 7). However, similar to the events of 1919, the participation of women was encouraged for practical gender interests. But, unlike in 1919, Egyptian feminists and women were challenged and pushed back into the private sphere.

The reactionary movement against women's strategic gender interests was strong. The ideological differences among the feminist organisations were once again stressed, and this time the Free Officers, that is, the officers who led the *coup d'état* against the British and the monarchy in Egypt in 1952, were in charge. Religious scholars appealed to their new military commanders and argued that the feminists, of both sexes, were manipulated and co-opted by the now ousted British powers and had 'encouraged women to go out to destroy the Islamic society' (Khamis, 1978), urging their suppression. This highlighted that women were once again exploited for national consolidation efforts and their participation was tolerated for its practical outcomes, yet the patriarchal gender roles were not challenged. After Egypt's functional independence from the British in 1952, Al-Azhar reaffirmed its conservative stance by issuing a statement commenting on women's political role 'No one can accept this nor Islam can approve it' (NYT, 1952), substantiating the argument that women were valued for their practical power, yet they would not be truly valued or be granted equal opportunity to foster their strategic gender interests, thereby maintaining the social status quo. It is important to note that Al-Azhar is a major social legitimising tool, which numerous Egyptian leaders used to solidify their power and control. It is also worth noting that, as an institution with such great social affluence, Al-Azhar was of strategic significance to the government. Therefore, when the statements of Al-Azhar were issued, the former leader Gamal Abdel Nasser was faced with the dilemma of having to either condemn Al-Azhar for promoting unequal gender roles and identities or condemn feminists for their noncompliance to the rules of the patriarchal system (NYT, 1952). This ultimately led to Nasser's decision to support Al-Azhar's statement and condemned feminists, such as Murqus Fahmi, Zainab Efflatoun, Huda Shaarawi, and Qasim Amin as 'enemies from within', and declared anti-feminists, like Mustafa Kamel, as social and political heroes. Badran attributed this disillusionment and reactionary move to be a rejection of the increased presence of women in the labour force. She argued that 'women were found in shops, factories, and professions and the social services in sufficient numbers to alarm the patriarchal sensibility of male fundamentalists' (Badran, 1991, p. 214). Yet, Badran (1991) overlooked the political audience cost Gamal Abdel-Nasser considered, disregarded the amount of time Egypt spent under British rule and its effects on social discourses and public opinion, and disregarded the pressures of being a newly independent country.

The sudden change of Egypt's political structure from a Monarchy to a Republic came with political constraints and uncertainty, particularly regarding National Development and Feminism. The struggle was investigated by scholars who concluded that Nasser attempted to implement his vision of a progressive and socialist Egypt while continuing to abide by religious codes (Kamal, 2017, p. 10). One scholar described Nasser's paradoxical ambition as 'increasingly alternating [between] ignoring and suppressing women's independent political initiatives to co-opting them into its own programme' (Bier, 2011, p. 55). Scholars described the manifestation as 'state feminism' (Bier, 2011; Hatem, 1992; Kamal, 2017). State feminism in the Egyptian context describes the simultaneous existence of a 'progressive framework' that governs public life and a 'conservative framework' that governs private life (Hatem, 1992, p. 232). As women were constricted to private life, the initiative of state-sponsored feminism allowed the government monopoly over gender interests (Kamal, 2017, p. 11). One would assume that this would end feminist activism in Egypt, but the DNU under the leadership of Doria Shafiq refused to accept being pushed back into the private sphere. Her activism and the persistence of the DNU led to Nasser granting women suffrage in 1956 and 'recognised women's equal status as citizens in building the new socialist union' (Kamal, 2017, p. 11). This reveals two things: first, before 1956 Egyptian women were indeed excluded from full-citizenship rights, confirming women's second-class citizenship, and second, it highlighted the first instance of substantive promotion and effective integration of women's strategic gender interests.

However, numerous Egyptians opposed the State's stance on women's issues and condemned feminist and women's movements. One of those scholars was Atiya Khamis who published a book called *Feminist Movements and Their Connection with Colonialism*, in which he declared women's movements as a group of corrupted women wishing to be harassed and degraded by going to work and be seen by everyone, adding 'her entry into public life is unnatural' (Khamis, 1978). Khamis' book reflected the general perception of women's strategic gender interests at the time, revealing that the patriarchal narratives in Egypt left no room for feminist negotiation. This meant that granting women suffrage did not translate into social change. This could explain why scholars such as Badran concluded that the second wave of Egyptian feminists failed to actualise a strong narrative in support of women's political representation and emancipation. Badran (1991) stated that 'women still lacked formal political rights, a symbol of their secondary status as citizens, while stalemate on the reform of personal status laws affirmed their unequal position within the family' (p. 215).

These remarks support the observation that a power struggle over who gets to define the Egyptian national identity and where women fit into that identity existed. Despite the alliance between secular and religious feminists, the patriarchal and conservative religious segment of society, legitimised by Al-Azhar, eventually secured more authority and popularity in Egypt. As a result, and to establish social stability for the nation, Nasser appeased the two forces by sponsoring legal reforms that grant women employment in 'education, health care and social services … [but] the judicial, diplomatic, and ministerial positions continued to exclude women' (Bier, 1992, p. 66) but personal status laws with regard to women's rights and roles were marginally reformed and focussed predominantly on implementing more rigorous child-care laws. The former appeased feminists and the latter appeased the reactionaries. The collected field data and observations confirmed that the same power struggle still exists in Egypt, and the discussion around women's status, political representation, and rights is still posing a threat to Egyptian women's full access to citizenship rights (see Chapter 5). The next section introduces the Third Feminist Wave in Egypt and expands on the journey of women gaining suffrage as well as the consequences of Nasser's model of State-sponsored Feminism on Egyptian women's strategic gender interests. The next sections continue to critically review historically relevant literature, with the aim of answering the second research question of 'to what extent did political Islam (including Islamist opposition) and religious institutions (including Al-Azhar) influence the promotion/suppression of women's strategic gender interests'? While this has been touched upon in earlier sections, the following sections highlight this relationship more prominently.

2.3. The Third Feminist Wave: State Feminism and Civil Society

From 1952 to the 1970s a publicised wave of suppression ruled Egypt, where any form of political expression, feminist or otherwise, was not tolerated by the regime. Although many feminist activists and multiple organisations fell prey to the new regime, Nasser ensured that women obtained a constitutional guarantee to equal opportunities in the public sphere, such as primary education and suffrage (Torunoglu, 2016). With the shutting down of many women's organisations, the State incorporated their services into the government apparatus as 'State

Feminism' (Abu-Odeh, 2004, p. 181). As a result, feminist leaders and pioneers at the time took advantage of the new opportunities accessible to them in terms of employment and education to nurture a new generation of young feminists. Two of the protégées of that era are Nawal al Saadawi (1931–2021), a medicine graduate from Cairo University, and Duriyya Shafiq (1908–1975), who in 1948 created the *Daughters of the Nile Union* and remained its president until 1953 (Badran, 1988; Nelson, 1996; Shafiq, 1956). Shafiq's feminism and activism had a direct effect on women's position and status in Egyptian society. For example, in 1953, before the crackdown of the State on a variety of women's organisations and civil societies, she published a book called *The White Paper on the Rights of the Egyptian Woman,* which was a 'compendium of pro-suffrage arguments by sympathetic liberals and politicians as well as pro and con views from within the Islamic establishment' (Badran, 1991, p. 216). The book highlighted the institutionalisation of female inferiority and criticised the constitutionally expressed 'acceptable' female identity. The activism of numerous Egyptian women and feminists, like Shafiq and her contemporaries, was regarded as radical and anti-Islamic. However, their efforts were recognised later by the society as they 'emerged from a veil of silence which shadowed women's existence in Egypt's crucial years of nationalisation eventually leading to a unique emergence of an incorporation of Islamism and feminism' (Jazzar, 2011, p. 87).

Her book had a direct influence on the proposed Electoral Law in Egypt. Sayyid Sabri, a constitutional lawyer, elaborated on the necessity of providing women with suffrage and supported Shafiq's quest by actively arguing for the benefit of social inclusivity and substantive representation of women in the constitution to reflect the social change (Tolino, 2018). However, the conservative opposition in Egypt reacted negatively to Shafiq's activism and released a joint public statement accusing women fighting for suffrage as God-less creatures who seek to cause *fitna*[7] (anarchy) (Ibrahim, 2002, p. 27). As a response to these accusations, Shafiq organised multiple marches and sit-ins at parliament and other government institutions and went on hunger strike to pressure the Government (Shafiq, 1953a, b). After 35 years of feminists demanding suffrage, in 1956 the Revolutionary Government finally obliged and granted women suffrage. The positive impact of gaining suffrage on women's identities has been well documented by scholars (Duveen, 2001, 2008; Galligan, 2007a, b; Kabeer, 2005, 2011; O'Neil et al., 2014; Spark & Cox, 2019), as was the case for Egyptian women, in terms of getting them a step closer to equal citizenship rights. Suffrage, and political representation more broadly, creates a social structure which dictates the rules and regulations that arise from social interactions and underline the patriarchal socio-cultural norm (Giddens, 2006).

As O'Neil et al. (2014) argued, it is 'impossible to talk about women gaining greater freedom and choice without reference to the structures that mediate both women's access to resources and their control and use of them' (p. 2). Their observations of feminist activism in the UK, which struggled for 60 years to gain women's suffrage, led them to the conclusion that the social structure in

---

[7]Oxford Dictionary: Unrest or rebellion, especially against a rightful ruler.

the UK protected the existing gender hierarchies and explained why 'men did not accept women as their equals and did not want to share political power' (O'Neil et al., 2014). Suffrage for Egyptian women, therefore, entailed more than the right to vote but signalled the potential to substantively represent women's strategic gender interests and challenge existing gender dynamics in Egypt. Capitalising on this momentum, feminists and women's organisations were motivated to continue the struggle against the patriarchy, institutionalised inferiority, and systemic subjugation by lobbying to change the personal status laws. The government, in the same year it granted women suffrage, banned most women's organisations and imprisoned multiple activists – Efflatoun was imprisoned, and Shafiq was put under house arrest – and co-opted[8] the 'tolerated activists'[9] such as the MS – which at that point were not considered as 'dangerous' as other women's organisations – into the government as to have direct control over them.

This crackdown on women's organisations and the absorption of feminist organisations by the State quickly ended this momentum. The MS suffered the same fate as other organisations and, in 1964, their leader Al-Ghazali was arrested and the MS were shut down. The State dismantled the EFU, as well as the Women's Committee for Electoral Awareness within the year. In 1959, the NFU lost its permit and had to forcibly shut down. After this development, many feminists realised that, while suffrage was a significant step forward, women are still exploited for practical gender interests, and their strategic interests and presence are not a priority for the government. By the end of 1964, the formation of women's organisation was officially a criminal offence – Law No. 32/1964 Concerning the Private Societies and Organisations/*Qanun al-Jam'iyyat wa al-Mu'assassat al-Khassa* (Human Rights Watch, 2004, p. 5), curtailing most feminist activism and promotion of Egyptian women's equal citizenship status. While the monopoly of the State over feminism dominated the socio-political climate, feminist and women political activists did not disappear entirely. The imprisoned leaders worked from behind the scenes by making contact with their respective protégées who agreed to operate within the parameters of this patriarchal bargain.

In the 1960s and early 1970s, subsidised family planning centres, contraceptive and birth control programmes, and scientific and technical support for mother and child care appeared in Egypt which is credited to Nasser's state-sponsored feminism project (Kamal, 2014, p. 12). This led to an observed decline in fertility

---

[8]There are different definitions for the word co-optation. In this context co-optation refers to 'being absorbed by powerful elites' and is employed 'to thwart potential challengers, even before the contestation has actually begun' (Holdo, 2019, p. 449). The purpose of co-optation is to increase the political leverage of a single insurgent group (McAdam, 2010, p. 42).

[9]In this context, tolerated activist is meant to denote the persons and/or organisations whose activism and activities do not threaten and/or challenge the power of the authoritarian leader. They are 'tolerated' in the sense that their function is utilitarian and is meant to depict a specific image of the authoritarian government which would gain them international audience cost and would assist in distracting the international community from human rights and other abuses.

as more women opted to receive an education and enter the labour force, moving away from the traditional lifestyle of getting married and having children (Haddad, 1982, p. 56). Additionally, a National Charter and the new Constitution were introduced which guaranteed the unrestricted mobility and access of women to the public sphere (Article 52 of the Egyptian Constitution). Furthermore, the free education ensured government position post-graduation significantly challenged traditional gender discourses and altered the narrative and orientation of the Egyptian identity. However, reactionary and conservative members of society still opposed the reforms Nasser's State-Sponsored Feminism articulated. This reactionary force could be attributed to conservative members' fear that the economic independence of women would challenge their authority over the public sphere, and specifically fearing that women's emancipation would result in a reduction in their dependency on men (Badran, 1991, p. 219). This is not only troubling but reflective of gender norms and relations in Egyptian society.

Aisha Abdel Rahman, *nom de plume,* Bint al Shati, attempted to reconcile this social structure by publishing a series of academic writings about the lives of the Prophet's wives to illustrate their unrestricted access and subsequent contribution to the status of women in Islam and the broader Muslim society. Amina al-Said (1914–1995), one of Aisha's contemporaries and followers, and the founder of the infamous women's magazine *Hawa* (Eve)[10] in 1954 utilised Aisha's innovativeness to a different aim. Recognising the patriarchal bargain she operates in, Amina al-Said recognised that confronting the system is not the most productive solution, and therefore wedded the concepts of liberal feminism to match the socialist state's feminist agenda. In multiple speeches, she expressed that '[women] as a group form the greatest obstacle to national progress to be found in their own country today', carefully noting that the seclusion and suppression of such an influential interest group are harmful to the development of the Arab nations. Additionally, she assured her Arab counterparts that emancipation is a right they must fight for if they wish to truly mimic the life of Prophet Mohamed. Despite Amina al-Said operating within a politically restrictive and socially conservative social structure, she creatively navigated a path to appease the reactionary forces and still advance women's realisation of their strategic gender interests. Mastering her abilities to negotiate, Amina criticised Nasser and advocated for remedying the inequalities set forth for women in the laws of the State and its representative institutions without directly challenging the system (Hammam, 1980, p. 53).

---

[10] Amina Sai'd (*see* p. 28) was an Egyptian journalist and writer, one of the first women to go to Cairo University in 1931, and one of the leading feminists in the new Arab Republic of Egypt. *Hawa* was the first women's magazine and Sai'd was its founder editor from 1954 until 1969 when the magazine was shut down by the Egyptian authorities for provocation and adult content. Despite that, she continued her work and became the Secretary General of the *Pan-Arab League Women's Union* and a chair of a well-established publishing house in Egypt (Lotha, 2016). The magazine *Hawa* is considered a 'family heirloom'. Copies of the magazine are currently auctioned because they are considered as part of history-making for Egyptians.

The efforts of Aisha and Amina were absorbed by young feminists like Hawa Idris (1908–1988). Idris carefully documented the double-burden Aisha and Amina identified, launching social service centres to help women affected by all forms of injustices and make up for the inadequacies of the state (Abdel Kader & Badran, 1988). Nawal El Saadawi respectively took an in-depth look at other social issues neglected by the state. As a medical doctor, she quickly realised the issue of female genital mutilation (FGM) in Egypt and the society's obsession of the society with a woman's virginity. In 1971, Saadawi published a book titled *Al Mar'a wa al Jins* (*The Woman and Sex*), she emphasised the interplay of social class, patriarchy, and religion in the creation of myths surrounding women's bodies and the subsequent harmful subjugation of girls. Her work could be considered, to an extent, radical and provocative, as she stipulated that the prevalence of sexual deviance, specifically incest, can be attributed to the sexual oppression of women and men, calling therewith for a sexual liberation revolution. By writing and publicly discussing women's sexual lives, Saadawi exposed herself to direct attack by the State. As sex and sexuality are taboo topics in Egypt, her writings was blacklisted, her books were banned by the government; she was ostracised by her community and disowned by her family (El Saadawi, 2016, p. 5). Most feminist voices were suppressed regardless of the nature of their activism, especially if they publicly engaged the society in any form of dialogue regarding 'traditional' practices and rituals, but they were never muted.

The three waves of feminist activism in Egypt showcased the struggle Egyptian women faced on the path to realise their strategic gender interests. Women's emancipation in Egypt was (re)defined and challenged with each wave of feminist activism, yet was also met by a strong conservative effort to reverse the expansion of women's rights. Arguably, Egyptian women's goal of greater autonomy and agency has been systematically curtailed by patriarchal and conservative social structures. This begs the question: why are those social structures so resilient? The next section offers one answer to this question: through the systemic use of dehumanisation as a tool to protect the patriarchal social structure, Egyptian women were denied autonomy and agency to pursue strategic gender interests. This explains how women's inferiority has been institutionalised, contributing to women's secondary citizenship status observed in Egypt today.

3. The Female Identity: Dehumanisation as an Explanation for Women's Inferiority

Dehumanisation is a process by which persons are 'denied uniquely human rights ... specific out-groups are therefore denied the privileges, activities, or agency that are ordinarily ascribed to in-groups' (Markowitz & Slovic, 2020, p. 9260). In-groups refer to persons who belong to the hegemonic and mainstream social group, and out-group refers to persons who belong to groups which are different from the hegemonic and mainstream group. The practice of dehumanisation is not necessarily overt and could covertly be disguised in subtleties. Markowitz and Slovic (2020) argue that dehumanisation could be divided into four categories: (a) dual perspective of humanness, (b) infrahumanisation theory, (c) dehumanised perception, and (c) mind perception framework. *Dual Perspective of Humanness* refers to the process by which specific members of groups, normally a minority or historically marginalised group, are perceived as 'animals' who lack 'refinement, self-control, intelligence, and rationality' (Haslam & Loughnan, 2014). The *Infrahumanisation Theory,* refers to the process by which secondary emotional faculties, such as humiliation or nostalgia, are 'withheld from out-groups', that is, the non-dominant social bloc (Leyens et al., 2003). *Dehumanised Perception* refers to the cognitive capacities of individuals and is a process by which a person is operating on automatic and unconscious cognitive biases by the in-group towards the out-group that ultimately lead to them being regarded as less than human (Harris & Fiske, 2006). The process could also be described as 'Othering' (Lévy-Strauss, 1961). Finally, the *Mind Perception Framework* refers to one's perception of others' cognitive abilities and capacities and is a fallacy where out-groups, that is, dehumanised groups are 'denied agency and experience because they are believed to not have the capacity for cognitive freedom, and are denied secondary psychological processes' (Markowitz & Slovic, 2020, p. 9261). Combined, these four theoretical categories interplay to formulate a perception of oneself and others, which is ultimately based on group membership and dynamics. For instance, should one belong to the in-group, that is, the social hegemonic bloc, where the probability of one denying attributes of humanness, humanity, human nature, and cognitive capacity becomes higher. Inversely, should one belong to the out-group, the probability of one internalising their dehumanisation becomes higher (Haslam, 2006).

For this section of the book, women's internalisation of their dehumanisation is argued for. The significance of this argument's validity is that, if women in Egypt have internalised their inferiority to their male counterparts and performatively conform to how they are perceived to be, the nuance of their secondary sociocultural status becomes more apparent. The discussion is meant to explain why strategic gender interests for Egyptian women have been suppressed by the maintenance of their second-class citizenship. To understand the relationship between women's identities and their citizenship status in Egypt, the following subheadings engage in a philosophical unpacking of the formation of one's identity, and perceptions of the self and others as an explanation for women's inferiority. This paved the way for the critical discussion of how the dehumanisation of women in Egypt survived the waves of feminist activism that promoted women's emancipation.

The concept of dehumanisation in theory and language used is surprisingly undeveloped in politics and international development studies. Manifestations and theories concerning dehumanisation in other fields have concluded two distinct forms in which denial of *humanness* is expressed: (1) in relation to ethnicity and race, where the usage of language that denies typical human characteristics to others by representing them as animal-like specimens; and (2) in relation to gender and sexuality, by utilising the comparison of humans as objects therewith denying them any human attributes and denying their claim to human nature (Haslam, 2006).

Martha Nussbaum (1999) approached the issue of women's equality and identity using the Sen's *Capabilities Approached.* The approach, developed over a substantial body of scholarship by Amartya Sen (1974, 1979a, 1979b, 1985a, 1985b, 1987, 1988, 1990, 1993, 1995, 1997, 1999, 2000), can be described as a

Moral Framework (Alkire, 2005). Sen (1990) developed the framework in which he challenged and critiqued the traditional economic evaluative accounts for not integrating human beings as 'the primary means of all production' (p. 41) and rather perceiving humans as means to an economic end. In his works, *Inequality Re-examined* (1992) and *Wellbeing, Agency, and Freedom* (1985a) he distinguished between two types of formulations of capabilities: *valuable beings and doings* (functionings) and *freedom*. The purpose of these reformulations was to highlight that the activities a person can undertake (doing) and the kind of person one can be (being) comprise the notion of capabilities. 'Real freedoms', as Sen argued, constitute the 'various things a person may value doing or being' (1999, p. 75), and the right to act on one's potential in terms of doing and being. This conceptualisation changes the narrative around productivity from a means based perspective – the resources people have – to an ends based perspective – what people are able to do with these resources. The 'real freedoms' the capabilities approach promotes are freedoms conceived as real opportunities (1985a, pp. 3–4; 1985b, p. 201; 2000). Nussbaum (1999) grew the approach and applied it to the case study of women's equality, arguing that

> All over the world, women are resisting inequality and claiming the right to be treated with respect ... In many cases these hardships are caused by their being women, and in many cases, laws and institutions construct or perpetuate these inequalities. (p. 117)

She continued to attribute women's lack of capabilities to 'existing value systems [being] highly paternalistic, particularly towards women. They treat them as unequal under the law, as lacking full civil capacity, as not having the property rights, associative liberties and employment rights of males' (Nussbaum, 1999, p. 231). While Nussbaum's case study was in India, her conclusion of 'women, unlike rocks and trees, have the potential to become capable of these human functions, given sufficient nutrition, education, and other support. That is why their unequal failure in capability is a problem of justice' (1999, p. 243) rings true for the Egyptian case.

In the same year, Nussbaum published a book titled *Sex and Social Justice* in which she argued that there are seven elements included in the objectification of women aside from pornography: (1) 'instrumentality', which views women as vessels for reproduction and homemakers; (2) 'ownership', which involves commodifying and the treatment of women as objects and tools of desire; (3) 'denial of autonomy', where women are perceived to lack secondary cognitive faculties that would allow them to act in accordance with objective morality; (4) 'inertness', which includes viewing women as agency-less and lacking in the cognitive ability to engage in deliberation and self-determination; (5) 'fungibility', which is viewing the individual women as an interchangeable object with other women or objects; (6) 'violability', which includes treating a woman as boundary-less, that is, permissibility to act on desires without requiring consent under a veil of entitlement and ownership; and finally (7) 'denial of subjectivity', which highlights the neglect of women's experiences and emotions and deems them insignificant and/or irrational. The components identified by Nussbaum are reflective of broader cultural and social contexts, which emphasise the portrayal of femininity and dictate how women should present themselves. The adoption of such socially constructed attitudes has not only dehumanised women but led to women dehumanising themselves; value is only ascribed to them through the male gaze and their 'price tags', a 'second sex' so to speak (de Bouvoir, 2009). Real freedoms and the dehumanisation of Egyptian women represent two mutually influential aspects, where women are perceived to lack humanness – rather they are perceived to resemble objects more than humans – and therefore denied functionings that would allow them to act on their potential, realising their strategic needs.

The dehumanisation process in Egypt can be attributed to the misuse of Islam as a legitimisation tool. Mahmood (2001) in her work *Feminist Theory, Embodiment, and the Docile Agent* reflected on the conservative and restrictive Islamic revival in Egypt. In an attempt to understand the relationship between religion and women's lack of agency and docility in Egypt, Mahmood (2001) found that 'this form reconceptualisation of power as a set of relations that do not simply dominate the subject, but also, importantly, form the conditions of its possibility', shedding light on the 'real freedoms' denied to Egyptian women (p. 210). The complex relationship between Islam and the inferiority of Egyptian women, Mahmood posited, is due to women's identities projecting their internalised objectification and dehumanisation:

> They pursue practices and ideals embedded within a tradition that has historically accorded women a subordinate status and seek to cultivate virtues that are associated with feminine passivity and submissiveness (e.g. shyness, modesty, perseverance, and humility. the very idioms that women use to assert their presence in previously male-defined spheres are also those that secure their subordination ... [through] false consciousness, or the internalisation of patriarchal norms through socialisation ... while women's bodies are made to bear the burden of modesty ... the larger conceptualisation of the body's relationship to the making of the self is quite different. (Mahmood, 2001, p. 205)

Mahmood (2001) concluded that the 'set of capacities inhering in a subject – the abilities that define its modes of agency – are not the residue of an undominated self that existed before the operations of power but are themselves the product of those operations', unveiling how repeated dehumanisation influenced Egyptian women's conceptualisation of their power and status, and provides a valid explanation to why efforts in pursuit of strategic women's interests were unsuccessful. Specifically, we can see how the denial of women's subjectivity and inertness (Nussbaum, 1999) serves to reinforce and reproduce the patriarchal system by limiting women's development to practical needs, and socialising women to abandon 'real freedoms' required to challenge their subordination and exclusion.

In this process of internalising their inferiority, Candi Cann (2016) in her work *Mothers and Spirits* argues that religion is 'used as a way to forge, cement, and create gender identity, constructing alternate discourses of power and inclusivity' by 'enforcing abstinence... constructing alternate discourses of belonging and exclusion in images of the afterlife and in everyday religiosity' (p. 149). Agreeing, Bosco B. Bae (2016) stated 'Belief ... enables our individual and collective agency ... [where] the individual is necessarily a reflection of on-going history and its many levels and intersections' (p. 16). Ritualised practices, embedded in the social structures and perpetuated through gender performativity, are therefore necessary for the endurance of belief and the survival of the status quo; the continuation of male hegemony and the denial of an independent female identity free of religious appropriation, and promises of a dignified afterlife exclusive for the 'good' women, wife, daughter, and mother (Atran & Norenzayan, 2004; Bae, 2016; Rappaport, 1999). So is Islam, as a religion and social institution, to blame for women's unrealised agency and strategic gender interests in Egypt? The short answer is that Islam on its own is not inherently promoting the objectification and subordination of women, but the social institution of Islam, which draws on the socially constructed understanding of women's status and role in the society, does. By applying scrutinous evaluation to scripture – here the Qur'an – we could subject the supposed customary foundations used as justification for women's inferiority, and didactically restricting women's autonomy and role in family and society we could observe that there is an inherent male bias in the dominant interpretations of texts. While there are scholars, such as Fatima Mernissi (1987, 1991a, 1991b), Leila Ahmed (1993), Asma Barles (2002), Margot Badran (Badran, 1995, 1999, 2005, pp. 6–29; Badran & Cooke, 2004), Riffat Hassan (1987), Ziba Mir Hosseini (1999, 2000), Amina Wadud (1999), and Barbara Stowasser (1996, 1998), who have provided an alternative exegesis that is women-centred, their efforts were systematically undermined for such scholarship by institutions such as Al-Azhar. As Offenhauer (2005, p. 28) rightfully criticised:

> These [male] scholars avoid questioning the sacrality of the scriptures, some out of personal belief and some out of conviction as to the strategic value of deploying a religious idiom to counter patriarchal religious discourse. They rehearse and criticise the justifications that are used by conservatives and radical Muslims to restrict women's rights (...) the scholars affirm only that it is worthwhile to undermine sexist discourse, since such discourse plays a legitimising role in women's second-class status. Religion is not the sole embodiment and conveyor of patriarchal ideology in Muslim or any other societies. However, Islamic modes of reasoning and argumentation play a prominent and explicit justificatory role, and, some argue, even an unusually prominent role, as religious discourse goes.

Ritualised practices, actively encouraged by the Egyptian Government, such as FGM, honour killings, and domestic violence, in addition to the use of religious institutions such as Al-Azhar by the government to legitimise the harmful practice that affects women, cemented by laws that reflect, reproduce, and perpetuate the social disenfranchisement of women, all lead to the observed sociopolitical and cultural secondary status of Egyptian women. In addition, the use of Islam to rationalise the inferiority of women is key in understanding how the dehumanisation process was operationalised. This leads to what Mahmood (2001) calls the embodiment of subordination, arguing that

> in order to explore the kinds of injury specific to women located in particular historical and cultural situations, it is not enough simply to point, for example, that a tradition of female piety or modesty serves to give legitimacy to women's subordination. Rather it is only by exploring these traditions in relation to the practical engagements and forms of life in which they are embedded that we can come to understand the significance of that subordination to the women who embody it. (p. 225)

The next section investigates how the dehumanisation of women has been operationalised in Egypt through religion. More specifically, the next section addresses the third research question: How is Egyptian women's inferiority and exclusion from full citizenship rationalised?

3.1. Rationalising the Dehumanisation of Women Using Religion

Caroline Moser (1993) in her book *Gender Planning and Development* posited that 'gender planning is not an end in itself but a means by which women, through a process of empowerment, can emancipate themselves' (p. 190). Moser (1993) believed that women's organisations play a crucial role in confronting women's subordination and subjugation and 'create alliances which will provide constructive support in negotiating women's needs'. Nonetheless, local and international women's organisations are subjected to the cultural environment within which they are erected. In the Egyptian context, religion plays a significant role in outlining the range of issues women's organisations can and cannot address. In this section, the role religion played in informing how the State 'controls women's strategic gender needs through family policy relating to domestic violence, reproductive rights, legal status and welfare policy' (Moser, 1993, p. 2) is explored. Specifically, this section highlights how religion has been utilised to justify and rationalise patriarchal control over women's bodies.

In 1994 the *United Nations International Conference on Population and Development* was held in Cairo, Egypt. The conference's objectives were to problematise diverse issues, ranging from family planning, population control, sexual and reproductive rights to human rights, and sustainable development. The conference was approached with scepticism and suspicion from various Muslim-majority states, such as Saudi Arabia, Lebanon, Iraq, and Sudan (Cohen & Richards, 1994, p. 273). Saudi Arabia's Council of Ulama[11] condemned the conference and described it as a 'ferocious assault on Islamic society' and prohibited Muslims from attending it (Gorman, 1994). Family planning and the use of contraceptives

---

[11]An advisory council composed of senior religious scholars who consult the Monarch on religious matters, especially the ones on which Islam is contested and up for interpretation.

to control population growth were regarded as 'Western imposition on Muslim societies and as an attempt to revive colonial and imperial ambition' (Noakes, 1995, p. 100). This demonstrates the incongruity between Islamic legacy and contemporary interpretations of Islamic traditions. To understand the rejection of modernisation and radicalisation of some Islamic scholars, and consequentially some Middle Eastern countries, a contextualisation and situating of the Muslim world into a matrix of post-colonial thought could assist.

The historical presence of Western colonial powers in the Middle East, for some countries, until the mid-20th century has informed and formed some of the current political and cultural resistance to Western influences, which included granting women greater agency and autonomy to pursue their emancipation. A vast and diverse scholarship emerged in the second half of the 20th century discussing the urgency of recuperating Muslim and Middle Eastern identity and culture and shielding it from 'Westoxication' or colonial influence (Al-e Ahmad, 1984; Keddie, 1983; Sharabi, 1988; Shariati, 1981), which is, in itself, insightful but not particularly relevant for this project. In the 21st century, the anti-colonial sentiment was exacerbated by the increasing interconnectedness of the world fuelled by modern technology and globalisation (Akbar & Donnan, 1994, p. 5), which may be perceived as an encroaching threat to some Middle Eastern societies and the authoritarian rule. Topics of discussion, such as the use of contraceptives, access to abortion, and family planning have often been mounted to 'conspiracy by Western powers to limit the growth and power of the Muslim world or as a reflection of a permissive sexual mores of Western society' (Shaikh, 2011, p. 341). Subscribing to anti-colonial sentimentalities, many Muslim-majority countries in the Middle East have assumed a particularly defensive position, and, albeit feminist opposition, the same notions are inversely used to define them as anti-modernisation and regressive (Noakes, 1995, p. 100).

Opponents of family planning often rely on a particular verse in the Qur'an, 'Kill not your children, on a plea of want, we provide sustenance for you and for them' (Qur'an 6:151), yet interpreters disregard the contextual basis which brought about this prophecy. According to Islamic belief, the 'Qur'an is the word of God, revealed to the Prophet Muhammad via the archangel Gabriel, and intended for all times and all places' (Abdel-Haleem, 2005, p. 2), but many scholars tend to dismiss the fact that when the Qur'an was supposedly revealed to Muhammad, it referenced specific situations and articulated wisdom and judgements on questions asked to the Prophet. The verse most cited and used by opponents of family planning was revealed to Muhammad after knowledge of female infanticides – being buried alive shortly after being born – in the pre-Islamic period known as *Jahiliah* [The Age of Ignorance]. The Qur'an captures this in the following verses 'And when one of them is informed of [the birth of] a female, his face becomes dark, and he suppresses grief. He hides himself from the people because of the ill of which he has been informed. Should he keep it in humiliation or bury it in the ground? Unquestionably, evil is what they decide' (Qur'an 16:59–60), to which the revelation of 6:151 was sent to Mohamed. Consequentially, the verse most used to negate and/or disallow abortion, the use of contraception, and, in contemporary times, family planning, under the pretence of it being *Haram* [forbidden] is taken out of historical context and appropriated to fit a specific narrative supported by conspiracy theories of the 'North versus Islam' (Daniel, 2009, p. 142; Jenkins, 2016, p. 538). The misreading of the verse has led proponents of family planning, particularly feminists, to urge the contextualisation of specific verses and separate which verses are responses pertaining to pre-Islamic Arabian customs, which are not obsolete, and which are commandments believers of the faith should adhere to (Rahman, 1982, p. 286).

Furthermore, most Islamic legal schools of thought[12] [*Madahib*] have advocated for the permissibility of contraceptive methods, specifically, *coitus interruptus*[13] also known as *azl* (Ministry of Information, 1994, p. 29; Omran, 1992, p. 175). Even with the conditions one must adhere to before engaging in *coitus interruptus* – one must obtain the woman's permission before withdrawing, as she has the right to a full sexual experience, and, one must seek permission to withdraw in case the woman desires a child – contraceptive measures were not considered *haram* (Musallam, 1983, p. 31). Even prominent Arab physicians and philosophers such as Ibn Sina (1025), Abu Bakr al-Razi (925), and Al-Ghazali (d. 1111) encouraged the use of contraception and proliferated their methods to include family planning and organisation utilising *fiqh*[14] as the premise of their arguments. Al-Ghazali, for example, supported the use of contraceptives for socio-economic purposes, proclaiming that dependents can economically burden families, imposing not only some financial restrictions on families but also psychological hardships (Farah, 1984, p. 111) due to the pressure of providing. His reasoning follows from the proposition that human beings possess an awareness of their economic capabilities, stating that *Allah* entrusted humans to uplift suffering, to engage in rational and just deliberation, but never intended for a child to suffer under His name (Farah, 1983, p. 113). The argument that Islam and family planning are not mutually exclusive was echoed centuries later by demographist Omran (1992), who concluded that

> Muslim countries have been forced to acquire debt, import food, and rely on foreign aid to cope with the needs of growing populations. The result is a vicious cycle of poverty, ill-health, illiteracy, overpopulation, and unemployment being compounded with social frustration, extremism, and social unrest. (p. 212)

---

[12]There are eight legal schools of thought recognised by *Al-Azhar*, the Muslim version Vatican, Hanafi (Sunni), Maliki (Sunni), Shafi'i (Sunni), Hanbali (Sunni), Ja'fari (including Mustaali-Taiyabi Ismaili) (Shia), Zaidiyyah (Shia), Ibadiyyah, and Zahiriyah. They are several interpretive possibilities in deriving the rule of Allah from the primary texts of the Qur'an and *Hadith* on a particular question.

[13]The withdrawal method of contraception is the practice of withdrawing the penis from the vagina and away from a woman's external genitals before ejaculation to prevent pregnancy. The goal of the withdrawal method is to prevent sperm from entering the vagina.

[14]The theory or philosophy of Islamic law based on deep understanding and rationalisation of the Qur'anic teachings and the traditions of the Prophet.

Amna Nosseir, Professor of Philosophy and Islamic Theology at Al-Azhar University and a member of the National Council for Women's Rights, in an interview Mada Masr, argued for the need to differentiate between *tahdeed* al-nasl (restricting reproduction) and *tanzeem al-nasl* (planning reproduction) (Kamel, 2017). She argued that *tanzeem* 'is an entrenched cornerstone of Muslim thought, meaning that a Muslim can plan the periods of pregnancies using their own mind's reasoning', but *tahdeed* involves the State's intervention to restrict reproduction by imposing legal controls, which she argues *is* against Islam (Ayad, 2013).

Nonetheless, these notions have erupted from a 'pseudo-Islamisation' (Liow, 2009, p. 83) of the main sources of Islamic legislation: the Qur'an and the *Hadith*. To discern interpretation from concrete commandments, contextualisation of the most commonly used verses must ensue. It is of importance to understand that central to the Islamic belief is the concept of *Al-Khalifah* (roughly translates to the successive authority and human moral agency), which connotes that every human being has a moral obligation to holistically address challenges of the everyday life, structural injustices, economic overburdens, and cultural and gender hierarchies; 'Indeed, I will make upon the earth a successive authority' (Qur'an 2:30, 2005), 'And it is He who has made you successors upon the earth and has raised some of you above others in degrees [of rank] that He may try you through what He has given you' (Qur'an 6:165, 2005), 'And if We willed, We could have made [instead] of you angels succeeding [one another] on the earth' (Qur'an 43:60, 2005). The essence of those verses is to shed light on the supposed purpose of human beings on earth. These verses are oftentimes used to undermine family planning, specifically to prohibit the use of contraceptives and block abortion policies, by arguing that true believers must enlarge the Islamic *Umma*[15] (Shapiro, 2014, p. 488). Moreover, most commonly opposers of contraceptives use the following *Hadith* as evidence for Islam's opposition to contraception and family planning: 'Abu Dawood (1050) narrated that Ma'qil ibn Yasaar said: A man came to the Prophet (peace and blessings of Allah be upon him) and said, 'I have found a woman who is of good lineage and is beautiful but does not want children. Should I marry her?' He said, 'No'. Then he came again with the same question, and he told him not to marry her. Then he came a third time with the same question, and he said: 'Marry those who are loving and fertile, for I will be proud of your great numbers before the other nations'. Classed as *saheeh* [authentic] by al-Albaani in Irwa' al-Ghaleel, 1784' (Abu Dawud, 2008, p. 2050). Furthermore, the concept of a successor, *Al-Khalifa*, implicitly shifts moral responsibility onto humanity, entrusting their ability to engage in rational deliberation, demanding humans to act justly towards ourselves and others. To further that claim, the Qur'an distinguishes humans from animals by designating them as the only species 'uniquely imbued with the spirit of God' (Shaikh, 2011, p. 342) – 'And when I have proportioned him and breathed into him of My [created] soul, then fall down to him in prostration' (Qur'an 15:29) – ascribing the

---

[15]It is the word used to describe the community of Muslims under the pretence that all Muslims are bound together by ties of religion.

capacity of logical inference and understanding to humans alone. This sequentially means that human beings are responsible for the cohesion of the world as they have a discernment capacity, shifting responsibility to act on, challenge, and fight moral, structural, and social injustices to the communities and individuals (Rahman, 1980, p. 18). Proponents of the faith describe it as progressive, tolerant, and encouraging of diversity, harmony, and peace (Hasan, 2011; Hussain, 2008; Kurcan & Erol, 1999). They argue that a fundamental virtue of Islam is that all humans are equal under God; there is 'a metaphysical sameness of all humans as creatures of God' (Al-Hibri, 2000, p. 52).

The proposition of sameness with *Allah* was echoed by *Sufis*[16] and *Sunnis*[17] who believe 'if we are true believers, we will not see any difference between others and ourselves. We will only see One. We will see one Allah, one human race, and one justice for all. That justice and truth is the strength of Islam' (Muhaiyadeen, 2008, p. 26), insinuating that each person, irrespective of race, nationality, gender, and so on, must enact the moral imperatives of justice and peace:

> O you who have believed, be persistently standing firm in justice, witnesses for Allah, even if it be against yourselves or parents and relatives. Whether one is rich or poor, Allah is more worthy of both. So, follow not [personal] inclination, lest you not be just. And if you distort [your testimony] or refuse [to give it], then indeed Allah is ever, with what you do, Acquainted. (Qur'an 4:135, 2005)

Nonetheless, it is difficult to perceive of an omnipresent, omnipotent, and eternal Supreme Being whose commandments dictate that we suffer, that we live in poverty and misery, and is thus against responsible and futuristic planning, may it be family planning or political organisation. Furthermore, the supposed mission of human beings on earth has failed as 1.3 billion people are living under the poverty line, 60% of whom are women already living in poor nations and who own less than 1% of the world's property yet account for two-thirds of the world's working hours (Alvaredo et al., 2018). While some could look at these statistical facts and engage in 'othering' – commonly, followers of the faith would generalise their experience and use these facts to make a case for Islam – it is more plausible to conclude that human lives are simply not equally valued.

From this investigation, it became apparent that Middle Eastern culture is heavily informed by Islam. Some contemporary Muslim scholars would argue that an improper application of the faith and its commandments explains why emotional, psychological, physical, and social distress exist in Egypt (Hassan, 2000; Wadud, 1999), attributing violence against women, human rights violations, honour killings, and clitoridectomy to the spiritual transgression of communities. The male-centeredness of cultural norms alludes to the insidious levels of female

---

[16] A sect of the Islamic faith, whose followers believe in *Tasawuf* as 'a science whose objective is the reparation of the heart and turning it away from all else but God'.
[17] Followers of the Islamic faith, who believe themselves to be the orthodox branch. The term literally translates to 'People of the Tradition'.

persecution, marginalisation, and subordination (Shaikh, 2011, p. 345). The cultural ideals encroached in the early ages of a Muslim person's life, the socially born values passed under the pretence of religiosity, and used interchangeably to ascribe gendered behaviours, are believed to result from 'tradition' and cultural norms, not religion (Shaikh, 2011). The promotion of women's subordination, silence, denial of access to higher education, restriction of women's mobility within the social hierarchies and from the private sphere to the public sphere, stripping women of their agency, and the renunciation of their full humanity, is therefore fundamentally 'un-Islamic'. Most women in the Middle East and Northern Africa region, indiscriminate of faiths and nationalities, are defined by their sexuality, viewed as objects of desire, deliberation, fixed in their pre-ascribed and expected roles as mothers, wives, and caretakers (El Feki et al., 2017; Ferrant et al., 2014). As Moghadam (2003) put it, Islam is 'no more or less patriarchal than other major religions, especially Hinduism and the other two Abrahamic religions, Judaism and Christianity, all of which share the view of woman as wife and mother' (p. 75). The structural violence and denial of the 'full-membership' to humanity women are subjugated to, therefore, is only religiously motivated in part, but can be fully attributed to the male interpretation of scripture.

It is for the aforementioned contextualisation that a female- and woman-centred interpretation of Islamic texts is necessary. Male Islamic jurists and scholars have co-opted, exploited, and misrepresented scripture for socio-political gains (Bailey, 1955; Richie, 2010, p. 724; Robinson, 2008). For most followers of Islam, it is the only Abrahamic-monotheistic religion to grant women an explicit right to honour, respect and dignity. Cesar and Casanova (2017, p. 15) urged for the distinction between Islam as a religion and Muslim Culture, explaining that:

> Interpretation of Islam is a modern construction that deviates from the tradition of Islam. It fails to take historical and cultural context into consideration and pushes women back into the tribal condition that was the norm during the time of the Prophet Mohammed. There is nothing in the Islamic tradition that prevents women from working, getting an education, or partaking in public social and political life. In fact, many times, the interpretations within the religious traditions have been ahead of the cultural norms and traditions common before Islam: for example, women cannot inherit lands in the Berber zones of North Africa – while such a custom contradicts Islamic rules. At the same time, the social and political advancement of women lags behind in most of the Middle East and North African countries.

Similarly, Jane I. Smith (1979) articulated 'historical circumstances through the centuries have often worked to the disfavour of Muslim women; predominant traditions of male authority and honour have made it difficult for women to avail themselves of the rights guaranteed by the Qur'an' (p. 517), revealing that Islam, in isolation, is not necessarily the reproducer of female inferiority, but male-interpretation of it are the drivers. The language used to refer to women in contemporary Islamic populations is one that absolves men of accountability, responsibility, and liability, and places the responsibility of male behaviours on women, furthering their victimisation, oppression, and inferiority. Many Muslim women critics have agreed that 'the problem is not simply that the woman is considered to be inferior. It is not an issue of female inferiority (...) but of laws and customs ensuring women's status as one of subjugation' (Smith, 1979, p. 527). One can thereby conclude that the Muslim female identity has been historically suppressed, and that no inborn, true Muslim female identity has made its way to public life and social discourse. One Egyptian woman interviewed by Smith (1979) went as far as to say

> the cause of liberation of women is too specifically Western to be applied unconditionally to the Arab world. Many Western scholars have disregarded what Muslim women think of themselves and have imposed their own value judgements on the condition of Women. (p. 529)

Smith was in essence urging researchers to collect narratives from the women affected by the patriarchal system and to seek them to understand how they perceive their roles and status in society, something this book set out to achieve. Considering that since the early 1980s, women's movements, scholarship, and organisations have partially or fully gone underground to survive political and legal persecution by the Egyptian state, this book served to localise the narrative of Muslim women and to reflect Egyptian Muslim women's voices, perceptions, and experiential realities as articulated by them.

This section highlighted two significant issues. First, male-dominated interpretations of religious scripture are problematic, as they guise patriarchal structures as religious mandates, when, as evidenced from the verses cited from the Qur'an, the scripture itself does not dictate that women are inherently inferior to men. Additionally, this highlighted how women's *less than human* status has been systematically operationalised to fit within the patriarchal framework. Second, this section shed light on the urgent need to employ intersectional and post-colonial feminist frameworks when investigating Egyptian women's subordination within the patriarchal system. This merits further research but falls beyond the scope of this particular book.

The upcoming chapter presents the legal framework which served to codify women's inferior status in Egyptian society. More specifically, the next chapter addresses the second research objective and serves to answer the fourth research question: what role did political Islam play in the resurgence of traditional conservative practices in Egypt such as the Hijab? And what consequences did this have on women's status and roles in Egyptian society? By reviewing the most relevant Articles from the Egypt Constitution, the personal status laws, and the Civil Codes, the preliminary findings suggest that they contain Articles and amendments that have been used to suppress and oppress women. By shedding light on these restrictive and prescriptive frameworks – that served to codify and institutionalise women's inferiority – the section unearthed how an emancipated Egyptian female identity was legally suppressed and sheds light on the role of political Islam played in legitimating women's inferiority and subordination.

Chapter 3

Codifying the Dehumanisation of Egyptian Women

1. State-sponsored Feminism and the Status of Egyptian Women

In the 1970s and 1980s, a resurgence of Islamic fundamentalism and feminism found new platforms for expression. The former Egyptian President Anwar Sadat, who succeeded Gamal Abdel Nasser after his assassination in 1970, employed a strategy of Islamism in hopes it would foster and groom social support for his Government and its objectives (Morsy, 2011). He is known as the first president to amend Article 2 of the Egyptian Constitution, which declared Islam the official religion of the state (Hamed, 2019, p. 110). He thereby transformed the state into a promoter of Islamic fundamentalism in hopes it would gain him social support, 'de facto turning Egypt from a secular into a religious country' (Lombardi, 1998). Agreeing, Guirguis (2012, p. 187) postulated that:

> [Under Nasser] Islamism was eclipsed by Arab nationalism, a secular, socialist ideology of pan-Arab unity and cooperation. Yet the defeat of Nasser's nationalist vision ushered the Islamists back to the forefront of national life. As Muslim fundamentalist movements proliferated and gained broader acceptance in the 1970s, religion became more culturally dominant and increasingly linked to politics, culminating in the assassination of Anwar Sadat in 1981.

Under Sadat's rule, Nasser's anti-Western rhetoric was reoriented and substituted by a pro-Western ideology. This is evidenced by his adoption and implementation of capitalist economic strategies, *Infitah* [open door policy], and political alliance with the USA (Lippman, 1989, p. 99). Simultaneously, a new face for Egyptian feminism emerged: the First Lady Jehan Sadat, wife of Sadat. She was praised for providing a platform for women to voice their opinions, and for her women's outreach programmes (Fowler, 2021). Her mission, coinciding with that of the State, was to contain communism and 'radical' feminism, now associated with Nawal Saadawi (Addison, 2020, p. 6), an Egyptian feminist who openly wrote about sex and sexual relations in Egypt, a topic which is considered taboo by some. By sidelining other feminist voices and using her power as the first lady, Jehan Sadat institutionalised a framework of state-tolerated and sponsored feminism (Fowler, 2021) and represented the Egyptian delegation at the 1975 International Women's Year Conference in Mexico City (Bennett, 2021). She is credited for the addition of Article 11 to the 1971 constitution, which states

> the state guarantees a balance and accord between a woman's duties towards her family on the one hand and towards her work in society and equality with man in the political, social and cultural spheres on the other without violating the laws of the Islamic *Sharia*. (Article 11, Egyptian Constitution, 1971)

Under Sadat's presidency and Jehan Sadat's activism, Egypt witnessed a resurgence of the Hijab which some Western-informed feminists had previously advocated against (Blakeman, 2014; Emil, 2014). Some scholars, such as Diffendal (2006), argued that the Hijab 'actually blinds women to the veil's political significance' (p. 134) and 'ultimately reinforces the very power structures that oppress them' (p. 136). While other scholars, such as Nancy Hirschmann (1997), concluded: 'that the veil is *both* a marker of autonomy, individuality and identity *and* a marker of inequality and sexist oppression' (p. 472). These arguments represent the existing debate about the *Hijab,* an issue discussed further in Chapter 4.

The 1970s and 1980s witnessed a measurable and significant increase in women wearing the *Hijab* and other types of traditional wear, which is believed to have been motivated by the ideological position of Sadat at the time. Yet, it could also be argued that this is reflective of a new patriarchal framework, influenced by political Islam and as a product of Nasserism and his political reorientation away from Western ideals. While the increase could be viewed solely as a rejection of the West, for those living and experiencing the framework, it holds a twofold meaning: on the one hand, the Hijab has a utilitarian value where it allows women to access the public sphere and work within the system, and on the other hand, it signals adherence to the Muslim identity and sexual codes (Ahmed, 1992, p. 224).

For feminists of that era, the Hijab was regarded as a liberating force, meant to counter the imagery of the Western superimposed 'Free women' (Al-Wazni, 2015, p. 326), and propelling the narrative that it 'is a piece of fabric, and, alongside other garments made of fabric, it does not violate rights' (Mancini, 2012, p. 522). The narrative assisted in 'preventing the drawing of clear-cut lines. There is no such thing as a monolithic "Muslim world" in which women are "monstrously oppressed"' (Ahmed, 1982a, b, p. 11). The Hijab particularly worked on changing the discursive notions of the Western Orientalist narrative towards the Muslim woman. As Laila Ahmed (1982a, b) asserted, the Western Orientaist narrative is that the Muslim world is irrational, backwards, and uncivilised, which are presented as 'facts' in Western society. Ahmed (1982a, b) vehemently argued that

> These are 'facts' manufactured in Western culture, by the same men who have also littered the culture with 'facts' about Western women and how

> inferior and irrational they are. And for centuries the Western world has been systematically falsifying and vilifying the Muslim World. (p. 523)

and pointed out that

> Western so-called knowledge about the Middle East consists largely of a heritage of malevolently fabricated mythologies, it is also impossible, in an environment already so negatively primed against us, to be freely critical – a task no less urgent for us than for Western feminists – of our own societies. (p. 527)

The supposed 'cultural superiority' of the West and the exportation of Western ideals served to radicalise Egyptian society (Lopez, 2001, p. 282). The frustration of Egyptian and Muslim feminists under Sadat's rule, and their opposition to his Western orientation, allowed for dissident voices to appear. Specifically, Islamists and the Muslim Brotherhood, which by the 1980s had gained access to public university campuses and were supported, funded and protected by the State (Grömüs, 2016, p. 62). Using the familiar strategy of the 'Muslim Identity' being 'under attack' which marked the 1919 Revolution, the MB propagated their organisation as one seeking to 'return' and 'reclaim' a Muslim identity to counter Western influence. As a result, the 1980s witnessed a conservative shift in Egyptian youths as 'with the political training and organisational skills they had acquired while working in the student unions … challenge the regime at every level, including in parliament and in civil society institutions such as the professional syndicates' (Fahmy, 1998, p. 554). The MB was able to radicalise the youth under the guise of anti-imperialism. The radicalisation efforts started by targeting and recruiting of a large number of lower and middle-class women and due to the relatively easy access they had to these stakeholders, recruitment was fast and ideological persuasion effective (Al-Anani, 2020; Gamal, 2019). Taraki (1996) noticed that the MB strongly believed that 'feminism was equated with cultural imperialism', and Ahmed (1992) similarly observed that 'Islamist discourse on women [was] a discourse of resistance' where women's public dress code and behaviours were weaponised to serve 'as proof of the moral bankruptcy of the West and the superiority of Muslims' (Ahmed, 1992, p. 63) and perpetuate the conservative narrative of the MB. Therefore, attempts to 'return to Islam' within this framework could have been attractive to many, particularly those who opposed Westernisation and Sadat's *Infitah* policies. As Hirschmann (1991) noted

> the West has tended to view Islam as a form of barbarism – fuelled in contemporary times by popular antipathy toward terrorist-bombing and hostage-taking – which is often seen as a source of women's inequality; and the veil is seen as the ultimate symbol, if not, tool, of this inequality. (p. 464)

However, Hirschman (1991) also recognised that 'many Islamic women not only seem to participate voluntarily in the practice but defend it as well, indeed claiming it as a mark of resistance, agency and cultural membership' (p. 165), revealing that the discourse around women's emancipation in Egypt was effectively influenced by the MB under Sadat's reign. This also highlighted the re-adoption of a national consolidation narrative, like that of the 1919 and 1952 Revolutions, where women's practical gender interests were advanced by the government to gain women's support.

Exploring how the discourse changed more concretely, we can see that the recruitment process followed the ideology of the MB which Hassan El-Banna had written back in 1928, in which he called for

> a campaign against ostentation in dress and loose behaviour (...) segregation of male and female students (...) a separate curriculum for girls (...) and [for private meetings between women and men] to be counted as a crime unless permitted degree of relationship. (al-Banna, 1978, p. 126)

Freer (2017) noted that the Muslim Sisters Group, which was established in 1932, was the actualisation of the gender segregation El Banna had envisioned. He posited that the 'primary issues for al-Banna, then, appeared to be the behaviour of women in public, their education, and the prevention of gender mixing, which he considered inappropriate'. Other scholars, such as Taraki (1996), who noted that the ideology of the MB is largely based on classical Islamic discourses, argue that women's issues are perceived as an 'essence' as opposed to a 'complex and living reality' leading to women's visibility and access to the public sphere receiving 'no more than lip service in the discourse of the *Ikhwan* [Muslim Brotherhood]' (Taraki, 1996, p. 141). This later led to her asserting that while the MB had reformed itself over time to keep up with new philosophical and social developments, hoping to remain relevant, their discourse still maintained that '[women can] work outside the home provided it does not conflict with women's domestic duties or involves contact with men, or the encouragement of female education in "appropriate" fields' (Taraki, 1996, p. 142). Saba Mahmood (2001) argued that the women who were subjected to the MB's discourses on a woman's place in society, and the duties of the 'good Muslim woman' later discovered that 'their participation is critically structured by, and seeks to uphold the limits of a discursive tradition that holds subordination to a transcendent will (and thus, in many instances, to male authority) as its coveted goal' (Mahmood, 2001, p. 204). This reveals that well into the 1980s and 1990s, Egyptian women were still trying to overcome the shortcomings of their gender-specific circumstances, that is, practical gender interests, yet there was no explicit hope that this would transform further into reforming the patriarchal system to realise women's strategic gender interests. The systemic recruitment of working and middle-class women, among other socio-economic and structural variables, have eventually led to a deeply embedded inferiority complex, where women perceive themselves as inferior to men (El Guindi, 1981; Mernissi, 1988b; Radwan, 1982; Williams, 1979). This confirms that women's status and roles in Egyptian society are subjugated by the structure of patriarchy. It additionally supports Kandiyoti's (1988) findings that 'women in areas of classic patriarchy [such as in the Middle East] often adhere as far and as long as they possibly can to rules (...) that result in their active collusion in the reproduction of their own subordination' (p. 289).

Furthermore, in 1971, a 'cult book' was disseminated titled *Al tabarruj* (Bodily Display). The author Ni'mat Sidqi, a young female university student at the time, wrote the book as a manifesto on why women should convert to traditional Islamic dress, adopt traditional gender roles, and remain hidden from the public eye in their quarters to protect their family honour. Studies conducted in the late 1970s on public university students found that 'Veiling, perceived as the symbol of Islamic authenticity, was theorised as a form of protest whether against the secular regime or against cultural dominance by the West' (van Nieuwkerk, 2021, p. 6). Other scholars, such as MacLeod (1991), who conducted similar studies in the 1980s, analysed the discourses around *Hijab* and found evidence of women's internalised inferiority complex, arguing that Egyptian women had accepted the *Hijab* in as much as they accepted the male control over their sexuality, bodies, and behaviours (MacLeod, 1991, p. 97). Read and Bartowski (2000) in their study titled *To Veil or Not to Veil* investigated the case study of identity negotiation among Muslim Women. They collected primary interviews of Muslim women asking them to identify the *Hijab*'s symbolic and substantive meaning to them. One of the participants in their study stated, 'The Veil keeps us [Muslim women] from getting mixed up in American culture' (Read & Bartowski, 2000, p. 407). Hirschmann (1997) in her studies confirmed the ambiguous position Egyptian women found themselves in, which is in between desiring strategic gender interests within the tenants of Islam, arguing:

> The veil is an important instrument in negotiating this ambiguity because it allows women to enter the public sphere of work while at the same time making a clear statement that they are good women, that is, attentive to the tenets of Islam, not Westernised.... The veil can be seen as a tool of women's agency in that it allows women to negotiate the strictures of patriarchal custom to gain what they want, to assert their independence, to claim their own identity. (pp. 480–481)

MacLeod (1991) expressed this as 'the women's dilemma', elaborating that 'the new veils enable women to regain control and create a new self-image, offering in symbolic fashion a partial resolution of the pressures women experience at the intersection of competing subcultural ideologies' (p. 120).

Given the Egyptian 'women's dilemma', it was unsurprising to see that with Sadat's presidency, and his reliance on the MB for public propaganda and support (Ibrahim, 1992), the Islamic dress spread among the wealthier classes who historically had shied away from it (Sa'id, 1972a, b, 1973). As the *Hijab* was most commonly worn by working women as a 'symbolic action by which they expressed their feelings of conflict and confusion about combining work outside the home with marriage and motherhood' (va Nieuwkerk, 2021, p. 6). This would mean those upper and upper middle-class women, who previously did not work because their financial circumstances did not require them to do so for survival, but now wished to enter the workforce, were adhering to the unspoken socially imposed dress-code to avoid social backlash (Diffendal, 2006, p. 132). An alternative perspective is that of MacLeod (1991), who argued that the expressed new wave of women putting on the *Hijab* is an act of political submission, where the Hijab 'takes place not as a remnant of traditional culture or a reactionary return to traditional patterns, but as a form of hegemonic politics in modernising environment, making its meaning relevant to women' (p. 121).

These observations can mostly be attributed to the conservative shift within the Egyptian society as informed by the political ideology of the President. Amina Said, the author of a woman's magazine called *Hawa* [Eve], was stunned by what she called, the 'reversal of female emancipation'. She noted that the influence of the MB on Egyptian youth and general discourse led to the decline of women's employment opportunities, and criticised the State for having an active role in convincing women to retreat into the private sphere (Zeidan, 2018). It was noted that these actions were not only reactionary but also illegal, as in 'certain practices that are contrary to the constitution and the Egyptian law [were noted] such as advertising in the newspapers for jobs specifying that applicants must be males' (Badran, 1991, p. 224). Unexpectedly, however, the government had enacted a law that ensures women 30 parliamentary seats, and, by presidential decree, Anwar Sadat amended the personal status law, granting women the right to initiate divorce, the right to contest polygamy in court, and added protections for women being divorced (Hussein, 1985, p. 231). These amendments later came to be known as 'Jehan's Laws', as the first lady, Jehan Sadat, pushed for these amendments. This upset many in the society, not only fundamentalists who believed it to be un-Islamic for a woman to divorce a man, but others who argued their status in society is being threatened by the first lady and feminists. Irrespective of how the general society perceived Jehan's Laws, they marked a substantial step towards realising women's strategic rights. Yet, as we observed with the 1956 constitutional Suffrage for Women amendment, just because the law changes, does not mean that the culture will change too. The enforcement of any law in Egypt has been historically problematic.

In subsequent years, the Sadat regime cracked down on all types of feminist activism. Nawaal El Saadawi as well as several female lawyers, medical doctors, and university professors struggled to obtain permits to establish women-led organisations, such as the Arab Women's Solidarity Association (AWSA). After failing to gain legal status in 1983 the organisation stated 'We knew that the liberation of the people as a whole could not take place without the liberation of women and this could not take place without the liberation of land, economy, culture, and information' (Bardan & Cooke, 1990). It registered as a nongovernmental organisation (NGO) with the UN in 1985. Feminists celebrated too early, as in 1985 – tremendous internal tension accumulated due to the peace treaty Sadat signed with Israel alienating the country from the rest of the Arab world – the decree amending the personal status laws was cancelled after turmoil and resistance soared in Egyptian society (Graham-Brown, 1985, p. 17). This was followed by a respected Al-Azhar scholar, Shaikh Metwally El Shaarawi declaring on national TV that a 'woman who works while she has a father brother or husband to support her, [is] a sinful woman' (Badran, 1991, p. 226; El Shaarawi, 1987). Al Ghazali, the founder of *The Muslim Sisters,* voiced her agreement with El Shaarawi stating that a woman seeking an occupation outside the household deserves the dangers awaiting her in the public arena – referring to sexual harassment and assault which rose substantially during that period and continued to increase up to present-day – blaming feminists for the encouragement of women to leave their homes and excusing men for their 'nature' and 'natural rights'. This narrative asserted that only a 'correct upbringing can protect women, not veiling' (Badran, 1991, p. 227).

Hirschmann (1997) asserted that this narrative led to women being 'systematically retrained by virtue of gender … [to tolerate] domestic violence, sexual harassment, rape, and sexual discrimination in the workplace' (p. 463). She continued to state that Egyptian women's first line of defence was to conform to the discourse and put the Hijab on, and supported that claim by stating:

> just as Western men used the veil as a symbol in their own political battles of imperialism, so did, and do, Eastern Islamic men use the veil in a similar fashion of resistance: in neither case do women take part in constructing the framework within which decisions about dress take place, but rather are forced to respond in conflicting directions to frameworks constructed by men. (Hirschmann (1991, p. 470)

Yet, Hirschmann (1997) also recognised the utility of the Hijab in forestalling patriarchal expressions of women's subservience, stating that 'the veil allows women entry into the working world by protecting women from sexual harassment and visibly demanding respect from a woman's husband, in the office, and even on the street' (p. 479). Whether the Hijab does protect a woman from sexual harassment, and how it does so, or whether this is simply a rationalisation to justify women's subordination and subjugation to male violence is a point of discussion in Chapter 4.

As observed, there has been oscillation of positions regarding feminism and women's issues. Throughout the 20th century, the state seems to have favoured the moderate view of an Islamic society without an Islamic governing system, realising the dangers of an Islamic state after observing the turn of events in Iran in the 1970s and 1980s. Radical views, such as those of Al Ghazali and El Saadawi, both lying on opposite sides of the spectrum, were suppressed and shut down by the regimes, regardless of their divergent political ideologies. At the turn of the century, feminist issues and their respective activists had gone underground with the rise of the Mubarak regime in the 1980s and well into 2011. The 25th January revolution, in 2011, gave some feminists hope for a better future, but this time, they became warier of the regimes in place. With the election of the MB member, Mohamed Morsi, into office in 2012, feminists believed that it would not be long until the regime cracked down on them, thus remaining an underground movement. With the impeachment of Morsi and the seizure of power by the military in 2014, embodied in Abdel-Fattah el Sisi, feminists realised the return of the Mubarak regime. To continue living a relatively normal life in the interim, one could argue, feminists chose to keep their activism hidden. The next section lays forward the reasons which have led feminist activists to choose to remain underground and not publicly support or promote the full emancipation of Egyptian women. Specifically, the next section builds on the issues addressed in this section and tackles the fifth research question: what role did political Islam play in constructing the status of Egyptian women?

2. The State and the Crackdown on Women's Movements

Civil societies are grassroots organisations meant to provide a platform for expression. They are an integral part of a democratic system as they mobilise public support for causes that affect a group within the society, utilising lobbying and campaigning to address local, national, or international concerns. It has been argued that civil societies in the Arab World specifically 'represent the competing ideologies and quest for power of political parties and the idealist concern of society at large through human rights advocacy' (Norton, 1995, p. 7). Therefore, the underlying purpose of such organisations is to provide a platform for the 'peaceful management of difference among individuals and collectivities sharing the same public space – i.e., the polity' (Ibrahim, 1995, p. 28). The following subsection investigates the strenuous status of civil society under Nasser, Sadat, and Mubarak, as it can be argued that civil societies have been suppressed in favour of personalised authoritarian regimes. Civil societies are 'credited for thwarting authoritarian designs and challenging arbitrary rules' (Norton, 1995, p. 7). Therefore, it is crucial for an authoritarian regime to tightly govern and reign over civil society, to avoid them reporting on 'internal corruption and hollow claims for legitimacy' that could eventually break down the regime (Al-Sayyid, 1995, p. 282). Feminist activism was perceived by the successive regimes to be a political organisation and opposition, therefore, feminist activism was encompassed under the umbrella of civil societies.

A senior Egyptian official once explained:

> Human rights mean having the right to pray, the right to your religion, the freedom of work, the freedom of movement .... How can [human rights] organisations get involved in politics of the State and say there is freedom or no freedom? This is none of their business. (Kassem, 2004, p. 119)

Protected by Article 11, the ruling authority has the legal right to 'label the activities of human rights advocates as political and therefore illegitimate' (Kassem, 2004), which means activists can be persecuted by the State and might be financially penalised or imprisoned under the guise of 'national security'. An example of such restriction is the police investigation filed by members of a Coptic village in Upper Egypt in 1998 against the government for the unlawful detention, murder, and torture of civilians. An human rights organisation, monitoring and reporting about the developments, was shortly after prosecuted by the government under suspicion of 'receiving money from a foreign country to damage the national interest, spreading rumours which affect the country's interest and violating the decree against collecting donations without obtaining permission from the appropriate authorities' (Aikman, 1999, p. 64). This indicted that reporting on human rights abuses is perceived by the government as a crime 'bordering treason' (Aikman, 1999) adding further restrictions on and relying on state-sponsored interpretations of what constitutes 'treason', 'political activity', and 'abuse'.

Specifically, women's rights organisations, most notably, AWSA (1982–1992) and *Egyptian Center for Women's Rights* (ECWR; 1996) have been targeted by the legislative and executive apparatuses. In 1992, in the case of *The Arab Republic of Egypt* vs *The Arab Women's Solidarity Association* and Dr Nawal El Saadawi (the scholar and founder of the organisation), the prosecution erected the law of association 57(4) in State Council's Administrative Judicial Court to condemn the practice of the organisation as a violation of 'rule of law and public order and morality by the practice of political and religious activities through its magazine and publication' (Human Rights Watch, 1997). AWSA's and ECWR's objectives were to lobby for an end to violence against women (VAW), the deprivation of women from equal access and legal right to participate in the public sphere, to raise awareness of the harmful practice of Female Genital Mutilation, and to end structural and institutional violence (UN, 2005).

After the 25th January revolution, in 2011, the government started cracking down even more on civil society and women's rights research institutions, most notably *Nazra for Feminist Studies* (shut down by the Government in 2016) and *El Nadeem Center for Rehabilitation of Victims of Violence and Torture* (shut down by the Government in 2017). *Nazra's* founder and executive director Mozn Hassan, in an interview with Al Ahram, explained 'the investigation with Nazra comes within the frame of taking escalating steps to close the public space by conducting a crackdown on independent civil society organisations in different ways' (Al Ahram, 2016), elaborating that civil societies and NGOs in Egypt are directly targeted by the government through the use of coercive means ranging from 'interrogations, to travel bans, summoning of organisations' staff members, and visits of inspection committees to some organisations' (Ford, 2016). Furthermore, *El Nadeem Center*, registered as a medical clinic with the Ministry of Health, had issued a press release articulating its condemnation of 'forced disappearances, arbitrary arrests and illegal detentions' (Raai, 2017), to which the government shortly afterwards responded with foreclosure of the clinic under the accusation it had 'violated the terms of license' (Raai, 2017).

Ever since the erection of Law 32 of 1964, and its revision in 2019 which added more restrictions (Cairo Institute for Human Rights, 2019), civil society organisations have been censored and persecuted by the Government (Nader, 2019) to suppress civil expression. These government efforts have been described by some organisations as 'deceptive and superficial (…) and seeks to subordinate them [civil societies and NGOs] to the security apparatus' (Cairo Institute for Human Rights, 2019). The repressive tension in Egypt apexed with the 25th January revolution, in 2011, where slogans of *'Esh, Horeya, Adala Egtema'ya* (Bread,

Freedom, and Social Equality) rampaged the streets of Cairo. The historically disadvantaged and abused minority groups, especially women, were major proponents and campaigners in the 25th January revolution, in 2011, onwards.

However, in 2018, the government renewed the state of emergency in Egypt, which was used to exercise censorship over social media platforms and media outlets. The censorship of social media has been used to detain at least 15 women under the guise of 'violating public morals' and 'undermining family values' (HRW, 2020a, b). For example, Amal Fathy, a human rights and women's activist in Egypt, posted a 12-minute video on the social platform, Facebook, detailing her experience with sexual harassment at a bank and the failure of the authorities to protect her. In a span of months, Fathy was arrested and charged with 'belonging to an outlawed group' and 'spreading false news' about the government (Mahfouz & Raghaven, 2018). Najia Bounaim, Amnesty International North Africa campaigns director, responded to the verdict stating '[it is an] outrageous case of injustice … [and] highlighted the vital issue of women's safety in Egypt … [describing Fathy as] not a criminal and should not be punished for her bravery' (Mahfouz & Raghaven, 2018). The summer of 2018 also witnessed the charge of a Lebanese tourist to Egypt with eight years in prison for the 'deliberately broadcasting false rumours which aim to undermine society and attack religions' (Specia, 2018) after she posted a video on Facebook detailing her experience with sexual harassment. The authorities justified the charge by claiming she deliberately engaged in 'defaming and insulting the Egyptian people', which is a crime punishable by law (Specia, 2018).

This section highlighted the different institutional responses to the opposition, which includes feminist and women's movements, and revealed the different levels of state-sponsored oppression inherent to authoritarian rule in Egypt. It additionally showcased the political and institutional conditions, which have led to women's inability to actualise and realise their strategic gender interests. Moreover, given this contextualisation, one can argue that Egyptian women resorted to the *Hijab* as a form of protection. Yet, Egyptian feminists are still fighting for women's emancipation. The following section builds on the literature and focusses specifically on how feminists and women's movements in Egypt have challenged the codification of Egyptian women's inferiority and second-class citizenship. Specifically, the next section tackles the sixth research question: To what extent does religion inform how women are perceived by society and the rights and liberties the legal framework protects?

3. Codifying the Dehumanisation of Egyptian Women

The first Egyptian constitution was created in 1923, four years after the Egyptian Revolution of 1919 which resulted in Egypt's independence, and was significantly influenced and inspired by the French legislative and government system (Meyer-Resende, 2014, p. 9). The legislative spirit in Egypt derives its principles from Sharia[1] as stated in Article 2 of the constitution (2014) 'Islam is the religion of the state and Arabic

---

[1] Islamic law.

is its official language. The principles of Islamic Sharia are the principal source of legislation' (Constitution of Egypt, 2014). According to the Egyptian constitution, the Qur'an, *Hadith*, and Islamic jurists[2] are the sources of deliberation when issues that have no explicit jurisprudence arise and require informed judgements based on interpretations (Moosa, 1997, p. 140). The Egyptian judiciary and legislative are heavily influenced by Sharia law, which is most conjured in issues regarding VAW, the protection of woman and child, marriage and divorce, passing on one's nationality, reproductive rights, and women's rights. As argued for and evidenced in the previous section, interpretation of Islam, and what is later rendered as Sharia law, is the male-narrative of what the scripture entails. Diffendal (2006) drew our attention to an important contextual issue, mainly that:

> Historically, Muslim women have had no hand in establishing the official parameters of Islam. Only men have had access to positions of power and influence within the tradition; they have interpreted religious texts, laid out and enforced prescriptions and proscriptions. One can and should call attention to women's agency within this context but must not lose sight of the fact that their choices and actions remain bound to this context. (p. 135)

One can therefore make a case that laws in Egypt are inherently 'anti-women' as the male interpretation of the scripture sees to the subordination and inferiority of women. Whether laws are a reflection of religious discourse or whether religious discourse was co-opted to constitute a law is beside the point of this argument, as both have the same result: women's social and cultural inferiority. It is significant to remember that for this book the *Hijab* is used as a proxy to understand and measure the female identity, status, and role within the Egyptian society. With that in mind, Diffendal (2006) argued that:

> Wearing the veil seemingly affords women a degree of autonomy and respect, but it fails to challenge the norms that work toward their overall disadvantage. Muslim women often can only legitimately assert themselves by adhering to the androcentric construction of a good Muslim woman. They must conceal themselves if they are to be taken seriously, accept responsibility for male sexuality, and deny their own sexuality in the process. Unfortunately, the Muslim women who do demand equality on their own terms are often accused of being sympathetic to Western, and therefore un-Islamic, ideals. In many Muslim contexts, women can defend and accommodate themselves to, but not create or criticise, norms. (p. 135)

---

[2]'Individuals informed by the spirit of the Qur'an and use their moral capacities for creative reasoning and judgement to arrive at relevant legal solutions' (Shaikh, 2011, p. 346).

Challenging cultural norms and creating new narratives which promote the strategic gender interests of women in Egypt was, and continues to be, a matter of contention. Egypt in the recent past has gone through drastic changes that erupted in post-revolutionary times. In four short years, three constitutional referendums occurred (2011, 2012, and 2014), each with its individual agenda, reflecting public, economic, and political priorities; In 2011, two days after the resignation of former Egyptian President Hosni Mubarak, the Supreme Council of the Armed Forces (SCAF) led the country during the transitional period until democratic elections were held January 11th of the next year (Casper & Serôdio, 2013), 2012, after the election of MB affiliate, Mohamed Morsi, to the presidency, a new draft constitution was passed in December of the same year (Casper & Serôdio, 2013); and January 2014 the latest draft constitution was passed after the second 'revolution', 30 June 2013, endorsed by SCAF, that ousted the MB president Morsi (Polimeno, 2015). The constitutional reforms were subtle and amounted to great controversies within the Egyptian community at large (Al-Atrush, 2014; Hussain, 2012; Shenker, 2011), and outraged women, who expressed their rage against the constitutional amendments by dancing on the streets of the capital Cairo, to oppose the restrictions imposed on the female body, development, and socio-economic mobility (Tadros, 2014).

The Constitution and the Penal Code are meant to declare the structure of government, create governmental institutions, empower the subjects of the State, protect the rights and set forth the obligations of individuals, and impose limits on violations of social order, for instance, corruption, abuse of power, the balance of power, *inter alia,* structural discrimination (Elkins et al., 2009, p. 36). Given this understanding, how can a constitution violate someone's autonomy or be used as a tool of oppression? The Egyptian constitution allows for statutory interpretation of the Constitution and Penal Code. Consequentially, legislative fallibility may occur, especially when it comes to controversial matters, such as marriage and divorce where a judge's discretion is lawful.

Women in Egypt have been disadvantaged by state and non-state actors, where the law's obscure language and elasticity have served in favour of the status quo and rarely has served the interests of women. The law is vaguest in issues pertaining to sexual, physical, and emotional VAW and the violation of women's rights. Gender ideologies underpin the judicial rulings in favour, or against, a victim in Egypt and the argument that *fear* is necessary to maintain a 'decent society' is reverberated and influenced by the idea that '[if you] remove this obstacle too and provide women with weak character assurance that they can safely surrender to their male friends you will see that the society will be plagued by the tide of moral licentiousness' (Maududi, 1974, p. 176). One could argue that this particular gender ideology is often used to rationalise sexual assault and the infliction of pain, physical and emotional, in the private and public sphere (Abdelhadi, 2016; Anderson, 2005; Baron, 2001; George & Martinez, 2002; Hubin & Haely, 1999; Kim, 2012; Miller, 2009; Ruggie, 1998; Schulhofer, 1998).

In the wake of the 25th January revolution, in 2011 in Egypt, where large numbers of women and men took their concerns to the streets of Cairo hoping to affect change, reports of mass sexual assaults, gang rapes, and more than

500 documented cases of sexual harassment accumulated (Amnesty International, 2013). As successive regimes have disregarded VAW in Egypt and failed to enforce the laws they created to protect women, issues affecting women fell on the reformative agendas of many politicians and lobbyists. Only recently, with the 2014 constitution, have we observed proactive steps to legal and institutional structures to combat VAW. According to UN Women (2018), 25.2% of married women between 15 and 49 have reported physical and/or sexual abuse by their spouses, 43.8% of women aged 10–29 reported being sexually harassed (Panel Survey of Young People in Egypt, 2014), 90% of men and 71% of women supported the toleration and silence of domestically abused wives to keep the family together (CAMPAS & UNICEF, 2017), 50% of men and 30% of women concurred that domestic violence is excusable and deserved, 30% of women and 20% of men reported bearing witness to their fathers abusing their mothers (CAMPAS & UNICEF, 2017), 17.4% of women were married before the age of 18 (EDHS, 2014), and 87.6% of married women between the ages of 15–19 have undergone FGM (EDHS, 2014). These statistics suggest a strong gravitation toward victim-blaming violations of women's rights, gender ideologies, and hint towards a deeply embedded internalised inferiority complex.

The Egyptian Government has collaboratively improved its constitutional and legal framework to establish more egalitarian and inclusive structures. Those improvements include a constitutional amendment to support eradicating VAW, child marriages, sexual harassment, and FGM. There have also been efforts on part of the State to launch support centres for victims, ranging from free legal services, counselling, and social and health services, such as the *National Strategy to Combat Violence against Women* (2015–2020), the *National Action Plan on Ending Violence Against Women* (2017), and an effort to extend and include *Ending Violence Against Women and Women's Empowerment* into national agenda (UN Women, 2018). The laws and policies of Egypt have been amended to be more accommodating and reflective of the issues and needs within the society. Article 11 of the constitution, added in 1971, reiterates the government's commitment to ending VAW, securing equal access for men and women to political participation and representation, socio-economic and cultural equality, and the right to hold public office without discrimination (Egy. Const., 1971:II, Article 11). Yet, amendments to the Penal Code, to support the iterations of Article 11, were only made 43 years later. Although the amendments' ambition seems to have been created to serve women's strategic interests, the language used is rather obscure and reflective of existing power relations, where the title of the article and its content can be interpreted subjectively and thus used for malicious purposes. The Article states:

> Article 11: The *place* [author's emphasis] of women, motherhood and childhood. The state commits to achieving equality between women and men in all civil, political, economic, social, and cultural rights in accordance with the provisions of this Constitution. The state commits to taking the necessary measures to ensure appropriate representation of women in the houses of parliament, in the manner specified by law. *It grants women* the right

> to hold public posts and high management posts in the state, and to appointment in judicial bodies and entities without discrimination. The state commits to the protection of women against all forms of violence, and ensures women empowerment to reconcile *the duties of a woman toward her family and her work requirements*. The state ensures care and protection and care for motherhood and childhood, and for breadwinning, and elderly women, and women most in need. (Egy. Penal Code, Article 11, 2014)

The italicisation was added by the researcher and is meant to emphasise potential problematic phrasing and use of language. The statement 'it grants women the right to hold public posts' is evidence of progressive thinking but can be misconstrued as giving women *permission* to work as opposed to them possessing that right by virtue of their humanity and their labour potential. Furthermore, the vernacular working of 'reconcile[ing] the duties of a woman towards her family and her work requirement' is extremely taxing as it codified, normalised and endorsed the double burden of women and thusly perpetuated the stereotyping of women as caretakers and free labourers, and also reproduced the traditional perception of women and their role in the society as 'home-makers'. Moreover, a study carried out by OECD in 2018 identified this as 'gender-based legal discrimination' and concluded that articles within Egypt's Constitution and personal status codes pose 'barriers to greater women's political representation in Egypt' particularly in relation 'to their socio-economic status (low levels of education, segregated employment, gender pay gaps) and discriminatory gender norms that encourage women to remain at home and out of the political spotlight' (OECD, 2018, p. 27). The report further detailed that women's political participation and representation comes at a high cost, as

> women who are successful in politics are often from wealthy or political families. Restrictive gender norms make it particularly difficult for women to see themselves as legitimate actors in the public sphere. Few women are encouraged to run for elections, whether for student body elections, local elections, parliament elections, and/or union elections. (OECD, 2018, p. 28)

Furthermore, Article 306 (A), intended to penalise sexual harassment, states that:

> A penalty of detention or a period not exceeding *one year* and a fine of not less than *two hundred Egyptian pounds* and not exceeding *one thousand Egyptian pounds* or either penalty shall be inflicted on whoever molests a female in a manner offending *her modesty* by words or deed on *a public road or a frequented place*' (Egy. Penal Code, Article 306 (A), 2014)

to which the following definition was added to include that 'any person who directs a lewd word, deed, or gesture on a public road in a populace place, including if the indecency takes place over the telephone or via any means of communication, wireless and otherwise, shall be punished by the aforementioned penalties' (Egy. Penal Code, Article 306 bis(B), 2014) amended via the Presidential Decree No. 50 of 2014 (Al-Jaridah Al-Rasmiyah, vol. 23(bis), 5 May 2014, p. 63: *in Arabic*). While on paper this seems to be a commitment by the government to protect strategic gender interests and grant women greater security, the most recent events prove this to be an unenforced commitment. In 2020, for example, Human Rights Watch issued a report in which they exposed the government for its lack of commitment, reporting:

> Egyptian authorities carried out an extensive campaign of arrests and prosecutions against women social media influencers, in violation of their rights to privacy, freedom of expression, and non-discrimination. Between April and time of writing, authorities arrested at least 15 people, including 11 women and a 17-year-old girl, on vague charges of violating 'public morals' and 'undermining family values'. Courts sentenced five of them to two and six years in jail. The prosecutions are based on videos and photos the women shared on social media apps showing themselves dancing and singing. Security forces arrested the 17-year-old girl after she published a video saying she was raped and assaulted by a group of men.

Moreover, Article 242-*bis* and Article 242-*bis*(A) of Law No. 58 of 1937 promulgating the Penal Code (as amended by Law No. 78 of 2016), attempted to discontinue the reproduction of dichotomous relationships, assuming that the private sphere is depoliticised, by providing punishment of enablers and perpetrators of VAW and women's bodies. Previously, Article 242 (bis) covered FGM as a misdemeanour. It imposed the penalty of imprisonment for between three months and two years on practitioners who commit the offence (Law No. 126 of 2008, amending Law No. 58 of 1937). Under the new amendment, individuals committing this crime will be punished with a period of imprisonment of between five and seven years. (*People's Assembly Strengthens the Penalty Against Female Genital Mutilation, supra.*) The article also punishes, with a penalty of imprisonment between one and three years, any individuals who escort the victims of such crimes to the perpetrators. Furthermore, the amendment punishes the crime with up to 15 years' imprisonment if the act of FGM leads to the death of the victim or a 'permanent deformity' [Law No. 78 of 2016, Al-Jaridah Al-Rasmiyah, vol.38 (Duplicate) (E), 26 Sept. 2016, p. 6 (in Arabic)]. However, in a report by 28TooMany (2018, p. 7), it was recorded that the lack of enforcement renders the laws ineffective and disputable, stating:

> There is a continuing failure to protect women and girls from FGM in Egypt and a lack of political will to implement and enforce the law. Punishments given to date do not reflect the penalties set out in the legislation and are not adequately followed through. Regarding the application of the law, it has also been observed that courts in Egypt to date appear to have only applied Article 242-*bis*, without accompanying criminal charges such as assault or

gross negligence (except in cases where the victim has died). Most notably, the courts have failed to apply Article 116-*bis* of the Child Act during Article 242-*bis* cases. Article 116-*bis* calls for doubled penalties if the crime of FGM is committed by an adult on a child.

To highlight the inefficacy of the domestic legal framework, 28TooMany constructed Table 1, to showcase that while Egypt may have ratified the *Convention for the eliminations of All Forms of Discrimination Against Women,* it 'did so with reservations that demonstrate how Islamic Sharia takes precedence over any international law or treaty. The new Constitution is also based on Islamic Sharia principles' (28TooMany, 2018, p. 2).

Nonetheless, these articles may be construed as a type of effort on behalf of the Egyptian Government to bring women into the public forum. Despite the lack of enforcement on behalf of the Government, it is an effort, nonetheless. However, the Egyptian Government has directly contributed to the codification and institutionalisation of women's inferiority and second-class citizenships with the addition of Article 291 to the personal status law. Identified as the most problematic personal status law it 'granted any individual who committed the offence of rape the option of marrying the victim in order to avoid the penalty imposed by the code' (Khalife, 2018). The law was verbally erected under British rule back in 1904 and formally codified in 1923. It was perceived as a way in which the family can restore their honour after a female family member was raped (Kitchen,

Table 1. Overview of Domestic Legal Framework in Egypt.

The Constitution explicitly prohibits:	
✓	Violence against women and girls
✗	Harmful practices
✗	Female genital mutilation (FGM)
National legislation:	
✓	Provides a clear definition of FGM
✓	Criminalises the performance of FGM
✗[a]	Criminalises the procurement, arrangement and/or assistance of acts of FGM
✗	Criminalises the failure to report incidents of FGM
✗[b]	Criminalises the participation of medical professionals in acts of FGM
✗	Criminalises the practice of cross-border FGM
✓	***Government has a strategy in place to end FGM***

[a]*Provision only for 'requesting' FGM.*
[b]*Ministerial Degree 271/2007 (see below) prohibits physicians and nurses from performing FGM but does not carry a criminal penalty.*
Source: 28TooMany (2018).

2015, p. 262). While this law was eradicated by presidential decree under Hosni Mubarak (Eltahway, 1999), it set two dangerous precedents: (1) the responsibility for protecting a family's honour is the woman's duty, which in turn absolves male members of the family from any responsibility towards maintaining the family's honour, and (2) it paints the victim of an assault as equally responsible for the attack as the perpetrator. The legal framework in Egypt has proven to be biased against women and systematically discriminates against their equal rights and equal status to their male counterparts. A report by the UNDP titled *Egypt Gender Justice and the Law* highlighted some of the problematic structures. The report investigated laws such as Article 375 in the Egyptian Penal Code which states:

> Whosoever surprises his wife, daughter, sister or mother in the act of adultery (in flagrante delicto) or in illegitimate sexual intercourse and immediately kills her or her partner or both in response to the assault that has affected his honour (sharaf) or the honour of his family, shall be liable to a prison sentence instead of the penalties provided for in Articles 234, 236.

Articles 234 and 236 pertain to the capital punishment and the prison sentence of murder, which has a maximum sentence of 25 years.

The UNDP (2018a, p. 17) reflected on this law stating:

> The law discriminates between women and men with regard to penalties and the location at which the crime is defined to occur. A wife proven guilty of adultery, inside or outside her marital home, shall be punishable by incarceration for a period of no more than two years. A husband proven guilty of adultery, only if it is inside the marital home, shall be punishable by incarceration for a period of no more than six months.

The report highlights the extent of the interplay between the political, social, and individual levels exposing how gender-based legal discrimination embedded within the Egyptian system is codifying the inferior status of Egyptian women. It also substantiates the argument that women are not considered equal citizens, because if they were, then the penalties should not vary depending on sex. This confirms the observation that women's second-class citizenship is codified within the legal framework and institutionalised socially. This was accentuated by the fact that all female participants for this book, like AU1e(3), a Hijabi, urban, upper-class woman, were told as young girls that, if they were harassed in public, they should say that the harasser stole something from them, because

> if you said that he harassed you then people would empathise with him and say 'it's because the economic situation is so abysmal and he can't get married, and men can't control their instincts' or worse, they would blame you for dressing a certain way or walking down a certain road. You would be at fault and not that pervert.

As women and men are not subject to the same penalties for crimes, men's livelihoods are not jeopardised by reporting violations, and women are socialised to believe in their own inferiority, the systematic institutionalisation of women's second-class citizenship is successful.

The evidence also supports the misuse of religion for political legitimation. This is highlighted by how quickly the presidential decree that abolished Article 291, was followed by a *fatwa* statement from Al-Azhar, which historically has been against commenting on rape, abortion, and VAW, in which the Grand Mufti stated that an 'unmarried rape victim should be permitted to have abortions' and continued to state 'government clinics should be allowed to perform operations on rape victims to reconstruct their hymens and 'restore' their virginity' (Eltahawy, 1999). Two obvious questions should be asked here: (1) Why is the restoration of the hymen necessary and what does it have to do with virginity? And (2) Why is the *fatwa* exclusive to 'unmarried' women? The answers are dependent on a cultural understanding of virginity. Virginity in Egypt is perceived as the existence of a physical hymen. This notion is problematic as almost half of women are born with an 'elastic hymen' meaning that the hymen does not break with penetration, and some women are born without a hymen altogether (Biggs et al., 1998; Mishori et al., 2019). This means that: (1) The hymen, in many cultures of the global South, is mistakenly confused with virginity and is used

> as 'proof' of the absence of sexual activity [which] has even led to an intersection of culture, religion, politics, law, economics, and medicine in the form of 'virginity testing', which involves the use of a vaginal examination to evaluate whether or not a woman's hymen is 'intact', in an attempt to ascertain whether a woman has had sexual intercourse. (Mishori et al., 2019, pp. 2, 3)

Moreover, the *fatwa* only pertains to 'unmarried' women because intermarital rape is not considered rape by the government, the law, or the religious apparatuses. This has grave societal consequences, where rape victims who happen to be married are not recognised by the law, culture, or even medical professionals as victims of rape.

The social discourse of men having the right to sexual satisfaction from women is not only perpetuated here but also reinforced by religious interpretations. As demonstrated in the earlier chapter, culture and tradition must be separated from scripture to fully comprehend what is responsible for women's inferiority to men in Egypt. With regard to sex, the Qur'an explicitly condemns the practice of premarital sex (Qur'an 24:2). However, intercourse also appeared in the following verse, which is commonly interpreted as the right of a man to sexual intercourse when he pleases 'Your wives are like farmland for you, so approach them consensually as you please. And send forth something good for yourselves. Be mindful of Allah, and know that you will meet Him. And give good news to the believers' (Qur'an 1:223). In its original language, Arabic, the word consensually appears as *Wa Akbelou* which has multiple connotations. The word in Arabic could imply 'and send forth (good deeds)', or 'and enter'. The first connotation can then be interpreted to mean consensually, but the second connotation can be interpreted to mean whenever a man wishes. The second connotation is the one adopted by Egyptian Muslims, which is supported by the evidence presented in the next sections.

From the collected field data, women who agreed to comment and were comfortable sharing their intermarital relationships revealed that they believed that their husbands have the right to demand sex even if they do not want to. One participant divulged that her mother told her that if she says no to his advances, Allah will not allow her into heaven. Participant observations confirmed that this is the adopted narrative of Egyptian women and men. This issue was pronounced when Nada Adel, the ex-wife of a famous Egyptian actor accused him of marital rape on her social media platforms (Samir, 2021). The video she posted caused an immense backlash from society. An Article by Samra Samir tracked the backlash and followed two Twitter users, Amr Sabry and Shaikh Abdullah Rushdy, who pioneered the backlash. In his investigative report, Samir (2021) cites Sabry who said:

> There is no such thing as #maritalrape in Islam and Egyptian law. Rather, it is forbidden for a woman (to refrain from her marital duties) as long as she does not have a great health excuse. And, a man should be MERCIFUL with his wife when she is tired.

Samir also cites Shaikh Abdullah Rushdy, who said:

> Some Westernised people are still promoting the so-called crime of marital rape! If a woman abstained from the husband without an excuse is forbidden. and the woman who does that is cursed, and her husband has the right to discipline [punish] her for that after advising and deserting her. If she responded, it is welcomed but if she refused, she should give him her dowry and be divorced.

These accounts, and the amount of support they received in Egypt speak to the social perception of women's status, rights, and rolesthere. Yet, the evidence suggests that, indeed, this is a cultural narrative and not a religious mandate. Marriage and sex are mentioned in the Qur'an in relation to harmony between spouses, where it says:

> And among His signs is that He has created for you spouses from among yourselves so that you may live in tranquillity with them, and He has created love and mercy between you. Verily, in that are signs for those who reflect. (Qur'an 30:21)

The *Hadith*, the second source of jurisprudence for Islamic Sharia, also contains explicit references to sexual etiquette, particularly with regard to sexual satisfaction for both partners, stating:

> 'When any of you wants to sleep with his wife, he must not rush her for indeed women have needs (too)' and even stressed the

significance of foreplay stating 'Do not engage in sexual intercourse with your wife like hens; rather, firstly engage in foreplay with your wife and flirt with her and then make love to her'.

In another *Hadith*, the prophet elaborated, 'Whoever wants to get close to his wife must not be hasty, because women before engaging in the act of lovemaking must be engaged in foreplay so that they are ready for making love to'. As Muslims believe that the Qur'an is the word of God and the *Hadith* is the decipherment tool for interpreting and understanding the Qur'an, both should be used concurrently to comprehend the religion. The evidence from the collected data as well as the reports reviewed for this project reveals the extent to which patriarchal interpretation of scripture influenced the status of women and how they are perceived by the society. The evidence demonstrates how patriarchal structures exploited theological despotism and

> drained Islam of all sense of ethics and morality but also all notions of humanity …. Everything that Muslim men have produced, from scriptural interpretations to Sharia Law to even our mysticism, is designed to keep women subjugated and isolated in a confined space. And our historic gift, patriarchy, ensure that things remain as they should. (Sarda, 2013, p. 4)

This also highlighted the gendered understanding of virginity for women and men – insisting on women remaining celibate but also encouraging men to be promiscuous as there are no socio-cultural, religious, or legal repercussions for their actions (ElTahawy, 2015, p. 137; Nosseir, 2019). These notions of virginity create a social dynamic in which women are denied sexual desires and their sexuality controlled and policed around the men's understanding of honour and purity, and sexuality and pleasure (Mensch et al., 2000). This gender dynamic is normalised through the process of gendered socialisation. In a study conducted by Mensch et al. (2003) on the gendered socialisation of Egyptian adolescents and its effects on gender dynamics in adulthood, the authors concluded that:

> The conventional view of gender relations is one in which women are generally submissive to men and are confined by social norms to roles within the family. For the most part, the findings support the prevailing view of gender roles in Egypt. By and large, young people appear to conform to traditional notions of what it means to be male and female in a Middle Eastern society (…) As girls enter puberty, they ex- perience an abrupt shift in what is considered appropriate behaviour, and at that point, if not earlier, they become aware of the restrictions placed upon them as women. (Mensch et al., 2003, p. 16)

Mensch et al. (2003) shed light on how 'power within' is suppressed by gendered socialisation, which could explain why Egyptian women have yet to actualise their strategic gender interests. Mona ElTahawy (2015, p. 109) expressed her outrage over the lack of autonomy and agency Egyptian women have over their bodies, stating even 'our hymens are not ours, they belong to our families'. Nawaal Saadawi (1977) similarly said

> An Arab family does not grieve as much at the loss of a girl's eye as it does if she happens to lose her virginity. In fact, if the girl lost her life, it would be considered less of a catastrophe than if she lost her hymen. (p. 54)

This speaks to the social perception of women as agency and autonomy, particularly to women's denial of humanness to express sexuality and strive for 'power within'. This is also reflected in marriage contracts where the father or legal guardian in Muslim wedding rituals must explicitly state that the wife-to-be is a virgin but no expressed statement of chastity is required for the husband-to-be (Wynn & Hassanein, 2017). The implication is also that the woman lacks the cognitive capacity to 'refinement, self-control, intelligence, and rationality' and requires a man to act and speak on her behalf. This dynamic is paternalistic in nature and is reminiscent of being a minor and requiring a legal guardian to be present when speaking to authority figures like a school principal, an issue unpacked later in this book.

Moreover, while the abolishment of this law was most certainly a celebration-worthy moment for Egyptian women, the reality is, that this presidential decree has effectively changed nothing. The researcher asked an established Egyptian lawyer about what these laws entail and what they mean. According to CU2p(98), the multiple dimensions of the law counteract the decree. This includes the allowance of judges to rule on cases using *Mahkamet El Orf* [customary courts] which reflect cultural traditions, values, and rituals. When asked what this means for real women, the lawyer reflected upon his own experiences in court, and with a pain-filled and antagonised expression said:

> This means that the formal abolishment of the law is effectively ceremonial and symbolic, because as long as the idea 'if he marries her, everything will go back to normal and honour will be restored' is still culturally reproduced, the judges can revert to the use of customary courts to circumvent state laws. For a judge to ascertain that customary law in a particular case ought to be employed, the male guardian of the unmarried woman, may that be the father, the brother, or a paternal male cousin simply has to stand in front of the court and state that the family wants the woman to be married off to her rapist. In these cases, this would grant the court the right to marry the victim off to her rapist. This is normally done under the guise of 'cultural preservation' and 'cultural relativism'. So if you were raped, and I'm your father, I would go to court with you. As your guardian is present, you do not speak, but your guardian speaks on your behalf. So I can tell a judge 'your honour, I want my daughter to marry this man to

protect my family from the dishonour she has brought upon us' is more than enough for the court to grant me my wish. I'm not saying I condone this, but it's just how it is done here. I've had many people, especially fathers and brothers of women from lower socio-economic classes who asked me to say those exact words to the judge, and they did indeed get their wish and the courts married their daughter to her rapist.

This testimony by an Egyptian lawyer substantiates the argument that gender-based legal discrimination and patriarchal interpretation of scripture served to codify and institutionalise women's inferiority. We can see evidence of women's lack of capabilities in 'existing value systems [being] highly paternalistic, particularly towards women. They treat them as unequal under the law, as lacking full civil capacity, as not having the property rights, associative liberties and employment rights of males' (Nussbaum, 1999, p. 231). We can also see clear evidence of six out of seven forms of dehumanisation Nussbaum (1999) identified. First, in the private sphere, women are valued for their 'instrumentality' as sexual objects, perceived to exist for male satisfaction and subject to men's claims of 'ownership'. Second, in the political sphere, the Egyptian legal framework served the 'denial of autonomy' and 'inertness' for Egyptian women by passing unequal penalties for the same crimes for women and men, not recognising the shortcomings of the legal framework in protecting women against gender-based violence in the private sphere or the public sphere and lack of proper enforcement of the laws that do. Third, in the social sphere, the social perception of women as inferior and the inadequate legal framework, which served to solidify it, normalised the 'violability' of women, and consequentially women's 'denial of subjectivity'. These six forms of dehumanisation worked to secure women's subordination in Egypt, through the systemic promotion of 'false consciousness, or the internalisation of patriarchal norms through socialisation' (Mahmood, 2011, p. 205).

This, in turn, corroborates the existence of three of the four categories of dehumanisation Markowitz and Slovic (2020) identified: *Dual Perspective of Humanness* where Egyptian women are regarded as sexual objects that can be owned, thereby normalising the perception of women lacking 'refinement, self-control, intelligence, and rationality' (Haslam & Loughnan, 2014); *Dehumanised Perception* of Egyptian women, where Egyptian men operate with impunity when committing crimes against women, ultimately leading to the social perception of women as inferior to men; and *Mind Perception Framework* where the patriarchal interpretation of scripture has 'denied [women] agency and experience because they are believed to not have the capacity for cognitive freedom, and are denied secondary psychological processes' (Markowitz & Slovic, 2020, p. 261). This section demonstrated how Egyptian women's inferiority and second-class citizenship were codified using dehumanising processes. Gender-based legal discrimination and the misuse of religion to perpetuate cultural discourses around women's rights in Islam normalised and solidified patriarchal practical gender interests and suppressed emancipatory strategic gender interests.

The next chapter presents the conceptual and methodological approaches used to address objective three of this book: understanding the types of patriarchal bargains identified by Egyptian citizens, and investigating what women have done to challenge/perpetuate their inferiority and second-class citizenship. Sylvia Walby (1990) in her book *Theorising Patriarchy* provides a conceptualisation of how different structures interact to perpetuate patriarchal systems and reproduce the dynamic of male domination and women's subordination. Walby's conceptual framework is adopted in this book to analyse the primary data. The adoption of Walby's conceptual framework facilitated the identification and extraction of social patterns from the primary data, believed to be the patriarchal bargains responsible for the perpetuation of the patriarchal system in Egypt, and the cause of Egyptian women's unrealised strategic gender interests (see Chapters 4–6). It also served to provide an account of how women navigated patriarchal bargains, that is, strategies developed and adopted by women to gain greater autonomy and security within the patriarchal structure. The next section presents the Walby's conceptional framework, *Six Structures of Patriarchy,* which is used for this book.

4. Conceptual Framework

Mona Eltahawy (2015) in her book *Headscarves and Hymens* argued that Egyptian women are socialised to believe in their inferiority and points to mothers as the main perpetrators of female inferiority and conformity to the roles ascribed by the patriarchal system. She states

> I recognise the need to conform. That need internalises misogyny and subjugation, so much so that mothers will deny daughters the same pleasure and desire they were denied, and will call them 'whores' for seeking it. To survive, women police their daughters' bodies and their own, subsuming desire for the 'honour' and the family's good name. (Eltahawy, 2015, p. 114)

In her book, Eltahawy (2015) interviewed Egypt's Nawal Saadawi, Egyptian feminist scholar and philosopher, who recalled her genital mutilation at the age of six, stating:

> I did not know what they had cut off from my body, and I did not try to find out. I just wept and called out to my mother for help. But the worst shock of all was when I looked around and found her standing by my side. Yes, it was her, I could not be mistaken, in the flesh and blood, right in the midst of these strangers, talking to them and smiling at them, as though they had not participated in slaughtering her daughter just a few moments ago. (p. 118)

Eltahawy's (2015) observations reveal how women's strategic gender interests are suppressed and denied, and confirm that a process of systematic dehumanisation exists in Egypt. It also confirmed Denz Kandiyoti's (1988) assertion that, 'in areas of classical patriarchy, women often adhere as far and as long as they possibly can to rules (...) that result in their active collusion in the reproduction of their own subordination' (p. 289). To investigate these findings further, we need to take a closer look at how different forms of patriarchal systems interact to produce and maintain women's inferiority and second-class citizenship.

Sylvia Walby (1990) in her book *Theorising Patriarchy* developed a conceptual framework called *Six Structures of Patriarchy* to investigate how patriarchal structures and systems interact to reproduce and perpetuate women's subordination. She argued that patriarchy is evident in: (1) Paid Employment, that is, gender pay gaps and gendered value of labour (p. 25); (2) Family/Household Production, that is, domestic division of labour and responsibilities (p. 61); (3) Culture, that is, cultural notions of femininity and masculinity and gender expectations (p. 90); (4) Sexuality, that is, attitudes towards sex as either a source of pleasure or as a tool for control and domination (p. 109); (5) Violence, that is, male VAW (p. 128); and (6) the State, that is, efforts to improve women's status in society through laws and political action (p. 150). Walby's identified *Six Structures of Patriarchy* are in essence a categorical organisation of Molyneux's (1985) *strategic gender interests*. Walby's structures were used in this book to outline the parameters for Egypt's patriarchal system. The qualitative data were then used to establish the extent to which women's strategic gender interests have been actualised in Egypt and to highlight patterns of strategies women employed to gain greater security and safety within the patriarchal bargains. Later on, a discussion of the findings is presented with findings on how the patriarchal system prevented women from achieving their of strategic gender interests, and by extension perpetuated their second-class citizenship in Egypt.

Walby's Six Structures of Patriarchy were adopted for this book as it is the most suitable for the investigation of classic patriarchal systems. Walby (2020, p. 414) in her work *Varieties Gender Regimes* offered a modified and developed version of the *Six Structures of Patriarchy* (Walby, 1990) in response to her critics. Walby's original conceptualisation was criticised for 'inevitably viewing women as victims and underestimating women's agency and capacity to political action' and 'for inappropriately suggesting that women actively create their own oppression' while the account ought to be theoretically led by the 'voluntarist concepts of women's actions' (Walby, 1996, p. 2). However, Walby qualified the move away from six structures of patriarchy to 'gender regimes' by drawing a distinction between premodern and modern manifestations of patriarchy. Walby argued that gender regime theory offers an alternative analysis of macro-level patriarchal transformation from the domestic and private sphere (premodern) into the public sphere (modern) (Walby, 2020, p. 416).

On the other hand, Walby built on Moghadam's (2020) theory of 'neopatriarchy'. Moghadam (2020, p. 470) described neopatriarchy as the state's introduction of 'women's social and spatial presence – public education, employment in the government sector, the vote – but retains patriarchal family laws that bind women and girls to the family and to protection (or control) by male kin'. Citing her earlier (1993 and 1999) work, Moghadam (2020) clarifies that she used the term 'neopatriarchy as an umbrella term for the different types of twentieth-century states and gender relations' (p. 469) as she believed 'classic patriarchy was on the wane'. The reason this book operationalises Walby's *Six Structures of Patriarchy* is that Egypt qualifies as a classic patriarchal system. While the developed version of Walby's *Six Structures of Patriarchy,* gender regimes is theoretically sound, it stresses the 'neopatriarchal form of public gender regime' and focusses on the macro-level of analysis. This may be appropriate for modern contexts, yet the conditions which would qualify Egypt as 'modern' have not been met and evidence of classic patriarchy is still prevalent.

Classic patriarchy is defined as a system in which women's autonomy and protest to unfavourable circumstances is not tolerated (Kandiyoti, 1988, p. 275), women's subservience is expected and reproduced through patrilocality (Kandiyoti, 1988, p. 278), and where 'woman's life cycle in the patriarchally extended family is such that the deprivation and hardship she experiences as a young bride is eventually superseded by the control and authority she will have over her own subservient daughters-in-law' (Kandiyoti, 1988, p. 279). Kandiyoti (1988) argued that in areas of classic patriarchy one could observe women's 'active collusion in the reproduction of their own subordination' (p. 280). She elaborated that women in areas of classic patriarchy 'would rather adopt interpersonal strategies that maximize their security through manipulation of the affections of their sons and husband ... [than] to alter the structurally unfavourable terms of the overall patriarchal script' (Kandiyoti, 1988, p. 280). Nonetheless, Kandiyoti (1988) recognised that some women engage with the patriarchal bargain of exchanging their autonomy for financial, physical, and emotional security, yet her study also revealed that:

> Despite the obstacles that classic patriarchy puts in women's way, which may far outweigh any actual economic and emotional security, women often resist the process of transition because they see the old normative order slipping away from them without any empowering alternatives. (p. 282)

The primary data collected for this book, the analysis of secondary legal and policy documents, and participant observations, suggest that Egypt qualifies as a system of classic patriarchy because empowering alternatives, such as emancipatory strategic gender interests, have not been realised. From the definition of what qualifies as 'premodern' and 'modern', the classification of Egypt as premodern is warranted. Therefore, this book chose Walby's (1990) conceptual framework of *Six Structures of Patriarchy* as it unpacks both the public (macro – in the form of Walby's patriarchal structures of Violence, Sexuality, Culture, and the State) and the private (micro – in the form of Walby's patriarchal structures of Family/Household Production and Paid Employment) levels of gender relations. The next section presents how Walby's Six Structures of Patriarchy are manifested in the Egyptian context.

4.1. Conceptual Diagram and Analytical Elements

Fig. 1 presents the patriarchal structures identified and studied by Walby and how these were translated to outline the parameters for Egypt's patriarchal system and measure the degree to which women can realise their strategic gender interests.

Walby (1990) identified Paid Employment as an essential strategic gender interest as 'Women have been increasingly entering paid employment in the post-war period' (p. 57). She posited that Paid Employment signified 'the entry into such an important aspect of the "public" sphere [which] has traditionally been seen as a sign of the emancipation of women' (Walby, 1990, p. 58). Walby (1990) also identified Family/Household Production as the second strategic gender interest where the Family is considered to be 'central to women's lives and to the determination of gender inequality ... and the structure through which women's labour is appropriated in the household' and the household is considered to be the site 'in which men oppress women, in that men benefit from women's domestic labour ... and women have committed themselves to the role of homemaker' (p. 87). In Fig. 2, these strategic gender interests were translated into the Egyptian context, to assess the extent to which these interests have been actualised.

Walby also identified Culture and Sexuality as two strategic gender interests where the patriarchal system prevails. Culture is defined by Walby (1990) as 'ideas about masculinity and femininity ... found in all areas of social relations. which go to make up patriarchal structures. which is important in the maintenance of gender relations' (p. 91). One can argue that the denial of women's strategic gender interest within this category can be attributed to 'a naturalisation ideology, to a dissimulative approach which denies the extent of the inequality' which places higher social value on masculinity over femininity.

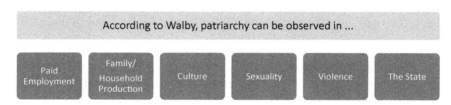

Fig. 1. Walby's Six Structures of Patriarchy.

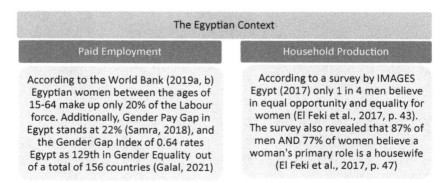

Fig. 2. Walby's Private/Domestic Sphere Structures.

Sexuality, in Walby's (1990) conceptualisation, is in a complementary position to Culture, as it can be viewed as a 'major source of pleasure that we seek in our lives, or the foundation of men's control over women' (p. 109). Walby (1990) particularly focussed on how 'sexual morality', meaning the imposition of the standard of chastity on women but not men, resulted in 'the sexual double standard and the sexual abuse' (p. 126). She also noted that 'birth control and divorce are means by which men gain greater sexual access to women's bodies', however, under a patriarchal system, 'a woman's status [is] crucially affected by her sexual "purity" and the negative consequences of pre or extra-marital sex [are] severe' (Walby, 1990, p. 124). She, therefore, concluded that control over women's sexuality extends men's control from the private sphere into the public sphere. The extent to which the patriarchal systems in Egypt appear within the concepts of Culture and Sexuality is presented in Fig. 3.

The last two structures of patriarchy identified by Walby are Violence and the State. Walby defined Violence in the constraints of male VAW including 'rape, sexual assault, wife-beating, workplace sexual harassment and child sexual abuse' elaborating that it is 'widely considered to be individually motivated and with few social consequences'. She argued that in the narrowest sense, Violence is most pronounced in the legal structures as 'these carry a certain authority because of their status. as a legal entity' and continued to state 'the rape of a wife by her husband; the woman is deemed to have consented to sexual intercourse on marriage' and 'the exclusion of husband-wife rape from criminalisation' are examples of the legal structure's authority in setting gender dynamics and ascribing social status. She further explained that in patriarchal contexts, 'judge's discretion is used to allow indirect evidence of women's sexuality to be routinely introduced in rape cases … to shift the balance of the courtroom away from the man accused of rape and towards the women' (1990, p. 148).

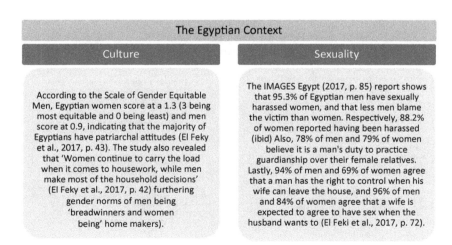

Fig. 3.   Walby's Public/Social Sphere Structures.

100 Recovering Women's Voices

The State, as defined by Walby (1990), can be 'engaged with gendered political forces, its actions have gender-differentiated effects, and its structure is highly gendered' (p. 150). However, she argued that 'the notion that the state has a monopoly over legitimate coercion' is problematic, particularly 'when in practice individual men are able to utilise considerable amounts of violence against women with impunity' (p. 150). She concluded that if 'improvements in the equal opportunity legislation, numbers of women in public office, and ease of divorce' are not committed to by The State, then women will disproportionately suffer. The extent to which the patriarchal system informed Violence and the State in Egypt is depicted in Fig. 4.

Walby's (1990) study concluded that women

> are not passive victims of oppressive structures. They have struggled to change both their immediate circumstances and the wider social structures ... however, it did not lead to an elimination of all the forms of inequality between men and women ... in response, patriarchy changed in form incorporating some of the hard-won changes into new traps for women. (p. 201)

This resonates with the participant observations of the Egyptian case study. From the analytical chapters preceding this, in addition to the descriptive quantitative data presented here, the following conclusions were established:

On Paid Employment and Family/Household Production. Chapter 1 addressed the first research objective: to identify the historical and political instances within which women's second-class citizenship in Egypt was established. This was achieved by reframing and re-examining the scholarship around women's

The Egyptian Context	
Violence	**The State**
More than half the men surveyed by IMAGES Egypt (2017) have physically abused their wives, and 80% of men admitted to emotionally abusing their wives. The Arab Barometer V (2020) report also found that 88% of domestic violence cases are never reoprted under the classification that it is a 'Private Family Matter' (Alayli, 2020). Additionally, the IMAGES survey (2017, p. 79) found that 70% of women and men interviewed agreed a woman should toleate physical violance to keep the family together. Furthermore, 21% of women and and 1.1% of men admitted to being forced to have sex with their husbands/wives. Also, 50% of women and 18.7% of men have admitted to being belittled and humiliated in public by their spouses. The survey also revealed that 64% of men and 60% of women believe a rape victim should marry her rapist (El Fekri et al., 2017, p. 82).	The findings of the IMAGES Egypt Survey suggests that while men do recognise that women could play a prominant role in leadership, two-thirds oppose women having political roles and authority (El Feki et al., 2017, p. 52). While Egypt has aligned some of its laws with the Convention on the Elimination of all forms of Discrimination Against Women (CEDAW), yet the government's approval provisioned that its new laws cannot violate Islamic Sharia, on which most its personal status law is based, thus effectively remaining the same. A comprehensive draft legislation for personal status proposed in 2021 attracted continues criticism for higlighting the 'regime's inability to maintain a religious and social balance (Ahmed, 2021). Unsurprisingly, the data highlights that 70% of men and 45% of women oppose criminalising marital rape and demostic violance, 78% of men and 33% of women agree that men should not be prevented from divorcing their wives without court proceedings (El Feki, 2017, p. 55)

Fig. 4. Walby's Political Sphere Structures.

movements in Egypt, and approaching them as efforts to actualise strategic gender interests for Egyptian women. Translating the findings into Walby's conceptual understandings of Paid Employment and Family/Household Production, the chapter highlighted how the actualisation of equal opportunity and status within both public and private spheres, has been historically suppressed, ranking Egypt today 129th on the Gender Gap Index. Further evidence of women's low degree of strategic gender interests includes how differential gender roles were normalised, specifically as many Egyptian men believe that if women leave their homes they 'have no shame and want to be raped' (Ramdani, 2013). Further evidence of this being a socially accepted narrative, was the statement of former Upper House of Parliament member Adel Afifi, who publicly stated, 'Women contribute 100% to their rape because they put themselves in that position [to be raped]' (Ramdani, 2013). This suggested a strong patriarchal bargain existing in Egypt which confined women to the private sphere where male control and domination are prominent. This contextual and conceptual understanding underlined the approach taken to code and analyse the collected data on *Personal Beliefs and Values*, using the proxy of the Hijab.

On Culture and Sexuality. Chapter 2 addressed the second research objective: to understand the intersectionality of the patriarchal system and Islam in reproducing women's inferior identities and identifying the patriarchal bargains set that deny women access to full citizenship status. The chapter highlighted the existence of gender-based legal discrimination in Egypt, particularly in terms of personal status laws. The chapter also demonstrated the presence of a convoluted understanding of what constitutes cultural tradition and what constitutes a religious mandate. The lack of separation led to the misuse of Islam to perpetuate and maintain the patriarchal system in Egypt. The analytical review demonstrated how political Islam was misrepresented to legitimate the social and cultural domination of men and normalise gender differentiating standards for sexual morality. This contextual and conceptual understanding underlined the approach taken to code and analyse the collected primary data from ordinary Egyptian citizens about their *Views and Experiences of Patriarchy and Oppression* in Egypt.

On Violence and the State. Chapter 2 additionally reviewed the legal structure in Egypt to investigate whether it contained elements that suppress women's attainment of strategic gender interests. The review concluded that the patriarchal system played a significant role in codifying what Walby categorised as the patriarchal structure of Violence. It also sheds light on how the State failed to commit to the emancipation of women by neglecting the enforcement of the few laws that protect women against male violence. The findings suggested that the patriarchal system of Violence is deeply embedded into Egypt's legal system, *de facto* institutionalising women's second-class citizenship and inferiority. This contextual and conceptual understanding underlined the analytical reviews within Chapters 1 and 2, however, no primary data could be collected about these patriarchal structures due to the research limitations imposed on this project.

So far, the findings suggest low levels of strategic gender interest attainment among Egyptian women and high levels of patriarchal bargains imposed within which women are struggling to gain equal opportunity, access, and citizenship status in Egypt. Thus far, the evidence suggests a multilayered patriarchal system in Egypt which develops women's practical gender interests but does not advance their strategic needs, thereby maintaining the social domination of men. This patriarchal system created an environment where women are excluded from full citizenship rights and benefits equal to their male counterparts, which the preliminary findings indicate can be attributed to women's lack of strategic gender interests. To confidently establish whether this observation is true in contemporary Egypt, the next few chapters present the primary data collected from the field, between January and August 2020, to identify which patriarchal bargains are most relevant to women today. The chapters also present data on the strategies women employ within the patriarchal structure to gain a greater 'ability to exercise agency on their own behalf, including the agency needed to challenge their [citizenship] exclusion' (Kabeer, 2006, p. 100).

Reflecting on Walby's conceptual framework, and the information that arose from the literature review, the addition of 'Religion' as a patriarchal structure seemed necessary and appropriate for the Egyptian case study. While 'Religion' is not inherently a patriarchal structure, in the context of Egypt where political Islam is a dominant political tool, the conceptual addition of Religion appeared to be essential. More specifically, as Article 2 of the Egyptian constitution declares that 'Islam is the religion of the state and Arabic is the official language. The principles of Islamic Sharia are the principal source of legislation' the establishment of Religion as a structure is fundamental to the unpacking of Egypt's patriarchal system. Nonetheless, it is critical to note that this expansion of Walby's conceptual framework is only applicable to case studies which produce similar sociopolitical, cultural, and legal emphasis on religion as Egypt does (Fig. 5).

Qur'an and *Sunnah* are the texts upon which *Sharia laws,* Islamic laws, are established. According to Shamsy and Coulson (2022), Sharia is:

> The religious law of Islam is seen as the expression of God's command for Muslims and, in application, constitutes a system of duties that are incumbent upon all Muslims by virtue of their religious belief. Known as Sharia … the law represents a divinely ordained path of conduct that guides Muslims toward a practical expression of religious conviction in this world and the goal of divine favour in the world to come.

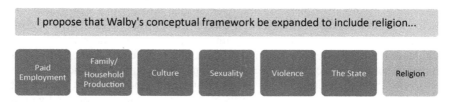

Fig. 5. ElMorally's Seven Structures of Patriarchy.

As the interpretation of the Qur'an and Hadith has been 'interpreted in varying ways, over time, the diversity of possible interpretations has produced a wide array of positions on almost every point of law' (Shamsy & Coulson, 2022). Nonetheless, the authors argued that 'social pressures and communal interests have played an important role in determining the practice of Islamic law in particular contexts – both in the premodern period and to an even greater extent in the modern era' (Shamsy & Coulson, 2022). In addition, the interpretation of scripture and the passing of religious rulings in contemporary Egypt is conducted by the Grand Mufti of Al-Azhar institution. The Grand Mufti, when approached by the government, can provide a religious stance on any issues, particularly with regard to the legality of municipal laws such as capital punishment. The problematic dynamic was pronounced in 2012 when the 'legislation on a on sharia-compliant state' was approved, leading to 'a crisis … [which] confirms the centrality of constitutional design choices for the operation of Sharia provision' (Parolin, 2015, p. 212). In an article by Cairo Scene (2017) it was noted that 'From the 1950s onward, Al-Azhar became void of authority, slowly turning into a bureaucratic religious symbol frequently used by the state to legitimise its actions and decisions'. To highlight the extent to which Al-Azhar is an extension of state power, the authors state:

> A prominent example of this is a *fatwa* issued by Al-Azhar in 1979 stressing that the time of peace with Israel has come (after years of calling for *Jihad* against the Israeli occupation of Palestine), which was a legitimizing force behind Sadat's Camp David peace accords after a number of condemnations from Muslims all over the world. The infamous fatwa, however, helped contain public anger in Egypt. (Cairo Scene, 2017)

Understanding this, Religion, embodied in the institution of Al-Azhar, has appeared as a patriarchal structure which ought to be separated from Walby's structure of the State. This particular distinction was motivated by the fact that while the State may be the structure which sets the laws and is responsible for their enforcement, Religion is the structure which legitimises it and makes it agreeable to the public. Religion as a patriarchal structure is thereby defined, in this book, as the use of Religion as a tool of political legitimation and justification for social control. Religion as a patriarchal structure in the context of the Egyptian case study appears in the employment of political Islam as an ideology by the state and will be referenced accordingly in the upcoming chapters.

Chapter 4

Methodology, Methods, and Tools

1. Research Methodology: Qualitative Interpretivism/The Interpretivist Paradigm

Thomas Kuhn (1970) said that paradigms are a 'tradition of claims, counter-claims, and debates over fundamentals', rendering the choice of a paradigm critical for any research endeavour (p. 22). The assumption that a paradigm is an unchanging set of conventions about the method of inquiry has provided scholars with the starting point. After discovering their paradigm, their world view, and how they will approach it and engage with it, scholars can move to understand the society they chose for their study.

For this book, I used an interpretivist paradigm. The interpretivist tradition, as George Herbert Mead (1982) stated, 'the individual mind can exist only in relation to other minds with shared meanings' (p. 5), thus insinuating that

> human beings interpret or 'define' each other's actions instead of merely reacting to each other's actions. Their 'response' is not made directly of one another but instead is based on the meaning which they attach to such actions. Thus, human interaction is mediated by the use of symbols, by interpretation, or by ascertaining the meaning of one another's actions. (Blumer, 1992, p. 82)

This means that knowledge is an intangible object that cannot be summarised but should be observed, as it is socially constructed and carries different value realities for every individual; that every mode through which information is disseminated is valid and bears value. The reason I chose to use an interpretivist paradigm is I am not attempting to measure knowledge or quantify information. Instead, I am attempting to understand the value system, the emotions, the core beliefs, and the diverse and divergent realities of Egyptian nationals to deconstruct *how* they have come to believe what they believe and *why* they attribute specific values to the consequent manifestations of those beliefs. As Clifford Geertz (1975) said, 'one cannot forcefully note meaning (…) rather [one ought to] understand a piece of behaviours in context and use one's knowledge to interpret it when one describes it' (p. 9).

The interpretivist worldview allows the researcher the space and flexibility to pursue their intuition and trust that their subconscious has the capacity to interpret realities before entering our conscious thought processes. Therefore, the purpose of employing the interpretivist paradigm in this book is, as Albert Einstein expressed, '[the scientific method] is trying in whatever way or manner is suitable, [to depict] a simplified and lucid image of the world .... There is no logical path, but only in intuition' (Holton & Sonnert, 1995, p. 168). As the process of inquiry in qualitative research endeavours is based on creating a narrative, one could easily 'play with ideas, try to create anomalies, try to find neat puzzle forms that we can apply to intractable troubles so that they can be turned into soluble problems' (Bruner, 1985, p. 126). Therefore, the purpose of this book is to identify and understand how people engage with the aforementioned problems.

2. Rationalising the Qualitative Methodology

This book is a qualitative inquiry into an observed social reality in Egypt. The reason the qualitative methodology is used is that the ontological and epistemological positions assumed by the researcher are better satisfied through the employment of qualitative techniques. The ontological position assumed in this book addressed the question of *what* led to the field observation that women are treated and perceived as second-class citizens in Egypt. This ontological position allowed the researcher to uncover the relativity of 'reality' and examine claims to 'truth' by triangulating the data using participant observation, interviews, and written documents.

The epistemological position of this book is postmodernist, which sought to address the question of *how* the female identity in Egypt is perceived by women and men, and *what* are the systematic ways we can use to understand the relationship between the women's identities and their citizenship. The book focussed on the subjective meanings regarding social phenomena, such as sexual harassment in public spaces as well as domestic violence, to arrive at answers to the ontological and epistemological questions. This was accomplished by considering the macro-, meso-, and micro-levels of analysis within the Egyptian context and how at each level claims to 'truth' are different. This also allowed the researcher to stray from the pressures of establishing grand explanatory schemes and dishonestly depicting an image where the social world seems predictable or decipherable by a set of recommendations.

3. Research Method: Auto-ethnography

The methodological choice for this book was inspired by James P. Spradley's (1979a, b) book *The Ethnographic Interview,* in which he stated,

> I want to understand the world from your point of view. I want to know what you know in the way you know it. I want to understand the meaning of your experience, to walk in your shoes, to feel things as you feel them, to explain things as you explain them. Will you become my teacher and help me understand? (p. 34)

Ethnographic research is a prominent research method, which at times can be taxing on the researcher, particularly if one's research involves engaging with vulnerable subjects. Recognising the significance of 'Enlightenment dreams' (Flax, 1990, p. 448), the relativity of objectivity and, ultimately, claims to truthful knowledge, was critical for the data collection process employed by the researcher to account for the multiplicity of knowledges and realities. By accounting for the variability of experiences and realities, the researcher attempted to avoid essentialising the lives of the voluntary subjects, and proportionally applied the postmodern school of thought. The purpose behind collecting interviews with primary sources was to enable a closer investigation of power, knowledge, and gendered superstructures that govern the Egyptian society with the objective of understanding why women in Egypt seem to be secondary citizens as compared to their male counterparts. Deconstructing traditions, religion, and religiosity, *inter alia,* history, and social movements to understand their weighted effects on socio-cultural, economic, and political outcomes observable was the primary objective of the fieldwork. Details of the book's objectives can be found in the introduction.

Having a clear and structured mission in mind, the field work commenced on 18 January 2020. After a successful pilot study conducted in July 2019, the study took its finalised form. Some questions were made redundant, and others replaced that seemed of higher significance for the participants involved. The ever-evolving nature of semi-structured interviews has enabled the researcher to claim some liberties throughout the interview, to highlight the unique reality of each participant, find patterns and commonalities, and identify experiential gaps. The fieldwork transformed into a challenge to binary and dichotomous notions of knowledge production and consumption. This in turn, as demonstrated in the chapters to follow, allowed for academic flexibility, unbound by the traditional scientific method, and free from the feminist epistemological and methodological rigidity which Effects Investigations bring about.

The adoption of the aforementioned allowed the researcher to present the findings with confidence in its internal validity. Internal validity in social science research is judged based on *Descriptive, Interpretative, and Theoretical Validities* (Maxwell, 1992); *Descriptive Validity* refers to the lack of distorted or dramatised information, that is, the reliance on facts 'reporting' (Maxwell, 1992) and 'primary understanding' (Runciman, 1983, p. 226). *Interpretative Validity*, respectively, refers to the mental processes researchers must adopt to 'capture and interpret/construct the meaning of the objects, events and behaviours of the people engaged and involved in the studies phenomena' (Hayashi et al., 2019, p. 100) and must encapsulate 'the conscious processes, hidden intentions, beliefs, concepts, and values of the participants' (Hayashi et al., 2019, p. 101). Finally, *Theoretical Validity* refers to the extent to which theoretical explanations are developed throughout the book and how consistent the handling of the data is (Onwuegbuzie & Johnson, 2006, p. 49). For Theoretical Validity it is important to note that theories traditionally possess two key components, concepts and subsequent categories that elaborate on the relation between concepts, without which the Theoretical Validity would not stand.

It is critical to acknowledge that this book utilises an auto-ethnographic approach, where the researcher is a participant in their own research. Auto-ethnographers vary in their definitions of the method, but most accurately and closely related to the one utilised in this book is Reed-Danahay's (1997, 2017) definitions. Hers is one based on Marcus and Fisher's (1986, p. 116) idea of 'anthropology as cultural critique' in which the realised extrapolations are based in anthropology as it 'expressed possibilities that are strictly within the conditions of life presented'. They additionally stated that:

> It is here that the power of ethnography as cultural critiques resides sincere there are always multiple sides and multiple expressions of possibilities active in any situation, some accommodating, others resistant to dominant cultural trends or interpretations, ethnography as cultural criticism locates alternatives by unearthing these multiple possibilities as they exist in reality. (Marcus & Fisher, 1986)

Reed-Danahay (2017) further explained

> autoethnography as lying at the intersection of insider and outsider perspectives, rather than setting up a dualism that privileges the insider account. Autoethnography reflects a view of ethnography as both a reflexive and a collaborative enterprise, in which the life experiences of the anthropologist and their relationships with others 'in the field' should be interrogated and explored. (p. 114)

She thereby removed the external as a barrier to examine validity of the research and stipulated the significance of reflexivity. Nevertheless, other scholars such as Ellis and Bochner (2000) categorise auto-ethnography as personal narrative, while Sparkes (1996) and Holt (2001) argued for the significance of auto-ethnography as a means to amalgamate theory and practice, that is, link literary concepts to personal experiences, with the purpose of elevating and substantively supporting the personal narrative (Duncan, 2004).

By appropriately applying auto-ethnography to one's research, the work can transcend to become relatable and identifiable for the masses, create a platform for voices of dissent, and give power and status to the localised narratives (Frank, 2000). This served to counter a Western-centric lens for analysis, explore issues of personal importance within a particular social context (Holt, 2001; Sparkes, 1996), a means to evaluate one's actions (Duncan, 2004), or critique existing literature on a topic with a personal dimension (Muncey, 2005). The creative latitude permissible in auto-ethnography, which Ellis and Bochner (2000) believed to undermine the scientific contribution of auto-ethnography, is, in fact, what makes it an appropriate method for this book, as it assists in answering the question of 'whose interests are being served'? Finally, as Boylorn and Orbe (2014) elaborated, auto-ethnographic research is designed 'to understand the lived experiences of real people in context, to examine social conditions and uncover oppressive power arrangements, and fuse theory and action to challenge processes of domination' (p. 25).

This is the interpretation and justification in defence of auto-ethnography adopted for this study.

As auto-ethnography begins with a personal narrative – in this book, the story of women whose lives have been altered, affected, and changed, by different structural and systemised notions of identity, women's status, and role in society, modesty, and family values. This is because said notions are intermingled and guised as 'socio-economic and political advancement', yet one can argue they are designed to subordinate women and institutionalise their status as second-class citizens. Narratives by local men and women – with the purposes of exposing the roots of women's suppression and oppression in mind – were used in this book and presented in a periodically, culturally, and socially relevant context. The role of the narratives is to reveal the ways in which these experiences and realities manifest, thereby establishing a portal into the public and private lives of the participants for a greater sociological, political, and anthropological comprehension (Ochs & Taylor, 1992).

As this study is based on my native society, it is necessary to consider my positionality, as it could bear advantages and disadvantages. I am a woman who was born and raised in the heart of Cairo, Egypt. I have two sisters and was born into a Muslim family. My father is a lawyer and my mother a housewife. I come from middle-class family and was educated predominantly in foreign languages (German and English). My educational background, coupled with my relatively privileged social status, has influenced the way I approach research, as well as my lifestyle. There is a certain responsibility associated with privilege, especially when it comes to researching your own country; this responsibility could either be assumed or be dismissed by individuals. I have chosen to provide a platform for the people, which enables those whose lives were historically, and are currently, affected by the systematic and institutionalised injustices of my government, to express their voice.

As I am an Egyptian woman myself, attempting to study the situation from *within* field work for me was both strenuous and straightforward, which is why I needed to acknowledge and critically engage with my positionality; as a native, I not only speak the common tongue, but have lived most of my life in Egypt and therefore can be relatable to my stakeholders, yet, I also lived in a particular part of Egypt, Cairo, the capital, which makes my experiences replicable in Cairo, but not in other parts of Egypt. Seeing as how I intended on providing people's truths and understand what *their* realities are, I did not only interview people from Cairo but travelled around Egypt. I believe that different people from different socio-economic and cultural backgrounds have different perceptions of reality. As I theorise that the ideology of the State is internalised by some people within the Egyptian society, it benefits this book to endeavour to know how far-reaching the influence of the State is in remote parts of Egypt. As James P. Spradley (1979a, b) stated

> field work ... involved the disciplined study of what the world is like for people who have learned to see, hear, speak, and act in ways that are different. Rather than studying people, ethnographers *learn* from people ... instead of collecting 'data' *about* people, the ethnographer seeks to be *taught* by them. (p. 3; italics in original)

As I am an Egyptian studying the Egyptian society, Naïve Realism was completely abandoned in my ethnographic research endeavour, as the assumption that 'love, rain, marriage, worship, trees, death, food and hundreds of other things have essentially the same meaning to all human beings' lacks depth, via its inherent essentialist qualities, and awareness of intersectionality of pressures and individuality of experiences (1979a, b, p. 4). Rather, as an ethnographer I engaged in participant observation, which

> is in some ways both the most natural and the most challenging of qualitative data collection methods. It connects the researcher to the most basic of human experiences, discovering through immersion and participation the *hows* and *whys* of human behaviours in a particular context. (Guest et al., 2013, p. 75)

Attempting neutrality in this book to maintain validity and objectivity of the study was most challenging as

> when we are participant observers in a more formal sense, we must, at least a little, systematise and organise an inherently fluid process. This means not only being a player in a particular social milieu but also fulfilling the role of researcher. (Guest et al., 2013, p. 75)

This expected dissociation from your stakeholders to fulfil the requirements of appropriate research conduct increases in difficulty when the subjects of the context are indistinguishable from the researcher. I chose participant observation as it permits 'the systematic description of events, behaviours, and artifacts in the social setting chosen for study' (Marshall & Rossman, 1989, p. 79), without disturbing the balance of objectivity and subjectivity of the researcher.

Consequentially, I decided to conduct an auto-ethnography. This type of ethnographic method allowed me to be a participant in my own research, whereby 'the researcher uses self-reflection and writing to explore anecdotal and personal experiences and connect this autobiographical story to wider cultural, political, and social meanings and understandings' (Thomas, 2017a, b, p. 168); thereby substantiating my argument to reflect and compare different understandings of the environment I was in. I chose to conduct an auto-ethnography because it not only 'challenges canonical ways of doing research and representing others and treats research as a political, socially just and socially conscious act' (Ellis et al., 2010, p. 10) but also establishes an evocative narrative where as a participant I could conduct a 'parallel exploration of the researcher's and the participants' experiences and about the experience of the researcher' (Méndez, 2013, p. 279).

As Carolyn Ellis (2000, p. 273) outlined, to be an auto-ethnographer one must: (1) become a full member of the group/setting they are situated in, (2) visibly be an ethnographer in their published work, and (3) be dedicated to and aware of the production and development of various theoretical considerations concerning social occurrences. Included in such a demanding method is reflexivity as it contains 'back-and-forth movement between experiencing and examining a valuable self and observing and revealing the broader context of that experience' (Ellis, 2007, p. 14). Yet, it assisted in distinguishing this piece from others as I intend to not only make my readers understand the research endeavour with the questions it answers, but I want 'readers to feel and care and desire' to understand the participants (Bochner & Ellis, 1996, p. 24). As Fine (2003) stated, qualitative data collection utilising 'peopled ethnographies' (p. 41) when conducted ethically is one of the strongest methods to collect knowledge-oriented data, to which this book aspired to contribute.

Adopting the recommendation of Ellis (2007, p. 273), the research for this book commenced with participant observation to become part of the groups outside the urban group. These participant observations were based on having informal and causal discussions with people in public spaces about current events in Egypt prior to any data collection. This process is easier in countries like Egypt where it is common practice for strangers to share tables in public and leisure spaces. These discussions informed the researcher's understanding of what significant issues Egyptians pay attention to as well as measuring the social awareness and attention paid to women's issues. These discussions assisted in the construction of indicative questions which were used to interview participants later on. Furthermore, these discussions facilitated the choice of the Hijab as a proxy-measure because it appeared multiple times in conversations with different random people. These participant observations were conducted between December 2018 and August 2020. This project commenced in September 2018, and participant observations were to be collected each time the researcher would visit Egypt.

These participant observations were motivated and facilitated by the researcher's volunteer work in Egypt and activism. As Egypt is the home of the researcher, engaging in participant observation was a straightforward task and no challenges were faced. Many of the discussions the researcher overheard, and participated in, were about how women 'ask for it' by dressing provocatively, such as a Hijab with tight-fitting clothes. Or, how the economic situation is dire and young people cannot marry or purchase houses were among other conversations about 'hot' topics during any particular period. Participant observations assisted in substantiating arguments and supporting claims. For example, the lack of law and regulation to protect women from male violence in Egypt was substantiated by the participant observation of Egypt's #MeToo protests of 2020, where numerous conversations were struck between the researcher and the random individuals about Egypt's policing and law enforcement systems. This benefitted the interpretation and analysis of the data as it highlighted how actions and behaviours which the law clearly states are criminal are not enforced. It also assisted in substantiating the claim of a presence of an apathetic or passive social policing system in Egypt which is male favouring. Finally, participant observations helped shed light on how mutually informing law and religion are for Egyptians, specifically as many tried to blame the woman's lack of 'piety', which is understood as women adopting the Islamic dress code and covering up in public spaces, to why women 'have no right to protest' her subjugation if they do not physically project the discourse of 'piety'. The participant observations positively influenced how the data were approached and interpreted, particularly by assisting in the contextualisation of data within its appropriate cultural area and extracting meanings and values conveyed through the interviews.

As researchers, being reflexive is potentially one of the more difficult parts of academia. It requires 'consciously *stepping back* from action in order to theorise what is taking place, and also *stepping up* to be an active part of that contextualised action' (Attia & Edge, 2017, p. 34). Nonetheless, allowing the private to become public is not an unreserved decision. As an Egyptian woman, I am an insider to the narrative, which is advantageous but also dangerous. In Egypt we have a concept called *'ishra*. This concept, as best explained, means 'a kind of expected solidarity and mutual assistance stemming from belonging to an *'asheera*, that is, a tribal community, clan, or kinsfolk' (Badawi & Hinds, 1986, p. 632). I have partially relied on this social construct to collect my data yet was conscious during data collection of how this social construct could be used against me within certain contexts. I recognise that reflexivity is most difficult on auto-ethnographers as the line between group membership and research is blurred but keeping a fieldwork journal during data collection and relying on my peers to point out unconscious biases, I may have inserted into the research that violate its academic efficacy, I consider that I mitigated the dangers. The journal was for personal use and not part of the data collected. I used the journal to write down impressions, feelings, and occurrences in which I felt emotionally charged, to reflect on them when I was in a calmer mindset. My peers were not shy about informing me when the information I was giving them did not make sense or seemed like my own impression and not the one that emerged from the collected data.

4. Textual Analysis and Selection of Legal and Policy Documents

The second objective of the book (see *Introduction*) relies on the selection and analysis of Articles from the Egyptian Constitution, Penal Code, and personal status code pertaining to women's strategic gender interests. The Constitution was chosen because it 'describes the basic principles of the State, the structures and processes of government and the fundamental rights of citizens in a higher law that cannot be unilaterally changed by an ordinary legislative act' (International IDEA, 2014, p. 1). The Constitution, therefore, was included to review how the Egyptian Government sets forth the status and rights of Egyptian women, and interpret the implications of it. The Penal Code was chosen because it sets the parameters of what is considered criminal behaviour and actions, and the punishments for violators of these set of laws. As punishments are reflective of the gravity of the crime, the Penal Code was chosen to analyse what punishments exist/for the protection of women from male violence in Egypt, and to identify potential gaps in the penal laws, such as the lack of a law that criminalises and punishes domestic violence and laws that recognise inter-martial rape.

Finally, the personal status code was chosen because 'the provisions of Egyptian personal status law, as applied today, are marked by their Islamic inspiration' (Bernard-Maugiron, 2010, p. 3). Bernard-Maugiron (2010) elaborated that while most branches of Egyptian law had been reformed and to an extent secularised throughout the 20th century, 'personal status law remained submitted to "the sharia [*sic*.]"' (p. 4), increasing the necessity to investigate this document. Furthermore, Bernard-Maugiron (2010) criticised the Egyptian Penal Code for not being 'codified in a comprehensive and exhaustive code', which she argued 'makes its knowledge and understanding quite difficult' (p. 5) – one of the challenges this book encountered. However, this issue was mitigated by relying on the assistance of legal and religious experts in Egypt to unpack the nuances of the personal status law and its religious dimension. Additionally, personal status laws in Egypt pose a legal problem for persons who may be negatively affected by them, as 'it is not easy to amend personal status laws in Egypt because of the resistance of the society and conservative religious groups'. Furthermore, the fact that 'rules of the sharia whose origin and significance are absolute (*al-ahk'm al-shar'i'ya al-qat'iyya fi thubutiha wa dalalatiha*), and these are the only ones for which interpretative reasoning (*ijtihad*) is not authorized' (Bernard-Maugiron, 2010, p. 4), encouraged the choice of the personal status law to analyse its limitations in prescribing rights and protections for women, and interpret their effects on the social perception of women's rights and status in Egypt.

The first step after the documents were chosen was to print out the Arabic version of the three documents and highlight Articles and Codes which related to the topics of my research and the ones that sounded interesting because of the word choice or tone to seek information about them and determine their relevance. The same process was also done to the Qur'an. These extracted quotes in their original language, Arabic, were put in a sheet manually using the format as in Table 2.

Step two, I used the information from the different lawyers as a baseline and started doing my desk research to review the literature around the impact of certain legal articles and Qur'anic verses on social understandings and discourses. This was the first attempt at trying to detect patterns and establish possible themes.

Step three, I used the hand-written sheet and approached individuals from my network of lawyers. I scheduled meetings with them and asked them to translate and explain the laws, particularly as I do not have legal background, thus, unfamiliar with its language. The reason it was significant to understand what these laws meant in practice provided me with insights regarding how the legal system in Egypt functions to substantiate the interpretations and arguments which emerged from the desk research. I additionally asked them about which laws they perceived to be problematic with regard to certain issues (harassment laws, divorce laws, labour laws, etc., i.e., issues I had identified as discussion points).

Step four, I used the information I learned from my network to start formulating interview questions. The interview questions were piloted in July 2019 and changed after the Confirmation of Registration in October 2019. These discussions were later used to probe questions for interviews with professional voluntary participants such as lawyers and religious clergy, to attain more detailed accounts regarding certain practices, such as court procedures regarding marriage/divorce, custody, assault, and commonly used and believed religious 'mandates' to investigate whether the social understanding of scripture is correct or misconstrued. The interviews from persons in both professions proved invaluable to the thematic analysis as it showcased discrepancies in legal structures within

114 *Recovering Women's Voices*

Table 2. Excerpts from Legal and Religious Texts: A Thematic Analysis.

Source (Constitution, Personal Status, Code, Penal Code)	Article/Code/Verse Number and Year That Law Passed	The Direct Quote from the Primary Source (Translated)	Related Articles (if Applicable)	Topic/Short Description
Example: The Constitution of the Arab Republic of Egypt	Example: Article 2 (2014)	Example: Islam is the religion of the state and Arabic is its official language. The principles of Islamic Sharia are the principal source of legislation	—	Relates to the significance and intersection of religion and law
Example: Personal Status Code	Example: Article 291 (1999)	Example: Grants any individual who committed the offence of rape the option of marrying the victim in order to avoid the penalty imposed by the code	Example: Article 17 of Penal Code: In accordance with principals of sentencing (…) clemency for any crime, subject to the discretion of the judge	Relates of women's bodily autonomy
Example: Quran	Example: Verse	Example: 3:34	Men are in charge of women by [right of] what Allah has given one over the other and what they spend [for maintenance] from their wealth. So righteous women are devoutly obedient, guarding in [the husband's] absence what Allah would have them guard (…)	Relates to perception of women's status as inferior

the patriarchal system and highlighted the difference between scripture and social practices that are believed to be religiously mandated.

To start the thematic analysis, I adopted Braun and Clarke's (2006) approach as it is the one most widely used. A thematic analysis is used for 'identifying, analysing and reporting patterns (themes) within data. It minimally organises and describes your data set in (rich) detail' (Braun & Clarke, 2006, p. 6). While thematic analysis closely resembles content analysis, it 'adds an experiential and emotional dimension to the material which illuminates intricacies of meaning … [where] the researcher plays an active role in identifying patterns and themes' (Ager et al., 2015, p. 903). The 'experiential and emotional dimension' was added in this project using the coded data from the semi-structured interviews and primary data collected from the field. The next section describes how Braun and Clarke's (2006) six-step guide to thematic analysis was used in this book using NVivo as a data management tool.

5. Research Tool: Semi-structured Interviews

In addition to the participant observations, I conducted interviews with the relevant stakeholders. Interviews are 'a discussion with someone in which you try to get information from them – facts, opinions, values or attitudes' (Thomas, 2017a, b, p. 202). This book is intended to understand opinions, values and attitudes towards women plus the social perception of women's identities and their place in society, as exemplified in the social perception and individual decision to put on/take off the *Hijab* as a proxy-measure to understanding identity, as well as forcing women to wear the *Hijab* to accumulate social capital and preserve and reproduce one's own beliefs. The interviews allowed me to ask women, as well as men, in the society about how they perceive women; what they understand to be individual responsibility and rights; and how they perceive *individual autonomy* and the *right to choose*. Coupling interviews with participant observation allows the integration of 'active looking, improving memory, informal interviewing, writing detailed field notes, and perhaps most importantly, patience' (DeWalt & DeWalt, 2002, p. vii), therefore equitably referencing people's experiences and outlooks.

Conducting interviews was challenging, especially because, for the purposes of this book, the interviews were more of a conversation between two people rather than a formal interview. Nonetheless, as the interviewer, a level of moderation is required to conduct the semi-structured interview. The structure of interviewers in this type of data collection is semi-structured interviews. Semi-structured interviews are

> a schematic presentation of questions or topics that need to be explored by the interviewer. To achieve optimum use of interview time [generally 30-40 minutes long], interview guides serve the useful purpose of exploring many respondents more systematically and comprehensively as well as to keep the interview focused on the desired line of action. (Jamshed, 2014, p. 88)

Semi-structured guidelines clarified the research domain and helped me uncover the myriad of belief and value systems existing in Egypt. Therefore, the questions asked were open- and close-ended to avoid the generic yes/no answers and encourage the participants to tell their stories and to establish their position on certain issues. Moreover, it assisted in guiding the narrative and gathering the information required in a structured manner. I was aware of the potential dubiousness of leading questions and therefore conducted a pilot study to ensure that the questions asked are properly formatted. It was also important to shy away from associating emotions to questions, negative or positive, so as not to influence the participant in any way by my personal frame.

The interview questions started with earlier events in their lives to establish a comfortable space for my interviewees and understand how they have built up specific values and beliefs. Moreover, I asked simple open-ended questions about their perceptions of society, through simple exercises like word associations, as a means for me to understand potential pre-existing biases within their answers. I constructed my questions in a culturally and periodically sensitive manner as to avoid offending my participants or violating social taboos. Nonetheless, during the interviews I challenged beliefs and values when it was appropriate, and I felt like the participant would not be offended. Most importantly, I prepared hand copies of the consent forms which were written in Arabic and reviewed by a lawyer and my primary supervisor to ensure that by requesting individuals to sign these forms I am not violating any municipal laws or the university's ethical guidelines.

I used a recording device, which the participants were made aware of. Yet, the recording device was switched off if interviewees so requested. I was aware of the appropriate decorum when conducting interviews, such as, not interrupting unless absolutely necessary to maintain the focus of the conversation on the main topic/theme, to avoid, to the best of my abilities, repeating questions if the participant seemed to try and evade them, timing myself as not to deviate too much from the topic and make sure I collected the information I needed in a timely manner, and finally, where time permitted, requested to sit with my interviewees after the recorded session to engage in an informal conversation about topics they would have liked to share during the interview but could not due to time constraints or nervousness because it is recorded. These informal conversations were later recalled in detail and reflected upon in my field notes, which were used to substantiate my participants' observations about their body language, how they were feeling during the interview, and any other information that might be useful for the analysis stage.

The interview guide was divided into five major subsections: (1) Background Information – this was used to better understand the background of the participants, and included questions about their family, siblings, their education (if any), their parents' education (if any), where they grew up in Egypt, a bit about their childhood, *inter alia,* and what religion they were raised in (if any); (2) Identity and Experiences – this section of the interview included questions about gendered differences, how each participant reacted to being of their sex and gender, and their perceptions on how their lives would change (for better or worse) if they were of the opposite sex and gender; (3) Views and Experiences of Patriarchy – section two flows into section three, and more specific questions about sexual harassment, abuse, exploitation, domestic abuse, marriage and divorce, and what the participant believed to be 'men's rights and obligations' and 'women's rights and obligations'; (4) Personal Beliefs and Values – complementary to sections three and four, this section was more particular about putting on/taking off the *Hijab*, the personal and social repercussions of each decision, and whether the decision ought to be made individually or collectively; and finally (5) Future Aspirations and Hopes – as a concluding section, where any grievances or comments not addressed throughout the interview can be articulated, and participants were asked what changes, if they could implement any, they would recommend to the Egyptian Government.

6. Conducting Culturally Appropriate and Sensitive Research

In this book, the thematic analysis helped me understand how historical, political, and socio-cultural factors have shaped the female experience and dictated women's realities in Egypt, which resulted in their seemingly 'secondary' citizen status relative to their male counterparts. By providing the local narrative with a platform of expression, the book also highlighted historic and contemporary political and social patterns, which in unison have contributed to the deteriorating status of women, and conceptually unpacked using Walby's (1990) *Six Structures of Patriarchy*.

Nonetheless, conducting research in a country where you are perceived to be 'inferior' posed its own set of challenges. El-Setouhy et al. (2008) recounted the challenges they faced conducting research in Egypt. The authors established that 'in every major Egyptian city there are traditions carried over from the time of the Pharaohs; other areas retain the tribal customs originated by the many invaders throughout the centuries' and urged researchers to develop 'cultural competence' (El-Setouhy et al., 2008, p. 35). Cultural competence, they argue, includes developing an understanding of the diversity of cultural beliefs within Egypt, a recognition of how religious the Egyptian society is as 'religious principles are noticeable in their daily lives' (El-Setouhy et al., 2008), and an understanding that 'there are often negative connotations associated with the words "investigation" and "study", and a suspicion of "experimenting"' (p. 36). The authors additionally stress that 'in Egypt, clan obligations unite extended families … Clan elders arbitrate disagreements, even those between husbands and wives, and give opinions on topics ranging from farming techniques to religious obligations' (El-Setouhy et al., 2008). However, as their research is in the medical discipline, their techniques to navigate the sensitive climate in Egypt are not directly applicable to social science research. The researchers conceded that medical doctors are held in high regard in Egypt (El-Setouhy et al., 2008, p. 36), which in turn can reduce a participant's autonomy as 'they do not question the medical competence in decision-making about their own care' (p. 36). They also argued that due to diverse attitudes and values in Egypt, a generalisable method of conducting research in Egypt cannot be established. El-Setouhy et al. (2008) concluded that due to Egypt's unique context innovative and creative solutions ought to be developed by researchers and recommended that researchers 'must apply their cultural experiences ... to develop cultural sensitivities among the research community and ensure that the rights of human subjects are protected' (p. 39).

To develop cultural competence, my research relied on the principles of ethnography, which 'takes a cultural lens to the study of people's lives within their communities' (Eriksson & Kovalainen, 2008, p. 149) to overcome the challenges identified by El-Setouhy et al. I travelled to the locations I intended on collecting my research from, prior to doing my fieldwork. I travelled there to understand and experience the different cultures of rural and indigenous communities. As I was born and raised in Cairo, Egypt, I had a foundational understanding of the cultural traditions and values within urban communities, which provided me with a potential advantage. Sequentially, I chose to use auto-ethnography which is 'an approach where the researcher's personal and reflective perspective is part of the research' (Eriksson & Kovalainen, 2008, p. 151). According to Adam et al. (2014), auto-ethnography provides researchers with an opportunity to articulate insider knowledge, as 'the writer can inform readers about aspects of cultural life that other researchers may not be able to know' (p. 3). The authors nonetheless urged that auto-ethnographers

> show how researchers are implicated by their observations and conclusions and to encourage auto-ethnographers to write against harmful ethnographic accounts made by others – especially cultural 'outsiders' – who try to take advantage of, or irresponsibly regulate, other cultures. (Adam et al., 2014, p. 4)

This means that within auto-ethnography a principal of nonintervention is crucial, and researchers ought not to violate existing cultural practices and must respect the environment they are studying.

To make sure I do not violate or offend participants, I relied on my existing network of friends and family who are from different areas in Egypt, such as my mother and her family as she was born and raised in Monufeya, to gain a better understanding of different cultural practices to be better able to establish rapport with participants. This is also referred to as the 'orientational process' which connotes that researchers begin their ethnographic research with participant observation, which is later complemented by other data (interviews and documents) [to record] everyday events (Eriksson & Kovalainen, 2008, p. 155). For this book, particularly in communities which were completely foreign to me, such as the Amazigh of Siwa, I conducted desk research on the history of Siwa first. Then upon arrival there I chose a café to sit at and strike conversations with others present. This part of my participant observations was meant to be an

> open ended collection of materials derived from learning the basic cultural rules and language used at the site ... to gain a rapport with the participants and test out whether the original research objectives are appropriate in the local situation. (Eriksson & Kovalainen, 2008)

Sitting at the café and talking to the people about why I am in Siwa, I was informed that the community has an official historian and spokesman, *Hakkay*. Prior to collecting data from anyone in the community, I organised a meeting with the *Hakkay* to gain insights into the cultural values, traditions and gauge which topics are 'off-limits' or taboo to discuss. This process was also referred to as 'the deep hanging out'. Coined by Clifford Geertz (1998), the term connotes immersing oneself physically and virtually within the community studied and participate in social or group experiences informally (p. 69). The aim of deep hanging out is to 'take into account what is meaningful to actors in those situations ... [and figure out what] relevant elements carry or convey meaning, what these meanings are, who is making them, and how they are being communicated' (Yanow, 2007, p. 111), which I tried to accomplish by sitting and socialising with the local community at cafés and later organising a meeting with relevant local people such as the *Hakkay* in Siwa.

During the orientational process in Siwa, for instance, I was taught about certain terminology and phrasing that Siwians use, which in urban communities may come across as offensive or vice versa, which helped avoid accidentally offending any participants. Additionally, I was taught about social routines, such as working hours. As the Siwian community is predominantly farmers, working hours are between 5–9 in the morning and 4–8 in the evening to avoid exhaustion or risk a heat stroke. Additionally, school hours in Siwa are between 9 in the morning and 2 in the afternoon, which is designed so that fathers can enjoy lunch with their children and spend time with them before the second working shift. Knowing this information, I scheduled interviews with Siwian women between the hours of 9 and noon, and interviews with Siwian men after 8 in the evening. I avoided scheduling any interviews between 2 and 4 in the afternoon so I would not disrupt family time.

Additionally, I learned that it is a local custom in Siwa to bring dates or olives as a gift when entering someone's home. This custom is meant to convey good will and respect for the household. As olives and dates are the most ubiquitous and accessible in Siwa, the custom is designed to be inclusive of all members of society and ensures that everyone is welcome irrespective of financial capability. According to the *Hakkay*, it also avoids embarrassing people regarding their financial status. Contrastingly, in urban and rural communities, a similar custom exists; however, the custom in urban and rural communities does stress financial capability and the belief is that the more expensive a gift is the more appreciation a person is conveying to the household members and the present can be material goods or traditional desserts. For my book, I followed the custom of bringing dates to the interviewees' homes, and in urban/rural areas I would bring a platter of mixed traditional desserts which had an average cost. Additionally, in Siwa, for example, a woman who is not a foreigner to Egypt is expected to wear face and head covering, and modest clothing; however, this is not socially imposed on any women. Nonetheless, I chose to wear both a wide-fitting dress, and face and head covering to signal respect to the local traditions, and solidify the rapport built with the community.

Second, Browne and Mcbride (2015) argued that in politically sensitive contexts, such as that of Egypt, ethnographic researchers are facing the challenge of 'gaining access, negotiating security, overcoming suspicion, as well as, at times, managing an outsider identity, retaining objectivity and appreciating cultural sensitivity' (p. 35). Additionally, Browne and Mcbride (2015) elaborated that these challenges are primarily an issue of building 'trust', and their observations concluded that the physical visibility of a researcher helps generate trust with 'research participants, and the communities of which they are part' because, in certain communities, people 'act on what they see to be true rather than the paper credentials of the researcher'. Responding to Goffman's (1969) recommendation of the necessity of 'presentation of self', Browne and Mcbride (2015) argued that politically sensitive communities arise from 'fragmented culturally, socially, and politically ... environments, [which] raised pointed issues of identity and positionality that, at times, situated the researchers as suspicious "others"' (p. 36). Therefore, they concluded that 'the nature of ... visibility thus became a crucial dimension in ... personal and professional relationships with the people ... engaged with' (Browne & Mcbride, 2015). For my book, despite the fact that it started in January 2020 and ended in August 2020, I chose to physically travel to the sites for my data collection. While travelling during a pandemic under changing restrictions was difficult, it was not only motivated by the significance of being visible in the communities I was collecting data from but also motivated by the fact that many members of these communities do not have access to technology, which would enable online interviews. As not to be technologically exclusionary and to establish trust between myself and the participants, I utilised both the hanging out method and the orientational process. Additionally, to circumvent potential 'othering' and suspicion, I affiliated myself with the American University in Cairo, conducting the interviews in Arabic.

Finally, to make sure that I do not violate any community traditions, I would always ask about potential dress codes and social norms within any community prior to travelling to it. For instance, in Kafr El-Shaikh men and women cannot meet in close-court private spaces, so interviews with men in that community were conducted in open spaces such as fields where there is a high degree of privacy, but is also a public space offering visibility. Nonetheless, by virtue of being a woman, I was able to interview women in the private and confidential spaces of their homes, which was an advantage that served to protect potentially vulnerable women from harm as well as conducting the interview in a space that is familiar to them and where they feel comfortable.

However, as Dickson-Swift et al. (2008) noted 'a researcher is rarely trained in such issues as managing distress, ending difficult interactions and identifying ways in which a person could be helped or encouraged to help themselves' (p. 135). Being a woman from Egypt, many of the sensitive and distressing experiences women would disclose to me were experiences I could predominantly identify with. As I am not a licenced counsellor I did not attempt to diagnose or counsel any participants, rather, where appropriate, I would simply listen to participants and where appropriate, I would give them a list of civil societies, nongovernmental institutions, and safe havens which they could utilise at their own discretion. In other instances, it seemed more appropriate to share my story with participants, in hopes it would alleviate feeling exposed. According to Bashir (2017), if a researcher manages to establish trust and rapport with participants, then 'participants may open up to someone for the first time, perhaps under the reassurances of confidentiality and an impartial stranger willing to listen' (p. 639). Bashir (2017) also noted that vulnerable participants 'value the opportunity to talk and adequately trust the researcher to disclose more intimate and personal experiences'.

I chose Kafr El-Shaikh and Fayoum because they had made national news in Egypt for atrocities committed against women. As this book attempted to represent the entire spectrum of the Egyptian society, from the most liberal to the most conservative, to be inclusive of the diversity and multiplicity of narratives in Egypt, including the voices of women from the most oppressed parts of Egypt was essential. Seeing as women in these places have also had it relatively the worst, it was only fair to provide them a platform to express themselves and their grievances.

Chapter 5

The Role of Religion and Class in Setting Patriarchal Bargains

The book so far has established that in Egypt women have realised few of their strategic gender interests. To reiterate, *strategic gender interests* are defined as the effort to actualise

> the abolition of the sexual division of labour, the alleviation of the burden of domestic labour and childcare, the removal of institutionalised forms of discrimination, the attainment of political equality, the establishment of freedom of choice over childbearing, and the adoption of adequate measures against male violence and control over women. (Molyneux, 1985, p. 233)

The secondary data highlighted that these emancipatory efforts aimed at gaining women greater agency, autonomy, opportunity, and greater status were either suppressed and/or rationalised using Islam as an instrument of legitimation or denied altogether. Evidence of that can be seen in the role political Islam played in structuring an inferior status for women (see Chapter 2), and in the statistical evidence provided earlier. Using the conceptualisation of Sylvia Walby's (1990) *Paid Employment* and *Family/Household Production* and applying it to the Egyptian context, it became clear that the patriarchal system in Egypt prevailed. The attitudes among Egyptians concerning gender equality within the private sphere, for instance, are nowhere near 'the abolition of sexual division of labour' or 'the alleviation of the burden of domestic labour and childcare' (Molyneux, 1985, p. 233). This is evidenced by the fact that under the conceptualisation of *Paid Labour,* women only make up 20% of the labour force in Egypt. Sylvia Walby (1990) argued that Paid Labour signifies women's access to the public sphere, which is 'seen as a sign of the emancipation of women' (p. 58), so low participation and presence of Egyptian women in the labour force also means low access to and presence in the public sphere.

Walby's conceptualisation of *Family/Household Production* appears to support the finding that in the context of Egypt 87% of men and 77% of women believe a woman's primary role is a housewife (El Feki et al., 2017, p. 47). Walby argued

124 *Recovering Women's Voices*

that the Family/Household is the site where domestic labour is devised and gender roles are assigned. The evidence suggests that Egyptian women's labour has been 'appropriated in the household ... men benefit from women's domestic labour ... and women have committed themselves to the role of homemaker' (Walby, 1990, p. 87). More significantly, these findings suggest three things: first, as 80% of the female population in Egypt is not employed, women are financially dependent on men, reinforcing the existing gender dynamic that men are the breadwinners and women are the caretakers; second, this gender dynamic within the household restricts women's access to and presence in the public sphere, leaving them fewer opportunities to challenge the existing power dynamics between men and women and work to realise their strategic gender interests; third, the statistic that 77% of women believe their primary role in society is to be a housewife corroborate the suggestion that women are financially dependent on men, and that women do not have equal opportunity and access to the public sphere. These findings indicate that women's role and 'place' in society are believed to be in the private sphere, and institute that Egyptian women have internalised this ascribed social role and have 'committed themselves to the role of homemaker' (Walby, 1990, p. 87).

Furthermore, Deniz Kandiyoti (1988) explained that gender dynamics in areas where classic patriarchy can be observed often make women 'adhere as far and as long as they possibly can to rules (...) that result in their active collusion in the reproduction of their own subordination' (p. 289). She argued that *patriarchal bargains*, that is, 'concrete constraints ... [that] influence both the potential for and specific forms of women's active or passive resistance in the face of their oppression' (Kandiyoti, 1998, p. 275), define the social rules and norms women have to carefully navigate. Kandiyoti (1998, p. 282) also noted that women have to adhere and conform to the patriarchal bargain if they wish to benefit emotionally/psychologically, financially, or socially; however, she also confirmed that lack of conformity to the socially ascribed roles and adherence to the gender norms can be socially sanctioned, double-binding women. In an earlier article by Kandiyoti (1984) she argued that the 'material base of classic patriarchy crumbles under the impact of new market forces', such as female labourers. This insinuates that, where women are excluded from the labour force, they are also excluded from having the power to affect change. Kandiyoti (1998, p. 283) concluded that:

> When classic patriarchy enters a crisis, many women may continue to use all the pressure they can muster to keep men living up to their obligations ... their passive resistance takes the form of claiming their half of this particular patriarchal bargain – protection in exchange for submissiveness and propriety.

Considering the findings of the previous chapters, one can conclude that Egypt does qualify as a classic patriarchal system. Knowing this, the significance of realising women's strategic gender interests becomes more pronounced, as it is the only path to achieving their equal citizenship status. This chapter explores the context within which the patriarchal system in Egypt appears. Relying on the collected primary data, the most significant social aspects of Egyptians appear to be,

The Role of Religion and Class in Setting Patriarchal Bargains **125**

class, education, and religion. Class, expressed in terms of wealth, signifies access to public services and public life. Respectively, education signifies an aspect of 'real freedoms' (Sen, 1999, p. 75), that is, freedoms conceived as real opportunities (Sen, 1985a, pp. 3–4; 1985b, p. 201; 2000) and the right to act on one's potential in terms of doing and being. On the other hand, religion signifies a set of oppressive structures which some women have to bargain with, while to others it signifies emancipation and a sense of belonging. Understanding why these social aspects are significant to Egyptians is critical to understanding why Egyptian women are assigned an inferior role and are excluded from full citizenship rights.

1. Growing Up in Classes

Class appeared to be an important contributor to many respondents' identities. In this section of the book, 'class' is used to reflect local connotations of social stratification. A class analysis, while beneficial, falls out of the scope of this book. CU1a(9), for instance, shared his experience of growing up with the awareness of class, stating:

> I grew up in Giza actually, specifically Al Haram. It's a small neighbourhood, so you can see a lot of different people from very different backgrounds. I wasn't born into the upper class (.) so it wasn't like I was born with a silver spoon in my mouth. You can say that this has exposed me to a variety of classes from the beginning. I was younger though, so I couldn't critically analyse the difference or even conceptualise it as a class and social system, but I noticed that there was something different in the way different people talked and dressed and so on. You can very distinctly see the difference in education and the way they carry themselves. Like in school [referring to a private international school] I would go and talk to people in a different way than I talk to my friends from the neighbourhood.

Echoing the significance of class was CU1l(1) who stated, 'I grew up in the suburbs of Cairo. It's usually quiet, it's isolated in terms of certain people, certain social classes that you interact with and so on'. When asked to elaborate, he stated:

> I get things more easily afforded to me than other social classes, such as getting good service, ease of interactions with banks and lenders, I can more easily get a credit card for example while other social classes can't get one as easily, for example. Being from this social class gets you more respect from people, and quality services are more afforded to us.

When another participant, CU1s(14) was asked what they meant by 'growing up in the nicer parts of Cairo' they stated, 'by nicer I mean the richer parts of

Cairo, the more upper-class parts'. This contribution suggests that class connotes wealth in Egyptian society, and wealth appears to be instrumental in accessing the public sphere. While this narrative is interesting, it would require an investigation of how class systems influence social dynamics, which scholars such as Ishaq Diwan (2012, 2013, 2019) and Melani Cammett (2012, 2021) have explored extensively. Despite this interesting dimension, it falls beyond the parameters of this book. Therefore, in this book class is used to broadly reflect the participant's understanding of social stratification, and not socio-economic class specifically.

Contrastingly, other participants exhibited high awareness of their feelings of class inferiority and how it affected their families, and, by extension, how they were raised and grew up. Growing up in a working-class family, for example, brings about its own set of social expectations, which, more often than not, confine women to the private sphere and reinforce their role as housewives. AR3u(39) felt compelled to negate these expectations, by stating:

> I was raised in a 1-bedroom which I shared with four sisters and two brothers. We are a poor family but a dignified one. We are a very respected family because we never did anything illegal for money like others. We also married poor men and we stood by them because we are honourable women. Because of us, our husbands now have some money.

The insinuation that those growing up in a working-class populated area in Egypt are inherently involved in illegal activities is a sentiment many interviewees of this background were eager to negate. This premise is not unfounded, as ethnographic researchers have consistently established evidence for the association between poverty, delinquency, and criminal behaviour in adulthood (Anderson, 1990; Sanchez Jankowski, 1991; Sullivan, 1989; Williams & Kornblum, 1985; Verme et al., 2014). Nonetheless, class segregation and discourses around class and socio-economic status appear to be significant in Egyptian society, as class seems to constitute access to a wider set of opportunities. While this book does not conduct an in-depth class analysis, this merits further research. In this section, class is used as a reflection of the local understanding of social stratification.

When asked, 'tell me a bit about yourself and where you grew up' different groups of people, depending on age group, vocation, gender, and other factors provided different responses. CR2p(6), for instance, provided a short timeline of historical events which have affected him and his family as farmers, stating:

> Since the 80s and until the mid-90s I lived in Kafr El Shaikh in a poor area, and all Egyptians were living in the very bad economic state, we didn't have any luxury in Egypt, and it was more apparent in rural villages, it was a very hard situation for us. Starting in the 90s things have started to get a bit better. Starting 2000s things got much better, at least there were job opportunities besides manual labour. We as farmers only had people work for two months during a whole year, the harvest times in the winter and summer.

AR2s(5) agreeingly added, 'In Kafr El Shaikh we sleep when the sun goes down, my friends and I don't abide by that, and we can stay out until 10 pm in a friend's house but not outside'. She continued to elaborate on her life as a woman in Kafr El Shaikh, stating:

> In Ramadan, we can stay as late as midnight and you can find women on the street till midnight! In grade 7 girls can't show their hair, so if a girl or someone from outside Kafr El Shaikh doesn't cover her hair, she will be known, they'll feel her. Even if I don't voluntarily put on the Hijab, or if my parents don't force me to wear it, the school will say I have to wear it, and they say it mockingly like I'm the stupid one.

What was pronounced here was the dress code imposed on women living in rural communities. The idea of coverage and the Hijab is unpacked in more detail in the following chapter. Echoing the sentiments of rural life and culture, was BU2s(34), who is originally from a rural community in Port Said, but moved to Cairo to attend university said:

> People are very narrow-minded in Port Said. The thinking and the interaction there are way different in Cairo and that was why I struggled when I came to the American University in Cairo. I was aware that people in Cairo are different, but there was still a cultural shock when I came to AUC. Port Said and AUC are two different extremes, and I struggled to know what's real and true. The more time I spent at AUC the more I started to think like them.

Using the American University in Cairo (AUC) as an example of the lifestyle and standards was most probably an unconscious decision on the part of the participant. Also, the use of the words 'cultural shock' served to reinforce the multiplicity of cultural understandings and realities cohabitating within one nation. This is significant, because it negates essentialism and reiterates the fact that 'one identity' is close to impossible even within the same borders. Furthermore, the use of AUC, a private elite educational institution, to refer to the 'culture in Cairo' serves to substantiate the point that class is a prevalent and conscious part of the social discourse.

Respondent CR2s(35) agreed with the social discourses of Caironese people being 'different' from rural communities, shedding light on how Caironese culture is viewed by other groups in other districts. He said:

> I realised that in Cairo the pace is very fast, life is so fast here. When I go back to Menoufia [a rural agrarian village in Egypt] I feel that the day is slow, and people are so calm. In Cairo people are more judging, especially they judge each other based on appearance. They're very shallow.

CR2s(35) mentioned appearance as a social bias in Cairo. Yet, judgements based on appearance are not a novelty in social research (Aspers & Godart, 2013;

Gronow, 1993; Smith, 1982, p. 194). Throughout history, the use of luxury items and goods has been

> a desirable characteristic, firstly, because it implies the possession of abundant resources that are required to buy luxury products in the first place. Secondly, wealth is desirable because it may demonstrate the abilities and skills to acquire resources. Luxury labels may thus act as costly signals that enhance status. (Nelissen & Meijers, 2010, p. 344)

Maintaining that 'they judge each other based on appearance. They're very shallow' is an indirect statement of the class differences and disparities one can observe in urban and rural areas in Egypt and is more pronounced in cities such as Cairo.

Class performance is epitomised for Egyptians in private education universities, like the AUC. CU1s(29) offered his thoughts about private institutions, saying 'The society in AUC is fake. I don't want to sound stereotypical or offensive, but they are very biased and spoiled to a very large extent. It's just people trying to be more western than ever. It's sad'. Private institutions, such as AUC, possess a symbolic connotation in Egypt: upper class, Westernised, elite, and fiscally conservative. Tuition fees for undergraduate courses at private universities in Egypt such as AUC (2020–2021) are approximately US$647 per credit hour, which is equivalent to ~EGP152,000/~GBP7250 per academic term for a minimum registration of 15 modules/15 credit hours. By comparison, Cairo University, a public university in Egypt, set its tuition fees at US$64, which is the equivalent to EGP1200/GBP47 per academic year (UniPage, 2020). The mean income per capita in Egypt is US$3020/year (World Bank, 2020), which is equivalent to ~EGP48000/GBP2258. Therefore, the presumption that AUC is 'reserved for the elite' is not implausible, as mean income and fees are incompatible, thus, only those who can afford fees can apply. One could argue that attending a private educational institution is a statement of wealth in itself, as income disparity in Egypt would make it unfeasible for certain groups to attend a private institution. With 60% of Egypt's population classified as poor or vulnerable by the World Bank, it would be a financial impossibility for persons within the 60% ($2/day), to apply for AUC (World Bank, 2019). Furthermore, by employing the Gini Coefficient/Index (a numerical value between 0 and 1, where 0 connotes perfect equality and 1 connotes perfect inequality), one can better understand why private institutions are oftentimes synonymous with 'elite'. The Gini Coefficient for Egypt is calculated to be at 0.756 (World Population Review, 2020), indicative of high levels of social and income inequalities, and reduced social mobility. This level of discrepancy and disparity between public and private institutions in Egypt applies to all levels of education, from nursery to university. This renders statements such as those made by CU1s(29) to mostly ring true.

Social class differences, epitomised in the AUC, are a significant discourse for Egyptians. Social Identity Theory stipulates that social groups can become part of the *self* (Smith, 1999; Tajfel, 1981; Turner, 1982) and that group membership has an emotional and psychological component attached to them, which make up one's self-concept (Tajfel, 1981). By realising the intersectionality of the self and the group, one can see how class disparities influenced the understanding and presentation of the self and identity (Argyle, 1994; Frable, 1997; Lott & Bullock, 2001; Ostrove & Cole, 2003; Phillips & Pittman, 2003; Wentworth & Peterson, 2001). Particularly, social class can dictate 'the possibilities they face and the decisions they make' (Massey et al., 1991, p. 197), as one's class 'provides the possibilities and limits for his or her personal identity (i.e., only a certain range of possibilities will occur because of prior socialisation specific to role location, or social customs and conventions)' (Côte & Levine, 2002, p. 135). Even if the actualisation of identity invokes a certain degree of choice and requires a degree of power and privilege, the class can 'shape, constrain, and mediate the development and expression of knowledge, beliefs, attitudes, motives, traits and symptoms' (Stewart & Ostrove, 1993, p. 476). It is, therefore, unsurprising that, when participants were asked about themselves and their upbringing, they predominantly cited their class. Social class evidently 'plays an important role both as an independent variable that shapes the formation of identity and as a domain of identity exploration' (Aries & Seider, 2007, p. 151). While the questions asked to the participants did not mention class, it is interesting that numerous participants touched upon it and presented it as common knowledge.

This also suggests that class struggle possesses a central role for ordinary Egyptian citizens because it connotes which 'real freedoms' a person has access to and can pursue. One can therefore make the argument that class struggle in Egypt could be classified as the 'unequal failure in capabilities' which 'is a problem of justice' (Nussbaum, 1999, p. 243). What was most revealing from this section was the reflection on the 'modest' dress code socially enforced in the rural community Kafr El Shaikh, an issue unpacked later in the book. This section provided a brief overview of how Egyptians perceive class and highlighted how the intersectionality of class differences and geographic location can influence a person's access to the public sphere, restrict their capabilities, and influence how they perceive the social environments around them. If men's access to the male-dominated public sphere can be restricted by their class, then it is logical to infer that women's access is further restricted. This becomes apparent when we view class from a wealth perspective. As most women in Egypt rely financially on male counterparts, may that be fathers, brothers or husbands), and constitute only one-fifth of the labour force, they have limited strategic presence in the public sphere. Adding the dimension of class, one can argue that adds a further barrier to this already unfavourable context. Critical awareness of how class differences affect women differently is essential so as not to essentialise women's experiences and to respect the complexity and uniqueness of each context. What is true for Egyptian women, however, is that the majority are subjugated and limited by the rules of the patriarchal system. Nonetheless, as Kandiyoti (1988, p. 289) noted, in areas of classic patriarchy, women employ strategies to gain greater control within the concrete confines set for them, that is, they bargain with patriarchy and enter a form of exchange. The next section tackles the second interesting social aspect that emerged from the data, Islam, to better comprehend how patriarchal bargains relate to it.

2. Islam: A Culture and a Religion

Another important social aspect was detected when participants were asked to reflect on their upbringing, religion. The Middle East and Northern Africa (MENA) region, made up of approximately 20 countries, is known as the birthplace of the *Kutub El Samaweya* (Holy Books from and by God only), Judaism, Christianity, and Islam. All monotheistic religions from this region can be considered an offspring of the same tradition. For instance, dietary rules are the same in Islam and Judaism, and both religions perceive the text of God to be the foundation for civil law within their countries (Ahmed & Ginsburg, 2014; Englard, 1968). While each religion follows the teachings of its own Prophets (for Islam it is Mohammed (peace be upon him), for Christians it is Jesus, and for Jews it is Moses) only Muslims have a didactic of respecting and believing in all Prophets of God. As the Following Qur'anic verse elaborates:

> We believe in Allah, and in what has been revealed to us, and in what has been revealed to Ibrāhīm, Ismā'īl (Ishmael), IsHāq (Isaac), Ya'qūb and his children, and in what has been given to Mūsā and 'Īsā (Jesus) and what has been given to the prophets from their Lord: We make no difference between any of them, and to Him, we submit ourselves. (Qur'an 2:136)

Religion diffuses into the ritualistic and rhythmic life of MENA inhabitants. Evidence is, not only, that they all share a ritualistic aspect of prayer with similar and shared guidelines on how to 'speak to God', but also religion determines the end of the work week, public holidays, and school terms (Baloch et al., 2014; Musharraf & Nabeel, 2015; Palomino, 2017). For instance, shops shut down in different neighbourhoods and places, Saturdays for the Jewish Sabbath, Sundays for the Christian day of Rest, and Fridays for the Muslim holy day. Common Arabic expressions such as *Allah* are used throughout the region, even in countries that do not speak Arabic such as Iran and Turkey (Perry, 1985). Additionally, we see religion seeping into daily conversations, so a normal response to 'how are you' is *El Hamdulellah* (Praise be God). Other daily conversations can include an expression of hope for a future event by saying *Inshallah* (God willing), or *Mashallah* (What God wills), and even in goodbyes *El Salam A'likom* (God's Peace/Peace be with you). Religion and life are therefore sometimes inseparable when studying cultures within MENA, which can make it difficult to discern which phenomena and events one ought to attribute to religion and which to culture.

So what is it like growing up with a religious identity assigned to you at birth? Here it is worth noting that, in Egypt, religious affiliation and declaration are legally required, that is, the religion of the father is passed down to the child and documented on their birth certificate, and later on their national ID and passport (HRW, 2007a, b). One can argue that the legal requirement to declare and assign a child a religious affiliation, in part, is influenced by Islam and, in part, has a utilitarian dimension. First, Muslims are actively encouraged to 'increase the Muslim *Umma*' (Ahmed, 1975, p. 28), as presented in Chapter 2. So, the assigning of religion at birth could influence the efforts of Egypt to quantitatively contribute to 'increasing the Umma'. Second, having one's religious affiliation on the national identification certificates and passports helps in burial ceremonies and legal proceedings such as inheritance; should a person die unexpectedly, their ID pass would highlight which manner their religion mandates they be buried, which differs between Muslims, Christians, and Jews (Ansari, 2007; Elias, 2020).

The cultural relevance of religion within Egypt cannot be overstated, as it directly impacts and governs a myriad of aspects of the life of an Egyptian from birth to death. Participants were thereby asked to reflect on how they grew up with religion. Answers varied, as some experienced a conservative and strict religious upbringing, while religion was on the margins for others and did not affect their upbringing. Many of the participants were taught about religion by their parents, siblings, and immediate family. Observational learning is a technique used by many to normalise and standardise religious practices, such as praying, eating with and entering places with the right hand and foot (a *Sunnah* from the Prophet Mohamed), and saying *Yarhamakum Allah* (May God have mercy on your soul) after someone sneezes. AU2l(36) for instance, upon reflecting on her childhood, said

> My dad and mom used to pray in front of me and they used to know what Islam really is and how to live a Muslim life. I used to learn about the Qur'an from my school and then I started reading it on my own every Ramadan like my mom does. My father used to never miss a prayer. We were raised knowing what Islam is. However, other religions were never discussed in my household.

AU1l(33) had a slightly different upbringing, where she enjoyed a more independent learning curve. She said:

> I learned about Islam from different books and my older sister always told me to pray and corrected me when I was doing it wrong. I also used to read the Qur'an a lot and listen to Shaikhs [Islamic preachers/scholars] on TV and read different interpretations of the Qur'an. So, this is how I learned about my religion, and I fell in love with it. Islam is about ease and simplicity, not harshness and strictness.

Similar to AU1l(33), BU1s(32) also enjoyed a degree of freedom to pursue knowledge regarding their assigned religion. She said:

> Unlike so many people, I was first taught to respect Islam, and then try to understand it with all its nuances. Yes, I was born with it, but I was taught to love it. We have a lot of 'you can't do this' but as I was raised to understand why I can't do this; I have respect for it. Faith is just a must in Islam because there is so much beauty in submitting to the unknown.

For some participants, religion was their calling, such as CU3c(12) who grew up in a Coptic Christian household. He said:

> I was taught to be committed to my religion and to serve it and my country. I was deeply connected to God from the beginning, and very committed to going to Sunday school. It's why I studied theology at university, and this path made me want to become a priest.

For other Catholic Christians, growing up with religion was different. BU2a(18), for instance, questioned some gender norms she observed in Church. She shared how questioning her father about her observations and what was perceived as normal helped her father change his behaviours. BU2a(18) said:

> My parents did not go to Catholic school like me (...) Their religious faith was important to them, but they emphasised forgiveness and tolerance as opposed to the harsh judgements of God and talk about hell. [At church] of course I always asked myself why women could not be priests. I would always question why girls were to serve the group of men and not the other way around. All those questions I posed to my dad. After asking him all those questions I started to see a change in his behaviours (...) he would help the women clean up the table [and] got more enlightened and gradually started abandoning racism.

For others, their religious experience was less dramatic and more relaxed, such as BU1s(22) who said:

> When I was younger I was forced to go to Church but I was never forced to go to Sunday school. My father would be happy to see me go to church and get closer to God, but he was never insisting. My dad knows that I am not religious, but he's not ecstatic about it, but he lets me do whatever I want.

As children are born into a religious affiliation, it was necessary to ask whether the participants were still practising that religion. Contributing to our understanding was CU1p(26), who said 'my mother, my father, grandfather, and uncles, everyone contributed with what they knew. They are not very religious or strict, they just follow the normal Islamic rituals such as praying and fasting'. When the participants were asked whether they still are a practising Muslims, however, they said:

> I am the kind of person who would try what is wrong so I can learn. My parents are not strict but I still wouldn't do anything *Haram* [prohibited by religion] because I know it's just not just wrong, but religion prohibits it and that must be for a reason that I don't know but must abide by. As a Muslim, I simply can't anger God like this. This is what they taught me: religion is about

discipline over your spirit and soul and not letting *Shaytan* [evil spirit/Satan] control me with my human desires.

Contrastingly, some participants chose to abandon organised religion altogether to follow their own paths. CU1a(9) for instance said, 'I was born and raised as a Muslim'. When he was asked whether he is a practising Muslim he said:

> As soon as you start exposing yourself to different materials and questioning things, like why should I or shouldn't I abide by that, why is something right or wrong, it's the beginning of the end. You start asking yourself these questions and then find that it's all a matter of relativity and subjectivity. How can I claim to be right and that others are wrong? What is the definition of right and wrong?

Tolerance and acceptance are something most participants grew up with. Yet, while it is culturally observed, it is not something to be generalised to any population. One participant, however, took their religious exploration to another level. CU2e(31) shared his journey away from Islam and his return to his faith. Utilising a myriad of arguments, spanning from his belief that Muslims cannot convert to Judaism, and that Christianity diminishes God by stating Jesus is the son of God, CU2e(31) argued that he is now a fulfilled Muslim. He said:

> My experience is way different in this. As I was growing up, I realised that I was a Muslim; I learned the basic principles of Islam, such as praying and going to the mosque (...)When I was 15/16 years old, I started to do my research on religion, as I always had Christian neighbours. What I learned while growing up is that Muslims are the only people who will go to heaven and others will go to hell. Then when asking the Christians, they would say that anyone who does not believe in Christ would go to hell. This forced me to do more research and dig deep.

He continued to elaborate by selectively citing the Bible and Torah as evidence for his efforts to reconcile the differences between what he learnt from his immediate surroundings and his research findings, stating:

> [for example] You cannot convert into Judaism; no one can. There are also unbelievable contradictions, such as that Jesus and God are one thing [in Christianity]. Then, when I started studying Islam I realised that there are no contradictions; all the do's and don'ts are one thing. Islam portrayed the prophets as ones with no mistakes. I was so relaxed and that was why I returned to Islam and became a Muslim, not just on paper.

Led by affluent and influential scholars and preachers who argue for 'Islamic Exceptionalism' (Hamid, 2016), the participant highlighted how irregular and unorthodox it is for Egyptians to 'be without religion' as it constitutes a major factor in the construction of the Egyptian identity; an abandonment of religion could cause a loss of identity (Hughes, 2013; Mohamad et al., 2020; Schirrmacher, 2020, p. 81). The participant is, nonetheless, not to blame; in a culture where the following verses of the Qur'an (3:19) are taught in schools:

> Certainly, Allah's only Way is Islam. Those who were given the Scripture did not dispute 'among themselves' out of mutual envy until the knowledge came to them. Whoever denies Allah's signs, then surely Allah is swift in reckoning.

And 'No religion other than Islam (submission to the will of God) will be accepted from anyone. Whoever follows a religion other than Islam will be lost on the Day of Judgment' (Qur'an 3:85), it is hardly surprising that his doubt has resulted in dissonance. Yet, even expressing doubt appeared to be taxing for the participant, who understandably worried about the researcher reporting him to the authorities for 'blasphemy'.

While some participants had sufficient freedom to explore, even if in secret, others were not as fortunate. CR2s(41) said,

> my father used to make us memorise the Qur'an when we were young and we used to go to Friday school every week to learn more about the Qur'an. So, I was forced into it until I was convinced with it.

Similarly, CR3c(11) said:

> Because my dad was a Shaikh [Islamic preacher] my family was very religious and I grew up in a very strict religious manner. We all had to memorise the Qur'an and we were all enrolled in Al-Azhar to learn more about it.

More than half the participants used paraphrased versions of CR2s(35)'s 'I was forced until I was convinced' to describe their upbringing with religion as a central theme, revealing that doubt is unbecoming of children. With strict and conservative upbringings, participants appeared to yearn for knowledge and answers to their most fundamental questions – as highlighted by BU2p(99s) who stated that questions 'how come God created the sky without columns holding it up?' are taboo – but the restrictive and prejudiced characteristic of the culture prevented them from seeking answers. This stems from the fear of being accused of 'blasphemy' or being an 'atheist', which 17 participants explicitly disclosed to the researcher.

One participant, despite the fear of persecution, detailed his resentment towards religion. As an 11-year-old boy, he was experimenting, and without realising it, exploring his sexuality. CI2s(19) said:

> Growing up as a human, a person becomes very curious especially when it comes to sexuality. I remember I had no other option,

but to have intimate friendships with guys. It started with games and acting; we started to create scenarios until the scenes became romantic and we started kissing. We used to do this for a while, but we never exceeded the kissing phase. I was once in a family house and playing games and I started kissing my boy cousin. My mother saw us doing so and she felt terrible. I wish someone had told me that this is not good; I would have avoided it. I now understand where she is coming from; she does not want her older son to be gay.

When asked what would be wrong if he had turned out gay, he hesitantly elaborated and said:

If you are born in a cage and you have no other life but this cage, you will have no idea how people are living outside this cage. This is the thing with our society in older generations. They have their own perimeter of what is right and wrong just like us. Some of those believe that every single person who is not really following Islam will go to hell. It is just completely crazy and my mom flipped on me. She used to call me names and was super scared of me spending time alone with my sister. She wanted to put me in a foster home I was 11 years old and did not know what was going on. She took it to another level. I remember an incident where she left me in the desert for 25 minutes alone when I was 11 years old to teach me about hell and what punishment is awaiting me as a gay boy.

Asked if they ever spoke to their mother about this, they said:

She told me that is this حرام (Haram) and that I will go to hell. However, she said it in a very aggressive way, but this was the only way she knew at that moment because she was young. My dad did not comment at all. He was only looking and not taking action; he did not have an opinion on this matter. It was my mom who changed my school to Al-Azhar [in Egypt this is the equivalent of being sent to military school] where they taught me everything about Islam in English.

The participant's experience revealed two taboo topics Egyptians shy from discussing: (1) sex and sexuality, and (2) fanaticism. As religion and culture are seemingly inseparable, and the dominant religion is male-interpreted Islam, it is unsurprising that homophobic sentiments are prevalent; the chauvinistic and machismo culture coupled with a confounded religious interpretation served to suppress homosexuality and the creation of new discourses (Siraj, 2012). While this testimony may not seem to have a direct relation to the topic of this book, it does support the argument that identities in Egypt are externally imposed. It also reveals how the patriarchal system in Egypt affects marginalised and vulnerable groups, such as women and the LGBTQ+ community equally, suggesting that the patriarchal system in Egypt is supressing any type of strategic gender interest realisation and is denying 'real freedoms' to anyone who challenges or even deviates from the social norms. Already vulnerable and marginalised groups are subjected to such high scrutiny, and proponents can be subjugated to social punishment and/or legal persecution for lack of conformity to the state and socially imposed gender roles (HRW, 2020a, b; Younes, 2020).

Another participant elaborated on how the 25th January revolution has made him turn his back on Islam. He said:

> [I grew up with] Salafi Islam. There was a mosque beside the house and my parents pushed me to go there. Since I was eight years old, I was part of the mosque and all the activities performed in the mosque. However, I left when I was in grade nine.

When asked why he left the mosque, he said:

> After the *Raba'a* massacre [the interim military government cracked down on Muslim Brotherhood supporting protestors, shot and killed 900 protestors, critically injured 1000+, and detained and sentenced 72 to the death penalty by labelling the protestors extremists (Soltan, 2018)], the Salafis views were so ignorant towards the Muslim Brotherhood (MB). I was very shocked. They gave me the poster of Abdel-Fatah El-Sisi to hang and I could not take it. He had just killed 1000 people, and they still supported him. I cut ties with the mosque and party in general. This was not religion; this was pure politics. Religion is just the cover and I believed them'. He continued to elaborate on why he abandoned Islam and concluded with 'it's all about doubt. Doubt everything'.

This testimony further supports the argument of religion being used in Egypt as a political tool to further the Government's *practical* interests and agenda. It also highlights how the line between religion and politics is blurry in Egypt.

Moreover, this section emphasised the extent to which religion impacts daily lives of Egyptian citizens and showcased how religion can be experienced as an oppressive force in Egypt. It also highlighted that the interpretation of religion can be problematic, particularly as certain interpretations reject any form of deviation from the supposed 'acceptable' behaviours or actions. Additionally, the *Raba'a* massacre accentuated the embeddedness of religion and politics. As Hamzawy (2017) highlighted that

> religious populism [in Egypt] elevates the ruler to the level of a moral paragon who has the right to speak in the name of religion—not just in the public and political spheres but also in terms of citizens' private lives and ethics.

Reflecting on the *Raba'a* massacre, Hamzawy (2017) concluded that

> the new authoritarian government is using official Islamic and Christian institutions to impose its own interpretations of religion on Egyptian society (...) [and] frames obedience to the ruling general and the approval of its policies as a religious duty (...) using religious symbols and statements in the public space to rationalise repression and human rights abuses.

This section, corroborated Hamzawy's observations and sheds light on how religion is a necessary dimension when analysing experiences and understandings in Egypt.

Chapters 1 and 2 tackled the intersection between religion and politics, and the testimonies of the primary sources confirm that this is still the case in Egypt. Additionally, this account substantiates the supposition that dehumanisation strategies are operationalised by the patriarchal system in Egypt which denies and/or sanctions anyone who does not conform to the concrete confinements and rules of the system. In reference to the events at *Raba'a,* the Government justified the massacre of protesters by labelling them fundamentals and terrorists from within (Al-Arian, 2014). Abdullah Al-Arian (2016) in anther editorial article reviewed the massacre in Egypt, stating:

> The dehumanisation of thousands of ordinary men, women, and children, many of whom are not even members of the Muslim Brotherhood, occurred as state officials and media personalities continually utilised the imagery of terrorism and violent extremism to depict the protestors (...) Given its enduring quality, however, it would be a mistake to assume that this incitement campaign against the Muslim Brotherhood is a recent incarnation. Far from being a makeshift construct that aided in Sisi's alarmingly rapid political ascent, the recent application of the 'war on terror' motif stems from a historic struggle over the Egyptian national narrative that pits the state against one of the country's oldest social movement organisations (...) By conflating the Muslim Brotherhood's legacy of oppositional politics with violent incarnations of anti-state contention, the terror metanarrative attempts to establish on a false basis the state's ability to respond to perceived threats with all means at its disposal.

Furthermore, Al-Arian's (2016) account of the mechanisms employed by the Egyptian Government to suppress and curtail movements which express a narrative that challenges the authority and power of the government. These mechanisms are employed by the government to solidify its executive power, which is evidenced by the ambiguous language used in the constitution. Specifically, the addition of the Penal Code law no. 175, which allows the State the power to interpret what constitutes a 'violation' on the basis of the national narrative.

By centralising power within the government, any person or group who expresses an opinion against existing structures in Egypt is persecuted by the State, in turn creating a culture of silence, fear, and passivity, and establishing an environment in which changes and social demands cannot be expressed. Consequentially, the State can maintain and reproduce patriarchal structures, for as long as it sees fit, by dehumanising and villainising the opposition. Moreover, it is crucial to understand that declaring yourself as an agnostic, atheist, or affiliating yourself with any other religion than the one assigned to you at birth is a crime punishable by law in Egypt as stipulated in Article 98(f) of the Penal Code, as amended by Law 147/2006 (Greenslade, 2015; Human Rights Watch, 2013). The Article also includes a judicial stipulation based on *Sharia* called *Hisba* which is 'an Islamic principle by which one Muslim can bring a case against another Muslim for perceived violations against Islam' (Freedom House, 2010). It additionally includes ambiguous language and phrasing such as 'stirring up sedition' or 'social harmony' which allows for the malleable and individual interpretation of the law. This ambiguity could, and has, resulted in discriminatory behaviours and persecution based on a judicial interpretation of the legal texts, as we observed in the 1995 case of Naser Abu-Zayed who 'an Egyptian Shariah court declared Dr Abu Zayd an apostate from Islam, annulled his marriage and effectively forced him and his wife into exile' (Reuters, 2010). This knowledge sheds light on the extent to which the State can exercise control over the private and public spheres in Egypt. Additionally, it highlights the role of religion in Egyptian society and the depth of control over 'real freedoms' the government has within the society. This also reveals the extent to which religion plays a central role in designating political rights and statuses, therefore supporting the earlier findings that religion is an instrument of socio-political legitimation of state-sponsored narratives.

Furthermore, Muslims wishing to convert or declare themselves as Christians can expect serious consequences, as 'The state does not recognise conversions from Islam and refuses to allow citizens legally to change their religious affiliation or to change a Muslim name to a Christian name on national identification documents' (Human Rights Watch, 2007). Yet the opposite is allowed, meaning a Christian can convert to Islam, adopt a Muslim name, and marry a Muslim person. This substantiates the argument that the dominant religion in Egypt, Islam, is highly influenced by the political apparatus. Additionally, to file a request of conversion the individual must be over the age of 16 and file an official request with the Security Directorate of the Ministry of Interior Affairs, and the police (HRW, 2007a, b; Rahman, 2017). The authorities then set forth a meeting with a representative of the religious denomination and advise them against conversion. However, if the convert does not accept the 'advise of his co-religionists' (HRW, 2007a, b) the local notary validates their conversion as stipulated in the civil status Law 143/1994. As there is no legal stipulation protecting the right of freedom of religion and belief, Article 1 of the Egyptian Civil Code (2020) is enacted, which states:

> Provisions of laws govern all matters to which these provisions apply in letter or spirit. In the absence of a provision of a law that is applicable, the Judge will decide according to custom and in the

absence of custom in accordance with the principles of Moslem Law. In the absence of such principles, the Judge will apply the principles of natural justice and the rules of equity.

This is significant as it highlights the malleability and subjectivity of the Egyptian constitution, the Penal Code, the Civil Code, and the personal status laws, highlighting the problematic assumption that the personal biases of judges would not influence their subjective and patriarchal interpretation of any law or code, thereby enforcing their belief onto individuals with whom they philosophically might disagree.

This is reinforced by Article 2 of the Egyptian Constitution which declares Sharia as the main source of legislation in Egypt. As Sharia law explicitly condemns and prohibits conversions from Islam to any other religious denomination or faith, *Al Riddah,* (roughly translates to defection or apostasy), and calls for *Al Hadd* (literally translates to border or limit, but in this context means the punishments stated and mandated by God for divergence or violation of Sharia laws) to be executed. The *Hadd* for apostasy is the death penalty, as mandated in the *Hadith* of the Prophet Mohamed, which states 'whoever changes his religion, kill him' (reliable *Hadith* from *Sahih Al Bukhari,* 2018, p. 1076).[1] As stated earlier, in Islam, the *Hadith* is considered to be the only source of legitimate jurisprudence and ought to be viewed as a supplementary source to Sharia Islam. This is stipulated in the Qur'anic verse 'And whoever obeys Allah and the – essenger – those will be with the ones upon whom Allah has bestowed favour of the prophets' (Qur'an 4:69) and 'you should love Allah, then follow me [Muhammad], ... Obey Allah, and obey the Messenger, and those charged with authority among you [Islamic jurists]' (Qur'an 3:31). These Qur'anic verses connote that the *Hadith* is not only complementary to the Qur'an, but one must obey the *Hadiths* as much as one would do the Qur'an. Nonetheless, it is important to state that 'there is no evidence to indicate that the Prophet Muhammad himself ever imposed the death penalty on any apostate for a simple act of conversion from Islam' (Saeed, 2011).

It is because of stipulations and religious laws in mind that Egyptians, who are born Muslim and wish to convert to a different religious denomination or faith, do not publicly or officially declare their orientations. This highlights that strategic needs and interests, which may divert from the 'acceptable' norms and identity the State imposes, that individuals may wish to pursue are oppressed by the governance system in Egypt. Additionally, it emphasises that women are not the only ones who need to bargain with patriarchy in Egypt, but that anyone who disagrees with the meta-narratives of the State must adhere to the rules of the bargain to avoid socio-political sanctions. This also suggests that second-class citizenship in Egypt is not only applicable to Egyptian women, but to the wider nonconforming

---

[1] Narrated 'Abdullah bin Mas'ud: that the Messenger of Allah (ﷺ) said: 'The blood of a Muslim man, who testifies that none has the right to be worshipped Allah, is not lawful except for one of three cases: The (previously married or) married adulterer, a life for a life, and the one who leaves the religion and parts from the Jama'ah (the community of Muslims)'.

groups within society. For this book, women's second-class citizenship is investigated and future research could investigate this issue further. Moreover, Muslims wishing to convert must:

> Confront the likelihood that they and their immediate families will face official as well as social discrimination, including the automatic nullification of marriage between the convert and his or her Muslim spouse and forced separation from children, who are compelled to reside with the Muslim spouse or a close Muslim relative. (See Cassation Court ruling in Case no. 1359/28 1984; Human Rights Watch, 2007)

These laws and regulations are therefore meant to actively deter individuals from disturbing 'social harmony'. As law 178 of the Penal Code states:

> Whoever makes or holds, for the purpose of trade, distribution, leasing, pasting or displaying printed matter, manuscripts, drawings, advertisements, carved or engraved pictures, manual or photographic drawings, symbolic signs, or other objects or pictures in general, if they are against public morals, shall be punished with detention for a period not exceeding two years and a fine of not less than five thousand pounds and not exceeding ten thousand pounds or either penalty. (Egyptian Penal Code, 1937)

Judges in Egypt set precedence for persecution based on 'violating public morals and decency' by persecuting and sentencing social media influencers for 'inciting immorality' (Hume, 2020), albeit international law and UN standards demand freedom of expression and religion (Siddiqui, 2020). As reported by Bahgat (2004):

> [the Egyptian Government] has been raising the banner of protection of public morality to justify intrusive surveillance of this new technological challenge to its control over Egyptian citizens. The Government's self-proclaimed moral battle with its Internet-using citizens has violated a right to freedom of expression that is not only internationally recognised but is also guaranteed by the Egyptian constitution.

Furthermore, perceived 'violators' are penalised under Article 176 of the Penal Code which states whoever 'incites, by any of the foregoing methods, to hate or deride a sect of people, if such incitement is liable to perturb public peace, shall be punished with detention'. As Freedom House's (2010) policy brief summarised:

> Despite constitutional provisions guaranteeing freedom of speech, the Egyptian Penal Code (EPC) criminalises religious insult and blasphemy; insults to the president; the dissemination of news, statistics, or information that could harm the reputation of Egypt abroad; and criticism of the constitution.

Nonetheless, what constitutes 'blasphemy' or 'insult' is left to the discretion of the General Prosecutor and the State Attorney to define and argue for. The ambiguities in the legal framework in Egypt are therefore abused to maintain a social order which aligns with the agenda of the hegemonic bloc and arms the institutionally dependent judiciary with the liberty to declare and prosecute actions and behaviours they subjectively deem 'indecent' or 'blasphemous' and still be considered lawful as whatever interpretation judges ascribe can, and does, fall within the spectrum of 'public order and social harmony'.

It is true that religion, may it be Islam or Christianity, with all their schools of thought, are influential components of the structure of the society. Given the institutional requirement to assign a religious affiliation to a new-born child, and the cultural influence of Islam on daily activities, one can proclaim that culture and faith are two sides of the same coin for Egyptians which constitute the social norms citizens have to abide by. By demonstrating the use of religious phrases in day-to-day interactions, and unpacking the socio-legal and cultural frameworks, one can state that religion and culture do not exist in opposition to one another but serve as complementary forces that are often employed to govern daily life as well as maintain social order. If one presumes that the social contract in Egypt demands mindfulness of, and submission to, religious authority *erga omnes,* then a natural conclusion would be the realisation of the embeddedness of religion within the culture, and its influence over what strategies women and minority groups choose to employ to bargain with the patriarchal system to gain greater control over their socio-political status, protect their rights, and pursue 'real freedoms'. Furthermore, one can deduce that organised religion not only affects and shapes the social configurations and arrangements we see in the Egyptian society, but more importantly for this book, it affects gender dynamics and assigns gendered roles and hierarchies based on particular interpretations of religious texts.

The next section tackles the last social aspect which arose from the primary data, education. The section sheds light on how differential educational outcomes are a result of the intersection between religion and class which set the social rules. Specifically, the idea of education as a means to access, opportunity, and individuals' pursuit of 'real freedoms' is unpacked. Education appears to be perceived as a strategic interest which is not afforded to all, making it a significant social contributor under Walby's conceptualisation of *Culture*. Walby (1990) argued that, within the category of Culture, the patriarchal system manifests in the 'naturalisation ideology, to a dissimulative approach which denies the extent of the inequality' (p. 107), thus, resulting in males having a higher social value over females. Also, within the context of Egypt, the statistical data highlight the prevalence of patriarchal attitudes among Egyptians (El Feky et al., 2017, p. 43). Diwan et al. (2016) in their working paper *Rates of Return to Education in Twenty Two Arab Countries* shed light on the relationship between education and employment in Egypt. Their survey revealed that:

> Countries with tight labour markets and high emigration rates, such as Egypt, Jordan, Lebanon and Tunisia, have better-performing students. Countries, where employment of nationals in the

public sector is more or less automatic, has the lowest performing students (for example, Kuwait, Oman, Qatar and Saudi Arabia).

The relevance of education to labour market needs is a more complicated issue. On the one hand, credentialism can be the driving force for investing in (wrong types of) education in countries where job seekers have an expectation of getting a job in the public sector. This has indisputably been the case in the past (for example, in Egypt) and still is (notably in the GCC). However, the public sector has reduced the rate of hiring in recent years. For example, the proportion of public sector employment in the first jobs of women with secondary education and above was more than 75 percent in Tunisia and Egypt and nearly 60 percent in Jordan in 1975 but it is now around 30 percent in all three countries.

This sheds light on the intersectionality and interconnectedness of Walby's concepts of Paid Employment, Family/Household Production and Culture. If there is a positive relationship between Egyptian women's unrealised strategic interests and citizenship status, then women's confinement to the role of homemaker and their unequal access and opportunity to paid employment, created a culture where men are placed at a higher status and valued more than Egyptian women. Therefore, one can argue that the system established the patriarchal structure in which women exchange equal and equitable opportunity for Paid Employment, and subordination within the Family/Household, in favour of security and financial benefits. However, this in turn has solidified women's inferior status and halted their ability to realise their strategic gender interests needed to challenge their exclusion. The next section further unpacks how the unequal valuation of men and women is manifested in education, particularly with regard to women's inferiority and maintaining the patriarchal notion that men are of higher value than women. Specifically, the next section looks at how 'Son Preference' is manifested in Egypt. UNICEF (2017) defines Son Preference as

> the practice of preferring male offspring over female offspring, most often in poor communities who view girl children as liabilities and boy children as assets to the family. This can result in families instilling superiority in male children and inferiority in female children, manifesting in such actions as sending boys to school, especially to higher levels, and not girls. (p. 7)

3. Education and Son Preference

Education is one of the primary indicators of human development. The challenges reflected in educational output and attainment are indicative of wider socio-economic and political challenges in the social experiences. In the current post-Mubarak era, there are several pressing demographic issues to be tackled, such as the fact that 34% of Egyptians are under the age of 14 (UNESCO, 2018), official estimates of 10.1% unemployment (World Bank, 2020), and staggering youth unemployment (age group 15–29) 30%, of which 15.8% are males and 31.7% are females (World Bank, 2020). The slow institutional responses to the 25th January revolution in 2011 posed large-scale shifts in society over the past years. The risk of literary deprivation and lack of adequate shifts to educational approaches might leave a generation ill-equipped to meet labour market demands and challenges in this ever evolving political and economic system. According to *Ingaz Al Arab*, a regional NGO, 'the poor quality of much of the state education system is the widespread reliance on private tutoring to supplement it, also contribute to Egypt's high level of economic inequality, raising concerns about social justice' (Loveluck, 2012a, b, p. 3). It additionally poses a barrier to entry where class is directly related to educational attainment; if a person is of lower socio-economic status in Egypt, given the reliance of Egyptians on private tutoring to supplement education, then one can make the logical leap that socio-economic status and class are precursive determinants to education.

As political and educational developments are closely interrelated, it is unsurprising that historical shifts in power and changes in the hegemonic bloc, that is, the ruling and powerful class, dynamics were accompanied by changes in the educational system and its structure. For instance, during the Ottoman rule of Egypt, the European style of education was introduced to the Egyptian society, to nurture a class of highly educated Army officers and public sector administrators (Loveluck, 2012a, b, p. 4). Respectively, British colonial powers (1882–1922) defunded education to curb disruptive and anti-colonial sentiments from aggregating, and concentrated efforts to educate and 'Britify' the local hegemonic elite, thereby reducing the risk of nationalist strives and instilling the belief in white superiority (Tignor, 1966, p. 320).

In 1952, Gamal Abdel-Nasser, the first president of Egypt and member of the *Free Officers* movement who fought against British rule, reoriented education to a more regionally acclaimed and appropriate system (Mirshak, 2020, p. 42). This included modernising the Arab curriculum, making primary education for all Egyptians mandatory and free of charge, investing in novel education infrastructures that would be more inclusive of all social classes and locations (as opposed to urban-focussed), and guaranteed vocations for secondary and tertiary graduates in public sector bureaus (Faksh, 1976, p. 235; Mansfield, 1965, p. 120; Mirshak, 2020). Nevertheless, as demand for secondary education and higher education increased, the public sector resources were unable to accommodate the increased demand, which ultimately led to the quality of education provided deteriorating (Faksh, 1976, p. 241). Nasser's sudden death and the appointment of Anwar Sadat in the 1970s and his 'Open Door' policies led to an increase in private schools and universities, which offered superior quality of education, and beneficiaries were predominantly from the upper and upper middle classes of society, as affiliates can afford the demanded tuition fees (Megahed et al., 2012, p. 42). Education is thereby a commodity which is closely related to life prospects and can be indicative of one's social status; the more 'exclusive' the school one attends, the more likely they are to attend a university with international accreditation and ranking, and the more likely they are to obtain well-paying jobs post-graduation.

The inequality of the educational system has gravely affected gender dynamics and relations in Egypt, as AR3m(60) elaborated, 'In rural areas, it is not a priority to educate a girl, as it is a priority to educate a boy. The girl ends up in her husband's house anyway', revealing that under calculated economic and financial restraints, families perpetuate the gendered social norms of men being providers and women being homemakers. This corroborates the participant observations as well as statistical data about the Gender Gap index in Egypt (El Feky et al., 2017, p. 43), and confirms the social institutionalisation of the patriarchal system. One can also argue that by monetising education, people of certain economic backgrounds are forced to choose between educating boys and girls. This highlights the differential social roles in Egypt and confirms the claim that women are perceived to 'belong' in the private sphere. As the women lack the agency to challenge this role and have to adhere for as far and as long as they could to the gendered exchange between agency and autonomy for financial security, they cannot challenge their secondary status and exclusion from full citizenship rights.

The notion of prescribed gender roles within the family is reflected in AR3m(59)'s experience where she elaborated that, as a woman in rural Egypt, education is not a priority, but home care is what she should be striving for. She stated:

> I am from Etfo, a rural village on the delta. I got my primary education at this local institute, I didn't go to school for it, but I can read and do the math. I got married after grade 7 and have been living with my husband for 11 years away from my village. We are *Falahin* [farmers] so my mother is a housewife and my dad works the field. This is how things are and how we divide responsibilities.

Among rural women in Kafr El Shaikh and Fayoum, AR3m(59)'s statement was reiterated in different words by 12 female participants, therefore it could be viewed as a summary of gendered responsibilities and roles. From a strategic interest realisation perspective and 'real freedoms', one can argue that motherhood and home-care responsibilities are signs of how the patriarchal exchange is set up. Women such as AR3m do not seem to doubt that a woman's primary role is in the domestic sphere, as such, there is no evidence to suggest that she desires a change of this dynamic. This can serve to confirm women's 'active collusion in the reproduction of their own subordination' (Kandiyoti, 1988, p. 289), and highlight the patriarchal structure of Culture which seems to gravitate towards naturalisation ideology (Mernissi, 1987, p. 89; Walby, 1990, p. 107) resulting in women internalising and reproducing their own inferiority.

For other women, the internalisation of gendered roles was a primary reason for them not to continue their education, such as AU2l(36) who said:

> In the 90s finding a job was so hard for a woman, so I didn't get one after finishing my secondary education. I didn't want to work either, I don't believe in having a job while I had my daughters waiting for me to come home.

Coupled with the social discourse around women's and men's roles in Egyptian society, these two accounts shed light on gender expectations. However, upon further reflection the discursive language within this statement can be interpreted as either that women in Egypt have internalised their inferiority, or that this is how they chose to live their lives. This is suggesting the construction of a social norm that, as an Egyptian woman, you are expected to *want* and *desire* motherhood specifically and homecare in general and stating otherwise is unorthodox and potentially disruptive. Furthermore, statements by women, such as AR3m(62) who emotionally recited her experiences said:

> I really wanted to do a lot of stuff with my life, like getting educated, but I couldn't do that because my father died before I was born and mom remarried and her husband did not believe in wasting money on educating me. I can't even read.

Yet not all parents in rural communities favour educating the boys. AR3m(7), for instance, was not educated herself, but answered the question of whether gender makes a difference she said:

> Of course not! How wouldn't we educate our girls? I would educate them so that they grow up to be 'enlightened' and aware of things around them in life so they can have a better life than me. I wasn't educated because of the circumstances of my father. We only had enough money to afford to eat and drink, that's it. Now that we are better off, we try to educate them all.

Respectively, some mothers interviewed seemed proud when asked about whether their daughters were educated. Others saw education as a social obligation, but motherhood as the ultimate goal, such as AU2l(36) who said:

> My oldest daughter is 40 and she graduated with a degree in Administration. She is not working as she is married and has three kids. My older son is in university now, and will *inshallah* find a good job after. My other daughter is 35, and she graduated from Cairo University with a philosophy major. She is also not working, as she is married and has one daughter who is seven.

This pattern of educated housewives was detected in the study and appeared to be a social expectation as opposed to a choice to become a full-time mother, which is another pattern detected. The extent to which society affects a woman's decision to enter into or leave the labour force is discussed in detail in later chapters. However, it is noteworthy to state that CR2p(6)'s recounting of events was not unique to his family. He said:

> At the time [the 70s and 80s Egypt] it was not normal for the whole family to get educated. Yes, everyone wanted to be educated, but in the end, it's the money that dictates who does. So usually in our families, the oldest brother gets educated and then teaches his siblings.

146   Recovering Women's Voices

This has also revealed that the opportunities afforded to different classes, such as larger access to higher education, do not necessarily connote more egalitarian and equitable attitudes, but more relevantly that observational learning and what a child is exposed to in the household determines their stances later on in life (Bandura, 1999, 2002, 2006; Frylin et al., 2011).

The interviews with 36 male participants and 34 female participants from urban areas, Cairo and Alexandria, and rural areas, Kafr El Shaikh and Fayoum, in Egypt have revealed the following social norms and gender expectations:

(1) Almost all women and men living in urban communities receive secondary education.
(2) Educational challenges are closely related to socio-economic issues.
(3) In rural communities some families still prefer to educate the boys and not the girls because it is considered futile to spend money on a girl's education, that is, Son Preference.
(4) Getting an education does not necessarily a guarantee obtaining a job, and in the instances one does, the society expects a woman to quit after marriage to fulfil her duties and responsibilities towards her husband and children.
(5) Women are more involved in diverse fields of labour in urban cities as opposed to being restricted to occupy 'women's' jobs [assistant, teacher, nurse etc.] in rural areas.
(6) In Egypt, fathers and husbands have the right to pull their daughters out of education for marriage and childbearing, and to command their wives to quit/not work in order to focus their energy to serve the home.

This section highlighted how the patriarchal system established a value-system where girls are denied equal opportunity for development and growth. It also sheds light on how social norms for women are constructed to put more emphasis on reproductive roles and childbearing, following the rules for women's social behaviour, and the consequences for women of not following these rules. This denial of women's autonomy as an independent individual with strategic needs served to reproduce the gender hierarchies, maintain male domination over strategically significant interests, and perpetuate women's subordinate social position. The next section builds on this understanding and tackles the seventh research question: what did the data reveal about the patriarchal bargains women employ to gain greater security and autonomy in Egypt?

4. Patriarchal Attitudes and Women's Subordination

The IMAGES Egypt 2017 report highlighted that 95.3% of Egyptian men have sexually harassed women and that fewer men blame the victim than women. The report also highlighted that 94% of men and 69% of women believe a man has the right to control women, for example, when his wife can leave the house, and 96% of men and 84% of women agree that a wife is expected to agree to have sex when the husband wants to (El Feky et al., 2017, pp. 72–85). The data from the IMAGES report shed light on the patriarchal values embedded within, what

Walby referred to as, the patriarchal structures of Sexuality, Culture, and Violence (see The First Feminists in Egypt, Chapter 2).

Moreover, the social consequence of patriarchal attitudes on the perception of female inferiority is evidenced by the statistic that 94% of men and 69% of women have agreed to the idea that a man has the right to control a woman. Upon further reflection, the evidence seemed to support the argument that the patriarchal structures of Violence and the State (Walby, 1990) are culpable in the solidification of patriarchal attitudes in Egypt. This is particularly evident in how the State enforces the few laws that protect women in the public sphere, such as sexual harassment laws, and the complete lack of laws to protect women within the private sphere, such as laws that would penalise domestic abuse and inter-marital rape. The patriarchal system in Egypt, therefore, allows men 'to utilise a considerable amount of violence against women with impunity' (Walby, 1990, p. 150). As a consequence, according to Bird (1996, p. 131), women's strategic gender interests cannot be realised unless the meanings of 'emotional detachment, competitiveness, and the sexual objectification of women ... cease to exist'. One could argue that this is especially significant as 'the beliefs, attitudes, and expectations that decree the valuation and/or devaluation of distinctive masculine and feminine [characteristics]' (Bird, 1996, p. 131), could be linked to the assignment of social status and rank, the right to enjoy socio-political and legal benefits, and the right to access the public sphere.

Evidence from the data highlighted that the classic patriarchal system in Egypt reinforced patriarchal structures which stress the gender expectations of women's primary role as homemakers. AU2a(64) shared how her father controlled her mother, stating 'the day she was contacted for a job my father asked her to marry him. He wanted her to stay home and promised he will give her all the money she needs so she doesn't have to work'. CR3s(56), on the other hand, confidently recounted why his mother did not finish her university degree, and left her job, stating:

> She left because she wouldn't have been able to balance between us and her work, and a mother's duty is first and foremost to care for her family. If she has a job that's great for her, but only if she can balance that with her home and family responsibilities. Why else would she get married?

These accounts of where women belong, and how the dominant discourse dictates a woman's 'place' and 'job' are pronounced here. Both participants recounted their experiences as normalised accounts: on the one hand, AU2a(64) perceived her father disallowing her mother to work as normal and socially acceptable, that is, not something she ought to question. On the other hand, CR3s(56), perhaps unconsciously, perpetuated the idea that a woman's role and her significance are prescribed by men, and her status is only relevant when contrasted to her male counterpart. Neither participants, even though they were explicitly asked about their mothers, provided an account of what their mothers expressed, but only provided an account of how their fathers ascribed and enforced his will, normalising women's inferiority and perpetuating male superiority.

Disagreeing with this narrative is CR3s(57) who elaborated on why women in rural communities are oftentimes perceived to belong in the home, stating:

> Because of traditional thoughts of how women only belong in the house with her husband many women like my mother were pulled out of education to fulfil their purpose as mothers and wives. Her needs and desires bore no consequence for her father, and she was married off. Just like that. But she wanted to be more educated. She used to take my schoolbooks and read them after my siblings were asleep and then ask me about them.

Unlike AU2a(64) and CR3s(56), CR3s(57) critically engaged with what seems to be taken for granted gendered social norms, identities, and roles, assuming that she *wants* to be a housewife, a caretaker, within the confines of the home.

Summarising the female experience from a male perspective was sociology major student CU1s(14) who said:

> Society here expects that a woman has to be married at a young age and look after her house and family. I think the Egyptian society constricts women's roles as just that. Even though it is changing, it is not effectively changing. Yes, women are now working, but it's still not okay for them to earn more than their husbands and to choose a career over their love life. This is why I said that societal pressure here is very high. However, the people surrounding her do not have the same expectations of society, she is lucky, like my mother.

Complementary to this statement was that of CU2s(38) who stated:

> My father does not believe it's okay for a woman to leave the house. But I do. If this work does not cause me any problems, I will allow my wife to work. However, I don't want her complaining that men are bothering her or flirting with her at work. Things like that will make me tell her to stop working. I am not against her working, I just don't want any problems.

He continued to say:

> My father is very strict, I'm not strict though. My father doesn't even allow my mother to leave the house without him. If he does not allow her to get something from the supermarket alone, of course, he will not allow her to work.

Critically approaching CU2s(38) word choice from the perspective of 'real freedoms' that women have access to in Egypt, then the words 'allowing' and 'strict' are operative. First, the use of the words 'allowing' and 'strict' suggests that a man does possess the right to both, even if it goes against the wishes and wants of the woman. Second, it highlights the presence of the *Mind Perception Framework* which 'denied [women] agency and experience because they are believed to not have the capacity for cognitive freedom, and are denied secondary psychological processes' (Markowitz & Slovic, 2020, p. 261) as highlighted at the end of Chapter 2.

Furthermore, CU2s(38)'s phrase 'bothering her or flirting with her at work' sheds light on what continues socially acceptable behaviour for men and women; the responsibility for not being harassed falls onto the woman, as opposed to her having the right to victimhood and physical safety, she is blamed for advances by her male colleagues for which she is not responsible. Furthermore, sexual and verbal harassment by males has become normalised in Egyptian society, to the point that it is a social expectation that women will be harassed in the workplace (Arab Barometer, 2021; UNFPA, 2018). This cultural discourse is also used to further limit women's autonomy and agency by setting patriarchal structures where women have to either exchange their agency and autonomy for the sake of security and protection from male violence or, if they choose to defy the patriarchal system, they are faced with sanctions for non-compliance (Kabeer, 1999, p. 45).

Vocalising the frustrations associated with a restrictive classic patriarchal system was BU2s(23) who said:

> My mom got her first job after 20 years of being married and now divorced from my father. She didn't work because dad wouldn't let her. He's very traditional and careful about what others say. Unfortunately in Egypt there is this stupid idea that if a woman has her own income she won't respect her man [husband] anymore, because they think she'll become too arrogant and will try and control her husband and ride him [in Egypt by 'riding' one is insinuating an animal analogy, where the belief is that the Jockey [father/husband] is the breadwinner and the horse is the caretaker (mother/wife)], so the man will lose his status and will be emasculated by the rest of the society if his woman is working. Men are expected to be in control and women are expected to be docile and obedient. They [men] use Qur'an 4:34[2] to justify this [control over women].

---

[2] 'Men are the protectors and maintainers of women, because Allah has made one of them to excel the other, and because they spend (to support them) from their means. Therefore, the righteous women are devoutly obedient (to Allah and to their husbands), and guard in the husband's absence what Allah orders them to guard (e.g., their chastity, their husband's property). As to those women on whose part you see ill-conduct, admonish them (first), (next), refuse to share their beds, (and last) beat them (lightly, if it is useful), but if they return to obedience, seek not against them means (of annoyance). Surely, Allah is Ever Most High, Most Great' (Qur'an, 4:34).

BU2s(23)'s statement confirms the earlier argument that patriarchal attitudes, when acted upon within Egypt's patriarchal system, maintain women's inferiority and their denial of full citizenship benefits and status.

This chapter tackled the question: what did the data reveal about the patriarchal bargains women employ to gain greater security and autonomy? According to the primary data, the patriarchal bargain is between women's agency and autonomy and women's safety and security. It also shed light on how the cultural domination of patriarchal attitudes serves to reinforce women's inferiority, particularly within the private sphere. Using Walby's conceptualisations, this chapter highlighted the prevalence and pervasiveness of the patriarchal system in Egypt, particularly in terms of *Paid Employment, Family/Household Production, Violence* and *Sexuality*. As these constitute the parameters against which women's strategic gender interests are measured, this chapter exhibited evidence of women's low realisation of strategic gender interest, which has solidified their inferiority and confined women to the private sphere where they cannot challenge their exclusion. The chapter also highlighted that class and religion are two significant social aspects which determine the extent of 'real freedoms' Egyptians can pursue. Lastly, the chapter also emphasised how education is key to challenging gender dynamics and relations in Egypt, which is believed to be the only path to emancipate women so they can realise their strategic gender interests and challenge male domination and violence. Education also seems to be a patriarchal bargain for men to gain greater autonomy within the framework of hegemonic masculinity the patriarchal system perpetuates through forced military drafting. While this observation is extremely valuable, and merits further research, it goes beyond the scope of this book. In light of that, the next chapter presents the strategies women, exclusively, have employed to gain greater agency and autonomy within the concrete confines of the patriarchal system. Specifically, the next chapter tackles the eighth question: what is the role of the *Hijab* in signalling adherence to the rules of the patriarchal bargain?

Chapter 6

The Role of the Hijab in Navigating the Patriarchal Bargain in Urban and Rural Egypt

> What happened to our society? Humanity altogether? I think it was our parents' generation. They treated men like kings because they were so damaged from the generation before, and from wars … they wanted to shield them so much that they f*cked it all up. Nour Badrawi[1]

The Hijab for many Middle Eastern countries specifically connotes a cultural and religious belief. It further signals a specific identity that these cultures attempt to export. However, the Hijab has become more controversial than ever in the past decade. From Nobel Peace Prize winner Malala Yousafzi being told if she wishes to teach in Quebec, Canada she would have to remove her Hijab (Ellsworth, 2019), to sovereign countries like France banning the Hijab in public schools (Fouka, 2020; Maurin & Naverete, 2019) and Belgium banning the Hijab at Universities (El Gharib, 2020).

The *Hijab* (veil) is not traditionally an Islamic cultural practice; many cultures practice veiling as well. The practice began long before the birth of the Islamic prophet Mohamed (PBUH). The Sassanids, Byzantines and many other cultures in the Middle East and Near East regions practised veiling and coverage (Slininger, 2014, p. 68). Some evidence suggests that Banū Isma'il and Banū Qahtān, pre-Islamic clans in Southwestern Arabia, practised veiling (El Guindi, 1999). In Mesopotamia, for example, wearing the veil was a sign of advanced social status and connoted respectability (Brooks, 1923, p. 187). In fact, in some ancient cultures, such as the Assyrian culture, the veil could only be worn by chaste and clean women, whereas slaves and harlots were prohibited by law from wearing it

---

[1]Employee at a private corporation in Ontario, Canada, of Egyptian and Muslim origin. Direct quotation from her reaction to the detrimental rise of predatory and paedophilic sexual advances by a psychiatrist in Egypt (Kharoshah & Sabh, 2020).

(Jastrow, 1921, p. 212). One can even argue that Islamic prophecy built on and formalised already established cultural practices in that region.

The tradition of the Hijab spread through the ancient world similarly to how any other ideology or practice has: through invasion and cultural imposition. Through invasion, cultural norms, rituals, and practices merged to create hybrid cultures (Clothier, 2005; Kapchan & Strong, 1999; Werbner, 2001). As we have seen with Mesopotamians, Persian, Greek, and recently British and Ottoman empires, Semitic people mixed and interacted with them, spreading the practice of veiling throughout the Middle East and parts of Asia. Evidence for this can be found in biblical texts such as Corinthians 11:5, which substantiates the argument that veiling preceded Islam as a cultural practice. One can thereby claim that the Hijab was appropriated by the Islamic prophecy and solidified face, body, and head covering as the appropriate and religiously preferred dress code for women. Furthermore, different religious faiths have different interpretations and conditions for veiling. For Christians, the woman's head is the man, the man's head is Christ, and the head of Christ is God. To dishonour Christ, a man would cover his head while praying, while a woman dishonours him if she does not (Corinthians, 11:3–4). This gendered mandate exists throughout religions and is not specific to Islam.

Prior to the Hijab being mandated in Islam, prophet Mohamed's (Peace Be Upon Him) wives used to wear a head covering, as it was the cultural norm to signal modesty, purity, and piety (Slininger, 2013, p. 70). It was not until the decades after the death of Mohamed (PBUH) that the practice became almost synonymous with Islam. It is important to acknowledge that the Hijab is not a mere fashion accessory, is representative of cultural and social identity, and does not connote a 'civilisation deficit' as assumed by some but is also a 'way of asserting identity and challenging stereotypical images and assumptions' (Wagner et al., 2012, p. 522). Many who do not observe the Islamic faith believe that the Hijab is a symbol of patriarchal and oppressive cultures (Mazumdar & Mazumdar, 2001; Ramazani, 1983; Sloan, 2011), albeit some observers of the faith negate this notion by repeatedly broadcasting it as a tool for liberation and resistance (Abu-Lughod, 2002; Alvi, 2013; Bartkowski & Read, 2000; Bullock, 2002; Hirschmann, 1998; Hoodfar, 1993; Kandiyoti, 1988; Khan, 2014; Ruby, 2006, p. 59).

To accomplish that, this book focussed the investigation on what the Hijab represents and what social cues it signals, to better understand the patriarchal system in Egypt. The researcher asked Egyptian men and women, Hijabi Muslim and non-Hijabis Muslim and non-Muslim women, about what they believe the Hijab represents, how they perceive Hijabi and non-Hijabi women, and whether there are any social repercussions, positive or negative, to a women putting it on or taking it off; in essence, the strategic uses of the Hijab to navigate the patriarchal bargain in Egypt. Diwan et al. (2017), who conducted the first empirical investigation of veiling patterns using the Gallop World Poll concluded that:

> It is possible that a woman's appearance may affect the threat of violence – that is, in Muslim majority countries, non-veiled women may be more at risk of assault. Recent survey evidence from Egypt

supports this hypothesis: 99% of women reported having suffered sexual harassment, and 91.5% have experienced unwelcome physical contact; at the same time, 96% of the male respondents attributed harassment to such factors as a woman's provocative clothing, enticing make-up application (95%), and disregard for cultural traditions (also cited by 95%).

The social aspects, such as class and religion, which the data revealed were significant for the ordinary Egyptian's perception of their 'real freedoms', or what Sen (1985a, pp. 3–4; 1985b, p. 201; 1990, p. 75; 2000) described under the capabilities approach as functionings conceived as real opportunities, were also highlighted in Diwan et al.'s (2017) study. Specifically, their study relied on education as an indicator of class, and the veil as an indicator of signalling adherence to the patriarchal bargain which shields women from various forms of violence and allows them to attain a greater degree of security. Similar to the findings of this book, education and paid employment constituted the arenas in which patterns of veiling were investigated in relation to their emancipatory value in making women aware of how to challenge the patriarchal system. With regard to paid employment (Walby, 1990), Diwan et al.'s (2017) study revealed that 'it is only for women with low education levels that veiling is associated with low labour force participation' and that 'women with secondary education who veil have a higher rate of labour force participation than similar women that do not veil' (p. 13).

Furthermore, consistent with the findings of this book, their study concluded that there is evidence between economic opportunities women can pursue and the frequency of veiling, religious belief and access to education for girls and boys, and evidence that the veil is utilised to 'enable their [women's] mobility outside the home, [and] a protective mechanism against the threat of violence' (Diwan et al., 2017, p. 13). Their study further revealed that 'women who have been assaulted tend to veil more. The effect was especially strong in urban areas' (Diwan et al., 2017, p. 9). The study also revealed other components associated with why women choose to wear the Hijab, including a woman's marital status (being married or widowed), age (older women specifically), and having children are all associated with a *higher* likelihood of veiling. Additionally, studies have shown that socio-economic status, i.e.,'being poorer is associated with more veiling, possibly [as] a sort of cache-misère phenomenon'(Diwan, et al., 2017, p.8). Similarly, according to the same study, 'the effect of education is strong', with 'more educated women veiling less, presumably due to the emancipative effects of education' (Diwan et al., 2017, p. 8). Lastly, their study revealed the condition of fear women can experience, motivating them to put on the Hijab, stating:

> The fear and experience of violence in public places was associated with higher rates of veiling, especially in high veiling countries – indicating that the relative rarity of not veiling may mean that such women risk feeling vulnerable. The strong correlation between being married and being veiled was suggestive of the power of husbands to influence their wives' decisions and behaviour. (Diwan et al., 2017, p. 14)

Combining this study's findings with Diwan et al. (2017) serves to reinforce the notion that the women in Egypt are operating within a patriarchal system that institutionalised women's inferiority and second-class citizenship by setting a double-bind patriarchal structure in which women are sanctioned for their non-compliance. The Hijab hereby appears to serve a strategic use by protecting women being subjugated to varying forms of violence. Reflecting on Walby's (1990) *Six Structures of Patriarchy*, we can see how the structure of patriarchy influenced women's attainment of strategic gender interests at the Family/Household Production, Paid Employment, Sexuality, Culture, and Violence levels. The following chapter tackles the eighth research question: what is the role of the Hijab in signalling adherence to the rule of the patriarchal bargain in Egypt?

The chapter is divided into three sections, the first of which aims to contextualise what the Hijab represents for Egyptians today. The second section revisits the notion of how religion was used to rationalise the dehumanisation of women, building on the earlier discussion in Chapter 1. The third section sheds light on new patterns from the data, which appear to confirm the active collusion of women with the patriarchal system. The last section expands on why women might actively collude with the patriarchal system by shedding light on the strategic uses of the Hijab in navigating patriarchal bargains in Egypt.

1. Contextualising the Hijab in Contemporary Egypt: What Does it Represent?

In Middle Eastern and Muslim-dominated countries how one is dressed is not as simple as a fashion statement or an accessory but connotes certain social values and religious obligations observable within this cultural context. The Hijab is representative of being an adherent of the Islamic Faith, the equivalent of which is growing beards in a particular style for men. To many non-Muslims, the Hijab has become a signal of 'oppressed women' who need 'saving' (Abou-Lughod, 2002; Droogsma, 2007, p. 294; Haddad, 2007, p. 261; Zeiger, 2008, p. 278). While some came to believe that the Hijab is only worn by women coerced into putting it on due to their oppressive Muslim environments (Nomani, 2016), Hijabi women argue that they choose to wear it, and that to them it is a tool of empowerment (El Guindi, 1999; Hopkings, 2016; Sloan, 2011; Zubair, 2019). Understanding what the Hijab is and the different manifestations of it throughout history contributes to our understanding of why women may choose to put on/take off their Hijab today. As Hirschmann (1997, p. 468) attested:

> Western attempts to 'liberate' women by removing the veil simply inscribed women's bodies as symbols of culture rather than individual agents; it replaced one form of social control with another. On the other hand, however, it provided women with a method language of resistance and agency; not only by intro Western concepts of individual rights and freedom but demonstrating the frequent inadequacy of these to Eastern cultural contexts. Indeed, although Westerners often men assaulting women who do not veil,

in fact among the first people in contemporary movements to use the veil as a symbol of resistance were Egyptian university women.

Hirschmann (1997) further insisted 'Does this mean that the veil, seen by Westerners as a mark of oppression, is, in fact, a mark of agency? Not quite, for the symbolic value also can be seen to entail the subjugation of women's subjectivity' (p. 468), which concurs with the findings of Chapters 1 and 2 which shed light on how women's inferiority is maintained by way of dehumanisation to deny women any claim over strategic gender interests. The Hijab arguably holds a symbolic utilitarian significance in navigating the system of classic patriarchal structure in Egypt, as opposed to being itself a religious patriarchal practice. This is evidenced by 'over four-fifths of respondents citing this [religiosity] as the reason for veiling in both the high and moderate veiling countries' (Diwan et al., 2017, p. 7) with Egypt being classified as a high veiling country, with 91% share of Muslim women wearing the Hijab (2017, p. 19).

According to the data, the Hijab can represent different things to different people and depending on one's positionality, exposure, and experiences, people attach their own individual meanings to it. One participant, AU1e(3), reflected on her understanding of the Hijab from her perspective as an elder-Hijabi woman, stating:

> It's fashionable to take it off sometimes. Because I'm older I can tell you that the entire female wardrobe in Egypt has had many trends throughout the past 40 years. Also, we were heavily exposed to fashion trends from the West [in the 80s], and we have Instagram and Facebook and so many other windows into the West ... even the way people talk and express themselves has radically changed and has been diluted with this cultural exposure. But most importantly, the liberal tide encouraged many women to take off their Hijab. It also subjugated us to other kinds of pressures, which was a natural outcome of globalisation, and it all started with Sadat [she's referring to the *Infitah,* open door economic policy former president Sadat implemented to re-orient Egypt's alliances to the West as opposed to the East]. Like now, men talk about whether the Hijab is a *Farida* [obligation or religious duty] or not and the religious scholars got involved too which made it even messier. Why can't men just stick to their own genitalia and leave stuff that concerns our bodies and our appearances alone?

As demonstrated in Chapter 2, the *Infitah* policy introduced Western values and mannerisms to Egyptians, which was exploited by the conservative and fundamental opposition, the Muslim Brotherhood, to infiltrate the political sphere claiming the Sadat system is betraying the Arab and Muslim identity. The chapter also highlighted how the Hijab was operationalised to promote the practical presence of women and galvanise the odds in favour of their political ideology. While this participant appeared aware of the political debates around the Hijab and how it was operationalised for political ends, other participants responded with more normative responses to the questions. An elderly female, AR2m(101), shared her story about the Hijab and how she came to wear it at the age of 38 stating:

> When I was younger, I lived with my parents in Saudi Arabia where my father worked as an Arabic teacher and my mom as a Mathematics teacher. As you know in Saudi all women must wear the Hijab and Niqab irrespective of their age or their faith, so even my Christian friends wore it.

Her statement supports the argument posed at the beginning of this chapter of the Hijab being a cultural practice as much as it is an Islamic one. She continued on to elaborate that, in Saudi Arabia, unlike Egypt where religion is taught in one class and the curriculum is 'poorly designed', she received '*Qur'an* [memorising scripture], *Fiqh* [Full Comprehension of Islamic Law], *Tawheed* [Asserting Oneness and the Nature of God], *'Akida* [Doctrine and Faith], and *Tafseer* [Qur'anic Commentary and Interpretations]' modules, and continued to state:

> We got a holistic understanding of what our religion entails, which made us be convinced that the Hijab is our way of protecting our bodies and having our privacy, away from all the fashion pressure of the West.

When asked why upon returning to Egypt she decided to take the Hijab and Niqab off she said:

> it was a mistake, but I wanted to fit in. I had no friends and had attended an all-girls school in Saudi, so coming to a mixed school I just wanted the boys and girls to like me and think I am pretty.

After the interview, she sat down for an informal conversation with the researcher to whom she said:

> Don't let people tell you to wear it. If you want to do it, do it because you're convinced and not because it is what people want. Don't live with regrets and don't let people pressure you. You are beautiful with it and without it.

This interview reinforced the argument that, while it is true that some women are forced to wear the Hijab and while it is indeed sometimes used as a tool for oppression, the consensus in Egypt is that it is an individual choice. Yet what degree of choice is there within a patriarchal system where women cannot actualise their strategic gender interests to challenge their inferiority and second-class status? According to the statements of women, it is their choice, but the secondary data seem to disagree with that. If women cannot realise strategic gender interests (Molyneux, 1985), then they lack the power to challenge their exclusion (Kabeer, 2006). This paradox could be explained if we accept the premise that women in Egypt have internalised their inferiority, then the paradox is justified – women have internalised their inferiority to an extent where they believe their inferiority is a choice – but if we reject it, then we must believe that women have not internalised their inferiority but choose to be inferior. The literature supports the former to be true, particularly as a mechanism of coping with oppression, internalising one's inferiority is a response to the psychological distress of 'learned helplessness, internalisation of hegemonic self-rejection view, and obedience to authority' (Prillentensky & Gonick, 1996, p. 132).

Accordingly, AR2m(101)'s perceived degree of 'choice' was challenged when the researcher asked other women what could motivate any woman to put on the Hijab, to confirm/negate that women in Egypt have internalised their inferiority. For instance, AU1e(3) stated:

> I felt like the Hijab just protected me from a lot of things ... I used to have a lot of issues when I wasn't veiled ... Harassment was just too much. Also, I would style my hair curly and put make-up on and perfume and everything, so my looks were very eye-catching, and I got a lot of unrequited attention from people on the streets. The men would cat call me, and the women would call me a sl*t, especially on public transport. The Hijab decreased these things a lot, so it's a lot better than when I wasn't veiled [nervous laughter]. I was scared to go out on the streets for quite some time, but I mainly put it on because God wants me to.

This sentiment was echoed by many Hijabi women. The Hijab as a clothing item does have protective qualities, in the sense that socially it provides a sense of uniformity for women, making them virtually invisible in the public sphere. This account spiralled a curiosity about why any woman might wish to be invisible, an issue discussed in further detail later on.

In juxtaposition, most women interviewed responded to the question of 'what can motivate a woman to take off her Hijab' in one of two ways: either they stated that she wants to be more attractive and wants more attention from those around her, or that she experienced some traumatic event which forced her to take it off, such as the loss of a parent. The rationality of both did not resonate with the researcher, but it did reveal that there is a dichotomous perception of Hijabi women. Yet, there were others, like AU1l(33), who approached the question with a religious lens, stating 'Just that she has not done what God obliged her to do', and BU2s(28) stating 'it is something that God obliges us to do, hence it is part of that obligation to continue wearing it and not take it off'. These statements highlight a narrative where religious interpretation is accepted without further deliberation by women over their origin or an awareness of the implications of having a male-dominated interpretation of scripture. This comes as a surprise, as Islam does preach critical thinking, deliberating commandments, seeking knowledge, and learning about the world (Qur'an 2:219, 16:12, 22:66–68, 17:14, 96:1–3).[2]

So why do women not question the mandate of the Hijab? One argument could be the lack of adequately developed curricula delivered in formal education institutions in Egypt. As AR2m(101) highlighted, religious studies are not as detailed or developed in Egypt as they are in other countries. Marwan Kamal (2013), Caroline Krafft, (2013), and Louisa Loveluck (2012) argued that this underdevelopment of curricula in Egypt is a deliberate political action to maintain the patriarchal system. Kamel (2013) identified some reasons for this observation, which included crowded classrooms, lack of adequate infrastructure for students to commute to schools, minimal government funding allocated to public schools and curriculum development, *inter alia*. The two most significant reasons they identified were that 'Classes are often based on what the Government decides people need to think, rather than what they should know' and that the mode of instruction is 'fear rather than respect (…) kids are kept in constant fear of being disciplined physically (usually) for not doing work (…) [so] the violent nature promotes violence in the students' lives' (Kamel, 2013). This provides one explanation of how women have internalised their inferiority, and touches upon the findings of Chapter 4 with regard to education and reiterated in Diwan et al.'s (2017) findings. Women's internalised inferiority is thereby a survival strategy: women had to adapt and protect themselves from the sanctions of non-compliance they are socialised at home and in educational settings to believe in (Mahmood, 2011, p. 205).

Another argument for the lack of analytical questioning is that the Egyptian Government

> fears the educated elite (…) [because] educated Egyptians who venture an opinion on the matter [of state-sponsored ignorance] aspire to be citizens of a democratic state—a state built on law, not on fear. But fear is already a part of modern law [in Egypt]. (Asad, 2012, p. 272)

The purpose of this discussion is to understand why Egyptian women do not question the rationality behind the Hijab. The evidence suggests that the way women are socialised – to be submissive, docile, obedient – coupled with society

---

[2]Qur'an 2:219 'They ask you about intoxicants and gambling. Say, 'There is gross sin in them, and some benefits for people, but their sinfulness outweighs their benefit'. And they ask you about what they should give: say, 'The sur- plus'. Thus, Allah explains the revelations to you, **so that you may think**'.Qur'an 16:12 'He regulated for you the night and the day; and the sun, and the moon, and the stars are disposed by His command. Surely in that are signs **for people who ponder**'.Qur'an 22:66-68 'My Verses were recited to you, but you turned back on your heels (66). Arrogant towards it – talked nonsense about it – disregarded it (67). **Have they not pondered the Word?** (68)'.Qur'an 17:14 '**Read** your book; today [day of judgement] there will be none but yourself to call you to account'.Qur'an 96:1-3 '**Read**: In the Name of your Lord who created (1). Created man from a clot (2). **Read**: And your Lord is the Most Generous (3)'.

favouring boys' education over girls' is the reason behind why some women do not question religious mandates or deliberately challenge the patriarchal structures set by their fathers, husbands, brothers, and in some instances, even sons. Some individuals assume that educating a girl is futile because 'she will eventually get married and have children' (Haddad, 1982, p. 56) and serve her primary role as a homemaker (Walby, 1990, p. 87) and thus will have a husband to do the thinking and deliberating for her.

Moreover, the argument that women are intentionally deterred from critical deliberation and analytical thinking is supported by the fact that, in Egypt's patriarchal society, women are regarded as some form of property (Kapoor, 2000; Moghadam, 1993; Nawar et al., 1995). The honour of their families depends on their 'biological and social hymens' (Abu-Odeh, 1996), that is, her virginity (Hirschon, 1984; Kandiyoti, 1988; Patai, 1967; Pitt-Rivers, 1977; Rubin, 1975; Tilhon, 1983; Wood, 1988). Simultaneously, a man's honour is perceived to come from a woman's obedience (Abu-Lughod, 1986). That argument is already established in Chapters 1, 2, and 3. A woman's obedience is believed to be one of the main inhibitors of her mobility and freedom, as the notion of *Ta'ah* (obedience) of wives (Fluehr-Loban & Sirios, 1990) is communally perceived to be religiously mandated. However, research shows that *Ta'ah* is in fact a socially constructed notion which has no religious foundation in Sunnah or in the Qur'an (Lane & Meleis, 1991). Yet, in the Egyptian Personal Status Law women can be sentenced by the court to *Beit Al Ta'ah* (the House of Obedience) – Law No. 25 of 1929 and Law No. 100 of 1985 – if her husband appeals the Family Court, solidifying her commodification and codifying her inferiority to her male counterpart. When and if the court accepts the appeal 'the police would arrest the woman wherever they found her – on the street, "n her parents" home – and hand her back to the aggrieved husband' and by law a husband is allowed to 'keep her locked in her room, as in a prison' (Time, 1960).

Under these laws, women are obliged to be obedient, and cannot leave the *Beit Al Ta'ah* until their husbands are satisfied. One woman recalled her experience stating, 'As I entered my husband's House of Obedience, he began to take revenge. He used to order me to stand naked most of the night and beat me' (Time, 1960). When interviewed by Human Rights Watch (HRW, 2004), a man who filed a *Ta'ah* case against his wife because she objected to him moving his second wife into her home with her children said, 'I do it [file an obedience complaint] to disgust her and wear her down'. The law states that in exchange for a man financially providing for his wife, she 'owes him' her obedience. This specific law is based on an interpretation of verse 3:34 in the Qur'an,[3] yet there is no mention in the Qur'an of allowing a husband to put his wife in a *Beit Al Ta'ah*, nor is

---

[3]'Men are in charge of women by [right of] what Allah has given one over the other and what they spend [for maintenance] from their wealth. So righteous women are devoutly obedient, guarding in [the husband's] absence what Allah would have them guard. But those [wives] from whom you fear arrogance – [first] advise them; [then if they persist], forsake them in bed; and [finally], strike them. But if they obey you [once more], seek no means against them. Indeed, Allah is ever Exalted and Grand' (Qur'an 3:34).

there an insinuation that a man is allowed to maltreat his wife until he is satisfied. This Qur'anic verse was therefore taken out of context and interpreted in a manner which serves the social hegemonic bloc and solidifies the social discourse of women being inferior to men. Furthermore, the elasticity of the legal framework and the absence of laws and regulations to protect women against domestic abuse has allowed some men to exploit the *Beit Al Ta'ah* as a loophole to avoid the payment of alimony during divorce procedures, because if a 'wife leaves her house [of obedience] without her husband's permission, she is considered disobedient and therefore must forfeit alimony upon divorce' (Susilastuti, 2003, p. 30).

Moreover, a pattern among the women interviewed was detected, where almost 80% of women believe that if a woman takes her Hijab off it is because she is trying to be more attractive. Rarely did the interviews lead to a critical evaluation of why women wear the Hijab. For instance, AR3u(3) operated under the impression that a woman's decision to take off the Hijab is related to her desire to be more attractive to her male counterpart, stating, 'Maybe she got engaged to a guy and she thinks taking it off will grab his attention'. Similarly, AU2s(36) said 'because she wants to wear tight clothes and show off her face ... she just wants to show off her whole body. So, when she finds a chance to take it off, she does'. Both statements reveal a social discourse where a woman's individual decisions over what to do with their own body are conditional on how men will perceive them, thereby covertly negating that a woman's actions could be reflective of subjective desires. Further supporting this notion, one man, CU1l(1), went so far as to state:

> Women in Egypt only put on the Hijab and take it off if it was forced on them at an earlier age or if they want to look like their friends, which transforms it to a fashion statement ... it's driven by something else that might be a fashion statement, or to signal modesty to a potential suitor.

CU1l(1) highlights the extent to which women are perceived to lack the 'capacity for cognitive freedom, and [therefore] denied secondary psychological processes' and agency (Markcitz & Slovic, 2020, p. 261). It is very important to note that not all women in Egypt wear the Hijab to avoid any particular social situation, even though, as shall be demonstrated in upcoming sections, many have cited protection as a motive for covering and veiling, that is, where veiling connotes the literal definition of the term: hiding. Some, like BI1s(27), held a different perspective on the matter. She attempted to holistically state the motives of women who wear the Hijab, saying:

> I think a big part of it is culture and not religion. Most of the people I know who wear the Hijab were motivated by society. Either they wanted to please their conservative parents, or to avoid being harassed, or her husband wanted her to. There is this belief that a good woman wears the Hijab. I know women who put on the Hijab while they don't pray because there was this Amr Khalid phase [Muslim televangelist] where everyone was just doing it.

Numerous participants cited Amr Khaled as the reason why they decided to put on their veil. As elaborated earlier, Egyptians can present as a contradictory people. Bayat (2002, p. 23) summarised why Amr Khaled was influential to Egyptian youth, stating:

> It is resonant of their aversion to patronising pedagogy and moral authority. This globalising youth display many seemingly contradictory orientations. They are religious believers, but distrust political Islam if they know anything about it; they swing back and forth from Amr Diab [pop singer] to Amr Khalid [preacher], from partying to prayers, and yet they feel the burden of the strong social control of their elders, teachers, and neighbours. As the Egyptian youth are socialised in a cultural condition and educational tradition which often restrain individuality and novelty, they are compelled to assert them in a 'social way', through fashion.

The next section unpacks the *Amr Khaled Phenomena* by expanding on how the televangelist is a state-sponsored promoter of conservative and traditional understandings of Islam. The section investigates how Amr Khaled was operationalised to reinforce women's inferiority and legitimise their lack of strategic gender interests, needed to challenge their exclusion from full citizenship benefits, by rebranding political Islam to target the growing globalised youth in Egypt, particularly since the early 2000s. Specifically, the next section builds on the discussion of Chapter 1, using primary sources to validate whether the secondary research findings – to justify women's secondary status political Islam was used to rationalise and normalise women's subordination – are still relevant to the Egyptian context today.

2. Rationalising the Dehumanisation of Women Using Religion in Contemporary Egypt

By 2011, attitudes towards the Hijab had changed, and the more conservative and traditional meanings associated with it were prevalent in the society. According to the data, the Hijab in Egypt symbolically distinguishes between which women are pious/impious, ergo it can be used as an instrument to measure which women are adhering to the rules of the patriarchal system, and which should be sanctioned for their non-compliance. Survey data from the Arab Barometer corroborated this, particularly the data on how participants rate their (dis)agreement with the statement: 'Women should wear modest clothes without needing to wear Hijab'. Figs. 6, 7, and 8 are the results from 2011, 2013, and 2018 surveys, which show a steady decline in public agreement with that statement, revealing a resurgence of a more conservative and traditional attitudes.

This had detrimental effects on women, as it further reinforced women's inferiority by rebranding political Islam to fit Egypt's youth, thereby actively maintaining the patriarchal system. This was particularly highlighted in the amount of state-sponsored violence targeting women during and after the 25th

162   Recovering Women's Voices

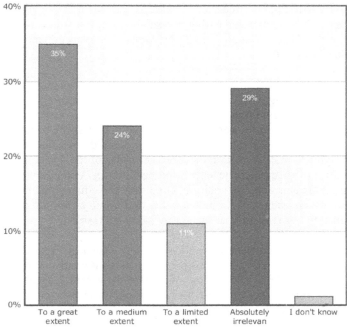

Fig. 6.   AB Wave II, 2011, Survey Results for "To what extent do you think wearing a hijab is a criterion for an individual's piety?"

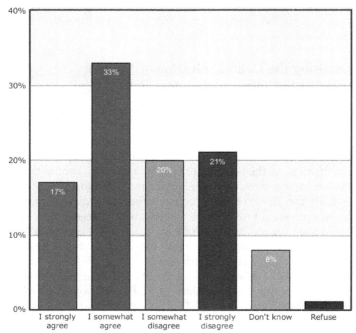

Fig. 7.   AB Wave II, 2013, Survey Results for "Women should wear modest clothes without needing to wear hijab"

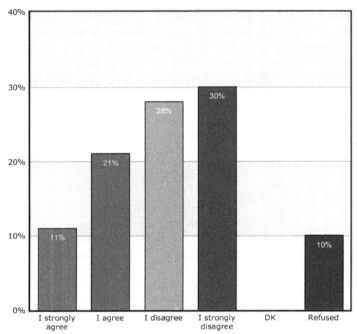

Fig. 8. AB Wave V, 2018, Survey Results for "A woman should dress modestly, but need not wear a hijab"

January revolution, in 2011. Dyer (2014) reported on the repercussions of state-commissioned political Islam and the damaging effects it had on the status of Egyptian women, which in effect nullified the efforts exerted over the years to attain women's strategic gender interests, stating:

> Under President Mohamed Morsi, the Shura Council, Egypt's upper house of parliament, even pushed for the convictions of victims of sexual assault. Last summer [2013], weeks before the military ouster of Morsi, the FJP's Shura Council human rights representative, Reda el-Hefnawy, insisted to me that there are 'so many reasons' why harassment remains the woman's fault. He said that if women choose to stand among men at the protests and fail to cover themselves up, sexual harassment is not only inevitable – it is their responsibility.

In another article, Emily Dyer (2013) reported on the numerous problematic actions taken by the Morsi regime following the 25th January revolution, in 2011, spanning from how Morsi's administration reduced women's political roles to administrative and support staff to how Morsi's administration 'pushed for the victims of sexual assaults during protests to be convicted' (Dyer, 2013, p. 31). A notable revelation from Dyer's (2013) article was regarding how Morsi's regime and political party, The Freedom and Justice Party, created a 'culture of acceptability surrounding sexual violence against women … in creating a blame culture against female victims of sexual harassment in both public and private spaces' (p. 9). Dyer (2013) further elaborated that the Morsi administration propagated women's sexuality as 'the main source of chaos, and a threat to its [the regime's] survival at a time of civil unrest and political instability' (p. 28). Morsi's administration accomplished that by introducing sexually segregated public spaces, legitimised harmful practices such as FGM, and curtailed efforts by various political and social organisations to reform harassment and assault laws (Dyer, 2013, p. 28). According to Dyer's findings, this led to an increase in reports of rape from 119 in 2011 to 129 in 2012, and reports of indecent assault have increased from 330 in 2011 to 349 in 2012. According to an interview Dyer (2013) conducted with Dr Nawla Darwiche, Director of the New Woman Foundation, assault cases are under-reported in Egypt as 'most people won't come out and say it happened because culturally it is not accepted' (p. 29).

With an increasingly unsafe environment in Egypt, more women starting conforming to the patriarchal rules to gain a greater degree of safety, such as dressing more conservatively and avoiding public spaces where women and men coexist. Moreover, Dyer's article sheds light on why an increasingly conservative attitude towards the Hijab and dress style was observed in the Arab Barometer data between 2011 and 2019. It further supports the presence of a double-bind Egyptian women are subjugated to by virtue of the increasingly aggressive patriarchal structures in Egypt. This also suggests the institutionalisation of patriarchal structures at the State level where 'men are able to utilise considerable amounts of violence against women with impunity' (Walby, 1990, p. 150). Noting Walby's findings, it becomes clearer that in the 25th January revolution, in 2011, women were 'not passive victims of oppressive structures. They have struggled to change both their immediate circumstances and the wider social structure'. However, their efforts to have a strategic presence in the public sphere and use the opportunity to advance their strategic gender interests were quickly extinguished by the political apparatus, which one can only assume was with the objective of maintaining the social status quo and restore political stability. During the collection of data, it became apparent that some women exacerbated the situation by colluding with the patriarchal system against their own strategic gender interests. The next section explores this dimension, to understand what could possibly lead a woman to stand against her own emancipation. A possible explanation would be that of Kabeer (2006), who attributes women's active collusion to their lack of agency. Similarly, Walby (1990) attributes the collusion to the successful interaction of the *Six Structures of Patriarchy*, which are designed to reproduce and perpetuate men's domination and women's subordination.

3. Women's Active Collusion in the Reproduction of Their Own Subordination

In 2008, amidst a period marked by social turmoil and a public outcry against the pervasive issue of sexual harassment in Egypt, a provocative image began to circulate widely across the internet and social media platforms. This image presented a stark visual analogy involving two lollipops: one covered and the other uncovered. The covered lollipop was labelled 'with the hijab', appearing neat, untouched by flies, and seemingly desirable. In contrast, the uncovered lollipop bore the caption 'without the hijab' and was depicted as surrounded by flies, appearing unappealing and tarnished. Accompanying this striking visual metaphor was a caption that read, 'You cannot avoid them, but God gave you the way to protect yourself from them'. This image ignited considerable debate and discussion, serving as a focal point for broader conversations about women's autonomy, the role of the hijab, and societal attitudes towards sexual harassment in Egypt.

As the image gained traction, discussions predominantly centred on its suggestion that women should adopt the hijab as a means of protecting themselves from sexual harassment, sparking widespread controversy over its implications. This narrative, deeply ingrained within the imagery, was criticised for perpetuating a problematic view of women's bodies as objects needing concealment to avoid unwanted attention. Yet, amidst the heated debates, a critical aspect of the analogy went largely unexamined – the depiction of men as flies. This comparison not only reduces men to base, instinct-driven creatures but also overlooks the broader societal and behavioural issues at play. By focussing solely on women's attire as a preventive measure against harassment, the dialogue neglected the need for a more profound examination of gender relations, respect, and the essential respect for personal boundaries and autonomy. This oversight highlighted a missed opportunity to address the root causes of sexual harassment and challenge the societal norms that enable such behaviour, instead of superficially attributing it to how women choose to dress.

It is widely accepted today that these depictions were inspired by the Egyptian-born cleric Shaikh Taj Aldin al-Hilali, who in 2006 said:

> If you take out uncovered meat and place it outside... without cover, and the cats come to eat it ... whose fault is it, the cats' or the uncovered meat's? The uncovered meat is the problem. If she was in her room, in her home, in her Hijab [the headdress worn by some Muslim women], no problem would have occurred. (Tran, 2006)

The influence of these images still reverberates today. For this book, 25% of participants cited the unwrapped lollipop to answer what they believe the Hijab represents and what can motivate women to put it on or take it off. As BU2s(23) stated:

> People here believe that [taking off the Hijab] is a gateway to destruction or that she has already been corrupted. There is this song by a local band called Cairokee where the lead singer says, 'a cigarette led to a joint, and a joint led to a pill, and the pill led to sex' and that's how it's seen here. If she took off that piece of cloth, then it's a slippery slope; bugs will flock to her and ruin her and she will no longer be the innocent unwrapped piece of candy. I was told this line when I took my Hijab off by so many people.

While less than 5% of participants stated that a woman's decision to take off/put on her Hijab is hers alone, like CR3c(11) who argued:

> If I wanted my girl to put on the Hijab, I would tell her that she's not wearing it for anyone but she's wearing it to follow the words of God. And if she tells me that she can't follow the word of God on this matter, then in this case all I have to say is that Hijab is a *Farida*. I would explain to her that there is action and there is subject: the action, in this case, is wearing the Hijab and the subject is in the hands of God, so if she wants God's mercy bestowed upon her, she should put it on.

However, the reality is that most women interviewed had other motives besides pleasing God in mind, namely protection from male violence (Diwan et al., 2017; El Feki et al., 2017). Protection for an Egyptian woman comes in a myriad of forms and signifies the patriarchal exchange Egyptian women are forced into; women need protection from social pressure, public humiliation, harassment and assault, and from their families and spouses, among many other things, but in exchange for protection and security they have to accept their subordination in the private sphere and exclusion from the public sphere. Hijabi women that were interviewed predominantly provided a paraphrased version of AR3p(70)'s statement, who said, 'When I was 8 years old it was not my choice, as my father forced me to put it on'. Similarly, AR3u(40) said 'I wore the veil in Middle School. My teacher just came in and distributed a white cloth to everyone and told us that we must wear it'. This phenomenon did not only occur in rural areas in Egypt but in urban ones too, as AU2a(64) shed light on the matter stating,

> When I was 12 years old, I put the Hijab on. My mother is a Niqabi woman, and all her family is like that. I grew up seeing all the women dressed like that, so I dressed like that too.

The fact that the immediate surroundings affect the personal choices of women was echoed by most participants. As CR3s(58) elaborated, social pressure is very powerful in Egypt,

> We are Muslims, and the Hijab is a *Farida* in Islam. This is how the culture is, so she has no option. It is also an obligation from society, it is not her choice. But my sister doesn't mind it.

While many female participants were more diplomatic in their answers, which may be due to the researcher being a Muslim non-Hijabi woman herself, a minority of women judged the non-Hijabis and those who reject the Hijab the harshest. Agreeing with this notion that it is sacrilegious to take off the Hijab 45% of men, who like CU2s(38), believe:

> Her friends [motivate her to take it off]. I'm not saying that they will influence her but seeing one of her girlfriends not wearing the

Hijab and looking beautiful could motivate a girl to take it off. Girls are jealous of one another, it's just their nature.

He continued to proudly state that he is exclusively attracted to Hijabi women and how his comments to a female friend about how ugly she looked after taking off her Hijab ultimately motivated her to put it back on. However, other men, such as CU3e(4) shed light on the heart of the controversy, stating:

> Unfortunately, there's some kind of discrimination, the woman with the Hijab thinks she's religiously at a higher level or is better morally than the non-Hijabi women, which I think is incorrect because we don't know whom God sees as better.

Yet, after some further discussion and when the researcher asked a direct personal question pertaining to the participant's wife, the tone and answers were different. Later in the interview, he said:

> When you're married to a man and not a *Khawal* [derogatory term used to refer to effeminate males and is derived from the practice of cross-dressing dancers popular in Egypt until the late 18th century] you have to listen to my opinion on everything. It ended up that she told me that I was very controlling, but I thought there should be restrictions for her because we're married, and I have the right to tell her how she should dress. After all, she is my wife and my honour.

This entitlement was even taken a step further by one participant, CU11(1), who said that if a woman takes off her Hijab, then she will inevitably be 'perceived as promiscuous' and is, therefore 'fair game'. He rationalised this by saying that if she took her Hijab off it is a signal that she wants to be looked at and approached by men, justifying sexual harassment and placing blame on the victims of harassment in the public sphere. These accounts shed light on the social understanding of Walby's concept of Culture, specifically the heterosocial hegemonic masculinity dynamic Bird (1997) shed light on, and suggests that her observation that naturalisation ideology would be a 'dissimulative approach which denies the extent of the inequality' (Walby, 1990, p. 109) in areas of classic patriarchy are true.

So why is it that men feel entitled to force their opinions onto their respective counterparts? The answer is twofold: first, gendered relations established in the private sphere have perpetuated and reproduced male-domination of the public sphere, that is, 'range of different symbolic activities, including the style of dress, patterns of consumption, ways of moving, as well as talking' are barriers to entry within the patriarchal structure (Edley, 2001, p. 191). Discourse 'refers to how knowledge, subjects, behaviours, and events are depicted and defined in statements, assumptions, concepts, themes, and shared ideas (…) a framework through which we see the world' (Braham, 2012, p. 58). Broadly, gender discourses are constructed and reproduced through the different social cues people observe and are exposed to, and by extension, the symbolic meaning behind them is altered; here the gender discourse is that a 'good' woman does not talk back and is obedient to her husband and father. This confirms the success the patriarchal system had in institutionalising women's inferiority and rationalising their *less than human* status using religion, and the role the gender discourse played in normalising male violence against women.

Second, reminiscent of the findings in Chapter 2, the majority of female participants expressed that it is a man's God-given right to dictate what women in his household wear, how they carry themselves, and sometimes even how they talk, as they are 'within his guardianship'. This 'guardianship' is a specific interpretation of the Qur'anic verse:

> Men are in charge of women by [right of] what Allah has given one over the other and what they spend [for maintenance] from their wealth. So righteous women are devoutly obedient, guarding in [the husband's] absence what Allah would have them guard. But those [wives] from whom you fear arrogance – [first] advise them; [then if they persist], forsake them in bed; and [finally], strike them. But if they obey you [once more], seek no means against them. Indeed, Allah is ever Exalted and Grand. (Qur'an 3:34)

To understand the extent to which this verse is culturally embedded and perpetuated, one needs to read about the repercussions of people who opposed this statement, that is, what would happen if a woman challenged the patriarchal system. A study conducted by UN Women in 2017 in which 87% of Egyptian men reported a woman's basic role is to be a housewife, 90% reported that a man should have the final word about decisions at home, 90% reported a woman should tolerate domestic violence for the sake of the family, 80% reported that boys (meaning boys <16) are responsible for the behaviours of their sisters, even if he is younger than them, and 78% reported that it is a man's duty to exercise guardianship and conservatorship (El Feki et al., 2017, p. 47). These statistics reveal the attitudes of Egyptians towards women, where on the one hand the propagated religious interpretation of the Qur'an embedded patriarchal gender norms, and on the other hand instilled the superiority-inferiority complex which is reflected in the primary testimonies. They further shed light on the role and magnitude of religion in attributing meaning and values to Egyptian society. This reveals that governing women's bodies appears to be integral to the survival of the status quo, which favours males and the patriarchal system.

The resurgence of politicised Islam, however, brought about more harm to women's movements and added further restrictions to women's social mobility, and agency. As stated above, most of the women interviewed agreed on one thing: a woman needs protection. To protect themselves from harassment, judgement, and social repercussions which are themselves politicised, Egyptian women had no option but to collude with the patriarchal system. The cost of noncompliance is set so high, that it may even be perceived as social suicide if a woman chooses to defy, resulting in the entire public sphere being a 'new form of trap' for women (Walby, 1990, p. 201). This confirms that, in patriarchal systems, women will adhere to the patriarchal bargain for 'as far and as long as they can' (Kandiyoti, 2006, p. 100) to ensure their basic right to security from male violence, that is, their practical needs are met. It is therefore not surprising that most Egyptian women would actively collude with the patriarchal system and reproduce the norm that the public sphere is not a woman's 'place'. The next section tackles the eighth research question: what is the role of the Hijab in signalling adherence to the rules of the patriarchal system?

4. Navigating Patriarchal Bargains: The Strategic Use of the Hijab in Urban/Rural Areas

The notion of modesty is culturally and historically contestable. For some African nations, it was argued that the notion of modesty was externally imposed by colonial cultural exportation and Christian missionary ambitions (Corrigan, 1988; Janz, 2018; Ruark, 2001) – by statements such as 'Let chaste and modest virgins shun the attire of the unchaste, the clothing of the immodest, the insignia of brothels, the adornment of harlots' and 'showy adornments and clothing and the allurement of beauty are not becoming in any except prostitutes and shameless women' (Cyprian cited in Corrigan, 1988, p. 5). This is not the case for the Egyptian society, however. For Egyptians, speculatively, although notions of modesty were marginally influenced by external forces, they are rather the result of male-dominated interpretations of Islam, which were later normalised through naturalisation theory and solidified through repeated cultural practice. Particularly, the following verse from the Qur'an:

> And tell the believing women to lower their gaze and guard their chastity, and not to reveal their adornments[1] except what normally appears. Let them draw their veils over their chests, and not reveal their hidden adornments except to their husbands, their fathers, their fathers-in-law, their sons, their stepsons, their brothers, their brothers' sons or sisters' sons, their fellow women, those bondwomen in their possession, male attendants with no desire, or children who are still unaware of women's nakedness. Let them not stomp their feet, drawing attention to their hidden adornments. Turn to Allah in repentance all together, O believers, so that you may be successful. (Qur'an, 24:31)

This verse is often used in reference to how 'modest' a Muslim woman needs to be. While there is no explicit mention of the private or the public sphere in this verse, Islamic jurists interpreted this as proof that a woman's 'place' in Muslim society is within the private sphere, particularly because a man's modesty is never mentioned, thus assumed to be the public sphere. The pre-identified proxy of the Hijab, allowed for the collection of data about the consequences of the claims set forward by the male-interpretation of Islam. Specifically, as the data highlighted the Hijab is symbolically relevant to signal adherence to the patriarchal structure, the researcher asked ordinary Egyptian citizens to reflect on what might influence a woman's decision to put on/take off the Hijab. It additionally holds and perpetuates a myriad of socio-cultural and political issues, including but not limited to, Hijabi women being perceived as more pious and modest and thus are granted 'more respect' in public spaces, while non-Hijabi women are perceived as 'westernised' and 'loose' (Gokariksel et al., 2009, 2012; Mahmoud, 2005; Moor, 2010). Another issue highlighted by using the Hijab as a criteria to measure public perception and women's status in the society, was public attention to harassment and assault. Hijabi women are less scrutinised when they call out predators and perpetrators in public as compared to non-Hijabi women who are perceived less like victims of predatory actions and more as 'asking for it' (Akkoc, 2004; Cinar, 2008), that is, they deserve to be sanctioned for their non-compliance to the rules set by the patriarchal system. In particular, non-Hijabi women are less likely to receive support in public spaces in assault and harassment instances (Yeğenoğlu, 2003). This was supported by the field work conducted, where the researcher was told that pretending to be a Hijabi woman would make her 'less visible' and 'less of a target' for public humiliation and shaming, particularly in non-urban areas. In this section, this ideas of 'does the Hijab protect women' and of 'invisibility' are examined as conditions imposed by the patriarchal system which require women to bargain with patriarchy. Specifically, the section sheds light on the idea that women's adherence to the patriarchal system does not necessarily mean that men will uphold their end of the patriarchal bargain.

First, the belief that the Hijab protects women was evidenced by the language used to attribute significance to it. However, as depicted below, we can see that the notion of *protection* is dependent on location and social class; in some lower income and rural locations in Egypt the Hijab does possess protective qualities, as it conforms with the cultural norm of said class and location, yet most women negated the notion that the Hijab protects a woman from harassment. Perspectives with regard to whether the Hijab possesses protective qualities or not varied across class, location and level of education. For instance, an urban, middle-class professor of sociology at a higher education institution in Egypt, a non-Hijabi woman, AU2a(20) said:

> I assigned an article to my students that stated that an increased number of women would wear حجاب (Hijab) because it was a public protection in the 80s until the late 2000s. People would look at her differently in the public space; they would look at her with respect. However, now it is different because you can be veiled and still be sexually harassed.

AU2a(20)'s statement reveals the significance of the Hijab to signal social conformity, employed by women to gain greater protection from male violence in the public sphere. Additionally, AU2a(20)'s assertion as a sociologist supports the argument that women use the Hijab strategically to bargain with patriarchy. According to Walby (1990), the patriarchal structures of Culture, Sexuality, the State, and Violence could be mutually inclusive and informative. On the one hand, the fact that a university professor assigns articles about the supposed protective qualities of the Hijab to disenchant students and enlighten them about the reality of the patriarchal system in Egypt stresses the binary understanding of women's rights and status in society. Understanding this, the patriarchal structure of Sexuality informs and perpetuates the Culture by placing the responsibility of avoiding male violence in the public sphere onto women, to signal that men who perpetrate violence do not and could not 'control' their urges and it is up for the woman to control their own behaviour if they wish to avoid violence. Simultaneously, the patriarchal structure of the State confirms men's inability to control their urges by allowing men to operate with almost complete impunity when perpetrating violence against women in the public sphere. This additionally reiterates the argument that while laws may exist in Egypt to protect women against male violence, if the patriarchal structure of Culture reproduces the cultural norm that men cannot control themselves and women ought to adhere to the patriarchal bargain to enter the public sphere with a relative degree of security and safety, then it is unsurprising that said laws are not adequately enforced nor comprehensively structured. Finally, as AU2a(20) is a professor of sociology at a private higher education institution in Egypt, the articles she assigns to her students are accessible to members of the society that belong to the upper-middle and upper classes of society, almost exclusively. While the upper-middle and upper classes in Egypt only make up less than 2% of Egyptian society, the knowledge that the Hijab may or may not possess protective qualities is moot, specifically as women from these socio-economic classes already possess a higher degree of protection within the social hierarchy than most women in Egyptian society. This argument is supported by Diwan et al.'s (2017) findings that patterns of veiling decrease in Egypt among women of higher socio-economic status because they do not require the same level of protection from male violence in public spaces as women of lower socio-economic status.

Confirming this observation was, an urban, upper-class, privately employed, Hijabi woman, BU1p(25) who stated:

> Not necessarily. It just protects them from daily harassment and any unnecessary comments. Those girls live in communities that are closely packed. It protects them from the daily commentary. However, it will not protect them from the ones who want to deliberately harass her. However, it will lend the image that she is a good girl, so they have to respect her. This is an idea that is imprinted in guys' minds. It does offer some sort of protection, but not a shield.

BU1p(25)'s word choice of 'protects them' and 'those girls' may have been an unconscious cognitive bias where she engaged in Othering of women from different socio-economic classes and areas in Egypt. Despite the participant being a Hijabi woman herself, her statement could be an expression of a subconscious dissonance where she is attempting to protect herself from being perceived as a victim of male violence in public spaces. Nonetheless, if we accept Kandiyoti's (1988, p. 289) assertion that women could actively collude with the patriarchal system, knowingly or unknowingly, then BU1p(25)'s statement could be interpreted as passive tolerance of the violations of women's rights the patriarchal system allows for. Furthermore, the insinuation that women of lower socio-economic classes are deluded into believing the Hijab possesses protective qualities is in fact not challenging the patriarchal system but challenging the intelligence of

172 Recovering Women's Voices

women from different classes and areas. This insinuation bears the consequence of perpetuating the patriarchal belief that some women lack the secondary cognitive faculties to recognise injustice and reproduces the Cultural structure of women's safety being the responsibility of women. This in turn normalises the idea that men are not in control of their urges and places the blame for women's subjugation onto women. Diffendal (2006, p. 130) argued that 'because Muslim cultures uphold modesty and obedience as the highest virtues of womanhood, women will inevitably desire to embody these ideals to achieve status and respect', which in turn 'demonstrates how the political origins of the veil have been displaced'. Coupled with the States' inability to enforce laws which ought to protect women from male violence, BU1p(25)'s statement is not only apathetic but also complicit in the continuation and maintenance of gender hierarchies in Egypt.

Contradicting this observation was an urban, middle-class university student at a higher education institution in Egypt, non-Hijabi woman, AU2s(8) said:

> The idea of the حجاب (Hijab) is not just to put a veil on your head and walk with it, you can protect yourself even if you don't have your hair covered, and you can wear wide clothes that cover your body but the idea that people wear the حجاب (Hijab) to protect themselves is unreasonable, I think that even women, who wear the 'niqab' get harassed.

Agreeing with AU2s(8) on the Hijab not possessing protective qualities, was an urban, working-class, student at a higher education institution in Egypt, Hijabi woman, BU3s(52) who stated:

> For some people, it could. I actually wore the veil for two months. I was living in a society where showing hair was something unacceptable and means the girl is not well-behaved. Because of that, you face harassment and bullying. I had to be in the same chain so I would not suffer from harassment. I was not convinced with the Hijab at all.

The statements reveal that a dichotomous narrative with regard to the Hijab's protective qualities exists in Egypt. The extent to which these dichotomies relate to a person's socio-economic status, educational level, and location in Egypt is evidenced in Diwan et al.'s (2006, 2017) articles, in which the authors' quantitative survey data revealed a positive correlation between the three variables of class, education and location. Additionally, the statements by AU2s(8) and BU3s(52) reiterate Diffendal's (2006, p. 130) observation that 'the veil can facilitate women's assertion of independence, but this assertion nonetheless occurs on male-defined terms and within male-oriented contexts', making the Hijab a tool of both oppression and agency. However, the statements of both women, to an extent, challenge the zero-sum game, or double bind, women are faced with; either complying with the patriarchal system or challenging it but also lose the right to object. Hirschmann (1997, p. 477) stated the patriarchal structures in Eastern societies 'redefines coercion as freedom and choice thereby denying individuals to see the control they are subject to, and making them instruments of their own oppression', which is concurrent with Kandiyoti's (1988) assertion. However, AU2s(8) and BU2s(52)'s statements contradict Hirschmann and Kandiyoti's observations, revealing that while some women may be complicit in the reproduction of the patriarchal system, the statement cannot be generalised and one must recognise that some women do desire to challenge the patriarchal norms and system but might lack the capabilities to actualise their 'real freedoms' (Sen, 2006). Therefore, for women to be able to challenge the patriarchal structure they must first recognise that patriarchal structures 'operate through the rules, norms and practices of different institutions to determine the resources, agency and achievement possibilities available to different groups of individuals in a society' (Kabeer, 2001, p. 26). Both women seem to have recognised the practices and norms which determine the possibilities available to them, yet are limited by the patriarchal structure which penalises noncompliance. One could argue that the cost of non-compliance, that is, harassment and the subjugation to male violence, is deliberately ignored by the patriarchal structures of the State, and perpetuated by the patriarchal structure of Culture, which normalises male violence and impunity in the public sphere. The cost of noncompliance is higher than the cost of compliance, that is, wearing the Hijab, which in turn makes compliance a rational choice.

Confirming the interpretation that compliance appears to be a logical choice was an indigenous, upper-class, student and Hijabi woman, BI1s(27) who defended the position that the Hijab does possess protective qualities for women, stating:

> Definitely! It was seen before as a way to liberate women, as it is a barrier between them and the outside world. They can be themselves without being noticed; it can make them blend with society even more. Some may think of it as a form of liberation and not something that oppresses them.

Contradicting the assertion made by BI1s(27) was an indigenous, middle-class, private-sector employee, Hijabi woman, BI2p(83) who answered:

> No, as men in Egypt have no manners. Even some women would harass women in the street [used by BI2p(82) in reference to the moral deterioration in Egypt]. Some men in Egypt see women as objects without a mind and soul.

While these statements may seem contradictory they are in fact similar. Where BI2s(27) believes that the Hijab creates a 'barrier between them and the outside world', BI2p(82) references the objectification and dehumanisation of women as the reason for the necessity of gender segregation in public spaces to shield women from victimisation and subjugation. This is particularly interesting, as both statements are from indigenous women in Siwa, who enjoy relatively more freedoms and a higher status in the community compared to urban and rural women (see Chapter 7). However, it is worth noting that public spaces in Siwa are divided into female and male spaces, which all indigenous women interviewed described as 'good'. All indigenous persons interviewed for this book referenced the researcher's location, Cairo, when discussing any issue, as if to make a clear distinction between urban women and indigenous women.

Moreover, messages of cultural superiority were sometimes conveyed in the way indigenous participants addressed the researcher, and evidenced by the need to draw a distinction between the cultural understandings and belief systems; urban and rural areas in Egypt often adhere to the Sunni interpretation of the Qur'an which is interpreted by predominantly male religious scholars, while the indigenous community of Siwa adheres to the Sufi interpretation of the Qur'an which is interpreted by both male and female religious scholars. The significance of which scholars were included in the construction of the Sufi and Sunni interpretation is investigated in Chapter 6. Back to the argument, women in Siwa who wish to receive higher education need to relocate to the closest city with a higher education institution, which for most persons interviewed, is Marsa Matrouh (400 km away from Siwa). As an urban city, Marsa Matrouh's culture is almost identical to that of Cairo, that is, women and men share public spaces, patterns of veiling are lower, and levels of harassment are higher. As is demonstrated in Chapter 6, the indigenous community of Siwa is protected under special group rights. Siwians abide by a different legal framework that based is on the Amazigh traditions and the Sufi interpretation of the Qur'an, known as *Orff Laws*. Siwa's legal framework severely punishes harassment and most forms of violence against women in public and private spheres, making Siwa the location with the lowest reported cases of male violence.

BI2s(27) and BI2p(8)'s statements could be interpreted as an expression of cultural shock, where their experiences as women in urban areas were the opposite of what they consider to be 'normal' behaviour in public spaces. Their accounts, one could argue, are therefore skewed by their understanding of appropriate behaviours, making them romanticise the culture of Siwa. These statements could also be perceived as a reiteration of the Siwian belief of their cultural superiority, particularly when they compared their culture to that prevalent in urban Egypt. Nonetheless, while there may be merit to the statements of both women, a problematic sentiment is conveyed here, where women are complicit in the reproduction of the patriarchal system. Both women argued for the perceived protection the Hijab offers, which could be an expression of Siwian women's cultural norm where all women are Hijabis and public spaces are segregated by gender. As in Siwa the law is rigidly enforced, both women could have established a false narrative which depicts an ideal where the way to protect women from male violence is analogous to enforcing a strict dress code and segregating public spaces. Yet, none of the indigenous women interviewed demonstrated a lack of awareness of how the legal framework and interpretation of the Qur'an have influenced the status and role of women in Siwian society. The perpetuation of the urban and rural patriarchal sentiment expressed by BI2s(27) and BI2p(8), that the Hijab possesses protective qualities, one can argue, is reflective of a more egalitarian cultural structure and understanding of Siwa and a critique of the oppressive patriarchal structure in urban areas, supporting the argument that one's location in Egypt is significant to their cultural understanding. It additionally sheds light on the possibility that gender segregation in public spaces may be appropriate for certain cultures and societies, and one ought not to label communities that operationalise gender segregation as invariably patriarchal and oppressive.

Reflecting a similarly divided position, were two rural, middle-class men. CR2p(45), who is privately employed, agreed with the position that the Hijab protects women, stating:

> It depends on where you are, as there are places where a Hijab can actually protect a girl from the people (...) I cannot say that it does. However, if the girl is from a lower social class, she will be normal and not seen as out of the society.

CR2s(35), a male student at a higher education institution in Egypt, took a proportional position to answer the questions regarding whether the Hijab does or does not protect women, stating:

> I can say yes and no. It does not protect in that we can see girls wearing the veil and are not protected, as they get harassed and everything. On the other hand, they are protected. The percentage of girls who get harassed is less for the veiled than the non-veiled. It is a matter of ratio and not yes or no.

These conflicting accounts inspired the separation between women's and men's perceptions of the Hijab as a patriarchal bargain to afford women access to the public sphere without violating the rules of the patriarchal system in Egypt. The two distinct accounts presented above, highlight how the patriarchal exchange is upheld by both women and men. Yet, as the patriarchal structure of the State, Walby argued, allows men to 'utilise considerable amounts of violence against women with impunity' (Walby, 1990, p. 150), the accounts demonstrated above may be predictable and logical.

4.1. 'Yes, the Hijab Protects ME'

Women and men were asked why they believe that the Hijab could protect women from harassment. AU2I(36) responded by stating, 'If she's wearing the correct Hijab that does not show the body, it will decrease the rate of harassment'. At first, the researcher thought that the issue might be specific to urban areas of Egypt, however, AR3m(62)'s account provided evidence that the discourse of 'Hijab being a protective tool' for women is ubiquitous and rings true with women cross sectionally in Egypt. She further added 'We are Falahein [farmers] and we cannot remove our veils because it protects us', which reveals a permissibility dimension previously dismissed. Reiterating the protective qualities of the Hijab in Egypt was AU1e(3), who stated:

> Harassment was just too much. Also, I would style my hair curly and put make-up on and perfume and everything, so my looks were eye-catching and I got a lot of unrequited attention from people on the streets. The men would cat-call me and the women would call

me a slut. Especially in public transport. The Hijab decreased these things a lot, so it's a lot better than when I wasn't veiled. I was scared to go out on the streets for quite some time as well.

The keywords that stood out were 'eye-catching' and 'scared'. The word 'eye-catching' reveals the understanding of modesty we find in Egyptian society. To be modest is to *not* stand out, and to disappear in a sea of other similarly dressed women. The idea of invisibility is pronounced here. This begs the question, is being invisible a desirable effect for women? The simple answer is no. As is natural for human beings, we are political animals, which by virtue of existing determines our desire to be seen and heard. This leads to the logical leap that desiring invisibility is socially constructed via existing power structures. As Mona ElTahawy (2016) observed and noted:

> Men grope and sexually assault us, and yet we are blamed for it because we were in the wrong place at the wrong time, wearing the wrong thing. Cairo has women-only subway cars to 'protect' us from wandering hands and worse. (p. 13)

Two distinctive conclusions can be drawn from these accounts: firstly, the public sphere is still a male-dominated space. Simply stated, the public sphere is a man's space, and if you wish and dare to walk with them, you must adopt a fly-on-the-wall approach and disappear into the background so as not to disrupt the flow. This ideology critically affects women's access and rights within the public sphere. To access this sphere a woman would have to adhere to the rules set forth for her by the hegemons occupying that space. These rules included covering oneself as not to 'tempt' or 'catch someone's eye' and are the result of both unequal gender relations which favour men over men, and male-dominant interpretation of scripture.

In Islam, the Hijab is meant to cover a woman's body so as not to tempt men. In the Qur'anic verse 24:32, it is stated:

> And say to the believing women that they should lower their gaze and guard their modesty; that they should not display their beauty and ornaments except what must ordinarily appear thereof; that they should draw their veils over their bosoms and not display their beauty except to their husbands, their fathers ... and that they should not strike their feet in order to draw attention to their hidden ornaments. (Qur'an, 24:32)

The idea of coverage in Egypt applies to all women. However, as discussed earlier, the line between religion and culture is almost invisible in Egyptian culture, so Christian and Muslim women alike are expected to wear some sort of veil. For Christian women, the verse 'man was not created for woman, but woman for man. Therefore, the woman ought to have a sign of authority over her head because of the angels' (Corinthians 11:3–10). The two dominant religions to which most of the Egyptian society ascribes mandate a woman be covered (Ibrahim et al., 1996, p. 23). For some Muslims, even the stomping of the feet could be regarded as impious and attention-seeking behaviour; by this logic, a woman speed-walking, jogging, and running in public spaces are also attention-seeking behaviours (Yaqin, 2007). This sheds light on why the public sphere is patriarchal and male-dominated; women are not naturally given the right to access public spaces according to both interpretations of the Bible and the Qur'an, which naturally allows the space to be exclusively accessible for men; should women wish to enter this space, she must do so unnoticed.

This lack of access to public space allowed for the domination of the patriarchal structure over sexuality (Walby, 1990, pp. 124–126) which generated a discourse that men do not possess any type of self-control to emerge, thus, absolving men from being held accountable. The mentality of 'out of sight, out of mind' is oftentimes used as an argument against women and against women in the public sphere. This narrative allowed for a shift in responsibility, where men have their 'God given right' to roam the public sphere unencumbered and a woman's access to it is regarded as an invasion and infestation. This has additionally created the discourse that women ought to practice self-control for both sexes. This simultaneously restricted women's access to public space and allowed an easy scapegoat for predators; by faulting the 'invaders' of men's space, especially those not adhering to the rules set forth by men and supported by a selective religious interpretation. This perpetuates victimhood and completely dilutes accountability for men's actions; As ElTahawy (2016, p. 17) summarised,

> Women are not to be seen or heard; even their voices are a temptation. Flowers instead of women's faces in the middle of a revolution in Egypt ... in which women were killed, beaten, shot at, and sexually assaulted while fighting alongside men to rid our country of Mubarak.

Mona ElTahawy's account shines the spotlight on how women are still exploited for their practical significance as observed in the 1919 and 2011 revolutions, respectively.

The second keyword that stood out from the accounts was the word 'scared'. After investigating access to the public sphere, and the real dangers associated with women's departure from the private sphere, the term 'scared' possesses a real and deep-rooted fear of the male-dominated public sphere. While many women reiterated this fear, framing it in terms of accessibility changes the narrative from access to the public sphere to surviving in the public sphere. By ascribing protective attributes and connotations to the Hijab, women started gradually leaving the private sphere and joining the public domain as a productive force. The perceived protection, however, did not alter men's feelings of women 'intruding' in or on their domain, nor did aggressive and hostile attitudes towards women travelling through the public sphere change.

It is thereby unsurprising that women believe the Hijab protects them from men to the point where women have internalised these patriarchal notions. Particularly unsettling was AR3m(60), for instance, who stated:

> Decency is good after all. When I see a girl wearing bad clothes [tight or revealing] on a public bus, I get very sad as a mother. Everyone is looking at her if she is dressed like that. All women in rural areas wear the same thing, a black *Abaya* [a type of full length dress] and a black *Tarha* [aka Hijab]. The uniformity protects because they cannot tell us apart so they worry they would harass their own mother or sister, so they don't harass at all [she laughs].

While Egyptians are known for their dark and morbid sense of humour, the researcher did not perceive AR3m(60)'s account as dark humour, but rather the truth masked in humour; men are not socially expected to practice self-control, even though Islam mandates it (Qur'an 24:30). The selective interpretation of the Qur'an has served and propagated the narrative that the public sphere is owned by men and access to it should be in adherence to their wishes and rules. As AR3m(59) elaborated 'My father refused that I wear pants and told me it is *haram* for a girl to show off her hair in my religion. Because this is my religion, I feel I should wear it'. Her sister, a 19-year-old girl, AR3u(53), additionally said 'I was told it protects me from the men who cannot marry and the guys who were not raised well. It will protect me from everything'. This provides evidence that women in Egypt are subscribing to the rules set for them by men (in this instance the father) who evidently himself does not believe that men in the public sphere are to be trusted to act piously. One might argue that this is an attempt by the father to strip his daughter from her personal autonomy and agency, but one can also regard it as a fatherly protective instinct who has first-hand knowledge of how vicious and merciless the public sphere is for women.

Problematically, a father's, a husband's, or a brother's desire to protect his female family members can and does inevitably lead to moral licencing, that is, 'cognitive bias, which enables individuals to behave immorally without threatening their self-image of being a moral person' (Simbrunner & Schlegelmilch, 2017, p. 201). Moral licencing is oftentimes used as a justification to excuse indulgence or temptation. Hereby, a cognitive dissonance resulting from licenced behaviours is unlikely to arise for Egyptian men; the idea of 'I made my daughter wear a Hijab and therefore I can indulge in harassing a couple of women who are not wearing it'. This is not a theoretical discussion, as CU1s(13), for example, said:

> Yes, it is a form of protection because the Hijab covers up and in Egypt being covered up is like protecting the woman. If she is wearing tight clothes she will be striking and attractive to men in the street.

In his account of why men are harassing women, he continued to state 'I know what I am saying is weird, but I want to be honest because he should not ever harass her to start with. I am not justifying, but it is known that wearing tight clothes does attract harassers'. The contradiction within his statement seemed to not have registered with the participant. However, it was revealing of how internalised and rooted the patriarchy, and its supposed remedy covering up, is and how it leads to moral licencing and deferral of responsibility and accountability to women.

4.2. 'Yes, the Hijab Protects HER'

The data emphasised that women believe wearing the Hijab would protect them from unrequited attention in the public sphere, with some even arguing that *invisibility* is the objective of the Hijab and a prerequisite to shield oneself from harassment and assault. While conducting interviews, one of the male respondents corroborated this field observation CR3s(71) stating, 'veiled women should not get harassed. But girls now do not wear the Hijab in the correct way in public, which means they are not raised well. It all goes back to how she was raised'. These statements licence harassment in public by shifting blame to the victim and excusing men's misconduct as a justifiable reaction to improper decorum. In other words, this account corroborates the fact that women in Egypt are sanctioned for non-compliance with the patriarchal system, using male violence as the means to maintain the patriarchal male-domination.

Nonetheless, over 60% of men interviewed agreed that the Hijab is not a form of protection from harassment. One participant, BU2s(22), confirmed media reports of harassment stating 'It is an epidemic'. Contextually, it is important to recognise that when the interviews were collected over the period of January to August 2020, an unexpected feminist movement shocked the status quo and sparked a 'MeToo' campaign. The spark was ignited by Nadeen Ashraf, an Egyptian 22-year-old female who 'In a moment of rage, created an Instagram page naming a man accused of being a sexual harasser. Within a week, it had 70,000 followers' (Walsh, 2020). Nadeen described as 'Egypt's #MeToo crusader' (Farouk, 2020) for her astonishing effort in raising public awareness about Violence Against Women (VAW), establishing a platform for victims of violence and abuse to submit allegations, and creating networks for victims of VAW to be protected and represented by an officer of the law *pro bono*. Her Instagram, much like the 25th January revolution, in 2011, which was also described as Egyptian Facebook Revolution of 2011, mobilised the urban community in Egypt. Over 50 women started submitting proof of abuse, sexual coercion, manipulation, and exploitation against the predator Ahmed Bassem Zaki, the person who inspired Nadeen to speak up (Mustafa, 2021). After months of struggle, which started in June 2020, the activism gained momentum and played a crucial role in the trial against him (Khairat, 2020). Due to Nadeen's activism, Ahmed Bassem Zaki has been sentenced to 8 years in prison for sexual assault (Mustafa, 2021). While respectively this may seem like an injustice to the women who came forward, this was the first modern high-profile sexual assault criminal trial in Cairo since the late 1980s. This moment marked a particularly interesting moment for feminists and activists in Egypt.

While this historic moment was challenging to the patriarchal system in Egypt, the interviewer was in the field collecting data. It was an unexpected but happy surprise for the researcher to be able to capture shifts in perception as they were unfolding. For instance, CU1s(14), responded to the question 'Does the Hijab provide women with a sort of protection' stated:

> I think people convince themselves that it protects and that is the argument they give, that harassment would stop if the woman was just properly dressed so the men would not feel enticed or provoked to harass her. But I do not think that it has this effect. I have seen two veiled women walking down the street and getting harassed and their private parts touched by a 5-year-old boy. That's why you cannot say that if a girl wears the Hijab, she won't get harassed. This boy watched his brothers or even his father probably and is mimicking what they did.

A more distressing account was that of CR3p(51) who pessimistically said 'Nope. Nor the *Niqab* [full face coverage]. Sexual harassment has become the norm. We can try to change the laws and convince the women that they have done nothing wrong, but this will take forever'. Shifting the conversation can easily cause a cognitive dissonance where one attempts to rationalise situations by appropriating the narrative to suit one's worldview. However, there are moments of dissonance. CR2s(35) first stated that the Hijab, when worn correctly, does protect a woman from harassment. However, when confronted with the statistic that 99% of Egyptians have been subjugated to at least one form of sexual harassment (Abdulaal, 2018; UN Women, 2013), he reacted by saying:

> I can now say yes and no. It does not protect by that we can see girls wearing the veil and are not protected, they still get harassed and everything. On the other hand, they are protected in relation to the percentage of girls who get harassed, as Hijabi girls get less harassed than non-Hijabis. It's a matter of the ratio.

Evidently, perception seemed scattered and the association of the Hijab with religion complicated the matter further, so the researcher asked a *Mufti*, a Muslim legal expert, with the power to give rulings on religious matters, from Al-Azhar institute to clarify what the Hijab represents and what mandates are to be followed on that topic. This action was inspired by an aspiration to discern social discourse from actual scripture to observe whether a discrepancy in perception and fact exists. As demonstrated above, most people in Egypt believe the Hijab is a *Farida* (mandate by God). To settle the dispute CR3m(1) elaborated:

> Hijab is not one of the pillars of Islam like some people argue. God gave us over 3000 commandments, and the Hijab is one of them. People forget that they need to fulfil the 5 pillars of Islam first before they move on to other mandates. If you have exams in 3000 subjects, and you fail one, does that mean you will fail the entire year? No. The same with the Hijab, it is one of 3000 tests, and if you do it that is good! You're one step closer to completing your exams and graduating and going to heaven. And if you fail

it, that is okay too, because you have 2999 tests to go. But the first thing you will be judged on is not the 3000, it's the 5 pillars.

This statement asserts that the Hijab is indeed one of the Islamic commandments, but disproves the widely held belief that it is one of Islam's pillars, thereby substantiating the argument that the Hijab is socially constructed, co-opted and appropriated to favour one group over the other. One participant, with whom the researcher had an established rapport, confirmed this argument by elaborating on what supposedly goes through a man's mind prior to harassing a woman on the streets. CR3p(54) challengingly said:

> I asked many *Shaikhs* [Muslim preachers] about women and their cover-ups. Most of them told me that a woman who is covered is more appealing than the ones who are not. Hence, you cannot say that sexual harassment is due to the girls' dress. I would harass a Niqabi and not a non-Niqabi. A Niqabi will not say anything, while a non-Niqabi could talk back and fight me. Hijab does not stop a girl from being harassed; it could actually increase it. Girls cannot be taught that Hijab is a form of protection, while there are *Shaikhs* who say the opposite to the boys. People look for something they have not experienced before. People want to know what a woman is and how she feels. If you can see her the curiosity is gone. It's the ones who are covered that intrigue us, we want to know what she is hiding beneath all of that, in hopes that it will feel good to touch her and extinguish that curiosity. The forbidden fruit theory you know. We are a psychotic society, and this is the reason for the problems we face.

His analysis of why the Hijab is not a form of protection for women, and conversely stating that it could be used to target women highlights three things: (1) Men are socialised to believe that a 'good' woman ought to be vulnerable, submissive, protective of her reputation, and silent; (2) women are socialised to believe that characteristics such as vulnerability and submissiveness are attractive and desirable, delegating the responsibility of not attracting a 'bad reputation' onto them; (3) unequal sexual morals in Egypt have allowed men to act with impunity and normalise the 'violability' of women (Nussbaum, 1999). This forces a double bind, if you cover up, men would be curious and harass and/or assault you, if you are not covered up then men would be provoked by you and harass and/or assault you. Summarising this conundrum was, BU1a(10), who said:

> it is the perception that if you are veiled you will protect yourself from harassment. It is a wrong perception and not a right one. In general, there is also the perception that if a girl disappears from the public space, either by sitting at home or covering herself up, she will protect herself. That is wrong too.

The findings of this chapter suggest that (1) some men have set the entry requirements for women through the imposition of patriarchal bargain; (2) most women have been excluded from the contemporary political and public spheres and possess minimal *de facto* and *de jure* power; and finally, (3) the social discourses of womanhood and manhood, which conversely denotes accessibility/deniability to the public sphere, are oftentimes socially perpetuated and reproduced by maintaining the guise of the public sphere being a dangerous space for women. The chapter specifically tackled how the Hijab plays a role in signalling adherence to the patriarchal bargain in Egypt but also revealed a double bind where even if women adhere to the rules set by the patriarchal system, there is no guarantee that men will hold up their end of the patriarchal bargain; while most Egyptian men perceived the Hijab as a social tool that signals piety and modesty, Egyptian women perceived the Hijab as virtually having no significant social function besides shielding a woman from social repercussions, such as stigmatisation for not adhering to the rules of the patriarchal system, but does not provide on its own merit guarantee protection beyond that.

Nonetheless, more than half of the men interviewed did not believe that the Hijab protects a woman against harassment, or assault, *inter alia,* there was compelling evidence to support the theory that men feel entitled to have unencumbered access to the public sphere and use this to rationalise and justify the harassment of women. By claiming the public sphere as the male sphere, most men interviewed did not perceive this effective gender segregation as male privilege. On the contrary, when asked about the female dress code most men reported that this dress code is for the protection of women and urged for the conformity and adherence of women to the dress codes they set forth to shield them from the 'dangers' of the public sphere.

However, some men's perception of the 'benefits' and 'drawbacks' of wearing/not wearing the Hijab bears critical weight, as it highlights the double bind women are positioned in. On the one hand, men are aware of the level of violence women are subjugated to in the public sphere, yet they play a passive and apathetic role in changing attitudes towards women. On the other hand, more than half the men interviewed admitted that the Hijab does not deter harassers and predators, yet they still advocated for its benefits for women who wish to enter the public sphere. These conflicting attitudes substantiate the argument that women are regarded as *less than human* which might explain the level of apathy men expressed. In the public sphere, a woman is expected to protect herself from male harassment by adhering to the male-prescribed dress code. Men, however, are not held accountable for the same social contract and do not comply with the rules of the patriarchal system, that is, wearing the Hijab as a patriarchal bargain, does not guarantee a woman's safety but is rather a practical need for women. Further, should the man choose to violate this patriarchal bargain, the blame still falls on the woman.

This means that the Hijab's supposed social value and protective qualities are in essence a façade erected by the patriarchal system to gate keep the public sphere and maintain the status quo without effectively changing anything. To further elaborate on this, the following chapter comparatively analyses how gender relations, patriarchal bargains, and the role of religion differ, if at all, in indigenous communities from urban and rural communities. The last chapter tackles the last research question: what purpose does the Hijab serve in challenging/perpetuating Egyptian women's secondary citizenship status and inferior social perception?

Chapter 7

Sufi Islam Versus Sunni Islam: The Role of Religious Interpretation on Women's Roles and Status in Society

Findings from the rural and urban research subject areas in Egypt (Cairo, Alexandria, Kafr El-Shaikh, and Fayoum) indicate similar cultural understandings, discourses, and manifestations, while the indigenous community of Siwa, the Amazigh, has different beliefs, ethnic backgrounds, legal structures, a separate government, and a different interpretation of Islam. Protected by Special Group Rights, Siwa is a self-governing indigenous community. The following chapter will build on the findings of Chapter 5, and comparatively analyse how this different and isolated indigenous community may have affected gender relations, how women are perceived, and women's status. The chapter is divided into four sections. The first section provides the reader with the history and contextual background of the Amazigh of Siwa. The second section sheds light on the strategic uses of the Hijab, building on Chapter 5's discussion of 'Navigating Patriarchal Bargains'. Also, the chapter highlights the unique circumstances of Siwian women and comparatively situates them within the broader context of Egypt. The third section specifically builds on the earlier discussion of the legal structure in Egypt, Chapter 2, and compares it to that of Siwa to gain further insights into whether the codification of the patriarchal structures of Violence, Sexuality, and Culture and the State are observable in Siwa. Particularly, the third section unpacks and analyses *Orff* (Customary Laws) in the tribal-indigenous communities, which, unlike urban and rural areas, are the only source of legislation among Siwa inhabitants. As indigenous communities abide by *Orff* as opposed to national laws – which as presented in Chapter 2 have systematically and codified women's inferiority by institutionalising their dehumanisation – to investigate whether women's rights and status are similarly codified in this separate system of laws and governance. As indigenous communities have their own set of laws, which are based on tradition, the Sufi religious interpretation of the Qur'an, and Amazigh customs, questions around marriage and divorce, the role of the Hijab, and women's 'place' in society assisted in comparing urban/rural understandings versus indigenous ones.

Recovering Women's Voices: Islam, Citizenship, and Patriarchy in Egypt, 183–206
Copyright © 2024 by Reham ElMorally
Published under exclusive licence by Emerald Publishing Limited
doi:10.1108/978-1-83608-248-420241008

It is important to note that Siwians do not have legal documents one could review such as a penal code, a written constitution, or personal status laws, which imposed some limitations on this book. First, the lack of written legal and policy documents prevented the possibility of using the documents as secondary resources to expand on and explore the field observations and data. Second, Siwians speak a different language, which is not written down and is only spoken by members of the community, so had there been legal documents available, the researcher would not have been able to read or analyse them. Having an unwritten constitution could have affect the rule of law negatively, particularly as 'in the absence of a written constitution or bill of rights, judges have to engage in interpretation of constitutional values' (Dyzenhaus, 2003, p. 843). This was the third research limitation faced. As Siwa follows a tribal governing system, the head of the tribe, *Shaikh Al Qabila,* acts as leader, judge, and jury. In the absence of written documents to analyse, decisions with regard to what constitutes a violation of the law are left to the discretion of *Shaikh Al Qabila.* Nonetheless, the Siwian governing structure relies on what is known as *Orff Laws* (roughly translates to Customary Laws), which draws on the Sufi interpretation and the Amazigh traditions as the source of legislation. As the indigenous Amazigh community of Siwa is an understudied and underrepresented group, limited secondary resources were available for the construction of a rigorous analysis. The analysis, therefore, focussed on the social implications of the interpretation of certain Qur'anic verses to gain insights into the Siwian structure and community. As the Qur'an is one of the sources the Siwian system draws on, it is approached in this chapter as a legal document to compare and contrast whether the Sufi interpretation of the Qur'an is different, if at all, from the Sunni interpretation most adopted in urban and rural communities. It is significant to remember that the Qur'an and *Sunnah* are the texts upon which *Sharia laws,* Islamic laws, are established. Sharia in Siwa, however, does not follow the *Sunnah/Sunni* understanding but instead follows the *Tasawuf/Sufi* understanding. Whether differences in interpretive approaches to the Qur'an produce different manifestations of the legal framework is explored in this chapter. This was particularly significant to the investigation of the influence political Islam may have on the status of women in society. As stated earlier, the term political Islam is used in this book to denote the use of Islam 'to a political end' (Knudsen, 2003, p. 2), that is, the selective use of scripture to justify, rationalise and gain acceptance for and of political gains by the political structure.

An interesting narrative emerged, which insinuated a possible difference between the Siwian identity and the Egyptian national identity. For example, one indigenous member said, 'we were proud to fight alongside the Egyptians. But we almost went extinct because of them. We needed to practice self-preservation' (AI3p78). Several keywords stood out in this testimony. First, the referral to the Egyptian Government and president as 'Egyptian' highlighted a possible lack of affinity to the Egyptian national identity. This was a pattern detected among the 30 interviewees, who mainly referred to themselves as 'Siwian' or 'Amazigh' as opposed to Egyptian when asked some background questions. Yet, as this book has a modestly sized sample, the analysis and findings drawn in this chapter should not be misconstrued as generalisable to the entire Siwian community. Siwa has a population of roughly

18,625 people, hence the collected interview only accounts for 0.16% of the total population, and does not meet the criteria of sample size sufficiency to allow for the generalisation of the findings (Vasileiou et al., 2018, p. 4). Another keyword which stood out from AI3p(78)'s testimony was the use of 'extinct' and 'self-preservation', which one could argue, read as isolationist terms. If this argument rings true, then the testimony could be interpreted as a deliberate action to convey either a fundamental distinction between the identity of the indigenous community of Siwa and the remainder of Egypt or as a reflection on the socio-political ideological difference between Siwa's governing system and the governing system of the rest of Egypt.

Supporting this observation is the knowledge that the three indigenous groups existing in Egypt – the Amazigh, the Arab Bedouins, and the Nubians – all have their own languages. These languages are spoken but not written, and therefore cannot be taught to 'Outsiders'. When asked about why the most common answer given by males was 'the Egyptians would ruin it as they did to the Qur'anic Arabic'. Respectively female members predominantly stated 'we raise the children to speak Amazigh so why would they have to learn it? They go to school to learn Arabic. They only need the second language to be good Muslims [The Qur'an, praying, and other religious rituals must be conducted in Arabic] so why waste time?' This revealed a possible negative perception about 'Egyptians', and a possible indirect reference to the narrative that there is a distinction between the Siwan identity and the Egyptian national.

Individualism and collectivism are two of the most prominent cultural phenomena investigated by scholars in social sciences. In general, individualistic cultures emphasise the 'self' and assign a distinguishable status to the individual within the society, highlighting independence and autonomy as the pillars of the individual (Ho & Chiu, 1994; Triandis, 2001). In an individualistic culture, one can observe more freedom of choice, the ability to set personal goals, and stresses the importance of self-reliance. Contrastingly, collectivist cultures are utilitarian, where the needs of the group, inter and intra-group harmony, and social awareness of hierarchical orders and relationships are pronounced (Hofstede, 2001; Oyserman & Lee, 2007). Within collectivist cultures, one can observe the prioritisation of the group over the individual, and accomplishments on the individual level ought to be of utility to the group (Triandis, 1994). The different cultural attachments and values are unsurprisingly reflected in the norms and behaviours one can observe within the respective societies. For instance, assertiveness is highly valued within individualistic cultures, but within collectivist cultures, the appropriate social behaviour is obedience to authority (Argyle, 1986; Parham et al., 2015; Triandis et al., 1986). It is commonly agreed that compared to Western cultures, Middle Easterners portray stronger sentiments towards collectivism (Bochner, 1994; Hofstede, 1980; Triandis, 1994) and 'perceive the self as an extension of significant others' (Koydemir et al., 2018, p. 116). Evidence of Koydemir et al.'s (2018) premise about the self as an extension of significant others was echoed in Siwa where, CI3p(75) stated:

> The Amazigh accepted to be neighbours with the Arabs, but Arabs do not like to be neighboured .... We are not considered Arabs or Amazigh; we are Siwans. The new identity from the mixture of

186 Recovering Women's Voices

both the Arab and Amazigh civilisations was the Siwan identity. This is Siwa and we are known for our simplicity, our strength, and our honour. Arabs are not.

Given the extensive research on cultural configurations, to be regarded as an extension of someone in collectivist cultures is unsurprising. Steven Hobfoll (1998, 2001, p. 361) argued that collectivism emerged as a survival mechanism and describes collectivism as a response to survival stress and is reproduced by social goals. Collectivism thereby entails that 'individuals are seen as embedded within their group identity, and the notion of a separate, autonomous self is deemphasised' (Kawamura, 2012, p. 95). In this context, women are viewed as an extension of the male honour in Egypt. While this does not necessarily hold a negative connotation in collectivist and communal societies – being regarded as a part of a whole as opposed to an autonomous individual – it does bear grave consequences for women and women's movements in Egypt. As CU1s(13) elaborated:

> There are three things no one can interfere with: your money, your religion, and your honour. In this case, this entails the mother, sister, and any woman in the family that pertains to you. Your mother and sister are your pride. Hence, women are secluded, and they cannot be seen or discussed in public.

Respectively, women are, to a degree, invisible from the public sphere. Their invisibility is both physical as well as normative. However, unlike urban and rural communities in Egypt, indigenous communities, particularly the Amazigh of Siwa Oasis, have a different understanding of honour, thus also a different understanding of invisibility (see Chapter 5). Prior to presenting the differences in social understandings, the next section provides a brief historical background of Siwa as recited by the designated spokesperson, the *Hakkay,* of the community to help the reader understand the context of Siwa.

1. Brief History of Siwa

The Oasis of Siwa is in the Great Sand Sea of Egypt's Western Desert and has a population of roughly 33,000. The closest city to the oasis is the city of Marsa Matrouh, located on the Western end of the North Coast of Egypt, and is 400 km away. The city is predominantly populated by Bedouin Arab tribes. The oasis is also only 80 km away from the Libyan border, making it a regular stop for travellers, nomads, and border-runners (the term refers to illegal immigrants, illegal arms dealers, and drug mules). Ancient Romans constructed approximately 203 naturally flowing springs in Siwa (Moghazy & Kaluarachchi, 2020, p. 2). Siwa consists of 11 Tribes, 10 Amazigh Tribes, and 1 Arab Bedouin Tribe. How that came about will be discussed in further detail later in this section. Each of the Tribes elects a leader. The tribe leaders operate like *Majlis Al-Shura* (Senate).

The 11 Tribe leaders then elect a Shaikh (like a President) whose responsibility includes, but is not limited to, resolving disputes between tribes, executing penalties, redistributing land, consulting on irrigation installations, *inter alia,* and voicing Siwa and Siwian interests in the capital, Cairo (like an ambassador).

According to the *Hakkay,* [spokesman and/or official historian] the oasis' history stretches back to Pharaonic times. According to CI3p(75), the belief is:

> Alexander the Great decided to visit the temple of Ammon without telling the priests of the temple of his arrival. Alexander the Great demanded to meet with Ammon alone, and the priests did not object. Coming out of the Ammon's temple, Alexander the Great told the priests Ammon considered him his son and bestowed the title of Son of God onto him.

The story continues to state that one of the secrets of the oasis is that Alexander the Great's grave is here, but its location is only known to those who are pure of heart and mind. The *Hakkay* continued to explain the transformation the oasis went through during the Roman expansion but stated:

> When Christianity started to spread, the Romans left the oasis and Siwa was an empty land with unending natural resources, and it stayed like that until Islam started to spread. However, Islam didn't appear in Siwa during the Prophet's era, but during Omar Ibn Khattab's era [father in-law of prophet Mohamed and the second caliph of Islam after the prophet's death] when the Amazigh were still nomadic and travelled across North Africa.

Naturally, the question of why the Amazigh chose Siwa specifically to settle down is a pertinent one. According to the *Hakkay,* it is because the Amazigh are themselves of royal descent. The *Hakkay* said:

> King *Sheshonk* was an Amazigh. He was a warrior and he had access to divine knowledge. He provided intel to his military and the strategies he designed are the same ones the Egyptian military uses today.

Siwians believe that they have been favoured by divine powers throughout history. Their blood lineage is believed to date back to Prophet Noah. The *Hakkay* said:

> Noah had three kids: She, Ham, and Japheth. Shem is the father of Arabs. Ham is the father of the Amazigh. Finally, Japheth is the father of Gomer, Magog, and many others. Ham was the father of Canaan and Canaan the father of Mazigh. The name transformed over time to Tamazight, and Arabs call us Amazigh.

The Siwian population is believed to have settled in Siwa because it has a spiritual as well as a blood-land connection to the place. The Hakkay continued the story and said:

> Amazigh means 'free man'. The Amazigh are shepherds and nomads, and we settled here after we investigated our ancestral lines. We came here with Shaikh Musallam. The name comes from the term Muslim, and he was the one who studies religion; that is why there is no other religion but Islam here ... Shaikh Musallam drew the constitution of Siwa, the same one we follow today. Our traditions, beliefs, and customs predate Islam and we preserved that. In Siwa we don't talk about religion; we do the pillars of Islam, but our history and customs are more important.

Upon arriving in Siwa, the researcher made a strange observation: there are no women to be seen or heard anywhere. While listening to the story of the Amazigh, the researcher asked the *Hakkay* where the women are. According to him:

> Siwa is divided into two: East and West. There are three doors: one for the East, one for the West, and one to connect the women of both areas. If problems occurred between tribes over land, the women would walk between East and West to tighten diplomatic ties and lead negotiations. They still do when tribes have issues, especially if it is about land. They are better than men at resolving conflict and bringing communities together.

According to the *Hakkay,* the tribes were at war with one another over natural resources and land division. According to online sources:

> After several endless disputes, Ahmad Madani, a Sufi from the Madanya[1] clan, brought peace by calling for all the men from the oasis to attend a meeting in the mountain village of Dakrour, near the oasis. He told them to pray to God and did not allow them to return home until they had settled down. Three days later they solved the problem, and that moment marked the beginning of the festival. (Gospodunov, n.d.)

According to the Hakkay, the women of the tribes played an integral role in resolving the conflict, as some of them had initially declined Madani's invitations.

---

[1] *Madanya* is a term used colloquially to refer to the *Madinah* district in Saudi Arabia, which is believed to be the location that the prophet Mohamed (pbuh) moved to after he received his prophecy. Furthermore, the term *Madanya* is used by Muslims to refer to a lifestyle which closely resembles that of prophet Mohamed (pbuh).

This day is now referred to as *Eid El Solh* (Concord Festival). A 3-day celebration is an annual event that starts on the first day of October's Full Moon. It is worth mentioning that the festival is held on Dakrour Mountain and is only attended by males and children up to the age of 12. Women spend the 3-day festival in the house of the Shaikh's wife (president's house).

The folklore and history of Siwa are intriguing, particularly the gender dynamics and how the society has organised itself. The researcher was able to get in touch with and interview the Shaikh (president) who happily shared the structure of Siwa's Government. Naturally, the first question asked was, 'What is the role of the Shaikh?'. According to CI3g(77):

> My role is to help solve people's problems, build peaceful relationships with the government, to be representative of our tribes, and be the one whom Siwians resort to and confide in. My role is to protect our heritage, which is something I personally am keen on doing. The Shaikh is responsible for the tribes and is the link between the tribes and the government.

When asked whether Siwa could have a female Shaikh he responded by saying 'It has yet not occurred and is not foretold'. It is important to consider that Siwians practice Black Magic and are extremely spiritual. When asked what they meant by 'foretold' the Shaikh simply answered with 'the secrets of the oasis are for its people'. The conversation evolved into understanding how Siwa governs itself within Egypt. While Egypt is not a federation, the spirit of the law devises its power from two sources: customary tradition and the Sufi interpretation of Sharia. The system was set up to protect the diverse culture existing in Egypt and protect minority ethnic groups from losing their heritage and allow them freedom of belief and cultural continuation (CU1p(98)). These courts are commonly referred to as '*Orff* Courts and Tribunals'. Indigenous communities, such as the Siwians, the Arab Bedouins of Sinai and Marsa Matrouh, and the Nubians of South Egypt, must elect a leader to liaise with the Government. The elected person must be approved by the Ministry of Internal Affairs. The Shaikh was asked whether he believes this is a form of censorship, to which he responded with:

> No because the ministry respects our privacy and heritage. They have seen that all Siwa wants is respect and for them to not interfere with our affairs. The Siwian people want the ministry to approve of the Shaikh so we can have a better relationship with the Government and can better lobby for our interests.

For instance, according to the *Hakkay*, the police forces have no presence in Siwa and rarely do they require police intervention. The police are only contacted under two circumstances: drug trafficking and to report foreigners who do not comply with and respect the rules, customs, and traditions of Siwa.

In addition to having a Shaikh and a *Hakkay,* Siwa also has a Caller. According to CI3p(75):

> You must know how organised Siwa is. The Caller is the black box of the tribes, he knows everything. He goes to the Shaikh and informs him of any problems and reports on progress such as harvest, irrigation etc. In addition, we have our customs board that advises the Shaikh.

One would expect the Shaikh to be held to a rigorous academic, theological, and cultural standard. However, as stated earlier, Siwians are spiritual and have a strong sense of community. When the researcher asked the Shaikh what criteria he would have to satisfy to qualify for the post his response was:

> He doesn't have to have formal education but must know how to read and write. He must be good natured, pure of heart, modest, well behaved, and proficient in *Orff* laws, and has enough money to spend on himself so the power of money doesn't corrupt him. He must be just, have excellent communication skills, and be proficient in Amazigh and Arabic so he can communicate eloquently with the government as well as be able to communicate with other Amazigh tribes, like those in Morocco, Libya, and Tunisia. He must know and fear God but doesn't have to have a formal theological education.

This led the researcher to conclude that quantifiable and material qualifications possess less meaning to the inhabitants of Siwa.[2] Rather, according to the *Hakkay* who serves as a representative for the Siwians, what differentiates them is their attention to normative values and skills, which are difficult to nurture, and they believe they are inborn. The Siwians pride themselves on living according to *Fitra* (roughly translates to instinct but also connotes a spiritual connection to nature, energy, and vibrations). The next section will further elaborate on the idea of *Fitra* and how it may relate to gender relations, particularly if it has any influence over patriarchal manifestations in Siwa. The section also presents findings concerning what the Hijab represents and how it affects the role and status of women in Siwa, particularly whether the Hijab has a strategic purpose within Siwa's structure or not. The first half of the chapter tackles the eighth research question: What is the role of the Hijab in signalling adherence to the rules of the patriarchal bargain? To address this, the section compares the findings of Chapter 5 on the strategic uses of the Hijab for urban/rural women to that of Siwian women, to better understand whether the uses of the Hijab are similar across different Egyptian women.

---

[2]While this may seem like an oversimplification of the power of money and its ability to corrupt, the readers should note that these conclusions are based on the reflections of the leaders of the Siwian community and not the researcher's interpretations.

2. Navigating Patriarchal Bargains: The Strategic Use of the Hijab in Siwa

As discussed in Chapter 5, the Hijab represents more than just an Islamic tradition and has a rich historical and cultural connotation to many communities. According to Akou (2010, p. 4), the Hijab and Niqab alike are

> Practical solution to the problem of living in a desert; covering the face protects the wearer's eyes, nose, and mouth from blowing sand. Even men are known to pull the edges of their garments over their faces during sandstorm.

Similar, to Akou's account of the practical use of coverage, Siwians hold a similar outlook. According to CI3m(79), the Hijab and Niqab are

> a form of protection and shield from the harsh weather conditions in Siwa. During winters it can go up to 40 degrees during the morning but drop to 15 degrees in the evening. So, the *Malaya* [Niqab] protects the woman. For us men, we wear the *Gallabiyah* [long loose garment], and we have our own scarves. (See images on *Siwa Live,* 2018)

Furthermore, according to Siwa's *Hakkay* the female garments are embroidered with secret messages. Traditionally, mothers embroider the garments with representations of prayers, blessings, and family secrets so that ancestry is preserved through the generations. Additionally, different tribes in Siwa have their own style of embroidery, which signals to other members of the community which tribe they belong to. According to CI3p(79), 'women wear Hijab out of modesty'. Due to the conservative culture in Siwa, the researcher was not able to speak to multiple women in the tribe, so collecting information about how they feel about the Hijab and what it represents to them was difficult to obtain. However, from the few women interviewed, they all provided a similar response to AI3m(85) who said, 'I put the Hijab on when I was one year old because it's traditional and customary for girls to wear it'. The interesting thing about this is that not a single female referenced Islam as the reason she wears the Hijab or Niqab, but exclusively referenced customs and tradition as their motivation to put it on. BI2I(84) even stated 'I wear it to feel like myself and to know my worth'. This statement connotes a culturally embedded understanding of coverage separate from Islam. When one woman, AI3m(92) was asked whether she thinks anyone would take off their Hijab she said 'No, because it's '*Eib* [immodest and/or indecent]' even though she stated 'it's optional to wear it but that won't happen because of our traditions'. Another participant, BI3m(79) was asked whether her father would mind her not wearing the Niqab to which she said:

> No, he wouldn't. But I realised that everyone is wearing it and I'm the only one who has her face revealed. As a result, everyone was looking at me strangely. However, I am also convinced with it. I want women to keep their Siwan identity, as this is what makes us different. I don't want us to copy the West blindly.

A male participant, CI3p(73), comparably was asked whether he would stop wearing the *Gallabiyah,* to which he responded with a simple 'No, as it is more comfortable in this weather and is part of my identity'. Paying closer attention to the purposeful use of language and the (un)conscious discursive choices is integral to understanding local narratives and realities (Mullet, 2018, p. 116). Here, 'copy the West blindly' and 'part of my identity' reveal the similarity between discourses in urban/rural centres and indigenous communities, showing that while Siwa may be isolated, anti-colonial sentiments and ideologies propagated in Egypt since the 1919 revolution reverberated throughout Egypt as a metanarrative. Interestingly, while Siwians approach social practices differently and are politically isolated from the remainder of Egypt, socio-political similarities are still found. More on the similarities later in the chapter.

This reinforces the observations in the introduction that Siwians seem to have an isolationist approach to governance and cultural preservation. Rituals and customary practices are systematically reproduced in hopes they would preserve and protect Siwa's heritage and the Amazigh cultural identity. Like other indigenous communities, such as the Nubians and Native Americans, the spoken language in Siwa is not written and is only taught orally to children. Broncho (2016), a Native-American professor of Shoshone Language, explained:

> Some speakers of oral languages do not necessarily even want a standard representation on paper. We Shoshone appreciate each other's individuality and embrace different pronunciations. With standardisation, we might lose that personalisation. Writing our language down also offers a path for outsiders to potentially exploit cultural knowledge intended only for Native people. As a whole, Native Americans have experienced years of forced assimilation.

He further explained 'our language is a living aspect of our culture: they go hand in hand' (Broncho, 2016). During the introductory phase of data collection, before conducting the recorded interviews with participants, Siwians had expressed similar sentiments, and informally informed the researcher, whose native language is Arabic, why their language is not written and only orally taught to members of the tribe. However, language is not the only aspect of the Siwian culture that they are adamant about preserving and protecting, social practices are equally protected.

In Siwa, the understanding of the Hijab is directly related to the Sufi interpretation of the practice. Where urban/rural women are predominantly subjected to the male dominated Sunni interpretation of Islam which preaches the inferiority of women (Chapter 1) and the role of women as subordinate and obedient homemakers, the Sufi interpretation relies on both male and female interpretations of scripture. According to the Threshold Society (2022), Sufis believe that:

> Since the beginning of consciousness, human beings, both female and male, have walked the path of reunion with the Source of Being. Though in this world of duality we may find ourselves in different forms, ultimately there is no male or female, only Being.

Within the Sufi traditions, the recognition of this truth has encouraged the spiritual maturation of women.

Furthermore, to spotlight how women are perceived in the Sufi interpretation and expand on why Siwians' understanding of the Hijab is different to that of rural/urban ones, one must understand that 'from the earliest days onward, women have played an important role in the development of Sufism, which is classically understood to have begun with the Prophet Muhammad' (The Threshold Society, 2022). Respectively, as women were included in the cohort of scholars to interpret scripture, the Sufi understanding is that 'the words of the Qur'an convey the equality of women and men before the eyes of God' (The Threshold Society, 2022), and not that men are superior to women as the Sunni interpretation holds.

An article by Specia (2017) also investigated 'who are the Sufi Muslims and why do some extremists hate them?' and concluded that the attacks on Sufi mosques in Egypt in 2017 are a result of Sunni hard-liners in Egypt who view Sufis as heretics, to justify their killing. Moreover, in an interview with Dr Alexander Knysh, Professor of Islamic Studies at Michigan University, explained to Specia (2017):

> The opponents of Sufism see the shrines and these living saints as idols (…) [according to Sunnis] their existence and their worship violate the main principle of Islam, which is the uniqueness of God and the uniqueness of the object of worship (…). They think the society is moving in the wrong direction and Sufis are aiding and abetting … this corrupt path.

However, while this may be the dominant perception of Sufi Muslims in Egypt, the evidence supports a much more problematic reason why Sunni Muslims persecute Sufis: the 'corrupt path' Sunni Muslims believe Sufis promote is the Sufi assertion that women and men are spiritually, cognitively, and physically equal in Islam. The Sufi interpretation, therefore, contradicts the Sunni assertion that men are the 'maintainers' of women and therefore women must be inferior to men. Furthermore, while Sufis rely on female and male scholars for the interpretation of scripture, Sunnis disavow female interpretations and only adhere to the male interpretations. The Threshold Society (2022) explained Sufis believe:

> As women, we come from the womb and carry the womb. We give birth from the womb and can find ourselves born into the womb of Being. Mary, the mother of Jesus, is very much revered in Sufism and Islam as an example of one who continually took refuge with the divine and opened to receive divine inspiration within the womb of her being. A contemporary male Sufi teacher once described an ideal guide as one who is like a mother. [Sufism] is a way of opening our minds in our own time for greater recognition of equal partnership. The male attributes of strength and determination also belong to women; the feminine attributes of receptivity and beauty also belong to men. As we look to the divine in

each other, encouraging each other to rise to the fullness of his or her own divine nature, we push against our limitations until they dissolve, and a gift unfolds.

Schimmel (1992) also corroborated how the role of women is central to the Sufi tradition, shedding light on how women played an active role in challenging other interpretations of Islam:

> Women played a positive role in Sufism. Even though the early ascetics were rather negative in their statements about women, it was a woman who introduced the concept of pure love into Islamic mysticism and has been venerated for this reason throughout the centuries. One meets women in almost every avenue of Sufism. They act as patrons of Sufi Khandaqs [prayer places] and as shaykhs of certain convents. They have been venerated as saints and accepted as spiritual guides. The symbol of the woman-soul who embodies the highest ambition of the God-seeking human being has been popular in the Sufi tradition.

This speaks to the difference between the Sufi and Sunni interpretations, shedding light on how the historical development of each school of thought affected how adherents of each interpretation understand the role and status of women in society. While the Sunni tradition appears to have resulted in the patriarchal attitudes in urban and rural areas of Egypt, the Sufi tradition appears to have resulted in a culture of harmonious coexistence between the sexes in Siwa. The integration of both female-dominated and male-dominated interpretations of scripture in Sufi Islam allowed the egalitarian meta-narrative to emerge, which might also explain why Siwians have different perceptions of what the Hijab represents.

However, the Sufi interpretation of Islam is not the only matter on which rural/urban and indigenous ones disagree. The Sufi interpretation also changed social practices such as marriage and divorce. As pointed out earlier, there is an expressed fear of losing the Amazigh identity. This is evidenced by participants referencing their traditions and customs as the source of their identity, their refusal to write down their language out of fear it would be diluted and changed, and their clear aversion to Western as well as Egyptian norms and ideals. However, the fear of losing their cultural identity enforced strict social behaviours and expectations. As 'the Siwian female is a diamond that has to be protected' (CI3p(71)) there are strict rules about marriage. For instance, a Siwian man is allowed to marry a Caironese woman, but the Siwian woman cannot marry a Caironese man. The rationality is

> the man carries the family name. If a woman marries outside of the tribe she must obey her husband, and he could take her away, so the family name and her heritage will die with her. A man can move his wife here and we can raise them.

This substantiates the claim that Siwians have adopted an isolationist approach in hopes it would protect their heritage and customs. Additionally, this supports the claim that while women may not be granted the same liberties as men, they are regarded as equals within their community; Men and women have different social roles, which superficially could be viewed as traditional or patriarchal, however, these roles are equally valued. Unlike in urban and rural communities, women in Siwa are not regarded as *less than,* but as autonomous, individuals who equally contributed to the structure of the public and private spheres, that is, women in Siwa are perceived as equal members of the community. It is crucial to note here that oppression and one's experience with patriarchy is observer-relative; what may appear to be oppressive for some women, may not be experienced as oppressive by other women. As Kandiyoti (1988, p. 275) argued 'women strategise within a set of concrete constraints that reveal and define the blueprint (...) of patriarchal bargains, [which for] any given society, may exhibit variations according to class, caste and ethnicity'. In the case of Egypt, class and ethnicity are not the only characteristics that could influence the variation in patriarchal bargains, Religion as a patriarchal structure and location are similarly influential in shaping women's experience of patriarchy and the patriarchal structure.

Furthermore, the idea of living according to *Fitra* (instinct) distinguishes the Siwians from any other community in Egypt. The idea is to live as one with their natural surroundings and quite literally follow their guts. During participant observations, the researcher noted that the nomadic community's clock is governed by the sun. They wake up at dawn and go to bed at dusk. They refer to their lifestyle as 'instinctive' (*Fitra*) and believe living in harmony with nature is crucial for a balanced, productive and fulfilled life. However, the researcher noted that *Fitra* extends beyond the productive capacity, it dictates a strong emotional and spiritual connection to the land. Siwians have accepted and adopted Sufi Islam, which aligns with their existing belief that inanimate objects possess energy which flows around and within them. Working the land is considered to be a spiritual practice and not a source of increasing food supply. Much like fasting during Ramadan is meant to discipline the spirit and teach the person to control their impulses, physical labour is approached similarly in Siwa. It is also considered a form of meditative practice, which connects the people with their land and disciplines their spirits. The Siwians rely on *Fitra* for almost every aspect of their lives, which contributed to the lack of consumeristic and materialist behaviours. As CI3m(79) elaborated:

> It is the natural instinct and how God created us. There are no external influences on Siwa. We have a tree and from the tree, we built everything else. We also set our own laws based on our *Fitra* and those laws are called *Al-Orff*. It all comes from *Al-Fitra.*

AI3e(83) respectively, defensively told the researcher:

> We used to live based on our natural instincts. We did not know how to lie, steal, hate, or any of that. Because of the strangers who entered Siwa [pointing towards the researcher], we changed.

> Before, people used to leave their doors open at night. Now, there are drugs and alcohol, which were not found here before. However, at least our girls are still protected and safe not like in Egypt.

The chapter thus far reiterated the role religion plays in cultural understandings and practices, particularly in Egypt. While for urban/rural Egyptians Sunni Islam is the dominant interpretation of Islamic scripture, in Siwa the Sufi denomination dominates. The development of each interpretation had visible consequences on gender relations in contemporary Egypt, which only became apparent after Siwa opened its borders to internal tourists from other areas in 2001. On the one hand, the Sunni interpretation appears to have been used to subordinate women while the Sufi interpretation seems to guarantee their equal status. On the other hand, they are two interpretations of the same scripture and seemed to create two distinct cultural understandings: gender-based discrimination and the unnaturalness of gender-based discrimination; while Sunni men expressed a woman's rightful place is in the private sphere as subordinate to her male counterpart, Sufi men expressed ridicule over the notion and perceive it as something that goes against *Fitra*. The fact that such radically different accounts could arise from the different readings of the same text is proof of the extent to which Egyptian culture is informed and legitimised by religion but also sheds light on how culture is not necessarily a direct result of religious scripture but of religious interpretation of scripture and political Islam. This is additionally highlighted in the patriarchal bargains that urban/rural women must adhere to and navigate by strategically using the Hijab, for which an equivalent patriarchal bargain could not be observed in Siwa.

Nonetheless, injustices were still observed in Siwa, and the extent to which they were informed by patriarchal culture and/or religious interpretation is investigated in the next section. The next section specifically looks at customary laws and their role in governing social relations. This includes a discussion about marriage, divorce, harassment, and domestic abuse, and an analysis of the Customary Laws, that is, *Orff* laws, to compare the gender-based legal discrimination affecting urban/rural women with the *Orff* laws affecting indigenous women. It is significant to note that *Orff* laws are based on the traditions and Qur'anic Scripture. The indigenous community in Siwa does not have a written constitution or any other form of legal documents which set out the rights, obligations, penalties, and regulations of the society. Rather, in Siwa, the head of the 11 tribes acts as judge, president, and jurist. The use of the term *customary laws* is a pragmatic approximation, as no equivalent to the word *Orff* exists in English. The purpose of the comparison is to tackle the last research question. Knowing that laws governing personal status laws are based on the *Sharia* of Islam, what role does religious interpretation play in challenging/perpetuating patriarchal structures?

3. Codifying the Status of Siwian Women

> Family is the most important thing. If a family member needs support, the whole tribe will stand by him. Connections are very important. AI3m(73)

This statement summarises the collective culture the researcher observed in Siwa. The idea of communal support and having a social responsibility to build strong familial and tribal connections were echoed by all participants interviewed in Siwa. As stated earlier in this chapter, there are ten Amazigh tribes and one Bedouin tribe in Siwa. According to the *Hakkay* Siwa's *Orff* (customary law) dictates that they cannot turn away those who seek help and refuge. The Arab Bedouin tribe in Siwa were members of the tribes in Marsa Matrouh (the closest city to Siwa). According to him, the tribe was exiled because a male member of the family, who is now deceased, had raped a young girl. The person in question received a harsh penalty, where his reproductive organs were removed with a knife, and he was stripped naked and put in the city square to bleed to death. According to the *Hakkay,* this is a tradition both ethnic groups share, and its objective is to humiliate as well as be a cautionary tale. The rapist's entire tribe was exiled as punishment for not raising their child 'properly' and sought refuge in Siwa. As the *Orff* dictated one cannot turn away those in need of help, the family was allowed to reside in Siwa until they are permitted back into their community. The family has been living in Siwa for over 50 years, and still has approximately 25 years left on their 75-year exile sentence. While the Siwians did accept the exiled tribe, they placed the family far from the tribes residing in Siwa.

A zero-tolerance *Orff* is also prominent in Siwa. AI3a(78) was asked whether she believed Siwa's society is patriarchal to which she said:

> If you ask a woman in Siwa, they will tell you no it's not. However, when you compare it to the West, it will be different because they think of our customs and traditions as patriarchal. The life of the man is all in the public sphere. As he has responsibilities, as well as rights. Those rights are that when he comes back home, he will find food and comfort. It is a social contract. For us. This is not patriarchy, but for the West it is. Women here believe that it is their role. They do not like it when their husbands help out in the house because this is their job. This is far from patriarchal and violent; this is a partnership in life that was set by our customs, traditions, and religion. I do not think this is only in Siwa but also in all the Eastern cultures. Additionally, violence against women is not accepted or tolerated in Siwa at all!

Indeed, Siwa superficially seems to have a gender discrepancy and segregates the sexes. While this could be interpreted as patriarchal or paternalistic, according to the women of Siwa it is far from it. To highlight the value system in Siwa, I asked participants about harassment, domestic abuse, and their approach to intermarital sex. Like any society, Siwa too has its dark side.

Generally, in Egypt, Personal Status Laws govern marriage and divorce and must be based on Islamic Sharia. As demonstrated in earlier chapters, the fact that personal status laws are fixed in the male-dominated interpretation of Islam is gravely problematic. First, Sunni Sharia Islam dictates that a Muslim man is allowed to marry a woman from any other faith, but is forbidden to marry an atheist. Respectively, a Muslim woman can only marry a Muslim man. The rationale behind it is sexist in nature: religion is passed down paternalistically, thus a Muslim man will automatically have Muslim children. The idea is to grow and sustain the *Muslim Umma* (see Chapter 4). Akou (2010, p. 1) elaborated on what the *Umma* entails, and explained:

> The concept of the *umma* as a global community of Muslims is quite old, going back to the earliest days of Islam. Originally, it was used in reference to the Muslim community established by the Prophet Mohammed and his Companions (peace be upon them) in Mecca, but over time the concept grew to include all Muslims in all lands regardless of time and space. In practice, however, it was difficult for individuals to experience the *umma*; only through extensive travel or undertaking the pilgrimage to Mecca (the *Hajj*) could the individual gain a sense of the true diversity of cultures within the larger Islamic community.

With that in mind, polygamy, as well as paternalism, were rationalised to be beneficial for the Muslims as a whole (see Chapter 2). As explained in earlier chapters, every child born to an Egyptian family must be declared Muslim, Coptic Christian, or Jewish. Legally, in Egypt, a child must be assigned a religious affiliation which appears on their birth certificate. When officials were asked why that is the case, one lawyer, CU1p(98) explained the religious affiliation of the deceased determines how their inheritance would be divided. He further explained the legal depth and necessity of knowing the person's religious affiliation, saying:

> There are two reasons we type down the religion of the person on their birth certificate and national ID, a social reason, and a religious reason. The social reason pertains to marriage and divorce; a Muslim woman cannot legally or religiously, marry a man from another faith. The same applies to Coptic Christian men and women who also are not allowed to marry from outside their faith. Divorce respectively also requires the identification of one's religious affiliation. For Muslims if a man has one wife or multiple wives, they all receive $1/8^{th}$ of the inheritance, for instance if a man is married to four women, each woman would receive a quarter of the $1/8^{th}$. Additionally, if a Muslim man has exclusive female children, they each get $2/3^{rd}$ and the remainder go to the father's siblings. If she is an only child, she gets half and the mother $1/8^{th}$ and the remainder go to the father's siblings. If the mother passes away first, then her husband inherits half of her inheritance, and the remainder goes to her siblings. If she has children, a quarter goes to the husband and the remainder is divided amongst the children depending on their sex. As a rule of thumb, a boy counts as two persons. So, if a person has two daughters and one son, the son gets twice as much as his sisters. However, the most important

thing to remember is that inheritance specifically is almost always on a case-by-case basis. Most of the time, the courts determine how much each family member gets because there is always a lot of disputes about it. As Sharia is what underlines the law in Egypt, Coptic Christians abide by the same rules for inheritance. However, a new law is now being drafted under the Personal Status Law which would allow Coptic Christians to: 1) choose to opt out of the Islamic inheritance guidelines, and 2) marry someone outside the church, but there are a lot of social and legal implications, so progress is slow. Lastly, if a person changes their religion, i.e., from Coptic to Muslim which is the only conversion you're allowed to do in Egypt, then their children and family members don't inherit anything and instead, their money is distributed to charities.

A representative from Al-Azhar who was interviewed verified this information. CR3c(11) added that a Muslim man inherits more than a woman because he has a religious responsibility to care for the female family members financially. He elaborated that this is what is meant by the Qur'anic verse (4:34) 'Men are the protectors and maintainers of women, because Allah has given the one more (strength) than the other, and because they support them from their means'. Furthermore, CR3c(11) also stated that if a brother is not able to financially support his sisters, then the inheritance should be divided equally, as men have an obligation to financially care, ergo why they receive a bigger portion from the inheritance. CU1p(98) verified that this is indeed the case, but very few women have pursued this in court, predominantly because it is considered shameful to take your brothers to court over money. He also disagreed with the dominant interpretation of this Qur'anic verse explaining that it is misappropriated by 'mankind' and does not resonate with the peaceful nature of Islamic scripture.

According to Mhajne (2020) Islam as a religion is viewed by secular and Islamist movements 'as the main point of reference for women's rights; they only differ in their interpretation and implementation of the texts'. Anwar Mhajne (2020) goes on to argue that 'the Egyptian government has used Islam and religious scholars to frame its gender reforms since the 1970s' and criticised the Egyptian government for its patriarchal exploitation of religion to frame 'any reforms as compliant with sharia and endorsed by religious institutions'. This, he argues, allows the regime to present itself as a champion of women's rights, while simultaneously pushing its ideological and political agenda. Agreeing, Saba Mahmood (2005) claimed that the government's co-optation of the discourse of freedom of choice and women's rights created the parameters of the patriarchal bargain Mahmood (2005) argued that patriarchal bargains women have to adhere to in Egypt are due to the confoundment of politics and religion, that is, political Islam, and asserted that women could utilise the social restrictions imposed on them to advance their emancipation. Mahmood stated that in order for this to be recognised and realised, feminist scholarship needs to be conceptually expanded. This, Mahmood (2005) stated, could be achieved by abandoning the assumption that women's agency must be accompanied by resistance to norms (p. 15). An example of this, Mahmood (2005, p. 146) explained, is women wearing the Hijab to signal piety, religiosity, and modesty in public spaces. It could be regarded as a strategy with a twofold purpose. On the one hand, it is a strategy employed by women to protect themselves from male violence when accessing the public sphere, and in this sense can be viewed as an adherence to the patriarchal bargain and as lack of resistance to patriarchal norms. On the other hand, capitalising on the supposed religious grounding of women's dress code, women who adhere to the patriarchal bargain could utilise the notions of piety, modesty, and religiosity to highlight that these are virtues mandated by Islam for all humans, not just women. In this sense, women 'do not regard authorised models of behaviour as an external social imposition that constrained the individual. Rather, they viewed socially prescribed forms of conduct as the potentialities, the "scaffolding" if you will, through which the self is realised' (Mahmood, 2005, p. 148). Respectively, Mhajne (2020) concluded that:

> To achieve any meaningful progress on women's issues in Egypt, a feminist engagement with religious texts is necessary. Any unilateral attempt by the government to enforce reforms will be rejected by religious institutions and large sectors of society. Female religious scholars must be better represented in religious institutions, and more support for women to study and critically engage with religious texts must be provided—without fear of retribution from the government.

The significance of including women in the critical engagement with religious texts is essential to both the contextual understanding of women's agency in Egypt, as well as the analysis of what constitutes resistance to social norms, the experience of patriarchy and patriarchal bargains. Back to the primary data, it must be noted that one man's disagreement with how scripture is misappropriated will have minimal effects in the real world, but for this book, the Al-Azhar representative's disagreement served to reinforce the necessary separation between religious interpretation and cultural practices (also highlighted in Chapters 1 and 2). While these are national laws, they do not directly apply to Special Groups, such as Siwians. Comparing urban/rural and indigenous communities, on the one hand, in urban/rural areas participants, such as BU3s(52), reported that 'the husband has a right to take all her money to force her to stay in this marriage. It, therefore, requires a great deal of audacity from the woman if she wants to get a *Khol'*[3][repudiation]' reflective of the patriarchal bargain in urban/rural areas of Egypt; in exchange for safety and financial security, women need to be subordinate to their male counterparts. On the other hand, in Siwa, according to CI3p(74):

> The Siwian female receives her entire inheritance, and she can manage it alone and her husband has no right to use it or even know how

---

[3]Roughly translates to repudiation or annulment and literally legally connotes the surrendering of all rights for the court to grant her the annulment, this includes the right to alimony, to the house, and to her children.

much it is. If she wants to use it to pay for things, like new clothes or some bills, this is considered a gift from her to her family, but she doesn't have to. But our women are good women. And because we are good men, the women happily share with us, especially during droughts when incomes are low. But we never ask for it.

This social practice reveals that the patriarchal bargain of urban/rural areas, which is set forth by the patriarchal system at the Family/Household Production, Culture and Violence Levels (Walby, 1990), are inapplicable within indigenous Siwa. From a theological perspective, Sharia Islam is applied almost perfectly in indigenous communities, which substantiates the argument that patriarchy and misogyny are not inherent to Islamic text but are dependent on interpretations of the text; there is a plethora of socially accepted and perpetuated attitudes and behaviours, particularly about women's rights and status, which are guised by the patriarchal system as 'Religious Mandates', when in fact, they are anthropic interpretations of decontextualised Qur'anic verses. As Mayer (2016) argued, the utilisation of religion to justify gender inequality could be perceived as an attempt to protect and reproduce the gendered status-quo, which serves the social hegemonic bloc, and strips Egyptian women of the right to agency and autonomy, rendering them helpless and powerless, second-class citizens.

Furthermore, investigating the role of religion in how the legal structure is designed, allows us to better measure how the interpretation of religion influenced patriarchal bargains. Specifically, the data used here touch upon the gender dynamics of marriage and divorce in Egypt to compare whether there are different legal frameworks that govern this social aspect for urban, rural, and indigenous women. Specifically, this section compares whether Walby's conceptualisation of Violence and the State are codifying and institutionalising male violence and domination in both contexts using the proxy of marriage and divorce. From the participant observations, it was noted that divorced women in urban and rural communities are stigmatised as 'bad women', while in the indigenous community of Siwa, a divorced woman is not subjugated to the same social stigmatisation. For instance, in rural communities, according to AR3m(60), 'society views divorced women very badly and will see them as a failure. They would say she should have tolerated the marriage and that the shadow of a man is better than the shadow of a wall'. AR2s(5) echoing the social discourse added:

> I've heard people say, 'don't acquaint yourself with this girl, her mother got divorced twice'. They humiliate the woman if she gets divorced. I think it's all about two people not getting along, but people always take it as a shameful thing and blame the woman'. A similar discourse was expressed in urban communities.

As AU2I(36) elaborated 'people see her as a divorced woman and nothing else. She is always to blame for the divorce and people always question her decency and say she is a bad woman'. BU2s(37) even went as far as to call it a 'taboo' and explained 'it's like she doesn't have a future anymore, as ridiculous as this might sound, this is the true reality of this country and society'. One male participant, reflecting on the unequal power distribution said that 'women who do not care about life anymore can file for divorce. If she has social-suicidal tendencies she can even file for *Khol'* [repudiation or annulment, legally surrendering]'. Respectively, AU2a(20) in an antagonised tone said '"Khol" is a law created by men for men with the objective to humiliate and punish a woman for daring to say "enough". Enough to abuse, enough to the humiliation, enough to life with this man'.

In juxtaposition, in Siwa, all participants who were asked to reflect on divorce and re-marriage provided answers along the lines of 'it is her fate'. When asked to elaborate, some participants, such as AI3m(73), said 'This is her destiny, her fate; it is not forbidden at all in our society. Once she gets a divorce she can re-marry after the three months of celibacy which God told us to do'. BI3p(87) enthusiastically added 'Not bad! It is okay and she will get married again. It's just her fate'. One of the male participants was asked whether he would be reserved if his daughter wanted to get a divorce, his response was:

> If she wants to get a divorce, I have no other option but to allow it. I am her father and I want what's best for her, and God told us to keep divorce as a last resort if arbitration between the parties doesn't work. But if she's mature enough to get married, she's mature enough to get a divorce. I raised her well.

Another father was asked the same question, to which he responded 'I must be wise and listen to her. It's her life'. CI3m(90) elaborated on the social context and said:

> We call a divorced woman a widow. People take care of her until she gets married. The girls go to her to learn what went wrong so they don't repeat the same mistakes, and the tribe takes care of her financially if she doesn't work or has her own money.

While superficially it may seem like Siwians approach divorce as a simple matter, there is a very rigorous hierarchical order and chain of command to the process. Most instances of divorce, which are few and far between in Siwa, result from domestic abuse cases. If abuse should occur, there are two simultaneous processes that ensue: inter-familial escalation and social escalation. Firstly, the wife who wants to get a divorce talks to her mother and expresses the desire to get divorced. The mother then approaches the mother-in-law and asks her to discipline the son. If the mother-in-law does not believe her son was in the wrong, the mother of the woman escalates the issue to the father. Repeating the process again. This normally ends with the father-in-law conceding and promising his son would behave better in the future. AI3m(73) shared her story with the researcher, saying:

> When I got married, he only slapped me once. I went to my mother, who told my father. My father stood by my side and spoke to my husband about how to treat me and how this violated our customs. My husband never touched me again. It is not accepted for

a husband to hit his wife at all. Then we met with our tribe's leader who set a financial compensation which my husband paid to me that I used to buy a new wardrobe. I only got slapped. My sister's husband punched her. Our tribe leader exiled him for 10 years and his entire family was responsible for paying compensation to her.

AI3m(80) was asked the same question, to which her initial response was, 'It doesn't happen. His family stops him from doing that'. After the question was paraphrased to sound more hypothetical the elderly woman said '[if it happened to me] I will just leave the house and go to my parents' house. A Siwian woman lives with her honour intact, and we are very proud and strong women'. This illuminates that pride and honour, virtues Siwian women enjoy, are inaccessible to some women in urban and rural communities, who are subjugated by the patriarchal system; where the patriarchal bargain dictates a woman exchanges any semblance of strategic interests for safety and financial security. Unlike the rural and urban contexts where the system is systematically subordinating women, Siwian women do not seem to be subjected to the same the patriarchal structures. Strategic gender interests positively affected the status of Siwian women, such as freedom from institutionalised male violence against women, equal opportunity to paid employment, equal distribution of domestic labour and gender responsibilities, and the equal recognition of the cultural, religious, and socio-political contributions of historical female figures. The Sufi interpretation also served to reinforce and promote the role of women in Islam as equal counterparts with men within the public and private spheres.

Nevertheless, life in Siwa is not perfect or ideal and there is evidence of a patriarchal side to Siwa's customs and traditions. Intermarital rape, for instance, is permissible and socially acceptable in Siwa, much like it is acceptable in urban and rural areas. The actions which warranted such a potent description are underage marriages. While most females in Siwa are married by the age of 16, and the age difference between them and the respective male suitors is 4–5 years, there is a dominant 'spinster' culture. A female unmarried by 20 is considered a spinster and is approached by suitors who seek a second or third wife, making the age difference bigger. Additionally, girls born with physical or psychological 'defects' are married off to older 'spinster' men. Due to the sensitivity of the topic, safety concerns, and the strong moral code of not violating community guidelines, offending participants, or losing credibility, the researcher only selected a few men with whom she had a strong rapport about the issue. One of the participants, CI3p(81) responded to the question 'is a husband allowed to force himself onto his wife', replied with:

> Yes, as he is free to do whatever he wants. The prophet said that even if a woman is riding a camel and the man asked her to do it right then and there, she must obey him. If a woman refuses and her husband is frustrated, the angels will be angry with her. If he asked her to bed, she must obey him.

The two other men interviewed cited the same supposed *Hadith* as evidence that Islam condones intermarital rape and grants men the right to seek sexual satisfaction with force. However, this attempt is reflective of Walby's concept of Sexuality being male-centred and speaks to how Violence is institutionalised globally. In the Egyptian context, however, the male domination over Sexuality and Violence are guised as thinly veiled as a religious mandate. This *Hadith,* evidently, does not exist and is considered ancient Egyptian folklore, demonstrating that Sexuality is universally male-centred and patriarchal, and negates that it is reflective of any religious framework. This incredible recitation of the *Hadith* and the pervasive number of cases of intermarital rape which are being passed as a Muslim man's God-given right, encouraged *Dar Al Ifta Al Masriyya* (the institute responsible for the passing of religious verdicts, and the only institute legally allowed to publish interpretations of Qur'an and *Hadith,* also called *Fatwa*) to issue the following statement:

> If the husband used violence to force his wife to sleep with him, he is legally a sinner, and she has the right to go to court and file a complaint against him to get punished. The woman also has the right to refuse to engage in sexual relations with her husband if he has a contagious disease or uses violence which hurts her body during sexual intercourse. The Islamic Sharia advised that the sexual intercourse between man and wife should be conducted with intimacy and love and made such amicable conduct as a sign of piety. God says in the Qur'an, 'Your wives are a place of sowing of seed for you, so come to your place of cultivation however you wish and make an introduction for yourselves. And fear Allah and know that you will meet Him. And give good tidings to the believers'. (2:223)

However, misinformation and illiteracy have caused the internalisation of this dynamic. The only woman, AI3m(92), who reluctantly agreed to answer this question stated, 'They are married so she is his right at the end of the day' and then declined the request to ask any follow-up questions. Respecting her right to privacy, the researcher did not ask any further questions and shied away from asking other women the same question.

Another patriarchal side of Siwian customs and traditions is the marrying-off of girls who have perceived physical deformities and/or psychological issues. AI3m(2) for example got married at 14-years-old because she was born with Phocomelia Syndrome.[4] When asked whether she understood the concept of marriage at such a young age, she said 'I knew some things, but the majority no. My friends told me some information'. Upon reflection on whether she thought this was acceptable or not, she said:

> It is wrong, as I lived four years with my husband, and he died after that. I became a widow with two kids when I was 18 years old.

---

[4]Phocomelia Syndrome is a genetically inherited disease which causes the underdevelopment of limbs and bones, particularly arms, the pelvic bone, and, more generally, bone density and structure.

> My life was destroyed too early. The woman who is widowed or divorced has a different lifestyle here. She cannot leave her house and no man is allowed to enter her house. She can remarry, and the tribe and family help, but they don't realise that I was just too young.

The researcher realised the woman's need to talk, to tell someone her story, and therefore remained quiet and listened to AI3m(2). During which she revealed that:

> The first one was 35 years old while I was 14 years old. He was sick and just died. The second one was in his 40s and I got a daughter from him, but then I got a divorce. He was beating me in front of my kids, so my brother took me and my children away and moved us into his house. My children suffered a lot from my second marriage.

After an emotionally devastating account of her life, AI3m(2) ended the monologue by saying 'I'm only alive for the kids. I want to die', after which the researcher immediately ended the conversation and stopped the recording.

In summation, while Siwa's *Orff* (customary laws) and traditions greatly favour women, there are some patriarchal cultural structures that oppress women, such as the allowance of intermarital rape and child brides, which reveal the darker nuances of the Siwian culture. While compared to urban and rural communities, women are more valued, respected, protected, and on next-to equal grounds to their male counterparts, the Siwian community is not free of misogynistic and patriarchal qualities. Despite, for instance, most acts of male violence against women being culturally unacceptable and legally criminal in Siwa – for example, harassers in Siwa are 'lashed 80 times and pay compensation to the family of the girl' (AI3m(80)), and the general perception is 'It is not the girl's fault at all. It is never justified' (CI3p(72)) Violating your wife is still accepted, however. Despite the zero-tolerance towards Violence Against Women (VAW), intermarital rape is not considered a form of VAW and is still considered a private matter and a taboo topic. Without so much as being allowed to discuss the issue, there does not seem to be any prospect that this patriarchal structure will change in the future. Therefore, from a third-party perspective, it is easy to assume that Siwa is as close to an egalitarian system as one can get, compared to the rest of Egypt, when you live among Siwians you are privy to the darker and hidden aspects of their life, which most certainly merits further research.

This chapter compared and contrasted women's social role and status in indigenous, rural and urban communities. The case study of Siwa highlighted that patriarchal notions and socially ascribed gender roles and hierarchies are not generalisable or applicable to all Egyptian women. The case of Siwa negated the claims that Islam is an inherently anti-woman and anti-feminist religion, by highlighting how different interpretations of the same scripture could generate two competing understandings of it. The chapter shed light on this marginalised religious denomination of Muslims and provided a platform for the Sufi narrative to be expressed by the indigenous community. By exploring how the Sufi interpretation influenced gender relations in Siwa and comparing the findings to how Sunni interpretations influenced gender relations, the chapter highlighted how discriminatory discourses are a product of male-dominated and patriarchal scripture interpretation; the Sufi interpretation challenges the Sunni interpretation of gender naturalisation which is exploited to legitimise the perpetuation of the patriarchal system. The next chapter discusses the implications of these findings and summarises more generally how the patriarchal system has prevented women from realising their strategic gender interests, and by extension perpetuated Egyptian women's second-class citizenship.

Chapter 8

Conclusion

This book set out to understand how the patriarchal system in Egypt prevented women from realising their strategic gender interests, and by extension perpetuating their second-class citizenship. The patriarchal system in Egypt exploited and manipulated women by advancing their practical gender interests, which served to maintain male domination and preserve the *status quo*, but prevented the actualisation of strategic interests and needs. The book highlighted how the perception of women as inferior is a social construct perpetuated and reproduced by the patriarchal system to consolidate and normalise women's second-class citizenship. Three objectives were set to tackle the research puzzle. The first objective investigated the historical and political instances within which women's second-class citizenship in Egypt was established. The second objective examined the intersectionality of the patriarchal system and Islam in reproducing women's inferiority to identify the patriarchal structures set, and which deny women access to full citizenship status. The third objective used the 100 interviews collected from 100 ordinary citizens (women $N=51$, men $N=49$) who were randomly selected and volunteered their time, to evaluate women's strategic use of the Hijab in navigating Egypt's patriarchal system. Each of the book's objectives were addressed using a set of questions designed to tackle the nuanced aspects of the issues covered. In this chapter, I present a summary of the findings, followed by a discussion of the implications of findings that emerged from the research questions. After the discussion, I conclude my findings and present my recommendations for future research.

1. Summary of Findings

Chapter 1 set out to address the first research objective: identifying the historical and political instances within which women's second-class citizenship in Egypt was established, tackling the first three research questions. The chapter started with a brief overview of feminist activism in Egypt throughout the 19th and 20th centuries. The literature was re-examined using the perspective of strategic gender interests. The re-examination from this perspective revealed that the Egyptian Government played an active role in suppressing the political and social status of Egyptian women. Nonetheless, the Egyptian Government exploited women for their practical presence during moments of national consolidation particularly in

2019 and again in 2011. However, after the liberation of Egypt in 1952, women's and feminists' efforts to attain women's strategic gender interests were quickly absorbed and monopolised by the State. The review of the literature also revealed that political Islam played an instrumental role in solidifying women's socio-political inferiority. Specifically, the findings suggest that political Islam is based on the male interpretation of scripture and is highly politicised. Political Islam was strategically used by the government to rationalise and legitimise denying women equal opportunities, rights, and access, that is, their strategic gender interests which are required to challenge existing power structures. The chapter also shed light on how the male-dominated Sunni interpretation of Islamic scripture resulted in the cultural understanding of naturalisation theory, which argues that women are naturally, and by divine order, subordinate to men and therefore occupy a *less than human* position. The chapter concluded that since 1952, Political Islam was operationalised by the government to gain and maintain men's control over the structures of Family/Household Production, Paid Labour, Sexuality, and Culture (Walby, 1990). The government also institutionalised the patriarchal system of male domination and control by creating a legal framework which favours men and discriminates against women using Islam as a political legitimation tool. Amr Hamzawy (2017) elaborated on the consequences of using Islam. His observations are consistent with the findings and showcase that the use of religion as a political tool is a longstanding political tradition in Egypt. Hamzawy (2017) stated:

> The new authoritarian government is using official Islamic and Christian institutions to impose its own interpretations of religion on Egyptian society ... the government frames obedience to the ruling general and the approval of its policies as a religious duty ... [and] the generals use religious symbols and statements in the public space to rationalise repression and human rights abuses and to demand popular support for the messiah in uniform.

Building on these observations, Chapter 2 unpacked gender-based legal discrimination in Egypt and set out to address the second research objective: understanding the intersectionality of the patriarchal system and Islam in reproducing women's inferiority, and identifying patriarchal structures which deny women access to full citizenship status. The chapter continued the discussion of the ramifications of state-sponsored feminism in the 1970s and 1980s in Egypt. The legal framework in Egypt which governs personal status laws, also known as Family laws, is based on the rules of Sharia Islam. As in the Sunni tradition, only male interpretations of scripture are included, the personal status laws reflected the male understanding of women's rights, status and 'place' in society. By critically analysing the legal framework in Egypt, the findings suggest that political Islam played a significant role in constructing the secondary status of Egyptian women. The chapter also highlighted that the resurgence of traditional and conservative practices in Egypt, such as the Hijab, is positively related to political Islam and the patriarchal system. Finally, the chapter concluded that how women are perceived by society is shaped by the patriarchal structures and legitimised by the male-dominant interpretation of scripture. The combination of both resulted in the codification of Egyptian women's inferiority and *less than human* secondary status.

The first two chapters critically re-examined and contextualised women's strategic gender interests in Egypt, and established what occurred in Egypt which led to the consolidation and normalisation of women's secondary citizenship status. Chapter 3, respectively, laid out the research approach, the methodology, method, tools, and conceptual framework adopted and used in the data collection for this project. The chapter qualified why the qualitative methodology was deemed the appropriate approach for the project, introduced, and explained the method of auto-ethnography and how it was operationalised during data collection. Most significantly, the chapter introduced Walby's *Six Structures of Patriarchy* and explained how they relate to the context of Egypt. Walby's conceptual framework underlined the analysis of the empirical chapters.

Chapters 4–6 constitute the empirical chapters of the book. The chapters relied on the collected data to address the third research objective: evaluating women's strategic use of the Hijab in navigating Egypt's patriarchal system. Each chapter addressed a specific research question. Chapter 4 specifically tackled the question: what did the data about patriarchal bargains women employ in Egypt to gain greater security and autonomy? Once Walby's conceptual framework was identified, it affected how the data were approached, so Chapter 4 starts with a short discussion reflecting on the first two chapters. The application of the conceptual framework to the Egyptian case study reframed the secondary data and highlighted that emancipatory efforts aimed at gaining women greater agency, autonomy, opportunity, and greater status were either suppressed, and/or rationalised, by using Islam as an instrument of legitimation, or denied altogether. The chapter then proceeded to analyse the primary data using Walby's conceptual framework and found that the women's unactualised strategic gender interests allowed the patriarchal system to prevail. The data highlighted that class and religion are two significant social aspects which determine the extent of 'real freedoms' (Sen, 2000) Egyptians can pursue. Additionally, it also emphasised how education is key in challenging gender dynamics and relations in Egypt, which is believed to be the only path to make women aware of their strategic gender interests so that they may pursue them and challenge male-domination and violence. The chapter concluded that the patriarchal bargain in Egypt entails women exchanging their strategic gender interests for financial security and protection from male violence, which resulted in women being categorically socialised to believe in their primary role as homemakers. The chapter concluded that the patriarchal bargain in Egypt is in essence an exchange between women's autonomy and agency for their safety and security.

Building on these findings, Chapter 5 addressed the question: what is the role of the Hijab in signalling adherence to the rules of the patriarchal bargain? The chapter started by first establishing what the Hijab represents for Egyptian women and men. After it was established that the Hijab is believed to gain women greater security within the public sphere and signal women's adherence to the patriarchal rules and bargains, the testimonies of women and men showcased that while women may believe the Hijab signals their adherence and therefore protects them from male violence, men do not believe in the Hijab's protective qualities. This was further investigated in accordance with the conceptual framework which revealed that while women believe the Hijab protects them from male violence, the patriarchal structures of Violence and the State (established in Chapters 1 and 2) institutionalised women's inferiority and second-class citizenship and codified male domination, creating a culture where 'men are able to utilise considerable amounts of violence against women with impunity' (Walby, 1990, p. 150). This unveiled that, while women may be adhering to the rules of the patriarchal bargain, Egyptian men do not uphold their end of the bargain, putting women in a double bind.

The double bind of the Egyptian patriarchal bargain however was not generalisable to all Egyptian women. The data were collected from two urban areas, Cairo and Alexandria, two rural areas, Kafr El Shaikh and Fayoum, and one indigenous community, the Amazigh of Siwa. This primary data reflected two types of ethnic communities, governing systems, and even religious interpretations. This previously unknown fact to the researcher emerged from the primary data and highlighted that while all areas are encompassed within the borders of Egypt, Siwa is self-governing and ethnically dissimilar to the rest of Egypt, belonging to and adopting a different religious denomination. Chapter 6, therefore, tackled the last research question: knowing that laws governing Person Status are based on the Sharia of Islam, what role did religious interpretation play in challenging/perpetuating patriarchal bargains? The chapter started by first introducing the Siwian population, which contributes to the limited knowledge we have about the Amazigh ethnic indigenous community. It then moved on to highlight the difference in cultural understanding, governing style, and legal framework between Siwa and other areas in Egypt. These differences explained why gender relations in Siwa are radically different from gender relations in urban/rural areas. The chapter built on the findings of Chapter 5 and compared the different positions of urban/rural women to that of Siwian indigenous women.

The contextual findings reinforced the argument that the male-dominant Sunni interpretation of Sharia played a key role in rationalising the dehumanisation of urban/rural women who the patriarchal system exploited to institutionalise Egyptian women's secondary citizenship status. This was substantiated by comparing the influence of the Sufi and Sunni interpretations on Walby's concepts of Culture, Sexuality, Violence, the State, and Family/Household Production. The Sufi interpretation was developed by incorporating both female and male scholarship, and the Sunni interpretation was developed exclusively on male scholarship. The chapter concluded that discriminatory discourses are a product of male-dominated and patriarchal scripture interpretation; the Sufi interpretation challenges the Sunni interpretation of gender naturalisation which is exploited to legitimise the perpetuation of the patriarchal structures in urban and rural areas.

While this study did not intentionally set out to conduct a comparative analysis, the data collected from Siwa produced these interesting findings. First, it is not common knowledge that Siwa is a self-governing, ethnically dissimilar, Sufi tribal population. Second, it is not common knowledge that Siwa is protected by Special Group Rights, which divides Egypt into two categories: those that self-govern and those that adhere to the laws established in the political capital, Cairo. It was during fieldwork that these comparative differences came to light. These revelations which emerged from the data critically affected this study's findings on how the patriarchal system advanced women's practical interests while supressing their realisation of strategic gender interests, effectively perpetuating and reproducing women's subordination and, by extension, their second-class citizenship.

2. Discussion

Religion plays a key role in Egypt. It appears to govern how Egyptians behave and what they believe to be truthful knowledge. Egyptian citizens in urban and rural areas appear to only be exposed to the male-dominant Sunni Interpretation of Islam, which informs their social identities, understandings, and perceptions. Religion appeared systematically in different contexts. First, the book highlighted how religion was significant in political liberation movements in constructing a national identity to counteract British colonialism. Second, religion appeared as an influencing factor in how the State approached policies and polity. This confounding of religion and politics, resulted in the State's adoption of political Islam, that is, 'any interpretation of Islam that serves as a basis for political identity and action [and] more specifically, refers to the movements representing modern political mobilisation in the name of Islam, a trend that emerged in the late 20th century' (Voll & Sonn, 2009).

This was recognised by Arthur Jeffery (1942) who explained that 'religious principals are an integral part of the Muslims conception of the State' (p. 393), to the extent where the discourse 'political victories were victories for Islam' emerged, underlying national liberation efforts. According to Jeffery (1942), the pan-Islamic colonial opposition arose as the common identity of colonised nations and created a political environment in Muslim majority countries where colonial powers, like the British in Egypt and the French in Morroco, were perceived as administering social, legal, and political systems that violated 'religious conviction' and the Muslim conception of the State, and 'defy not man but Allah' (pp. 390–393). This explains the findings of Chapter 1 by shedding light on how political Islam came to be the *raison d'étre* for Egyptian opposition. Notably, this underlined the national identity in Egypt upon which the government is constructed. It is thereby unsurprising that the first chapter noted how women were mobilised for the *practical* (Molyneux, 1985) presence during movements of resistance.

This *raison d'étre* was instilled in 1919 and continued to develop for years until the functioning liberation of Egypt in 1952. By that time, political Islam had become the political ideology of the State and the baseline for Egyptian culture and social structure. It proliferated into other aspects of policy and polity. This book looked at how it affected women's status and found that the male-dominant Sunni interpretation of Islam upon which political Islam in Egypt is structured was the interpretation adopted in Egypt. Kandiyoti (1991a, b) noted that after national consolidation, and in areas where classic patriarchy is prevalent, conservative reactionary forces will attempt to 'reverse what appeared to be the steady expansion of women's rights in the early stages of national consolidation' (p. 12). This observation is true for the Egyptian context, where this reversal manifested in the State granting women suffrage in 1956 and then immediately outlawing feminist and women's organisations which demanded the emancipation of women – the attainment of strategic gender interests so that women may challenge their exclusion and the patriarchal structures. The findings of Chapter 1 also showcased how this appearance of state-sponsored feminism systematically suppressed the actualisation of women's strategic gender interests: to maintain the patriarchal system the State's legal framework was refined to ascribe and institutionalise gender roles. Kabeer (2001) argued that for a person to challenge patriarchal structures they must recognise that structures 'operate through the rules, norms and practices of different institutions to determine the resources, agency and achievement possibilities available to different groups of individuals in a society' (p. 26). In essence, rephrasing Amaraty Sen's (1985a, b, 1992, 1990, 1995) 'capabilities as real freedoms', Kabeer (2006) posited that investigating the 'deeper hidden structures' is essential as they dictate the 'distribution of resources and power in a society and reproduce it over time' (Kabeer, 2001, p. 27). Concurring with the findings of Kabeer (2001), this book also found that for

> change to translate into meaningful and sustainable processes of empowerment, it must ultimately encompass both individual and structural levels. The institution of rights within the legal framework of a society is meaningless unless these rights have a real impact on the range of possibilities available to all individuals in that society. (p. 28)

The critical review of secondary data revealed that the legal framework in Egypt institutionalised gender-based violence and discrimination, upon which the society constructed the parameters of the patriarchal structures to which women had to adhere to or face sanctions for noncompliance. Specifically, the adoption of the male-dominant Sunni interpretation of Islam proved to be detrimental to the construction of a meaningful and sustainable legal framework to govern Personal Status Laws in Egypt. This was evident in the State's continued insistence to maintain Personal Status Laws under Islamic Sharia. The fact that Sunni interpretation is the dominant one in urban/rural areas of Egypt, personal status laws project a male narrative of what are believed to be women's rights. Through the use of dehumanisation strategies, these laws, in essence, codified women's inferiority and created an institutional structure where 'men are able to utilise considerable amounts of violence against women with impunity' (Walby, 1990, p. 150). Similar to Kabeer, this book also found that the lack of enforcement of the few laws that do protect women's rights in the personal status law rendered it 'meaningless'. In essence, the law does not have a 'real impact', nor does it protect 'the range of possibilities available to all individuals in society' (Kabeer, 2001, p. 28), rather it protects male control, perpetuates male violence against women, and reproduces the patriarchal system.

The continued prevalence of the patriarchal system in Egypt is attributed to the systematic dehumanisation of women, particularly as the Sunni interpretation of Islam actively supports gender naturalisation. As highlighted in Chapter 2, gender-based legal discrimination and patriarchal Sunni interpretation of scripture served to codify and institutionalise women's inferiority. We can see evidence of women's lack of capabilities in 'existing value systems [being] highly paternalistic, particularly towards women. They treat them as unequal under the law, as lacking full civil capacity, as not having the property rights, associative liberties and employment rights of males' (Nussbaum, 1999, p. 231). We can also see clear evidence of six out of the seven forms of dehumanisation Nussbaum (1999) identified. First, in the private sphere, women are valued for their 'instrumentality' as sexual objects, perceived to exist for male satisfaction and subject to men's claims of 'ownership'. Second, in the political sphere, the Egyptian legal framework served the 'denial of autonomy' and 'inertness' for Egyptian women by passing unequal penalties for the same crimes for women and men, not recognising the shortcomings of the legal framework in protecting women against gender-based violence in the private sphere or the public sphere and lack of proper enforcement of the laws that do. Third, in the social sphere, the social perception of women as inferior and the inadequate and gender discriminatory legal framework, which served to solidify it, normalise the 'violability' of women, led to women's 'denial of subjectivity'. These six types of dehumanisation processes worked to maintain women's subordination in Egypt, through the systemic promotion of 'false consciousness, or the internalisation of patriarchal norms through socialisation' (Mahmood, 2011, p. 205).

To further investigate how the dehumanisation process affected the status of Egyptian women in contemporary Egypt, I operationalised Walby's (1990) *Six Structures of Patriarchy* conceptual framework. Walby (1990, p. 20) defined a patriarchal system as a 'system of social structures and practices in which men dominate, oppress and exploit women'. She identified six levels that encompass the significant 'social structures' that she believes can assist in measuring low/high levels of oppression within the patriarchal system. These six levels are: (1) Paid Employment, that is, gender pay gaps and gendered value of labour (p. 25); (2) Household production, that is, domestic division of labour and responsibilities (p. 61); (3) Culture, that is, cultural notions of femininity and masculinity and gender expectations (p. 90); (4) Sexuality, that is, attitudes towards sex as either a source of pleasure or as a tool for control and domination (p. 109); (5) Violence, that is, male violence against women (p. 128); and (6) the State, that is, efforts to improve women's status in society through laws and political action (p. 150). Similarly, this book draws on the different structures of patriarchy to understand how these social structures operate within the Egyptian context. Dissimilar to Walby, who focussed on studying women's subordination in the Western context, this study focussed on the Egyptian context. The primary data revealed that Egyptian women have marginal agency and autonomy to realise their strategic gender interests. Their inability to enact their agency and autonomy is a direct result of the patriarchal system preventing women from realising and actualising their strategic gender interests. Walby's conceptual framework was situated within the Egyptian context and crystalised the extent to which the patriarchal system restrained women's realisation of their strategic gender interests. At each level where women could assert their equal power and exert control on matters which affect them.

The patriarchal structure in Egypt blocked women's realisation of their strategic gender interests. In the private sphere, in terms of Paid Employment and

Family/Household Production, women can be denied the opportunity to enter the public sphere by their male 'guardians'. Their domestic labour is exploited by men and reproduced by the Sunni interpretation that it is a woman's duty to be a homemaker. In the public sphere, in terms of Culture and Sexuality, women are deterred by the threat of male violence and socialised to believe that their rightful 'place' in society is in the private sphere. To manoeuvre this patriarchal bargain, the Hijab emerged as a strategy for women to navigate the patriarchal system, therefore making 'invisibility' within the public sphere a strategic necessity and the Hijab a means to satisfy this necessity. Nonetheless, the patriarchal notions embedded within Egypt's legal framework institutionalised male violence against women, leading men to perceive women as 'violable' aggravating women's dehumanisation. In addition, at the State level, the government failed to enforce the few laws that do protect women's interests and rights, thereby giving men to ability to use 'considerable amounts of violence against women with impunity' (Walby, 1990, p. 150).

The choices available to women with their limited agency and autonomy were described by Mona ElTahawy (2015) as hateful violence against women. In her book *Headscarves and Hymens,* she asked 'why do those men hate us?'. Her answer reflects the anger many Egyptian women interviewed for this book expressed,

> they hate us because they need us, they fear us, they understand how much control it takes to keep us in line, to keep us good girls with our hymens intact until it's time for them to f**k us into mothers who raise future generations of misogynists to forever fuel their patriarchy. (ElTahawy, 2015, p. 25)

The author continued to urge her readers to recognise how patriarchy harms men as well, which this book also highlighted, and declares that 'once we rid ourselves of the alliance of State and Street that works in tandem to control us, we will demand a reckoning' (ElTahawy, 2015, p. 25). In other words, ElTahawy (2015) shed light on the brewing anger and frustrations Egyptian women feel, nonetheless, the research data also shed light on how some women reproduce and perpetuate the patriarchal structures, which subjugate them, with their offspring.

Moreover, Deniz Kandiyoti (1988) observed that 'women in areas of classic patriarchy often adhere as far and as long as they possibly can to rules' of the patriarchal bargain, positioning women in a setting where they are in active 'collusion in the reproduction of their own subordination' (p. 289). The primary data suggests that some Egyptian women also actively collude and reproduce the patriarchal system. The rules of the patriarchal bargain in Egypt dictate that in exchange for safety and financial security women have to give up their agency and autonomy and accept their primary role of homemaker. The data also revealed that women in Egypt have a desire to enter the public sphere (Chapter 4), yet to do so without violating the patriarchal bargain, women strategically used the Hijab to be 'invisible' within the public sphere. The strategic use of the Hijab to avoid being subjected to male violence in the public sphere was also confirmed by Diwan et al. (2017), who highlighted that 'It is possible that a woman's appearance may affect the threat of violence – that is, in Muslim majority countries, non-veiled women may be more at risk of assault' (p. 14). This survey study also revealed that 96% of male participants in the study attribute harassment to enticing make up application and provocative clothing, and a woman's disregard to 'cultural traditions' (Diwan et al., 2017). The survey also revealed that 99% of female participants in the study admitted to having been sexually harassed, with 91.5% of these female participants stating they experienced unrequited physical harassment. The study concluded that the Hijab is operationalised by Egyptian women strategically to protect themselves from male violence in public spaces.

However, the strategic use of the Hijab to navigate the patriarchal bargain and gain greater safety within the public sphere is not a strategy all Egyptian women employ. The indigenous community of Siwa perceive women as equal counterparts, and women's rights, roles, and status are protected by their *Orff* Laws – oral Customary Laws which are based on the Amazigh traditions and the Qur'an and make up their legal framework. The considerably different perceptions of Siwian women are believed to be the result of their adoption of the Sufi interpretation of scripture, which Chapter 6 detailed was historically developed using female and male scholarship, and not just male scholarship like the Sunni interpretation. The Sufi interpretation was reflected in every aspect of social and political life for Siwians. First, the Sufi interpretation of the Qur'an perceives women as equal counterparts to males and dismisses claims of male hegemony which the patriarchal Sunni interpretation assumed. The legal framework in Siwa, therefore, is designed to punish any violator and was described as being especially relentless on any form of male violence against women.

Second, the Hijab was historically used by the nomadic tribes of Siwa to protect the skin from the harmful effects while wandering through the Sahara. When the 10 tribes which now make up the population of Siwa settled in the oasis they converted to Islam and particularly adopted the Sufi interpretation as it was the one most compatible with their traditional nomadic beliefs and values, and their traditional and customary practices. With the drawing of national borders, the redefinition of the world map by colonial powers, and other significant historical factors, Siwa was encompassed by the Egyptian nation's borders. Years later, the legal framework in Egypt recognised their status as a Special Group and granted them Special Group Rights which included self-governance. Being self-governing, and recognising the major role religion played in rationalising and legitimating the patriarchal system, radically changed the socio-political and cultural understanding of Siwian women. For instance, there was little to no evidence that the same or equivalent process of dehumanisation, which solidified and consolidated urban/rural women's inferiority, occurred in Siwa. As women's dehumanisation was rationalised and legitimised using the patriarchal and male-dominated Sunni interpretation of Islam, and then institutionalised in the form of Sharia-informed personal status laws. This solidified the argument that religion is a significant instrument of the patriarchal system as it is virtually codependent on it for its legitimation and power consolidation. It additionally substantiates the argument that religion can be a political and patriarchal tool. This study revealed that the *Six Structures of Patriarchy* are not inclusive of the added dimension of religion.

Reflecting on the conceptual framework and contribution this book made, Fig. 9 is an alternative diagram with 'Religion' as a patriarchal structure, which could be operationalised for future research on the subordination of women in Muslim Majority countries.

However, the primary data which were collected from Egypt revealed that religion affects every aspect of life, which is why this book proposes that it be included concurrently while operationalising Walby's conceptual framework. This study demonstrated how religion interacts with each of Walby's concepts, making it a significant contributor to participants' worldviews and experiences. Fig. 10 demonstrates an alternative diagram to how religion could also interact with the *Six Structures of Patriarchy*.

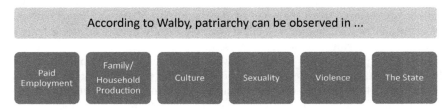

Fig. 9.   Walby's Six Structures of Patriarchy.

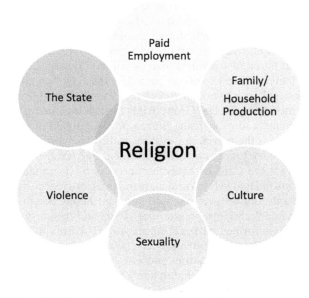

Fig. 10.   ElMorally's Seven Structures of Patriarchy.

3. Conclusion

This book recommends that researchers conducting similar qualitative studies recognise the role religion plays in constituting discourses, maintaining structures, and reproducing dominance and inferiority. The book particularly highlighted that the significance of religious interpretation cannot be overstated when examining gender relations and/or trying to figure out how women are prevented from realising their strategic gender interests within the confines of the patriarchal system. Furthermore, caution is advised when collecting data from sensitive political and social environments of Middle Eastern and Northern African nations and the use of the Hijab is recommended as a proxy measure when investigating women's issues. In this study, the Hijab was pre-identified as a proxy to inquire sensitively about women's subordination. The findings revealed that fewer women wear the Hijab for religious reasons than do for strategic ones. The Hijab needs to be recognised within whatever context future researchers investigate. The Hijab has different meanings, representations, and connotations for different Muslim women within different nations. While this study concluded that the Hijab is a strategy to navigate the patriarchal bargain in Egypt, the patriarchal system is double-binding women as men do not hold up their end of the bargain. However, it also revealed that this is untrue for indigenous Siwian women, who do not have a strategic use for wearing the Hijab. If these differences exist within one nation, they inevitably exist between nations.

This book set out to understand how the patriarchal system in Egypt prevented women from realising their strategic gender interests, and by extension perpetuated their second-class citizenship. The book concluded that the patriarchal system in Egypt succeeded in preventing women from realising their strategic gender interests by socially and structurally institutionalising women's inferiority. The systematic oppression of Egyptian women led to some women internalising their inferiority while perceiving themselves as naturally, and by divine order, subordinate to men. This resulted in Egyptian women actively colluding with the patriarchal structure and reproducing their inferiority. The Hijab as a strategy to navigate the patriarchal bargain is evidence that most women are resisting the patriarchal structure with the limited agency and autonomy they possess, which has deemed them as second-class citizens. However, unless women's 'real freedoms', including political freedoms, social equality, equal opportunity and economic empowerment, and protective security, are recognised, the patriarchal system will continue to exploit and manipulate women for their practical gender interests, which served to maintain male domination and preserve the status quo.

Bibliography

28TooMany. (2018). *Egypt: The law and FGM*. 28TooMany. Retrieved April 29, 2022, from https://www.28toomany.org/static/media/uploads/Law%20Reports/egypt_law_report_v1_(june_2018).pdf
Abbott, P., & Teti, A. (2017). *Against the tide: Why women's equality remains a distant dream in Arab countries*. The Conversation. https://theconversation.com/against-the-tide-why-womens-equality-remains-a-distant-dream-in-arab-countries-74410
Abdelhadi, M. (2006). *Sadat's legacy of peace and conflict*. BBC archives. http://news.bbc.co.uk/1/hi/world/middle_east/5412590.stm
Abdelhadi, E. (2016). Women's rights in Egypt: An overview of legislative reforms. *Journal of Egyptian Studies, 22*(1), 112–129.
Abdelhady, W. (2016). *Honor crimes and violence against women: Preventing and punishing honor killings*. Tilburg University Press.
Abdel-Haleem, M. A. S. (2005). *The Qur'an: A New Translation*. Oxford University Press.
Abdulaal, M. (2018). *Are 99% of Egyptian women sexually harassed?* Egyptian Streets. https://egyptianstreets.com/2018/11/28/are-99-of-egyptian-women-harassed/
Abu Dawud, H. (2008). *Sunnan Abu Dawud* (Y. Qadhi, Trans.). Maktaba Dar-us-Salam.
Abu-Lughod, L. (1988). The marriage of feminism and Islamism in Egypt: Selective repudiation as a dynamic of postcolonial cultural politics. In L. Abu-Lughod (Ed.), *Remaking women: Feminism and modernity in the Middle East* (pp. 243–269). Princeton University Press.
Abu-Lughod, L. (2002). Do Muslim women really need saving? Anthropological reflections on cultural relativism and its others. *American Anthropologist, 104*(3), 783–790.
Abu-Lughod, L. (2010). The active social life of "Muslim Women's Rights": A plea for ethnography, not polemic, with cases from Egypt and Palestine. *Journal of Middle East Women's Studies, 6*(1), 1–45.
Abu-Lughod, L. (2013). *Do Muslim women need saving?* Harvard University Press.
Abu-Odeh, L. (2004). *Modernizing Muslim family law: The case of Egypt*. Georgetown Law Faculty Publications and Other Works, 38.
Ackerman, S. R. (2007). Judicial independence and corruption. In D. Rodriguez & L. Ehrichs (Eds.), *Global corruption report: Corruption in judicial systems*. Transparency International and Cambridge University Press.
Adams, T., Ellis, C., & Jones, S. H. (2014). Autoethnography. In J. Matthes, C. S. Davis, & R. F. Potter (Eds.), *The international encyclopedia of communication research methods* (pp. 1–11). John Wiley & Sons.
Adams, V., & Pegg, S. L. (2005). Sex in development: Science, sexuality, and morality in global perspective. *Archives of Sexual Behavior, 40*(5), 1079–1080.
Adang, C. (2002). Women's access to public space according to al-Muhalla bil-Athar. In N. Marin & R. Deguilhem (Eds.), *Writing the feminine: Women in Arab sources* (pp. 75–94). I. B. Tauris.
Addison, C. (2020). Radical feminism and androcide in Nawal El Saadawi's woman at point zero. *English Studies in Africa, 63*(2), 1–13.
Adorno, T., & Horkheimer, M. (1991). The schema of mass culture. In J. Bernstein (Ed.), *The culture industry*. Routledge.

Bibliography

Ager, K., Albrecht, N. J., & Cohen, M. (2015). Mindfulness in schools research project: Exploring students' perspectives of mindfulness. *Psychology, 6*, 896–914.

Ahluwalia, P. (2002). The struggle for African identity: Thabo Mbeki's African renaissance. *African and Asian Studies, 1*(4), 265–277.

Ahmed, D., & Ginsburg, T. (2014). Constitutional Islamization and human rights: The surprising origin and spread of Islamic supremacy in constitutions. *Virginia Journal of International Law, 54*(3), 615–695.

Ahmed, L. (1982a). Feminism and feminist movements in the Middle East. Preliminary explorations in Turkey, Egypt, Algeria and the People's Republic of Yemen. In A. Al-Hibri (Ed.), *Women and Islam* (pp. 153–168). Pergamon Press.

Ahmed, L. (1982b). Western ethnocentrism and perceptions of the Harem. *Feminist Studies, 8*(3), 521–534.

Ahmed, L. (1992). *Women and gender and Islam*. Yale University Press.

Ahmed, L. (1993). *Women and gender in Islam: Historical roots of a modern debate*. Yale University Press.

Ahmed, L. (2011). The 1970s: Seeds of resurgence. In *A quiet revolution: The veil's resurgence, from Middle East to America* (pp. 68–92). Yale University Press.

Ahmed, M. (1975). Umma: The idea of a universal community. *Islamic Studies, 14*(1), 27–54.

Ahmed, R. S. (2010). Who killed Nasser? *Egypt Independent*. https://egyptindependent.com/who-killed-nasser/

Ahmed, S. (2017). Mayim Bialik, if you think modest clothing protects you from sexual harassment, you need to listen to these Muslim women. *The Independent*. Retrieved June 3, 2019, from https://www.independent.co.uk/voices/modest-clothing-mayim-bialik-harvey-weinstein-sexual-harassment-muslim-women-a8004501.html

Ahmed, S. (2018). *On this day: Egypt's remarkable 1952 revolution anniversary*. Egyptian Streets. https://egyptianstreets.com/2018/07/23/on-this-day-egypts-remarkable-1952-revolution-anniversary/

Ahmed, S. (2021). *The regime between stability and stumbling: Family law in Egypt*. Carnegie Endowment for International Peace. https://carnegieendowment.org/sada/85081

Ahram Online. (2014). Egypt's referendum poll results 1956–2012. *Ahram Online*. https://english.ahram.org.eg/NewsPrint/91674.aspx

Aikman, D. (1999). Egypt's human wrongs. *American Spectator, 32*(3), 64–66.

Akbar, S. A., & Donnan, H. (1994). Islam in the age of postmodernity. In S. A. Akbar & H. Donnan (Eds.), *Islam, globalization and postmodernity* (pp. 1–20). Routledge.

Akkoç, N. (2004). The cultural basis of violence in the name of honour. In S. Mojab & N. Abdo (Eds.), *Violence in the name of honour* (pp. 113–126). Bilgi Üniversitesi Press House.

Akou, H. M. (2007). Building a new "world fashion": Islamic dress in the twenty-first century. *Fashion Theory, 11*, 403–421.

Akou, H. M. (2010). Head coverings in the virtual Umma: The case of Niqab. *Textile Society of American Symposium Proceedings, 3*, 1–6.

Akyol, M. (2019). *Turkey's troubled experiment with secularism*. The Century Foundation. https://tcf.org/content/report/turkeys-troubled-experiment-secularism/?session=1

Al Ahram. (2016). New legislative reforms in Egypt. *Al Ahram Weekly*. http://english.ahram.org.eg/

Al-Ali, N. (1997). Feminism and contemporary debates in Egypt. In D. Chatty & A. Rabo (Eds.), *Organizing women: Formal and informal women's groups in the Middle East*. Berg.

Al-Ali, N. (2000). *Secularism, gender and the state in the middle east: The Egyptian women's movement*. Cambridge University Press.

Al-Ali, N. (2002). *The Women's Movement in Egypt, with selected references to Turkey* (Civil Society and Social Movements Programme Paper, pp. 5–19). United Nations Research Institute for Social Development.

Al-Anani, K. (2020). Devout neoliberalism?! Explaining Egypt's Muslim Brotherhood's socio-economic perspective and policies. *Politics and Religion, 13*(4), 748–767.

Al-Arian, A. (2016). *Answering the call: Popular Islamic activism in Sadat's Egypt.* Oxford University Press.
Al-Arian, A. (2014). The terror metanarrative and the Rabaa massacre [Blog]. Oxford University Press. https://blog.oup.com/2014/08/terror-metanarrative-rabaa-massacre/
Al-Atrush, S. (2014). Egyptians vote for new constitution in controversial referendum. *Mail and Guardian.* Retrieved December 11, 2018, from https://mg.co.za/article/2014-01-14-egyptians-vote-for-new-constitution-in-referendum
Al-Awa, M. S. (2012). FGM in the context of Islam (pp. 366–367). UNFPA. https://egypt.unfpa.org/sites/default/files/pub-pdf/d9174a63-2960-459b-9f78-b33ad795445e.pdf
Al-Banna, H. (1978). Toward the light. In *Five tracts of Hasan al-Banna* (C. Wendall, Trans.). University of California Press.
Al-Bukhari, M. (2000). Sahih al-Bukhari. In S. Abd al-Aziz (Ed.), *Mawsu'ah al-Hadith al-Sharif al-Kutub al-Sittah* (p. 256). Dar al-Salam.
Aldeeb Abu-Sahlieh, S. (1994). The Islamic conception of migration. *International Migration Review, 28*(1), 7–26.
Al-e Ahmad, J. (1984). *Occidentosis: A plague from the west [Gharbzadegi].* (R. Campbell, Trans., from Arabic). Mizan Press.
Al-Fawwaz, Z. (1892). Fair and equal treatment. *Digital collections: The American University in Cairo.* Retrieved January 30, 2019, from http://digitalcollections.aucegypt.edu/cdm/singleitem/collection/p15795coll19/id/165
Al-Ghazali, A. H. (2015). Book on the etiquette of marriage. In *Ihia' 'Ulum al-Din [The book of knowledge: Book 1 of the revival of the religious sciences]* (M. Farah, Trans., pp. 46–167). Islamic Book Trust.
Al-Hakim, A. (2002). Ibn 'Arabi's twofold perception of woman as human being and cosmic principal. *Journal of Muhyiddin Ibn 'Arabi Society, XXXI,* 1–29.
Al-Hibri, A. (2000). An introduction to Muslim women's rights. In G. Webb (Ed.), *Windows of faith: Muslim scholar-activists in North America* (pp. 51–71). Syracuse University Press.
Alkire, S. (2005). *Valuing Freedoms: Sen's Capability Approach and Poverty Reduction.* Oxford University Press.
Al-Razi, A. B. (1955). *Kitab Al Hawi fi al Tibb [The comprehensive book on medicine].* Matba'at Majlis Dai'rat al-Ma'rif al'Uthmaniyah.
Al-Sabaki, A. K. B. (1987). *Al-Haraka Al-Nissa'iyah fi Misr bayn al-thawratayn 1919–1953 [The women's movement in Egypt between the two revolutions 1919–1953].* Hay'at al-Kitab al-Amaa.
Al-Sayyid, M. K. (1995). A civil society in Egypt? In A. R. Norton (Ed.), *Civil society in the Middle East* (Vol. 1, pp. 269–293). E. J. Brill.
Alberg, B. M., & Kulane, A. (2011). Sexual and reproductive health and rights. In S. Tamale (Ed.), *African sexualities: A reader* (pp. 313–339). Pambazuka Press.
Almroth-Berggren, V., Almroth, L., Bergström, S., Hassanein, O. M., El Hadi, N., & Lithell, U. B. (2001). Reinfibulation among women in rural area in Central Sudan. *Health Care for Women International, 22*(8), 711–721.
Alvaredo, F. L., Piketty, T., Saez, E., & Zucman, G. (2018). *Global inequality report* (pp. 38–66). World Inequality Database. https://wir2018.wid.world/files/download/wir2018-full-report-english.pdf
Alvi, A. (2013). Concealment and revealment: The Muslim veil in context. *Current Anthropology, 54*(3), 177–199.
Alyali, A. (2020). *Domestic violence and Arab women's false choice during COVID-19.* Arab Barometer. https://www.arabbarometer.org/2020/06/domestic-violence-and-arab-womens-false-choice-during-covid-19-pandemic/
Al-Wazni, A. (2015). Muslim women in America and hijab: A study of empowerment, feminist identity, and body image. *Social Work, 60*(4), 325–333.
American University in Cairo (AUC). (2020–2021). *Tuition and fees.* American University in Cairo. https://www.aucegypt.edu/admissions/tuition-and-fees#undergraduate

222   Bibliography

Amin, G. (1982). External factors in the reorientation of Egypt's economic policy. In M. H. Kerr & Y. El Sayed (Eds.), *Rich and poor states in the Middle East* (p. 303). Routledge.
Amin, G. (2011). *Egypt in the era of Hosni Mubarak*. American University in Cairo Press.
Amin, Q. (2000). The liberation of women. In M. Moaddel & K. Talattof (Eds.), *Modernist and fundamentalist debates in Islam*. Palgrave Macmillan.
Amnesty International. (2013). *Gender based violence against women around Tahrir Square* (pp. 5–10). Amnesty International Publications.
Anderson, C., & S. Kirkpatrick. (2016). Narrative interviewing. *International Journal of Clinical Pharmacy, 38*, 631–634.
Anderson, E. (1990). *Streetwise: Race, class, and change in an urban community*. University of Chicago Press.
Anderson, E. (2015). The white space. *Sociology of Race and Ethnicity, 1*(1), 10–21.
Anderson, L. (1997). State policy and Islamist radicalism. In J. L. Espositio (Ed.), *Political Islam: Revolution, radicalism, or reform?* (pp. 17–32). Lynne Rienner Publishers.
Anderson, L. (2001). Arab democracy: Dismal prospects. *World Policy Journal, 18*(3), 53–60.
Anderson, M. (2005). Negotiating sex. *Southern California Law Review, 78*, 1401–1438.
Ansari, H. (2007). 'Burying the dead': Making Muslim space in Britain. *Historical Research, 80*, 545–566.
Appiah, K. A. (1992). *In my father's house: Africa in the philosophy of culture*. Oxford University Press.
Appiah, K. A. (2005). *The ethics of identity*. Princeton University Press.
Arab Barometer. (2020). *Gender dynamics: Examining public opinion data in light of Covid-19 crisis*. Arab Barometer. https://www.arabbarometer.org/wp-content/uploads/Gender-Data-in-Light-of-Covid-19-Crisis.pdf
Arab Barometer. (2021). *Egypt's sexual harassment problem: Encouraging reporting as a possible remedy*. Arab Barometer. https://www.arabbarometer.org/2020/03/egypts-sexual-harassment-problem-encouraging-reporting-as-a-possible-remedy-2/
Arab Barometer. (2011). *Criterion for an individual's piety: Wearing a Hijab*. Arab Barometer. https://www.arabbarometer.org/survey-data/data-analysis-tool/
Arab Barometer. (2011, 2013, 2018). *AB Wave II, AB Wave III, and AB Wave V – Data analysis tool: Arab Barometer*. https://www.arabbarometer.org/survey-data/data-analysis-tool/
Aran, A., & Ginat, R. (2014). Revisiting Egyptian foreign policy towards Israel under Mubarak: From cold peace to strategic peace. *The Journal of Strategic Studies, 37*(4), 556–583.
Ardovini, L. (2017). 'Preachers not Leaders': The rise and fall of the Freedom and Justice Party. In *The 'failure' of political Islam? The Muslim Brotherhood's experience in government* (pp. 135–178). Lancaster University Press.
Arendt, H. (1994). *The origins of totalitarianism* (pp. 123–157). Harcourt.
Argyle, M. (1986). Rules for social relationships in four cultures. *Australian Journal of Psychology, 38*, 309–318.
Argyle, M. (1994). *The psychology of social class*. Routledge.
Aries, E., & Seider, M. (2007). The role of social class in the formation of identity: A study of public and elite private college students. *The Journal of Social Psychology, 147*(2), 137–157.
Arifin, S. R. (2018). Ethical considerations in qualitative study. *International Journal of Care Scholars, 1*(2), 30–33.
Aris, G. (2007). The power and politics of dress in Africa. *Undergraduate Humanities Forum 2006-7, Travel 1*, 1–18.
Armbrust, W. (2014). Media review: "al-Da'iyya" (The preacher). *Journal of the American Academy of Religion, 82*(3), 841–856.
Arvin, M., Tuck, E., & Morrill, A. (2013). Decolonizing feminism: Challenging connections between settler colonialism and heteropatriarchy. *Feminist Formations, 25*(1), 8–34.

Asad, T. (2012). Fear and the ruptured state: Reflections on Egypt after Mubarak. *Social Research*, *79*(2), 271–298.
Ashley, R. K., & Walker, R. B. J. (1990). Introduction: Speaking the language of exile: Dissident thought in international studies. *International Studies Quarterly*, *34*(3), 259–268.
Aslan, R. (2010). *Mohamed ElBaradei plots to topple Mubarak regime in Egypt*. The Daily Beast. https://www.thedailybeast.com/mohamed-elbaradei-plots-to-topple-mubarak-regime-in-egypt
Aspers, P., & Godart, F. (2013). Sociology of fashion: Order and change. *The Annual Review of Sociology*, *39*, 171–192.
Atia, M. (2012). 'A way to paradise': Pious neoliberalism, Islam, and faith-based development. *Annals of the Association of American Geographers*, *102*(4), 808–827.
Atiya, A. (1968). *History of eastern Christianity*. University of Notre Dame and Mathuen and Co. Ltd.
Atran, S., & Norenzayan, A. (2004). Religion's evolutionary landscape: Counterintuition, commitment, compassion, communion. *Behavioral and Brain Sciences*, *27*, 713–770.
Attia, M., & Edge, J. (2017). Be(com)ing a reflexive researcher: A developmental approach to research methodology. *Open Review of Educational Research*, *4*(1), 33–45.
Awan, M. A. (2017). Gamal Abdel Nasser's pan-Arabism and formation of the United Arab Republic: An appraisal. *Journal of Research and Society of Pakistan*, *54*(1), 107–128.
Ayad, S. (2013). *Watani talks to Amna Nosseir*. English Wataninet. Retrieved December 6, 2018, from http://en.wataninet.com/interviews/watani-talks-to-amna-nosseir/2418/
Ayoob, M. (2004). Political Islam: Image and reality. *World Policy Journal*, *21*(3), 1–14.
Aziz, S. F. (2014). Bringing down an uprising: Egypt's stillborn revolution. *Connecticut Journal of International Law*, *30*(1), 1–28.
Baaklini, A., Denoeux, G., & Springborg, R. (Eds.). (1999a). *Legislative politics in the Arab world: The resurgence of democratic institutions*. Lynne Rienner.
Baaklini, A., Denoeux, G., & Springborg, R. (1999b). The neglect and rediscovery of Arab parliaments. In *Legislative politics in the Arab world: Resurgence of the democratic institutions* (pp. 11–28). Lynne Rienner Publishers.
Bandai, E., & Hinds, M. (1986). *A dictionary of Egyptian Arabic* (pp. 576–634). Librairie du Liban.
Badran, M. (1988a). Huda Sha'rawi and the liberation of the Egyptian woman. *British Society for Middle Eastern Studies*, *15*(2), 370–386.
Badran, M. (1988b). The feminist vision in the writings of three turn-of-the-century Egyptian women. *Bulletin – British Society for Middle Eastern Studies*, *15*(112), 11–20.
Badran, M. (1991). Competing agenda: Feminists, Islam and the state in 19th and 20th century Egypt. In D. Kandiyoti (Ed.), *Women, Islam and the state* (pp. 201–236). Temple University Press.
Badran, M. (1993). Independent women: More than a century of feminism in Egypt. In J. E. Tucker (Ed.), *Arab women old boundaries, new frontiers* (pp. 132–134). Indiana University Press.
Badran, M. (1995). *Feminists, Islam, and nation: Gender and the making of modern Egypt*. Princeton University Press.
Badran, M. (1996). Educating the nation. In *Feminists, Islam and the nation: Gender and the making of modern Egypt* (pp. 142–164). Princeton University Press.
Badran, M. (1999). Toward Islamic feminisms: A look at the Middle East. In A. Afsaruddin (Ed.), *Hermeneutics of honour: Negotiating female 'public' space in Islamic/late societies* (pp. 159–188). Harvard University, Center for Middle Eastern Studies.
Badran, M. (2005). Between secular and Islamic feminism/s: Reflections on the Middle East and beyond. *Journal of Middle East Women's Studies*, *1*(1), 6–28.
Badran, M., & Cooke, M. (Eds.). (1990). Challenges facing Arab women. In E. Perry (Rev.), *Opening the gates: A century of Arab feminist writings*. Virago and Bloomington.

Badran, M., & Cooke, M. (Eds.). (2004). *Opening the gates: An anthology of Arab feminist writing* (2nd ed.). Indiana University Press.

Bae, B. B. (2016). Believing selves and cognitive dissonance: Connecting individual and society via "belief". *Religions, 7*(7), 86.

Bagnol, B., & Mariano, E. (2008a). Elongation of the labia minora and use of vaginal products to enhance eroticism: Can these practices be considered FGM? *Finnish Journal of Ethnicity and Migration, 3*, 42–53.

Bagnol, B., & Mariano, E. (2008b). Vaginal practices: Eroticism and implications for women's health and condom use in Mozambique. *Culture, Health and Sexuality, 10*(6), 573–585.

Bahgat, H. (2004). *Egypt's virtue protection of morality*. Middle East Research and Information Project: Critical Coverage of the Middle East Since 1971. https://merip.org/2004/03/egypts-virtual-protection-of-morality/

Bailey, D. S. (1955). *Homosexuality and the western Christian tradition*. Longmans.

Baizerman, S., Eicher, J. B., & Cerny, C. (2008). Eurocentrism in the study of ethnic dress. In *The visible self: Global perspectives on dress, culture, and society* (pp. 123–132). Fairchild Publications, Inc.

Baker, P., Gabrielatos, C., & McEnery, T. (2013). Discourse analysis and media attitudes: The representation of Islam in the British press. In R. Wodak, B. Mral, & M. Khosravinik (Eds.), *Right wing populism in Europe: Politics and discourse*. Bloomsbury Academic.

Baker, R. (1981). Sadat's open door: Opposition from within. *Social Problems, 28*(4), 378–384.

Baloch, G. M., Chhachhar, A. R., & Singutt, W. V. (2014). Influence of religion on life style and social behavior in Christianity: Perspective of Malaysian Christian students. *Journal of Basic and Applied Scientific Research, 4*(4), 300–307.

Bandura, A. (1999). Social cognitive theory of personality. In L. A. Pervin & O. P. John (Eds.), *Handbook of personality: Theory and research* (pp. 154–196). Guilford Press.

Bandura, A. (2002). Social foundations of thought and action. In D. F. Marks (Ed.), *The health psychology reader* (pp. 94–106). SAGE Publications.

Bandura, A. (2006). Toward a psychology of human agency. *Perspectives on Psychological Science, 1*(2), 164–180.

Baring, E. (1916). *Modern Egypt*. The Macmillan Company.

Barlas, A. (2002). *Believing women' in Islam: Unreading patriarchal interpretations of the Qur'an*. University of Texas Press.

Baron, B. (1994). *The women's awakening in Egypt: Culture, society, and the press*. Yale University Press.

Baron, M. (2001). I thought she consented. *Philosophical Issues, 11*, 1–32.

Bartels, A., Eckstein, L., Waller, N., & Wiemann, D. (2019). Postcolonial feminism and intersectionality. In *Postcolonial literatures in English* (pp. 115–167). J. B. Metzler.

Bartkowski, J., & Read, J. (2000). To veil or not to veil? A case study of identity negotiation among Muslim women in Austin, Texas. *Gender and Society, 14*(3), 395–417.

Bashir, N. (2017). Doing research in peoples' homes: Fieldwork, ethics and safety – on the practical challenges of researching and representing life on the margins. *Qualitative Research, 18*(6), 638–653.

Bassiouni, C. (2012). *Schools of thought in Islam*. The Middle East Institute. https://www.mei.edu/publications/schools-thought-islam

Bayat, A. (2002). Piety, privilege, and Egyptian youth. *ISIM Review Articles, 10*(1), 1–23.

Bayat, A. (Ed.). (2017). 8. Half Revolution, No Revolution. In *Revolution without Revolutionaries: Making Sense of the Arab Spring* (pp. 153–178). Stanford University Press. https://doi.org/10.1515/9781503603073-009

Battle, M. (2013). *African passages, low country adaptations*. College of Charleston. https://ldhi.library.cofc.edu/exhibits/show/africanpassageslowcountryadapt/sources

BBC News. (2012). *Muslim Brotherhood's Mursi declared Egypt's president*. BBC News. https://www.bbc.co.uk/news/world-18571580

BBC News. (2013a). *Egypt crisis: Army ousts President Mohammed Morsi.* BBC News. https://www.bbc.co.uk/news/world-middle-east-23173794
BBC News. (2013b). *Profile: Interim Egyptian President Adly Mansour.* BBC News. https://www.bbc.co.uk/news/world-middle-east-23176293
BBC News. (2019). *Mohamed Morsi's trials and convictions.* BBC News. https://www.bbc.co.uk/news/world-middle-east-24772806
BBC News. (2020). *Egypt President Abdul Fattah El Sisis: Ruler with an iron grip.* BBC News. https://www.bbc.co.uk/news/world-middle-east-19256730
Beauvoir, S. de (2009). *The Second Sex.* Vintage Books. (Originally published in 1949)
Beck, U. (1999). *World risk society.* Polity Press.
Bello, W., & Ambrose, S. (2006). *Take the IMF off life support.* http://www.voltairenet.org/article139668.html
Belzen, J. A. (1999). The cultural psychological approach to religion: Contemporary debates on the object of the discipline. *Theory and Psychology, 9*, 229–225.
Belzen, J. A. (2010). *Towards cultural psychology of religion: Principles, approaches, applications.* SAGE Publications.
Benigni, E. (2018). Translating Machiavelli in Egypt: *The Prince* and the shaping of a new political vocabulary in the nineteenth-century Arab Mediterranean. In L. Biasiori & G. Marcocci (Eds.), *Machiavelli, Islam and the east* (pp. 199–224). Palgrave Macmillan.
Bennett, A. (2021). *Remembering Jehan Sadat.* The Cairo Review. https://www.thecairoreview.com/midan/remembering-jehan-sadat/
Bennett, J. (2011). Subversion and resistance: Activist initiatives. In S. Tamale (Ed.), *African sexualities: A reader* (pp. 77–100). Pambazuka Press.
Bereiter, C. (2005). Aspects of knowledgeability. In *Education and mind in the knowledge age* (pp. 131–173). Routledge.
Bernard-Maugiron, N. (2010). Gender equality in Muslim family law. *International Journal of Law, Policy and the Family, 24*(3), 361–387.
Bernard-Maugiron, N., & Dupret, B. (2002). From Jihan to Suzanne: Twenty years of personal status in Egypt. *Recht van de Islam, 19*, 1–19.
Berry, J. W. (1999). Aboriginal cultural identity. *Canadian Journal of Native Studies, XIX*(1), 1–36.
Bier, L. (1992). Islamic feminism in Egypt: Between accommodation and resistance. *Journal of Middle East Women's Studies, 7*(1), 101–121.
Bier, L. (2011). *Revolutionary womanhood: Feminism, modernity and the state in Nasser's Egypt.* Stanford University Press.
Big Think. (2011). *Judith Butler: Your behavior creates your gender | Big Think.* YouTube. https://www.youtube.com/watch?v=Bo7o2LYATDc
Biggs, M., Stermac, L. E., & Divinsky, M. (1998). Genital injuries following sexual assault of women with and without prior sexual intercourse experience. *CMAJ, 159*(1), 33–37.
Billet, B. L. (2007). The case of female circumcision. In *Cultural relativism in the face of the west* (pp. 19–51). Palgrave Macmillan.
Binder, L. (1988). The prospect for liberal government in the Middle East. In *Islamic liberalism: A critique of development ideologies* (pp. 339–360). University of Chicago Press.
Bird, S. R. (1996). Welcome to the men's club: Homosociality and the maintainer of hegemonic masculinity. *Gender and Society The Conversation 10*(2), 120–132.
Bishop, A. J. (1990). Western mathematics: The secret weapon of cultural imperialism. *Race and Class, 32*(2), 51–65.
Black, I. (2007). A country in crisis as fearful government cracks down on Islamist opposition. *The Guardian.* https://www.theguardian.com/world/2007/jul/19/egypt.ianblack
Blakeman, J. (2014). *Social movements and public policy: Impact, manifestation, and the political arena.* Routledge.
Blumer, H. (1969). *Symbolic interactionism: Perspective and method.* University of California Press.

Blumer, H. (1992). Society and symbolic interaction. In *Symbolic interactionism: Perspective and method* (pp. 78–90). University of California Press.
Bochner, A. P., & Ellis, C. (1996). Talking over ethnography. In C. Ellis & A. P. Bochner (Eds.), *Composing ethnography: Alternative forms of qualitative writing* (pp. 13–45). Alta Mira Press.
Bochner, S. (1994). Cross-cultural differences in the self concept: A test of Hofstede's individualism/collectivism distinction. *Journal of Cross-Cultural Psychology, 25*(2), 273–283.
Bodnar, J. (1992). *Remaking America: Public memory, commemoration, and patriotism in the twentieth century.* Princeton University Press.
Bohlen, H. (2013). Universal moral standards and the problem of cultural relativism in Hue's 'A Dialogue'. *Philosophy, 88*(4), 593–606.
Bonds, A., & In wood, J. (2016). Beyond white privilege: Geographies of white supremacy and settler colonialism. *Progress in Human Geography, 40*(6), 715–733.
Booth, M. (2001). Woman in Islam: Men and the "Women's press" in turn-of-the-20th-century Egypt. *International Journal of Middle East Studies, 33*(2), 171–201.
Borger, J. (2001). 9/11: Three hours of terror and chaos that brought a nation to a halt. *The Guardian.* https://www.theguardian.com/world/2001/sep/12/september11-usa
Boswell, J. (1980). *Christianity social tolerance and homosexuality: Gay people in western Europe from the beginning of the Christian era to the beginning of the fourteenth century.* University of Chicago Press.
Botman, S. (1988). The experience of women in the Egyptian Communist Movement, 1939–1954. *Women's Studies International Forum, II,* 117–126.
Boulanouar, A. W. (2006). The notion of modesty in Muslim women's clothing: An Islamic point of view. *New Zealand Journal of Asian Studies, 8,* 134–156.
Bourdieu, P., & Wacquant, L. (1992). *An invitation to reflexive sociology.* University of Chicago Press.
Boutayeb, A. (2009). The impact of HIV/AIDS on human development in African countries. *BMC Public Health, 9*(Supplement 1), S3.
Bowen, J. R. (2007). *Why the French don't like headscarves: Islam, the state, and public space.* Princeton University Press.
Bowen, J. R. (2010). *Can Islam be French. Pluralism and pragmatism in a secularist state.* Princeton University Press.
Bowen, J. R. (2017). *1967 war: Six days that changed the Middle East.* BBC News. https://www.bbc.co.uk/news/world-middle-east-39960461
Boyce, C. D., & Fido, E. S. (1990). *Out of Kumbla.* Africa World Press.
Boylorn, R. M., & Orbe, M. P. (Eds.). (2014). *Critical autoethnography: Intersecting cultural identities in everyday life.* Left Coast Press.
Brah, A. (1992). Difference, diversity and differentiation. In J. Donald & A. Rattansi (Eds.), *Race, culture and difference.* SAGE Publications.
Braham, P. (2012). Chapter 13: Discourse. In *Key concepts in sociology* (pp. 57–61). SAGE Publications.
Braun, V., & Clarke, V. (2006). Using thematic analysis in psychology. *Qualitative Research in Psychology, 3,* 77–101.
Brechenmacher, S. (2017). Institutionalized repression in Egypt. In *Civil society under assault: Repression and responses in Russia, Egypt, and Ethiopia* (pp. 37–64). Carnegie Endowment for International Peace.
Brennan, W. (1995). *Dehumanizing the vulnerable: When word games take lives.* Loyola University Press.
Brescoll, V. L. (2016). Leading with their hearts? How gender stereotypes of emotion lead to biased evaluations of female leaders. *The Leadership Quarterly, 27,* 415–428.
Broncho, S. (2016). *How do you learn a language that is not written down?* British Council. https://www.britishcouncil.org/voices-magazine/how-do-you-learn-language-isnt-written-down

Brooks, B. (1923). Some observations concerning ancient Mesopotamian women. *The American Journal of Semitic Languages and Literatures, 39*(3), 187–194.
Brown, N. J. (2011). *Post-revolutionary Al-Azhar* [The Carnegie Papers]. Carnegie Endowment for International Peace. https://carnegieendowment.org/files/al_azhar.pdf
Brown, N. J., & Dunne, M. (2021). Who will speak for Islam in Egypt – And who will listen? In F. Wehrey (Ed.), *Islamic institutions in Arab states: Mapping the dynamic of co-optation, and contention*. Carnegie Endowment for International Peace.
Brownlee, J. (2011). Peace before freedom: Diplomacy and repression in Sadat's Egypt. *Political Science Quarterly, 126*(4), 641–668.
Bruce-Lockhart, K. (2014). Unsound minds and broken bodies: The detention of hardcore Mau Mau women at Kamiti and Gitmayu detention camps in Kenya, 1954–1960. *Journal of Eastern African Studies, 8*(iv), 590–608.
Bruner, J. (1985). Narrative and paradigmatic modes of thought. In J. Bruner (Ed.), *In search of pedagogy. The selected works of Jerome Bruner* (Vol. 2, pp. 116–128). Routledge.
Bruner, J. (2002). *Making stories: Law, literature, life*. Harvard University Press.
Bullock, K. (2002). *Rethinking Muslim women and the veil: Challenging historical & modern stereotypes*. IIIT Publishers.
Burcar, L. (2012). The new world order and the unmasking of the neo-colonial present. *ELOPE: English Language Overseas Perspectives and Enquiries, 9*(1), 29–40.
Bureau of Democracy. (1997). *Egypt country report on human rights practices for 1996*. U.S. Department of State. Retrieved January 24, 2019, from https://1997-2001.state.gov/global/human_rights/1996_hrp_report/egypt.html
Bush, R. (1999). Economic reforms and Egyptian agriculture. In *Economic crisis and the politics of reform in Egypt* (pp. 9–29). Westview Press.
Butler, J. (1988). Performative acts and gender constitution: An essay in phenomenology and feminist theory. *Theatre Journal, 40*(4), 519–531.
Butler, J. (1990a). *Gender trouble: Feminism and the subversion of identity*. Routledge.
Butler, J. (1990b). Subjects of gender/sex/desire. In *Gender trouble* (pp. 1–34). Routledge Classics.
Butler, J. (1993). Bodies that matter. In *Bodies that matter: On the discursive limits of "Sex"* (pp. 3–27). Routledge Classics.
Butler, J. (1994). Gender as performance: An interview with Judith Butler. *Radical Philosophy: A Journal of Socialist and Feminist Philosophy, 67*(summer), 32–39.
Butler, J. (1999). *Gender trouble: Feminism and the subversion of identity* (anniversary Ed.). Routledge. (Original work published 1990)
Cabrera, A. F., & Nora, A. (1994). College students' perceptions of prejudice and discrimination and their feelings on alienation: A construct validation approach. *The Review of Education/Pedagogy/Cultural Studies, 16*(3–4), 387–409.
Cairo Institute for Human Rights Studies. (2019). *Egypt: Draft NGO law before parliament is simply rebranded repression, must be rejected*. Cairo Institute for Human Rights Studies. https://cihrs.org/egypt-ngo-bill-before-parliament-is-simply-rebranded-repression-must-be-rejected/?lang=en
Cairo Review. (2011). *Faith and hope in Egypt*. The Cairo Review of Global Affairs. https://www.thecairoreview.com/q-a/faith-and-hope-in-egypt/
Cairo Scene. (2017). *Al-Azhar: Minaret of moderation or tool of oppression?* Cairo Scene. https://cairoscene.com/In-Depth/Al-Azhar-Minaret-of-Moderation-or-Tool-of-Oppression
Calhoun, C. (Ed.). (1994). *Social theory and the politics of identity*. Blackwell.
Camfield, D. (2016). Elements of a historical-materialist theory of racism. *Historical Materialism, 24*(1), 31–70.
Cammett, M. (2012). Power-sharing in post-conflict societies: Implications for peace and governance. *Journal of Conflict Resolution, 56*(6), 982–1016.
Cammett, M. (2021). What's religion got to do with it? In M. Cammett & P. Jones (Eds.), *The Oxford handbook of politics in Muslim societies*. Oxford University Press.

Campbell, C. (2009). From local to global: Contextualizing women's sexual health in the shadow of AIDS – Book review: *AIDS, sex and culture: Global politics and survival in South Africa* by Ida Susser. *Journal of Health Psychology, 14*(6), 833–835.

Cañar, A. (2008). Subversion and subjugation in the public sphere: Secularism and the Islamic headscarf. *Signs: Journal of Women in Culture & Society, 33*(4), 891–913.

Cann, C. (2016). Mothers and spirits: Religious identity, alcohol, and death. In D. J. Davies & M. J. Thate (Eds.), *Religion and the individual: Belief, practice, and identity* (pp. 47–62). MDPI AG. http://www.mdpi.com/journal/religions

Casper, J., & Serôdio, D. (2013). The development of Egypt's constitution: Analysis, assessment, and sorting through the rhetoric. In *Arab-West report* (pp. 16–62). The Center for Intercultural Dialogue and Translations.

CBS News. (2011). *Egyptians riot in the streets since 1977*. CBS News. https://www.cbsnews.com/news/egyptians-riot-in-the-streets-in-1977/

Central Agency for Public Mobilization and Statistics (CAMPAS) and UNICEF. (2017). *UNICEF annual report*. The United Nations International Children's Emergency Fund. Retrieved December 12, 2018, from https://www.unicef.org/about/annual-report/files/Egypt_2017_COAR.pdf

Cesar, S. M., & Casanova, M. (2017). *Title of the Work*. Publisher.

Chambers, R. (2004). *Ideas for development: Reflecting forward* [IDS Working Paper 238, pp. 7–22]. Institute for Development Studies.

Chang, L. T. (2018). Egyptian women and the fight for the right to work. *The New Yorker*. https://www.newyorker.com/news/news-desk/egyptian-women-and-the-fight-for-the-right-to-work

Chang, M. J. (2002). Preservation or transformation: Where's the real educational discourse on diversity? *Review of Higher Education, 25*(2), 125–140.

Chatham House. (2009). Egypt's regional role. In *Middle East and North Africa programme workshop summary* (pp. 2–9). Chatham House.

Check, J., & Guloine, T. (1989). Reported proclivity for coercive sex following repeated exposure to sexually violent pornography, non-violent dehumanising pornography, and erotica. In D. Zillmann & J. Bryant (Eds.), *Pornography: Recent research, interpretations, and policy considerations* (pp. 159–184). Lawrence Erlbaum Associates, Inc.

Chehabi, H. E., & Linz, J. (1998). A theory of Sultanism: A type of neodemocratic rule. In H. E. Chehabi & J. Linz (Eds.), *Sultanistic regimes* (pp. 3–23). John Hopkins University Press.

Chemers, M. M., & Ayman, R. (Eds.), *Leadership theory and research: Perspectives and directions* (pp. 167–188). Academic Press.

Cheref, A. (2020). *Don't call us Berber, we are Amazigh*. The National News. https://www.thenationalnews.com/opinion/comment/don-t-call-us-berber-we-are-amazigh-1.965334

Chiha, I. I. (2013). Redefining terrorism under the Mubarak regime: Towards a new definition of terrorism in Egypt. *The Comparative and International Law Journal of Southern Africa, 46*(1), 90–120.

Christie, C. (2000). *Gender and language: Towards a feminist pragmatics*. Edinburgh University Press.

Civantos, C. (2013a). Narrating the Nile: Latin American autobiography and the Egyptian water crisis. *Comparative Literature Studies, 50*(3), 460–482.

Civantos, C. (2013b). The challenges of gender equality in the Arab world. *Gender & Development, 21*(3), 513–528.

Clendenin, D. J., & Connelly, F. M. (2000). *Narrative inquiry: Experience and story in qualitative research*. Jossey-Bass.

Clarke, V., & Braun, V. (2017). Thematic analysis. *Journal of Positive Psychology, 12*(3), 297–298.

Clothier, I. M. (2005). Created identities: Hybrid-cultures and the internet. *Convergence*, *11*(4), 44–59.
Cochran, J. (1986). *Education in Egypt*. Routledge.
Cohen, S., & Azar, E. (1981). From war to peace: The transition between Egypt and Israel. *The Journal of Conflict Resolution*, *25*(1), 87–114.
Cohen, S. A., & Richards, C. I. (1994). The Cairo consensus: Population, development and women. *Family Planning Perspectives*, *26*, 272–277.
Cole, J. R. (1981). Feminism, class and Islam in turn-of-the-century Egypt. *International Journal of Middle East Studies*, *13*, 387–407.
Coller, I. (2020). Introduction. In *Muslims and citizens: Islam, politics, and the French Revolution* (pp. 1–14). Yale University Press.
Commons, L. (1993). Savage sexuality: Images of the African woman in Victorian literature. *Latitude*, *3*. http://ssmu.mcgill.ca/journals/latitudes/3vsex.htm
Condorcet, M., & Caritat, M. J. (1790). On the admission of women to the rights of citizenship. In *The first essay on the political rights of women* (A. Vickery, Trans.). Garden City Press Limited.
Connell, R. W. (1995). *Masculinities*. University of California Press.
Connell, R. W. (1987). *Gender and power: Society, the person, and sexual politics*. Stanford University Press.
Connell, R. W. (2005). Change among the gatekeepers: Men, masculinities, and gender equality in the global arena. *Signs*, *30*(3), 1801–1825.
Connell, R. W. (2007). *Southern theory: The global dynamics of knowledge in social science*. Allen and Unwin Publishing.
Constitution of the Arab Republic of Egypt (*Dustur Juinhuriyat Misr al-Arabiyah*) [Egyptian constitution] (2014). (Chapter I, Article II): 12.
Cooper, F. (1988). Mau Mau and the discourses of decolonization. *Journal of African History*, *29*(2), 313–320.
Cornwall, A., & Bock, K. (2005). What do buzzwords do for development policy? A critical look at 'participation', 'empowerment' and 'poverty reduction'. *Third World Quarterly*, *26*(7), 1043–1060.
Corrigan, P. (1988). The body of intellectuals/the intellectuals' body (remarks for Roland). *The Sociological Review*, *36*(2), 368–380.
Côté, J. E., & Levine, C. G. (2002). *Identity formation, agency, and culture: A social psychological synthesis*. Erlbaum.
Cox, R. W. (1981). Social forces, states and world orders: Beyond international relations theory. *Millennium*, *10*(2), 126–155.
Craciun, M. (2015). The Islamic fashion industry in Turkey: An anthropological perspective. Everyday Muslim: Documenting Muslim Heritage in the UK. https://www.everydaymuslim.org/blog/the-islamic-fashion-industry-in-turkey-an-anthropological-perspective/
Crais, C. C., & Scully, P. (2009). *Sara Baartman and the Hottentot Venus: A ghost story and a biography*. Wits University Press.
Craven, M. (2012). Colonialism and domination. In B. Fassbender & A. Peters (Eds.), *The Oxford handbook of history and international law* (pp. 862–889). School of Oriental and African Studies.
Crenshaw, K. (1991). Mapping the margins: Intersectionality, identity politics, and violence against women of color. *Stanford Law Review*, *43*, 1241–1299.
Daniel, N. (2009). *Islam and the west: The making of an image* (pp. 133–151). Oneworld Publications.
Danielson, V. (2007). *The voice of Egypt: Umm Kulthum, Arabic song, and Egyptian society in the twentieth century*. University of Chicago Press.
Dar Al-Ifta Al-Massriyya. (n.d.). *Fatwa, society and family, marriage*. Dar Al-Ifta Al-Masrsriyya. https://www.dar-alifta.org/Foreign/ViewFatwa.aspx?ID=6033

Darwish, A. E., & Huber, G. L. (2003). Individualism vs collectivism in different cultures: A cross-cultural study. *Intercultural Education, 14*(1), 47–56.
David Tal, D. (2009). The making, operation and failure of the May 1950 Tripartite Declaration on Middle East Security. *British Journal of Middle Eastern Studies, 36*(2), 177–193.
Davison, J. (1989). *Voices from Mathira: Lives of rural Gikuyu women.* Lynne Reinner.
Davison, P. W. (2020). *Public opinion.* Encyclopedia Britannica. https://www.britannica.com/topic/public-opinion
De Beauvoir, S. (2009). Lived experiences, Chapter 2: The girl. In *The second sex* (pp. 395–440). Vintage books.
Deaton, A. (2013). *The great escape: Health, wealth, and the origins of inequality.* Princeton University Press.
Derrida, J. (1970). Structure, sign and play in the discourse of the human sciences. In R. Macksey & E. Donato (Eds.), *The structuralist controversy* (pp. 247–272). Johns Hopkins University Press.
DeWalt, K. M., & DeWalt, B. R. (2002). *Participant observation: A guide for fieldworkers.* AltaMira Press.
Dickson-Swift, V., James, E. L., Kippen, S., & Liamputtong, P. (2008). Risk to researchers in qualitative research on sensitive topics: Issues and strategies. *Qualitative Health Research, 18*(1), 133–144.
Diffendal, C. (2006). The modern Hijab: Tool of agency, tool of oppression. *Annual Review of Undergraduate Research, School of Humanities and Social Sciences, School of Languages, Cultures, and World Affairs, College of Charleston, 5,* 129–136.
Diwan, I. (2012). Liberals, Islamists, and the role of the middle class in the demise of the Arab autocracies. *Harvard Journal of Middle Eastern Politics and Policy, 1,* 31–54.
Diwan, I. (2013). Understanding revolution in the Middle East: The central role of the middle class. *Middle East Development Journal, 5*(1), 1350004-1–1350004-30.
Diwan, I. (2016a). The political effects of changing public opinion in Egypt: A story of revolution. In E. A. Sayre & T. M. Yousef (Eds.), *Young generation awakening* (pp. 123–150). Oxford University Press.
Diwan, I. (2016b). *The emancipation gap in Arab education.* Project Syndicate. https://www.project-syndicate.org/commentary/gaps-in-arab-education-by-ishac-diwan-2016-04?barrier=accesspaylog
Diwan, I. (2019). *The middle east economies in times of transition.* Palgrave Macmillan.
Diwan, I., & Klugman, J. (2016). *Patterns of veiling among Muslim women* [Working Paper No. 1007, pp. 2–28]. The Economic Research Forum.
Diwan, I., Malik, A., & Atiyas, I. (2017). *Crony capitalism in the Middle East: Business and politics from liberalization to the Arab spring.* Oxford University Press.
Diwan, I., Tzannatos, Z., & Abdel Ahad. J. (2016). *Rates of return to education in twenty two Arab countries: An update and comparison between MENA and the rest of the world* [Working Paper No. 995, pp. 3–17]. The Economic Research Forum.
Dorfman, A., & Mattelart, A. (1975). *How to read Donald Duck: Imperialist ideology in the Disney comic.* International General.
Driessens, O. (2013). Celebrity capital: Redefining celebrity using field theory. *Theory and Society, 42*(5), 543–560.
Droogsma, R. A. (2007). Redefining Hijab: American Muslim women's standpoints on veiling. *Journal of Applied Communication Research, 35*(3), 294–319.
Dryberg, J. (1997). Power, identity and political authority: Foucault's power analysis. In *The circular structure of power: Politics, identity and community* (pp. 85–99). Verso.
Dryer, C. (2010). *A call for Muslims in the west to serve their societies.* Qantara. https://en.qantara.de/content/interview-with-amr-khaled-a-call-for-muslims-in-the-west-to-serve-their-societies

Duncan, M. (2004). Autoethnography: Critical appreciation of an emerging art. *International Journal of Qualitative Methods, 3*(4), Article 3. https://sites.ualberta.ca/~iiqm/backissues/3_4/html/duncan.html

Dunch, R. (2002). Beyond cultural imperialism: Cultural theory, Christian missions, and global modernity. *History and Theory, 41*(3), 301–325.

Dupret, B. (2011). Law in action: A paradoxical approach to law and justice. In *Adjudication in action: An ethnomethodology of law, morality and justice* (P. Ghazaleh, Trans., pp. 63–92). Routledge.

Duveen, G. (2001). Representations, identities, resistance. In K. Deaux & G. Philogène (Eds.), *Representations of the social: Bridging theoretical traditions* (pp. 257–270). Blackwell Publishing.

Duveen, G. (2008). Social actors and social groups: A return to heterogeneity in social psychology. *Journal of the Theory of Social Behavior, 38*, 369–374.

Dyer, E. (2013). *Marginalising Egyptian women*. Henry Jackson Society. https://henryjacksonsociety.org/wp-content/uploads/2013/12/Marginalising-Egyptian-Women.pdf

Dyer, E. (2014). Egypt's shame: Why violence against women has soared after Mubarak. *Foreign Affairs*. https://www.foreignaffairs.com/articles/egypt/2014-01-27/egypts-shame

Dyzenhaus, D. (2003). The unwritten constitution, and the rule of law. In I. Brodie, G. Huscroft, & I. Ross (Eds.), *Constitutionalism in the charter era* (pp. 383–412). York University Press.

Eckentein, L. (2016). *History of Sinai*. Forgotten Books.

EDHS. (2014). *Egypt demographic and health survey 2014*. Cairo: Ministry of Health and Population.

Edris, A. M., Hegazy, A. A., & Etman, W. M. (2017). Vaginal tightening surgery: A new technique. *Annals International Medical and Dental Research, 3*(10), 32–36.

Eegunlusi, T. R. E. (2017). Mental alienation and African identity: Exploring historical perspectives in response to the crises of African societies. *Open Journal of Philosophy, 7*, 1–24.

Efflaton, S. (2014). Women's rights and the new Egyptian constitution. *Journal of Middle Eastern Women's Studies, 10*(1), 34–55.

Efflatoun, I. (2014). *Muzakarat Inji Efflatoun: Min Al-Toufoula ila Al-Sign* [*Inji Efflatoun's memoirs: From childhood to prison*] (p. 247). Dar Al-Thaqafa Al-Jadida.

Egan, K. (2002). *Getting it wrong from the beginning*. Yale University Press.

Egyptian Constitution. (1923). *Constitution of the Arab republic of Egypt*. Official Gazette.

Egyptian Constitution. (2014). *Constitution of the Arab republic of Egypt*. Official Gazette.

Egyptian Streets. (2019). *Man confesses to stabbing his wife and three children*. Egyptian Streets. https://egyptianstreets.com/2019/01/03/egyptian-man-confesses-to-stabbinghis-wife-and-three-children/

Egyptian Penal Code. (1937). Egyptian Penal Code, Law No. 58 of 1937.

Egypt Independent. (2019a). Egypt executes man convicted of raping 20-month-old baby. *Al-Masry Al-Youm*. https://egyptindependent.com/egypt-executes-man-convicted-of-raping-20-month-old-baby/

Egypt Independent. (2019b). Egyptian prosecution dismisses murder charges against 15-year old girl who killed rapist in self-defense. *Al-Masry Al-Youm*. https://egyptindependent.com/egyptian-prosecution-dismisses-murder-charges-against-15-year-old-girl-who-killed-rapist-in-self-defense/

Egypt Today. (2019). 32.5% of Egyptians live in extreme poverty: CAPMAS. *Egypt Today*. https://www.egypttoday.com/Article/1/73437/32-5-of-Egyptians-live-in-extreme-poverty-CAPMAS

Eisner, E. W. (1998). *The enlightened eye: Qualitative inquiry and the enlightenment of educational practice*. Prentice Hall.

Ekant, V., Becirovic, I., & Martin, B. (2010). If Kate voted conservative would you? The role of celebrity endorsements in political party advertising. *European Journal of Marketing, 44*(3/4), 436–450.

232   Bibliography

El Feki, S. Heilman, B., & Baker, G. (Eds.). (2017). Chapter 3: Egypt. In *Understanding masculinities: Results from the International Men and Gender Equality Survey (IMAGES) – Middle East and North Africa* (pp. 40–87). UN Women and Promundo-US.

El Feky, O., Ibrahim, I., & Soliman, S. (2017). Women's economic participation in Egypt: Constraints and opportunities. *Journal of Economic Development, 42*(2), 85–102.

El Gharib, S. (2020). *#HijabisFightBack: In Brussles, thousands protest Belgium's College headscarf ban*. Global Citizen. https://www.globalcitizen.org/en/content/hijabis-fight-back-brussels-headscarf-ban/

El Guindi, F. (1981). Veiling *Infitah* with Muslim ethics: Egypt's contemporary Islamic Movement. *Social Problems, 28*(4), 465–485.

El Guindi, F. (1999). The Veil: Modesty, privacy, and resistance. In B. Shiemer (Ed.), *Veil: Modesty, privacy and resistance* (pp. 3–27). Berg Publishers.

El Guide, F. (2002). Veil: Modesty, privacy and resistance. *Society for Visual Anthropology Newsletter, 18*(1), 112–113.

El Nagger, S. (2014). The impact of digitization on the religious sphere: Televangelism as an example. *Indonesian Journal of Islam and Muslim Societies, 4*(2), 189–211.

El Saharawi, N. (1988). The political challenges facing Arab women at the end of the 20th century. In N. Toubia (Ed.), *Women of the Arab world* (pp. 8–26). Zed Publishing.

El Saadawi, N. (2016). Introduction: Why is Nawal El Saadawi banned? In *Diary of a child called Souad. Giants of contemporary Arab literature* (pp. 1–24). Palgrave Macmillan.

El-Sayyed, H. (2009). طالبة الإعدادى التى أجبرها شيخ الأزهر على خلع النقاب: أعلم أنه على حق ولكنه أفسد فرحتى بالدراسة. وزميلاتها يشعرن بـ"الإهانة" ويقلن: "عرفناه على حقيقته" [High School student forced by Azhar Sheikh to take off her Veil: 'I know he was right but he ruined the joy of going to school for me ... and my friends feel humiliated and said 'now we see him for what he truly is']. *Al Youm al-Sabe'*. https://www.youm7.com/story/2009/10/8/ النقاب-أعلم/143533 طالبة-الإعدادى-التى-أجبرها-شيخ-الأزهر-على-خلع-

El-Setouhy, M., Crouch, M. M., & Earhart, K. C. (2008). Developing cultural competence and overcoming challenges in the informed consent process: An experience from Egypt. *The Journal of Research Administration, XXXIX*(2), 33–40.

El Shaaraw, M. (1987). *Al Mar'a kama aradaha Allah* [*The woman like god wants her to be*]. Maktabat Al Quran.

El Sherif, A. (2014, July, 3–21). *The Egyptian Muslim Brotherhood's failure – Part 1 of a series on political Islam in Egypt*. Carnegie Endowment for International Peace.

Elias, A. A. (2018). *Hadith on Jannah*. Daily Hadith Online: Wisdom of Prophet Muhammad in Arabic and English. https://abuaminaelias.com/dailyhadithonline/2018/06/10/poor-jannah-before-rich/

Elias, J. P. (2020). Chapter 11: Coptic burial wrapping. In *The Phoebe A. Hearst expedition to Naga ed-Deir, Cemeteries N 2000 and N 2500* (pp. 453–482). Brill.

Elkins, Z., Ginsburg, T., & Melton, J. (2009). Conceptualizing constitutions. In *The endurance of national constitutions* (pp. 36–62). Cambridge University Press.

Ellis, C. (2000). Creating criteria: An ethnographic short story. *Qualitative Inquiry, 6*, 273–277.

Ellis, C. (2007). Telling secrets, revealing lives: Relational ethics in research with intimate others. *Qualitative Inquiry, 13*, 3–29.

Ellis, C., Adams, T., & Bochner, A. (2010). Autoethnography: An overview. *Forum Qualitative Sozialforschung/Forum: Qualitative Social Research, 12*(1), Article 10.

Ellis, C., & Bochner, A. P. (2000). Autoethnography, personal narrative, reflexivity. In N. K. Denzin & Y. S. Lincoln (Eds.), *Handbook of qualitative research* (2nd ed., pp. 733–768). SAGE Publications.

Ellsworth, B. (2019). *Canada: Malala can teach in Quebec if she removes Hijab*. Anadolu Agency. https://www.aa.com.tr/en/americas/canada-malala-can-teach-in-quebec-if-she-removes-hijab/1525582

Elsadda, H. (2012). *Gender, nation, and the Arabic novel: Egypt, 1892–2008*. Edinburgh University Press.

Elsadda, H., & Abu-Ghazi, E. (2001). *Significant moments in the history of Egyptian women* (H. Kamal, Trans.). National Council for Women.
ElTahawy, M. (1999). Egypt ends legal opt-out for rapists. *The Guardian.* https://www.theguardian.com/world/1999/apr/06/8
ElTahawy, M. (2015). *Headscarves and hymens: Why the Middle East needs a sexual revolution.* Faber & Faber.
ElTahawy, M. (2016a). The god of virginity. In *Headscarves and Hymens: Why the Middle East needs a sexual revolution* (pp. 109–139). Weidenfeld and Nicolson.
ElTahawy, M. (2016b). Why they hate us. In *Headscarves and Hymens: Why the Middle East needs a sexual revolution* (pp. 3–32). Weidenfeld and Nicolson.
Emechta, B. (1974). *Second class citizen.* Allison and Busby.
Emil, B. (2014). The dynamics of female participation in the Egyptian labor market. *Journal of Middle Eastern Women's Studies, 10*(2), 123–145.
Emil, S. (2021). Don't use an instrument of oppression as a symbol of diversity and inclusion. *Canadian Medical Association Journal, 193*(51), E1936.
England, K. V. L. (1994). Getting personal: Reflexivity, positionality, and feminist research. *The Professional Geographer, 46*(1), 80–89.
Englard, I. (1968). The problem of Jewish law in a Jewish state. *Israel Law Review, 3*(2), 254–278.
Erikson, E. H. (1968). *Identity, youth and crisis.* W. W. Norton.
Eriksson, P., & Kovalainen, A. (2008). Chapter 12: Ethnographic research. In *Qualitative methods in business research* (pp. 149–163). SAGE Publications.
Ernst, J. (2021). *World leaders hail Egypt-brokered Gaza ceasefire.* France 24. https://www.france24.com/en/diplomacy/20210520-us-uk-hail-egypt-brokered-gaza-ceasefire
Eshag, E., & Kamal, S. (1968). The economic development of Egypt. *World Development, 16*(3), 427–441.
Essam al-Din, G. (2000). Three more years of emergency. *Al-Ahram Weekly* (2–8 March 2003). Retrieved January 24, 2019, from http://weekly.ahram.org.eg/archive/2003/627/eg4.htm
Essam al-Din, G. (2003). Egyptian women and the dynamics of the public sphere. *Middle East Review of International Affairs, 7*(2), 47–60.
European Parliament Committee on Women's Rights and Gender Equality. (2012). *Resolution P7_TA(2012)026: Female genital mutilation.* http://www.europarl.europa.eu/sides/getDoc.do?pubRef=-//EP//NONSGML+TA+P7-TA-2012-0261+0+DOC+PDF+V0//EN
Evans, E. W., & Richardson, D. (1995). Hunting for rents: The economics of slaving in pre-colonial Africa. *Economic History Review, 48*(4), 665–686.
Fahmy, K. (1998). The era of Muhammad 'Ali Pasha, 1805–1848. In M. Daly (Ed.), *The Cambridge history of Egypt* (pp. 139–179). Cambridge University Press.
Fahmy, N. S. (1998). The performance of the Muslim Brotherhood in the Egyptian syndicates: An alternative formula for reform? *Middle East Journal, 52*(4), 551–562.
Faksh, M. A. (1976). An historical survey of educational system in Egypt. *International Review for Education, 22*(2), 234–244.
Fanack. (2017). *Amr Khaled: Egypt's once hip preacher turned symbol of the past.* Fanack. https://fanack.com/egypt/faces-of-egypt/amr-khaled/
Farah, N. (1983). *Naked Needle.* Heinemann.
Farah, N. (1984). *Maps.* Vintage Books.
Farid, S. (2015). *Will a 'remove the hijab' campaign turn heads in Egypt?* Al Arabeya News. https://english.alarabiya.net/perspective/analysis/2015/01/15/Will-a-remove-the-hijab-campaign-turn-heads-in-Egypt-
Farouk, M. A. (2020). *Egypt's #MeToo crusader fights sex crimes via Instagram.* Reuters. https://www.reuters.com/article/us-egypt-women-internet/egypts-metoo-crusader-fights-sex-crimes-via-instagram-idUSKBN25U2B8?edition-redirect=uk

Farouk, M. A. (2021). *Egyptian women oppose 'repressive' bill to strip them of rights and freedoms*. Reuters. https://www.reuters.com/article/us-egypt-women-laws-trfn-idUSKB N2B22KU
Fausto-Sterling, A. (2000). *Sexing the body: Gender politics and the construction of sexuality*. Basic Books.
Ferranti, G., Pisano, L. M., & Nowacka, K. (2014). Unpaid care work: The missing link in the analysis of gender gaps in labour outcomes. OECD Development Center. https://www.oecd.org/dev/development-gender/Unpaid_care_work.pdf
Fetouri, M. (2018). Four decades on, is Sadat viewed as a traitor or a hero? *Middle East Monitor*. https://www.middleeastmonitor.com/20181115-four-decades-on-is-sadat-viewed-as-a-traitor-or-a-hero/
Fine, G. A. (2003). Towards a peopled ethnography developing theory from group life. *Ethnography*, 4(1), 41–60.
Fisaha, J. (2016). Female genital mutilation: A violation of human rights. *Journal of Political Sciences and Public Affairs*, 4(2), 198–204.
Flax, J. (1990). Postmodernism: Thinking in fragments. In *Thinking fragments: Psychoanalysis, feminism and postmodernism in the contemporary west* (pp. 187–221). University of California Press.
Flax, J. (1992). The end of innocence. In J. Butler & J. W. Scott (Eds.), *Feminists theorize the political* (pp. 445–463). Routledge.
Fleischer, H. (1965). The essence of historical materialism. In H. Fleischer (Ed.), *Short handbook of communist ideology* (Sovietica Book Series 20), (pp. 7–12). Brill.
Fluehr-Loban, C., & Sirois, L. B. (1990). Obedience (Ta') in Muslim marriage: Religious interpretation and applied law in Egypt. *Journal of Comparative Family Studies*, 21(1), 41–54.
Ford, L. (2016). Egyptian feminist leader Mozn Hassan resolute in face of official investigation. *The Guardian*. Retrieved January 25, 2019, from https://www.theguardian.com/global-development/2016/mar/31/egyptian-feminist-leader-mozn-hassan-resolute-investigation
Foucault, M. (1977). Part one: Torture. In A. Sheridan (translated from French), *Discipline and punish: The birth of the prison*. Vintage Books.
Foucault, M. (1980a). The confession of the flesh. In C. Gordon (Ed.), *Power/knowledge: Selected interviews and other writings 1972–77 by Michel Foucault* (pp. 194–228). Pantheon Books.
Foucault, M. (1980b). Truth and power. In C. Gordon (Ed.), *Power/knowledge: Selected interviews and other writings 1972–77 by Michel Foucault* (pp. 109–133). Harvester Wheatsheaf.
Foucault, M. (1984). *The history of sexuality Vol. I*. Penguin.
Foucault, M. (1985) [1984]. *The use of pleasure: The history of sexuality, Volume Two* (R. Hurley, Trans., pp. 1–25). Random House.
Foucault, M. (1988). The ethic of care for the self as a practice of freedom. In J. Bernauer & D. Rasmussen (Eds.), *The final Foucault* (pp. 1–20). MIT-Press.
Foucault, M. (1991). *Discipline and punish: The birth of the prison*. Penguin.
Foucault, M. (1993). About the beginning of the hermeneutics of the self (transcription of two lectures in Darthmouth on Nov. 17 and 24, 1980, ed. by Mark Blasius). *Political Theory*, 21(2), 198–227.
Fouka, V. (2020). *French ban on headscarves in public schools hindered Muslim girls' ability to finish school*. Stanford University: School of Humanities and Sciences. https://humsci.stanford.edu/feature/stanford-scholars-report-french-headscarf-ban-adversely-impacts-muslim-girls
Fowler, S. (2021). *Jehan Sadat: Egypt's first lady who transformed women's rights*. BBC. https://www.bbc.co.uk/news/world-middle-east-57672706
Frable, D. E. S. (1997). Gender, racial, ethnic, sexual, and class identities. *Annual Review of Psychology*, 48, 139–162.

Frank, A. W. (2000). The standpoint of storyteller. *Qualitative Health Research, 10*(3), 354–365.
Franke, L. M. (2021). Muslimness on demand: Critical voices of Islam in Egypt. *Religions, 12*, 152.
Freedom House. (2010). *Policing belief: The impact of Blasphemy laws on human rights – Egypt*. United Nations High Commissioner for Refugees. https://www.refworld.org/cgi-bin/texis/vtx/rwmain?page=printdoc&docid=4d5a700b2d
Freer, C. (2017). Egypt's secular opposition. *Middle East Journal, 71*(4), 559–578.
Freire, P. (2000). *Pedagogy of the oppressed* (30th anniversary ed.). Continuum.
Fries-Britt, S. L., & Turner, B. (2001). Facing stereotypes: A case study of Black students on a White campus. *Journal of College Student Development, 42*(5), 420–429.
Fryling, M. J., Johnston, C., & Hayes, L. J. (2011). Understanding observational learning: An interbehavioral approach. *The Analysis of Verbal Behavior, 27*(1), 191–203.
Gadallah, M., Verme, P., Milanovic, B., Al-Shawarby, S., El Tawila, S., & El-Majeed, A. A. (2014). The measurement of inequality in the Arab Republic of Egypt: A historical survey. In *Inside inequality in the Arab Republic of Egypt – A World Bank study* (pp. 13–32). International Bank for Reconstruction and Development/The World Bank.
Gaden, É. (2019). *L'Égyptienne 1925–1940*. Bibliothèques d'Orient. https://heritage.bnf.fr/bibliothequesorient/en/egyptienne-magazine-art
Galal, S. (2021). *Gender gap index in Egypt from 2016–2021*. Statista. https://www.statista.com/statistics/1253939/gender-gap-index-in-egypt/
Galbraith, J. K. (2006). Global macroeconomics and global inequality. In D. Held & A. Kaya (Eds.), *Global inequality: Patterns and explanations*. Polity Press.
Galligan, Y. (2007a). Women and politics in contemporary Egypt. *Middle East Journal, 61*(3), 423–446.
Galligan, Y. (2007b). *Women and politics in the third world*. Routledge.
Gamal, W. (2019). *Lost capital: The Egyptian Muslim Brotherhood's neoliberal transformation*. Carnegie Middle East Center. https://carnegieendowment.org/files/2-1-19_Gamal_Muslim_Brotherhood.pdf
Gamal El-Din, S. (2019). Egyptian man sentenced to death for killing wife, three children. *Ahram Online*. http://english.ahram.org.eg/News/324917.aspx
Garcia, J. (1996). The heart of racism. *Journal of Social Philosophy, 27*, 5–45.
Geertz, C. (1998). Deep hanging out: Review of James Clifford, *Routes, Travel, and Translation in the Late 20th Century and Pierre Clastres, Chronicle of the Guayaki Indians. The New York Review of Books, 45*(1), 69.
George, W., & Martinez, L. (2002). Victim blaming in rape: Effects of victim and perpetrator race, type of rape, and participant racism. *Psychology of Women Quarterly, 26*, 110–119.
Geshekter, C. (1995). Outbreak? AIDS, Africa and the medicalization of poverty. *Transitions, 5*(3), 4–14.
Ghoussoub, M. (1985). Feminism – or the eternal masculine – in the Arab world. *New Left Review, 161*, 3–18.
Gibson, A. (2005). Veneratation and vigilance: James Madison and public opinion, 1785–1800. *The Review of Politics, 67*(1), 5–35.
Giddens, A. (1991). *Modernity and self-identity*. Stanford University Press.
Giddens, A. (2006). *Sociology*. Polity Press.
Giddings, F. H. (1896). *The principles of sociology*. Columbia University Press.
Gilbert, J. (1953). The composition and structure of Machiavelli's Discourse. *Journal of the History of Ideas, 14*(1), 136–156.
Gillies, D. (1996). Frameworks of human rights analysis. In *Between principle and practice: Human rights in north–south relations* (pp. 3–32). McGill-Queens University Press.
Gilman, S. (1985). Black bodies, white bodies: Toward and iconography of female sexuality in late nineteenth century art, medicine and literature. In H. L. Gates (Ed.), *Race, writing and difference*. University of Chicago Press.

Glaser, B. G. (1978). *Theoretical sensitivity*. The Sociology Press.
Glass, A. (2019). Egypt, Israel conclude peace treaty, March 26, 1979. Politico. https://www.politico.com/story/2019/03/26/egypt-israel-peace-treaty-1233742
Goetz, A. M. (1990a). From feminist knowledge to data for development: The bureaucratic management of information on women and development. *IDS Bulletin*, *21*(3), 34–39.
Goetz, A. M. (1990b). Women's political effectiveness in rural Africa. *World Development*, *18*(2), 175–191.
Goetz, A. M. (1995). *The politics of integrating gender to state development processes: Trends, opportunities and constraints in Bangladesh, Chile, Jamaica, Mali, Morocco and Uganda* [UNRISD Occasional Paper, No. 2]. United Nations Research Institute for Social Development (UNRISD).
Gokariksel, B., & Secor, A. (2009). New transnational geographies of Islamism, capitalism and subjectivity: The veiling-fashion industry in Turkey. *Area*, *41*(1), 6–18.
Gokariksel, B., & Secor, A. (2012). 'Even I was tempted': The moral ambivalence and ethical practice of veiling-fashion in Turkey. *Annals of the Association of American Geographers*, *102*(4), 1–16.
Goldschmidt, A., Jr. (2008). Chronology. In *A brief history of Egypt* (pp. 244–254). Facts on File Inc.
Golley, N. (2003). Huda Shaarawi's *Harem Years:* The memoirs of an Egyptian feminist. In *Reading Arab women's autobiographies: Shahrazad tells her story* (pp. 35–52). University of Texas Press.
Goodarzi, S. (2019). I was forced to wear the Hijab. It wasn't liberating: Why World Hijab Day is an insult to girls like me. *The Spectator*. Retrieved June 3, 2019, from https://www.spectator.co.uk/2019/02/i-was-forced-to-wear-a-hijab-it-wasnt-liberating/
Gordon, J. (2016). *Nasser's blessed movement: Egypt's free officers and the July revolution*. The American University in Cairo Press.
Gorman, C. (1994). Clash of Wills in Cairo. *Time Magazine*. Retrieved December 6, 2018, from http://content.time.com/time/magazine/article/0,9171,981409,00.html
Gospodunov, P. (n.d.). *Siwa festival in Egypt*. Thousand Voyages. https://thousandvoyages.net/the-siwa-festival-in-egypt/
Gowans, C. (2004). A priori, refutations of disagreement arguments against moral objectivity: Why experience matters. *Journal of Value Inquiry*, *38*, 141–157.
Gowans, C. (2018). Moral relativism. In E. N. Zalta (Ed.), *The Stanford encyclopedia of philosophy*. The Metaphysics Research Lab, Center for the Study of Language and Information (CSLI), Stanford University. https://plato.stanford.edu/archives/sum2018/entries/moral-relativism/
Graham-Brown, S. (1985, June). After Jihan's law: A new battle over women's rights. *The Middle East*, 17–20.
Greenslade, R. (2015). Egyptian student jailed for proclaiming he is an atheist. *The Guardian*. https://www.theguardian.com/media/greenslade/2015/jan/13/egyptian-student-jailed-for-proclaiming-that-he-is-an-atheist
Greges, F. (2002). The end of Islamist insurgency in Egypt? Costs and prospects. *Middle East Journal*, *54*(4), 592–612.
Grömüs, E. (2016). The economic ideology of the Egyptian Muslim Brotherhood: The changing discourse and practices. *Journal of Emerging Economies and Islamic Research*, *4*(3), 60–74.
Gronemeyer, M. (1992). Helping. In W. Sachs (Ed.), *The development dictionary: A guide to knowledge as power* (pp. 55–73). Zed Books.
Gronow, J. (1993). Taste and fashion: The social function of fashion and style. *Acta Sociologica*, *36*, 89–100.
Gruenbaum, E. (2005a). Feminist activism for the abolition of FGC in Sudan. *Journal of Middle East Women's Studies*, *1*(2), 89–113.

Gruenbaum, E. (2005b). Socio-cultural dynamics of female genital cutting: Research findings, gaps and directions. *Culture, Health & Sexuality*, 7(5), 429–441.
Guest, G., Namey, E. E., & Mitchell, M. (2013). Participant observation. In *Collecting qualitative data: A field manual for applied research* (pp. 75–112). SAGE Publications.
Giurgiu's, M. (2012). Islamic resurgence and its consequences in the Egyptian experience. *Mediterranean Studies*, 20(2), 187–226.
Habermas, J. (2006). Religion in the public sphere. *European Journal of Philosophy*, 14(1), 1–25.
Haddad, M. (2020). A Muslim reformist: Muhammad Abduh in Muslim reformism – A critical history. *Philosophy and Politics – Critical Explorations*, 11, 15–47.
Haddad, Y. (1982). The case of feminist movement. In *Contemporary Islam and the challenge of history* (pp. 54–70). State University of New York Press.
Haddad, Y. Y. (2007). The post-9/11 Hijab as icon. *Sociology of Religion*, 68(3), 253–267.
Hamad, S. (2018). *Gender and politics in Sudan: Women's struggles in a violent context*. Palgrave Macmillan.
Hamed, A. E. (2019). Globalization in higher education in Egypt in a historical context. *Research in Globalization*, 1, 1–5.
Hamid, S. (2016). *Islamic exceptionalism: How the struggle over Islam is reshaping the world*. St. Martin's Press.
Hammam, M. (1980). Women and industrial work in Egypt: The Chubra El-Kheima case. *Arab Studies Quarterly*, 2, 50–69.
Hamzawy, A. (2017, March 16). *Legislating authoritarianism: Egypt's new era of repression*. Carnegie Endowment for International Peace. https://carnegieendowment.org/2017/03/16/legislating-authoritarianism-egypt-s-new-era-of-repression-pub-68285
Hardaker, D. (2006). Amr Khaled: Islam's Billy Graham. *The Independent*. https://www.independent.co.uk/news/world/middle-east/amr-khaled-islam-s-billy-graham-6112733.html
Harris, L. T., & Fiske, S. T. (2006). Dehumanizing the lowest of the low: Neuroimaging responses to extreme out-groups. *Psychological Science*, 17, 847–853.
Hasan, A. H. H. (2011). An Islamic perspective of the interfaith dialogue amidst current inter-religious tensions worldwide. *Global Journal of Al-Thaqafah*, 1, 25–35.
Hashim, S. (2011a). *Politics and Islam in contemporary Sudan*. Routledge.
Hashim, S. (2011b). The role of women in the Sudanese economy. *African Development Review*, 23(4), 341–355.
Haslam, N. (2006). Dehumanization: An integrative review. *Personality and Social Psychology Review*, 10(3), 252–264.
Haslam, N., & Loughnan, S. (2014). Dehumanization and infra-huminisation. *Annual Review of Psychology*, 65, 399–423.
Hassan, R. (1987, January–May). Equal before Allah: Woman/man equality in the Islamic tradition. *Harvard Divinity Bulletin*, 7(2), 2–4.
Hassan, R. (2000). Human rights in the Qur'anic perspective. In G. Webb (Ed.), *Windows of faith: Muslim scholar-activists in North America* (pp. 241–248). Syracuse University Press.
Hatem, M. (1986). The enduring alliance of nationalism and patriarchy in Muslim personal status laws: The case of modern Egypt. *Feminist Issues*, 6(1), 19–43.
Hatem, M. (1992). Economic and political liberation in Egypt and the demise of state feminism. *International Journal of Middle East Studies*, 24, 231–251.
Hatem, M. (1993). Toward the development of post-Islamist and post-nationalist feminist discourses in the Middle East. In J. Tucker (Ed.), *Arab women: Old boundaries, new frontiers* (pp. 29–48). Indiana University Press.
Hayashi, P., Abib, G., & Hoppen, N. (2019). Validity in qualitative research: A processual approach. *The Qualitative Report*, 24(1), 98–112.
Hayford, S. R. (2011). Religious differences in female genital cutting: A case study from Burkina Faso. *Journal for the Scientific Study of Religion*, 50(2), 252–271.

Haywood, C. (1994a). Masculinities in education: Work and the politics of representation. *Gender and Education*, *6*(1), 43–51.
Haywood, C. (1994b). Masculinities, gender relations, and generation. *Educational Review*, *46*(2), 211–217.
Hegel, G. W. F., Miller, A. V., Findlay, J. N., & Hoffmeister, J. (1979). *Phenomenology of spirit*. Clarendon Press.
Heikal, M. (1983). *Autumn of fury: The assassination of Sadat*. Andre Deutsche.
Helle-Velle, J. (2004). Understanding sexuality in Africa: Diversity and contextualized dividuality. In S. Arnfred (Ed.), *Rethinking sexualities in Africa* (pp. 195–207). The Nordic African Institute.
Helliwell, C. (2000). 'It's only a penis': Rape, feminism and difference. *Signs*, *25*(3), 789–816.
Henley, A. D. (2016). Religious leaders and the problem of sectarianism. In *Religious authority and sectarianism in Lebanon* (pp. 14–19). Carnegie Endowment for International Peace.
Herman, J. (1997). *Trauma and recovery: The aftermath of violence—From domestic abuse to political terror*. Basic Books.
Hess, A. (1973). The Ottoman conquest of Egypt (1517) and the beginning of the sixteenth-century World War. *International Journal of Middle East Studies*, *4*(1), 55–76.
Hessler, P. (2019). Mohamed Morsi, who brought Muslim Brotherhood to the Egyptian Presidency. *The New Yorker*. https://www.newyorker.com/news/news-desk/mohamed-morsi-who-brought-the-muslim-brotherhood-to-the-egyptian-presidency
Hijab, N. (1997). Women and work in the Arab world. In S. Sabbagh (Ed.), *Arab women: Between defiance and restraint*. Olive Branch Press.
Hill, E. (1979). *Mahkama!* In *Studies in the Egyptian legal system: Courts and crimes, laws and society* (pp. 11–49). Ithaca Press.
Hinchman, L. P., & Hinchman, S. K. (1997). Introduction. In L. P. Hinchman & S. K. Hinchman (Eds.), *Memory, identity, community: The idea of narrative in the human sciences* (pp. xiii–xxxii). State University of New York.
Hinnenbusch, R. (1981). Egypt under Sadat: Elites, power structure, and political change in a post-populist state. *Social Problems*, *28*(4), 442–464.
Hinnebusch, R. (1990). Authoritarian power and state formation in Ba'thist Syria: Army, party, and peasant. *Middle East Journal*, *44*(3), 327–343.
Hinnebusch, R. A. (2001). The formation of modern Syria. In *Syria: Revolution from above* (pp. 14–44). Routledge.
Hirschmann, N. J. (1991). Freedom, recognition, and obligation: A feminist approach to political theory. *American Political Science Review*, *85*(2), 445–456.
Hirschmann, N. (1997). Eastern veiling, western freedom? *The Review of Politics*, *59*(3), 461–488.
Hirschmann, N. (1998). Western feminism, eastern veiling, and the question of free agency. *Constellations*, *5*(3), 345–368.
Hirschon, R. (1984). Introduction: Property, power and gender relations. In R. Hirschon (Ed.), *Women and property – Women as property* (pp. 1–22). St. Martin's Press.
Ho, D. Y. F., & Chiu, C. (1994). Component ideas of individualism, collectivism, and social organization: An application in the study of Chinese culture. In U. Kim, H. C. Triandis, C. Kagitcibasi, S. C. Choi, & G. Yoon, G. (Eds.), *Individualism and collectivism: Theory, method, and applications* (pp. 123–136). SAGE Publications.
Hobfoll, S. E. (1998). *Stress, culture, and community: The psychology and philosophy of stress*. Plenum Press.
Hobfoll, S. E. (2001). The influence of culture, community, and nested-self in the stress process: Advancing conservation of resources theory. *Applied Psychology*, *50*, 337–421.
Hofstede, G. (1980). *Culture's consequences*. SAGE Publications.
Hosted, G. (1991). *Cultures and organizations: Software of the mind*. McGraw Hill.
Hofstede, G. (2001). *Culture's consequences: Comparing values, behaviors, institutions and organizations across nations* (2nd ed.). SAGE Publications.

Holdo, M. (2019). Cooptation and non-cooptation: Elite strategies in response to social protest. *Social Movement Studies*, *18*(4), 444–462.
Holland, J., Ramazanoglu, C., Sharpe, S., & Thomson, R. (1998). *The male in the head: Young people, heterosexuality and power*. Tufnell Press.
Holmes, R. (2007). *The Hottentot Venus: The life and death of Saartjie Baartman born 1789–buried 2002*. Jonathan Ball, published in association with Bloomsbury Publishing Plc.
Holt, N. L. (2001). Beyond technical reflection: Demonstrating the modification of teaching behaviors using three levels of reflection. *Avante*, *7*(2), 66–76.
Holton, G., & Sonnert, G. (1995). Mapping scientists' careers. In *Who succeeds in science? The gender dimension* (pp. 164–179). Rutgers University Press.
Home Office. (2019). Domestic abuse. In *Country policy and information note – Egypt: Women* (pp. 13–39). Home Office.
Hood far, H. (1993). The veil in their minds and on our heads: The persistence of colonial images of Muslim women. *Resources Feminist Research*, *22*(3), 5–18.
hooks, b. (1990). *Yearning: Race, gender and cultural politics*. South End Press.
Hopkins, P. (2016). *Five truths about the hijab that need to be told*. The Conversation. https://theconversation.com/five-truths-about-the-hijab-that-need-to-be-told-63892
Hosken, F. (1987). *The Hosken report: Genital and sexual mutilation of females*. Women's International News Network.
Hsu, L. (2009). Social and cultural alienation in Toni Morrison's *Tar Baby*. *Sun Yat-sen Journal of Humanities*, *29*, 51–70. http://www.un.org/womenwatch/daw/beijing/pdf/Beijing%20full%20report%20E.pdf
Hubin, D., & Haely, K. (1999). Rape and the reasonable man. *Law and Philosophy*, *18*, 113–139.
Hudge, G. D. M. (1978). *Education in modern Egypt: Ideals and realities*. Routledge and Kegan Paul.
Hudson, M. C. (1996). The political culture approach to Arab democratization: The case for bringing it back in, carefully. In R. Brynen, B. Korany, & P. Noble (Eds.), *Political liberalization and democratization in the Arab world: Theoretical perspectives* (Vol. 1, pp. 61–77). Lynne Reinner.
Hudson, M. C. (1998). The political and cultural approach to Arab democratization: The case study of bringing it back in, carefully. In B. Korany, R. Brynen, & P. Noble (Eds.), *Political liberalization and democratization in the Arab world* (Vol. 2, pp. 61–76). Lynne Rienner Publishers.
Hughes, A. (2013). The performance of Muslim identities. In *Muslim identities: An introduction to Islam* (pp. 203–222). Columbia University Press.
Hughes, M., & Taylor, J. (2011). Rape 'impossible' in marriage, says Muslim clerk. *The Independent*. https://www.independent.co.uk/news/uk/home-news/rape-impossible-marriage-says-muslim-cleric-2106161.html
Human Development Report. (2020). *The next frontier – Human development and anthropocene* [United Nations Development Program, Human Development Report]. https://www.eg.undp.org/content/egypt/en/home/presscenter/pressreleases/2020/human-development-report-2020-the-next-frontier-human-developm.html
Human Development Report Office (HDRO). (2015). *What is human development* [United Nations Development Program, Human Development Report]. http://hdr.undp.org/en/content/what-human-development
Human Rights Watch (HRW). (1992). *Egypt: Court upholds closure of women's organizations* (Vol. 4, No. 2). Human Rights Watch. https://www.hrw.org/reports/1992/egypt/
Human Rights Watch. (1997). *The repression of women in the Islamic world*. Human Rights Watch.
Human Rights Watch (HRW). (2004a). *Egypt: Margins of repression state limits on nongovernmental organization activism* (Vol. 17, No. 8E, pp. 1–41). Human Rights Watch. https://www.hrw.org/reports/2004/egypt0704/egypt0704.pdf

240 Bibliography

Human Rights Watch (HRW). (2004b). *The pains and perils of unequal divorce system.* Human Rights Watch. https://www.hrw.org/reports/2004/egypt1204/4.htm

Human Rights Watch (HRW). (2004c). *War in Iraq: Not a humanitarian intervention.* Human Rights Watch. https://www.hrw.org/news/2004/01/25/war-iraq-not-humanitarian-intervention

Human Rights Watch (HRW). (2007a). *Conversion and freedom of religion.* Human Rights Watch. https://www.hrw.org/reports/2007/egypt1107/5.htm#_ftn129

Human Rights Watch (HRW). (2007b). *Religious and national identity in Egypt: Identity documents and religion.* Human Rights Watch. https://www.hrw.org/reports/2007/egypt1107/3.htm

Human Rights Watch (HRW). (2013). *Egypt: 3-year sentence for atheist convicted under Blasphemy Law.* Human Rights Watch. https://www.hrw.org/news/2015/01/13/egypt-3-year-sentence-atheist

Human Rights Watch (HRW). (2019). *Egypt: New NGO law renews Draconian restrictions.* Human Rights Watch. https://www.hrw.org/news/2019/07/24/egypt-new-ngo-law-renews-draconian-restrictions

Human Rights Watch (HRW). (2020a). *Egypt: Security forces abuse, torture LGBTQ people – Arbitrary arrests, discrimination, entrapment, privacy violations.* Human Rights Watch. https://www.hrw.org/news/2020/10/01/egypt-security-forces-abuse-torture-lgbt-people

Human Rights Watch (HRW). (2020b). *Egypt: Spate of 'morality' persecutions of women – Arrests, jail for violating 'family values'.* Human Rights Watch. https://www.hrw.org/news/2020/08/17/egypt-spate-morality-prosecutions-women

Human Rights Watch (HRW)/Africa. (1996). *Shattered lives: Sexual violence during the Rwandan genocide and its aftermath.* Human Rights Watch Women's Rights Project. Library of Congress. https://www.hrw.org/reports/1996/Rwanda.htm

Hume, T. (2020). Influencers Haneen Hossam and Mowada al-Adham were sentenced to two years in prison for inciting "immorality" on the social media platform. *Vice.* https://www.vice.com/en/article/pkymak/egypt-jailed-tiktok-haneen-hossam-mowada-al-adham

Hundley, T. (1991). Egyptians abandoned by Gulf War allies. *Chicago Tribune.* https://www.chicagotribune.com/news/ct-xpm-1991-07-07-9103170485-story.html

Husband, C. (2005). Doing good by stealth, whilst flirting with racism. Some contradictory dynamics of British multiculturalism. In W. Bosswick & C. Husband (Eds.), *Comparative European research in migration, diversity and identities* (pp. 191–206). University of Deusto.

Husband, C. (2010). Counter-narratives to multiculturalism and the assimilationist drift in British policy. *Translocations,* 6(2), 1–23.

Hussain, A. (2008). From tolerance to dialogue: A Muslim perspective on interfaith dialogue with Christians. *Asian Christian Review,* 2, 85–97.

Hussain, A. (2012). Egypt opposition group to boycott 'irresponsible' vote on new constitution. *The Guardian Online.* Retrieved December 11, 2018, from https://www.theguardian.com/world/2012/dec/09/egypt-opposition-vote-constitution

Hussein, A. (1985). Recent amendments to Egypt's personal status law. In E. Fernea (Ed.), *Women and the family in the Middle East* (pp. 231–232). University of Texas Press.

Ibn 'Arabi, M. (1911). *al-Futūḥāt al Makkīyah.* Dar al-Tiba'ah.

Ibn Sina, A. (1999). *Qanun al-Tibb* [*The cannon of medicine*]. Kazi Publications.

Ibrahim, S. (1982). An Islamic alternative in Egypt: The Muslim Brotherhood and Sadat. *Arab Studies Quarterly,* 4(1/2), 75–93.

Ibrahim, S. E. (1992). The troubled triangle: Populism, Islam and civil society in the Arab world. *International Political Science Review,* 13(4), 407–424.

Ibrahim, S. E. (1995). Democratization in the Arab world. In A. R. Norton (Ed.), *Civil society in the Middle East* (Vol. 1, pp. 27–54). E. J. Brill.

Bibliography 241

Ibrahim, S. E. (2002). "Anatomy of Egypt's Militant Islamic Groups" and "Islamic Activism and Political Opposition in Egypt". In S. E. Ibrahim (Ed.), *Egypt, Islam and democracy: Critical essays*. The American University Press.

Ibrahim, S. E., Taros, M. R. I., El-Fiki, M. A., & Soliman, S. S. (1996). Copts today. In *The Copts of Egypt* (pp. 23–36). Minority Rights Group.

Ichheiser, G. (1949). *Misunderstandings in human relations: A study in false social perception*. University of Chicago Press.

IMF. (2021). *World economic outlook database April 2021*. International Monetary Fund. https://www.imf.org/en/Publications/GFSR/Issues/2021/04/06/global-financial-stability-report-april-2021#FullReport

'Inān, Muḥammad 'Abd Allāh. (1958). *Tarikh al-Jami' al-Azhar [History of the mosque and University of Al-Azhar]*. Mu'assasat al-Khanjī.

Inbar, E. (2017). Israel's costs vs. its benefits: The six-day war. *The Middle East Quarterly*, *24*(3), Article 6267.

International Institute for Democracy and Electoral Assistance (IDEA). (2014). *What is a constitution? Principals and concepts* (pp. 1–12). International Institute for Democracy and Electoral Assistance (IDEA), Constitution Building Primers.

IRIN. (2005). Razor's edge – The controversy of female genital mutilation. *The Inside Story on Emergencies (IRIN)*. Retrieved October 12, 2018, from http://www.irinnews.org/video/2005/03/08/razors-edge-controversy-female-genital-mutilation

Islami, I. (2016). Political history of modern Egypt. *ILIRIA International Review*, *6*(1), 189–206.

Islam Web. (2013). *Fatwa: Why are Muslims discouraged from questioning the essence of god?* Islam Web. https://www.islamweb.net/ar/fatwa/231082/النهي-عن-التفكر-في-ذات-الله-عز-وجل

Ismi, A. (2004). *Impoverishing a continent: The World Bank and the IMF in Africa* (pp. 7–11). Canadian Centre for Policy Alternatives.

Jackson, R., & Roseber, C. G. (1982). Clientelism, corruption and pluralism. In *Personal rule in Black Africa: Prince, autocrat, prophet, tyrant* (pp. 37–47). University of California Press.

Jackson, S. (1995). Gender and heterosexuality: A materialist feminist analysis. In M. Maynard & J. Purvis (Eds.), *(Hetero)sexual politics*. Taylor and Francis.

Jahoda, G. (1999). *Images of savages: Ancient roots of modern prejudice in western culture*. Routledge & Kegan Paul.

Jamshed, S. (2014). Qualitative research method: Interviewing and observation. *Journal of Basic and Clinical Pharmacy*, *5*(4), 87–88.

Janz, M. (2018). From Kente to colonialism: African fashion over time. *BIAS Journal of Fashion Studies*. https://adht.parsons.edu/fashionstudies/bias-post/from-kente-to-colonialism-african-fashion-over-time/

Jastrow, M. (1921). Veiling in ancient Assyria. *Revue Archéologique*, *14*, 209–238.

Jawad, H. A. (1991). Islam and women's education. In *The rights of women in Islam* (pp. 16–29). Palgrave Macmillan.

Jaynes, W. H. (2011). Race, racism and Darwinism. *Education and Urban Society*, *43*(5), 535–559.

Jazzar, R. (2011, December). *The Egyptian Women's Movement – Identity politics and the process of liberation in the nineteenth and twentieth centuries* (pp. 82–128). Arizona State University Press.

Jeffery, A. (1942). The political importance of Islam. *Journal of Near Eastern Studies*, *1*(4), 383–395.

Jehl, D. (1997). 70 die in attach at Egypt temple. *The New York Times*. https://www.nytimes.com/1997/11/18/world/70-die-in-attack-at-egypt-temple.html

Jenkins, B. (2016). Islam and the west: Interplay with modernity. *Journal of Alternative Perspectives in the Social Sciences*, *7*(4), 516–548.

Jenkins, P. (2007). *God's Continent: Christianity, Islam, and Europe's Religious Crisis (The Future of Christianity)*. Oxford University Press.

Johan Malmqvist, J., Hellberg, K., Möllås, G., Rose, R., & Shevlin, M. (2019). Conducting the pilot study: A neglected part of the research process? Methodological findings supporting the importance of piloting in qualitative research studies. *International Journal of Qualitative Methods, 18*, 1–11.

John, R. (2021). *Gamal Abdel-Nasser*. Encyclopedia Britannica. https://www.britannica.com/biography/Gamal-Abdel-Nasser

Johnson-Agbakwu, C., & Warren, N. (2017). Interventions to address sexual function in women affected by female genital cutting: A scoping review. *Current Sexual Health Reports, 9*(1), 20–31.

Joseph, S. (1997). The public/private – The imagined boundary in the imagined nation/state/community: The Lebanese case. *Feminist Review, 57*, 73–92.

Kabeer, N. (1999). *The conditions and consequences of choice: Reflections on the measurement of women's empowerment* [Discussion Paper No. 108, pp. 2–43]. United Nations Research Institute for Social Development.

Kabeer, N. (2001). Reflections on the measurement of women's empowerment. *Discussing Women's Empowerment: Theory and Practice, 3*, 17–57.

Kabeer, N. (2005). Gender equality and women's empowerment: A critical analysis of the third millennium development goal 1. *Gender & Development, 13*(1), 13–24.

Kabeer, N. (2006). Citizenship, affiliation and exclusion: Perspectives from the south. *IDS Bulletin, 37*(4), 91–101.

Kabeer, N. (2011). Between affiliation and autonomy: Navigating pathways of women's empowerment and gender justice in rural Bangladesh. *Development and Change, 42*(2), 499–528.

Kaegi, W. (1998). Egypt on the eve of the Muslim conquest. In C. F. Petry (Ed.), *The Cambridge history of Egypt* (Vol. 1, pp. 34–61). Cambridge University Press.

Kaler, A. (2009). African perspective on female circumcision. *Canadian Journal of African Studies, 43*(1), 178–183.

Kalev, H. D. (2004). Cultural rights or human rights: The case of female genital mutilation. *Sex Roles, 51*(5–6), 339–348.

Kamal, H. (2014). A century of Egyptian women's demands: The four waves of the Egyptian feminist movement. In *gender and race matter: Global perspectives on being a woman*. https://doi.org/10.1108/S1529-212620160000021002

Kamal, H. (2016). A century of Egyptian women's demands: The four waves of the Egyptian feminist movement. In S. Takhar (Ed.), *Gender and race matter: Global perspectives on being a woman* (pp. 3–22). Emerald Publishing Limited.

Kamal, H. (2017). A century of Egyptian women's demands: The four waves of the Egyptian feminist movement. *Gender and Race Matter: Global Perspectives on Being a Woman, 21*, 3–22.

Kamel, M. (2013). *A to Z reasons why Egypt's education system is lacking*. Egyptian Streets. https://egyptianstreets.com/2013/12/15/a-to-z-reasons-why-egypts-education-system-is-lacking/

Kamel, H. (2017). *Overpopulation, religion, and fatwas on demand in Egypt*. Mada Masr.

Kanchana, R. (2019). How do Muslim states treat their "outsiders"?: Is Islamic practice of naturalisation synonymous with Jus Sanguinis? In *Migration and Islamic ethics* (pp. 136–155). Brill.

Kandiyoti, D. (1984). Bargaining with patriarchy. *Gender & Society, 2*(3), 274–290.

Kandiyoti, D. (1988). Bargaining with patriarchy. *Gender and Society, 2*(3), 274–290.

Kandiyoti, D. (1991a). Identity and its discontents: Women and the nation. *Millennium: Journal of International Studies, 20*(3), 429–443.

Kandiyoti, D. (1991b). Islam and patriarchy: A comparative perspective. In B. Baron and N. R. Keddie (Eds.), *Women in Middle Eastern history: Shifting boundaries in sex and gender*. Yale University Press.

Kandiyoti, D. (1995). Reflections on the politics of gender in Muslim societies: From Nairobi to Beijing. In M. Afkhami (Ed.), *Faith and freedom: Women s human rights in the Muslim world* (pp. 19–32). I. B. Tauris.
Kandiyoti, D. (1998). Bargaining with patriarchy. *Gender & Society*, *2*(3), 274–290.
Kapchan, D., & Strong, P. (1999). Theorizing the hybrid. *The Journal of American Folklore*, *112*(445), 239–253.
Kapoor, S. (2000). Domestic violence against women and girls. *Innocenti Digest*, *6*, 1–19.
Karam, A. (1998). *Women, Islamisms and the state: Contemporary feminisms in Egypt*. Macmillan Press.
Karshenas, M., & Moghadam, V. M. (2001). Female labor force participation and economic adjustment in the MENA region. In M. Cinar (Ed.), *The economics of women and work in the Middle East and North Africa* (pp. 51–74). JAI Press.
Kartch, F. (2017). Narrative interviewing. In M. Allen (Ed.), *The SAGE encyclopedia of communication research methods* (pp. 1073–1075). SAGE Publications.
Kassem, M. (1999). The presidency. In *In the guise of democracy: Governance in contemporary Egypt* (pp. 31–74). Ithaca Press.
Kassem, M. (2004a). Civil society. In *Egyptian politics: The dynamics of authoritarian rule* (pp. 87–132). Lynne Rienner Publishers.
Kassem, M. (2004b). Egypt's Islamists: From fundamentalists to 'Terrorist'. In *Egyptian politics: The dynamics of authoritarian rule* (pp. 133–166). Lynne Rienner Publishers.
Kassem, M. (2004c). Governance from Nasser to Mubarak. In *Egyptian politics: The dynamics of authoritarian rule* (pp. 11–48). Lynne Rienner Publishers.
Kassem, M. (2004d). Introduction. In *Egyptian politics: The dynamics of authoritarian rule* (pp. 1–11). Lynne Rienner Publishers.
Kassem, M. (2014). *Egyptian politics: The dynamics of authoritarian rule*. Lynne Rienner Publishers.
Kawamura, K. Y. (2012). Body image among Asian Americans. In T. Cash (Ed.), *Encyclopedia of body image and human appearance* (Vol. 1, pp. 95–102). Academic Press.
Kazai, H., & Shah, Z. (2001). *US bombed Afghan Power Plant*. BBC News. http://news.bbc.co.uk/1/hi/world/south_asia/1632304.stm
Keddie, N. (1983). *An Islamic response to imperialism: Political and religious writings of Sayyid Jamāl ad-Dīn 'al-Afghānī'*. University of California Press.
Keikelame, M. J., & Swartz, L. (2019). Decolonizing research methodologies: Lessons from a qualitative research project, Cape Town, South Africa. *Global Health Action*, *12*(2), 1–7.
Kelemen, B. (2019). *Egyptian leadership in historical perspective: Abdel Fattah El-Sisi & Gamal Abdel Nasser*. London School of Economics and Political Science. https://blogs.lse.ac.uk/lseih/2019/05/08/egyptian-leadership-in-historical-perspective-abdel-fattah-el-sisi-gamal-abdel-nasser/
Kelly, E., Hillard, P., & Adams, B. (2005). Female genital mutilation. *Current Opinion Obstetrics and Gynecology*, *17*(5), 490–494.
Kendiyoti, D. (1991). Women, Islam and the state. *Middle East Report*, *173*, 9–14.
Kenny, L. (1967). 'Alī Mubārak: Nineteenth century Egyptian educator and administrator. *Middle East Journal*, *21*(1), 35–51.
Kepel, G. (1999a). From one ordeal to another: 1944–66. In *Muslim extremism in Egypt: The prophet and the pharaoh* (J. Rothschild, Trans., pp. 26–68). Ithaca Press.
Kepel, G. (1999b). The vanguard of the 'Umma'. In *Muslim extremism in Egypt: The prophet and the pharaoh* (J. Rothschild, Trans., pp. 129–164). Ithaca Press.
Kershaw, S. (2003). Cairo, once 'the scene,' cracks down on gays. *The New York Times*. Retrieved January 24, 2019, from http://www.radicalparty.org/en/content/cairo-once-scene-cracks-down-gays
Key, V. O. (2015)[1961]. Public opinion and American democracy. In M. Lodge, E. C. Page, & S. J. Balla (Eds.), *The Oxford handbook of classics in public policy and administration* (pp. 2–19). Oxford University Press.

Kezar, A. (2002). Reconstructing static images of leadership: An application of positionality theory. *Journal of Leadership Studies, 8*(3), 94–109.

Khairat, F. (2020). *Meet assault police's Nadeed Ashraf: The student behind Egypt's Anti-Harassment Revolution.* Egyptian Streets. https://egyptianstreets.com/2020/09/20/meet-nadeen-ashraf-the-student-behind-egypts-anti-harrassment-social-media-revolution/

Khaled, A. (2010). *Reward for wearing Hijab – Amr Khaled* [Video]. YouTube. https://www.youtube.com/watch?v=sUyIOKqHn30

Khalifa, E. (1973a). The development of Egyptian Law. *International and Comparative Law Quarterly, 22*(1), 170–189.

Khalifa, E. (1973b). Women in the Egyptian labor market. *Middle East Journal, 27*(3), 299–311.

Khalifa, I. (1998). *Women, Islamisms and the state: Contemporary feminisms in Egypt.* Macmillan Press.

Khalife, L. (2018). These Arab Countries repealed their 'marry the rapist' law before Lebanon. *StepFeed.* https://stepfeed.com/these-arab-countries-repealed-their-marry-the-rapist-law-before-lebanon-2383

Khamis, A. (1978). *Al Harakat al nisa'iyya wa silatuha ma'al ist'amar* [*Feminist movements and their relations with imperialism*]. Dar Al Ansar.

Khan, M. (2014). The Muslim veiling: A symbol of oppression or a tool of liberation. *UMASA Journal, 32,* 1–11.

Kharoshah, E., & Sabah, H. (2020). *'Years of sexual abuse': Egyptian psychiatrist accused of assaulting underage girls exposed.* Egyptian Streets. https://egyptianstreets.com/2020/10/04/years-of-sexual-abuse-egyptian-psychiatrist-accused-of-assaulting-underage-girls-exposed/

Khater, A., & Nelson, C. (1988). Al Harakat Al Nissa'iyah: The women's movement and political participation in modern Egypt. *Women's Studies International Forum II,* 465–483.

Kholoussi, S. (2017). Not so dangerous liaisons: Interstitial subjectivities and the autobiography of Arab women. *English Language and Literature Studies, 7*(4), 11–24.

Kiger, M. E., & Varpio, L. (2020). Thematic analysis of qualitative data: Amee Guide No. 131. *Medical Teacher, 42*(8), 846–854.

Kim, J. (2012). Taking rape seriously: Rape as slavery. *Harvard Journal of Law & Gender, 35,* 263–310.

Kingsley, P. (2015). How Mohamed Morsi, Egypt's first elected president, ended up on death row. *The Guardian.* https://www.theguardian.com/world/2015/jun/01/mohamed-morsi-execution-death-sentence-egypt

Kitchen, J. E. (2015). Violence in defense of empire. *Journal of Modern European History, 13*(2), 249–267.

Kitzinger, C. (2000). Doing feminist conversation analysis. *Feminism and Psychology, 10,* 163–193.

Knudsen, A. (2003). *Fishing for development: Small-scale fisheries, technological change and women in Kerala, India.* VDM Verlag.

Korany, B., Noble, P., & Brynen, R. (1998). *Political liberalization and democratization in the Arab world.* Lynne Rienner Publishers.

Korzeniewicz, R. P., & Moran, T. P. (2009). *Unveiling inequality: A world-historical perspective.* Russel Sage Foundation.

Koydemir, S., Cecilia, A. & Essau, C. A. (2018). Chapter 5 – Anxiety and anxiety disorders in young people: A cross-cultural perspective. In M. Hodes, S. Shur-Fen Gau, & P. J. Veries (Eds.), *Understanding uniqueness and diversity in child and adolescent mental health* (pp. 115–134). Academic Press.

Krafft, C. (2012). *Challenges facing the Egyptian educational system: Access, quality, and inequality* [Survey of Young People in Egypt Policy Brief No. 2]. Population Council.

Kramer, E. M. (2003). Cosmopoly: Occidentalism and the new world order. In E. M. Kramer (Ed.), *The emerging monoculture: Assimilation and the "model minority"* (pp. 234–291). Praeger.
Kramer, G. (1994). The integration of the integrists. In G. Salame (Ed.), *Democracy without democrats: The renewal of politics in the Muslim world* (pp. 200–226). I. B. Tauris.
Kreshaw, K. (2003). *Reproductive rights and wrongs: The global politics of population control.* South End Press.
Kroeber, A. L., & Kluckhohn, C. (1952). Culture: A critical review of concepts and definitions. *Papers. Peabody Museum of Archaeology and Ethnology, Harvard University, 47*(1), viii, 223.
Kudsi-Zadeh, A. A. (1972). Afghani and Freemasonary in Egypt. *Journal of the American Oriental Society, 92*(1), 25–35.
Kuhn, T. S. (1962). *The structure of scientific revolutions* (pp. 1–10). University of Chicago Press.
Kuhn, T. S. (1970). Logic of discovery or psychology of research? In I. Lakatos & A. Musgrave (Eds.), *Criticism and the growth of knowledge* (p. 22). Cambridge University Press.
Kukathas, C. (1995). Are there any cultural rights? *Political Theory, 20*, 105–139.
Kukathas, C. (2003). *The liberal archipelago: A theory of diversity and freedom.* Oxford University Press.
Kurcan, A., & Erol, M. K. (1999). *Dialogue in Islam, Qur'an, Sunnah, History* (pp. 12–125). Dialogue Society.
Kymlicka, W. (1995). Multicultural citizenship: A liberal theory of minority rights. In W. Kymlicka (Ed.), *The rights of minority cultures.* Oxford University Press.
Labov, W. (1997). Some further steps in narrative analysis. *Journal of Narrative and Life History, 7*(1–4), 395–415.
Labov, W., & Waletzky, J. (1967). Narrative analysis. In J. Helm (Ed.), *Essays on the verbal and visual arts* (pp. 12–44). University of Washington Press.
Laczo, M. (2003a). The changing identity of 'women's issues' in Egypt. *Feminist Review, 73*(1), 66–89.
Laczo, M. (2003b). Women's economic rights in Egypt: Pathways to gender equality in employment. *Journal of Middle East Women's Studies, 4*(1), 24–45.
Lafranchi-Shaarawi, S. (2011). *Casting off the veil: The life of Huda Shaarawi, Egypt's first feminist (1879–1947).* I. B. Tauris.
Lane, S. D., & Meleis, A. I. (1991). Roles, work, health perceptions and health resources of women: A study in an Egyptian hamlet. *Social Science Medicine, 33*(10), 1197–1208.
Lapidus, I. M., & Salaymeh, L. (2002). Women in the Middle East: Nineteenth to twenty-first century. In I. M. Lapidus (Ed.), *A history of Islamic societies.* Cambridge University Press.
Laquer, T. (1986). Orgasm, generation, and the politics of reproductive biology. *Representations, 14*, 1–41.
Laquer, T. (1990). *Making sex, body and gender from the Greeks to Freud.* Harvard University Press.
Latif, N. (2002). *Women, Islam and human rights* [Doctoral thesis, University of Newcastle-upon-Tyne]. https://core.ac.uk/download/pdf/153776035.pdf
Lax, R. F. (2000). Socially sanctioned violence against women: Female genital mutilation is its most brutal form. *Clinical Social Work Journal, 28*(4), 403–412.
Leclerc-Madlala, S. (2001). AIDS in Africa: A pandemic of silence. *Lola Press – International Feminist Journal, 15*, 34–40.
Leclerc-Madlala, S. (2002). Youth HIV/AIDS and the importance of sexual culture and context. *Social Dynamics, 28*, 20–41.
Leitz, L. (2015). *The Arab feminist union.* Britannica. https://www.britannica.com/topic/Arab-Feminist-Union

246 Bibliography

LeMoncheck, L. (1985). *Dehumanizing women: Treating persons as sex objects*. Rowman and Allanheld.
Lens ink, R., & White, H. (2001). Are there negative returns to aid? *Journal of Development Studies, 37*(6), 42–65.
Leotti, L. A., Iyengar, S. S., & Ochsner, K. N. (2010). Born to choose: The origins and value of the need for control. *Trends in Cognitive Sciences, 14*(10), 457–463.
Lesley, N. (2001). Analyzing masculinity: Interpreting repertoires, ideological dilemmas and subject positions. In M. Wetherell, S. Taylor, & S. J. Yates (Eds.), *Discourse as data: A guide for analysis* (p. 191). SAGE Publications.
Levy, J. T. (1997). Classifying cultural rights. In I. Shapiro & W. Kymlicka (Eds.), *Ethnicity and group rights*. New York University Press.
Lévy-Strauss, C. (1961). *Race and history*. UNESCO.
Lévy-Strauss, C. (1962). The science of the concrete. In *The savage mind* (G. Weidenfield & Nicholson Ltd., Trans., pp. 1–22). University of Chicago Press.
Lewis, D. (2011). Representing African sexualities. In S. Tamale (Ed.), *African sexualities: A reader* (pp. 199–216). Pambazuka Press.
Lewis, R. (2013). Hijab on the shop floor: Muslims in fashion retail in Britain. In *Islamic fashion and anti-fashion: New perspectives from Europe and North America* (pp. 181–200). Bloomsbury Academic.
Lewis, R. (2015). *Muslim fashion: Contemporary style culture*. Duke University Press.
Leyens, J. P., Cortes, B., Demoulin, S., Dovidio, J. F., Fiske, S. T., Gaunt, R., Paladino, M.-P., Rodriguez-Perez, A., Rodriguez-Torres, R., & Vaes, J. (2003). Emotional prejudice, essentialism, and nationalism the 2002 Tajfel lecture. *European Journal of Social Psychology, 33*, 703–717.
Library of Congress. (2012). *Why use primary sources*. University of Technology Sydney UTS. https://www.lib.uts.edu.au/guides/primary-sources/primary-sources/benefits
Liow, J. C. (2009). Reconstructing and reinforcing Islamism. In *Piety and politics* (pp. 73–112). Oxford University Press.
Lippman, T. W. (1989). *Egypt after Nasser: Sadat, peace, and the mirage of prosperity*. Paragon House Publishers.
Lofgren, H. (1993). Economic policy in Egypt: A breakdown in reform resistance? *International Journal of Middle East Studies, 25*(3), 407–421.
Lombardi, C. (1998). Islamic law as a source of constitutional law in Egypt: The constitutionalization of Sharia in a modern Arab state. *Columbia Journal of Transnational Law, 37*(1), 82–123.
Lopez, A. S. M. (2001). Ethnocentrism and feminism: Using a contextual methodology in international women's rights advocacy and education. *Southern Law Review, 28*(3), 279–287.
Lotfi, A. M. (1978). The revolutionary gentlewomen in Egypt. In L. Beck & N. Keddie (Eds.), *Women in the Muslim world*. Harvard University Press.
Lotha, G. (2016). *Aminah al-Sa'id: Egyptian journalist and writer*. Encyclopedia Britannica. https://www.britannica.com/biography/Aminah-al-Said#ref794928
Lott, B., & Bullock, H. E. (2001). Who are the poor? *Journal of Social Issues, 57*, 189–206.
Loveluck, L. (2012a). *Education in Egypt: Key challenges* [Background Paper for the Middle East and North Africa Programme]. Chatham House. https://www.chathamhouse.org/sites/default/files/public/Research/Middle%20East/0312egyptedu_background.pdf
Loveluck, L. (2012b). *Education in Egypt: Key challenges*. Chatham House. https://www.chathamhouse.org/sites/default/files/public/Research/Middle%20East/0312egyptedu_background.pdf
Lyotard, J. F. (1984) [1979]. *The postmodern condition: A report on knowledge* (G. Bennington & B. Massumi, Trans.). University of Minnesota Press.
Maathai, W. (2009). *The challenge for Africa*. Pantheon Books.

Mabro, R. (2006). *Egypt's oil and gas: Some crucial issues* (2006 Distinguished Lecture Series, pp. 3–24). The Egyptian Center for Economic Studies.
Machiavellu, N. (1981). Of new principalities that are acquired by others' arms and fortune. In *The prince* (H. C. Mansfield, Trans., pp. 25–34). University of Chicago Press.
Machiavelli, N., *1469-1527* (1981). Chapter 12: Concerning the secretaries of princes. In *The prince* (H. C. Mansfield, Trans., pp. 92–93). University of Chicago Press.
MacKinnon, C. (1987). *Feminism unmodified: Discourses on life and law*. Harvard University Press.
MacLeod, A. E. (1991). *Accommodating protest: Working women veiling, and change in Cairo*. Columbia University Press.
MacLeod, A. E. (1993). *Accommodating protest*. Columbia University Press.
MacManus, S. A. (2007). *Young v. old: Generational combat in the 21st century*. Westview Press.
MacManus, J. (2010). From the archive, 7 October 1981: President Sadat assassinated at army parade. *The Guardian*. https://www.theguardian.com/theguardian/2010/oct/07/archive-president-sadat-assassinated
Magubane, Z. (2001). Which bodies matter? Feminism, poststructuralism, race, and the curious theoretical odyssey of the 'Hottentot Venus'. *Gender and Society*, *15*(6), 816–834.
Mahfouz, H. F., & Raghaven, F. (2018). In Egypt, a #MeToo complaint can land a woman in jail. *The Washington Post*. Retrieved January 25, 2019, from https://www.washingtonpost.com/world/in-egypt-a-metoo-complaint-can-land-a-woman-in-jail/2018/10/24/3a2fe5a0-d6db-11e8-a10f-b51546b10756_story.html??noredirect=on
Mahmood, S. (2001). Feminist theory, embodiment, and the docile agent: Some reflections on the Egyptian Islamic revival. *Cultural Anthropology*, *16*(2), 202–236.
Mahmood, S. (2005). *Politics of piety: The Islamic revival and the feminist subject*. Princeton University Press.
Mahmood, S. (2011). *Politics of piety: The Islamic revival and the feminist subject*. Princeton University Press.
Maktouf, L. (2015). The separation of church and state under the 'Islamist Protocol'. *Turkish Policy Quarterly*. http://turkishpolicy.com/article/770/the-separation-of-church-and-state-under-the-islamist-protocol
Malik, K. (2015). The failure of multiculturalism: Community versus society in Europe. *Foreign Affairs*. https://www.foreignaffairs.com/articles/western-europe/failure-multiculturalism
Mama, A. (1996). *Women's studies and studies of women in Africa during the 1990s* [Working Paper Series 5/96]. CODESRIA.
Mama, A. (2007). Is it ethical to study Africa? Preliminary thoughts on scholarship and freedom. *African Studies Review*, *50*(1), 1–26.
Mancini, J. (2012). *American Catholicism transformed: From the sixties to the fifteen years after the millennium*. Oxford University Press.
Mann, B. L. (2006). An intrinsic, quantitative case study of WebCT developers. In *Selected styles in web-based research* (pp. 71–80). Information Science Publishing.
Mansfield, P. (1965). *Nasser's Egypt*. Penguin Books.
Mansfield, E. (1971). *Microeconomic theory: A mathematical approach*. W. W. Norton.
Mansfield, P. (1973). Nasser and Nasserism. *International Journal*, *28*(4), 670–688.
Manstead, A. S. R. (2018). The psychology of social class: How socioeconomic status impacts thought, feelings, and behaviour. *British Psychological Society*, *57*, 267–291.
Marcus, G. E., & Fisher, M. F. (1986). *Anthropology as cultural critique: An experimental moment in the human sciences*. Chicago University Press.
Markowitz, D., & Slovic, P. (2020). Social, psychological, and demographic characteristics of dehumanization towards immigrants. *Proceedings of the National Academy of Science of the United States*, *17*, 9260–9269.

Markus, H. R., & Kitayama, S. (1991). Culture and the self: Implications for cognition, emotion, and motivation. *Psychological Review, 98*(2), 224–253.
Marshall, C., & Rossman, G. B. (1989). *Designing qualitative research*. SAGE Publications.
Marx, K., & Davis, R. (1994). A contribution to the critique of Hegel's philosophy of right: Introduction. In J. O'Malley (Ed.), *Marx: Early political writings* (pp. 57–70). Cambridge University Press.
Massey, D. S., Gross, A. B., & Eggers, M. L. (1991). Segregation, the concentration of poverty, and the life chances of individuals. *Social Science Research, 20*, 397–420.
Masud, N., & Yontcheva, B. (2005). *Does foreign aid reduce poverty? Empirical evidence from nongovernmental and bilateral aid* [IMF Working Paper]. International Monetary Fund Institute.
Matsumoto, D. (2007). Culture, context and behavior. *Personality, 75*, 1285–1320.
Maududi, M. (1974). *Birth control: It's social, political, economic, moral and religious aspect* (K. Ahmad & M. I. Faruqi, Trans., pp. 155–177). Islamic Publications Ltd.
Maurin, E., & Navarrete, N. H. (2019). *Behind the veil: The effect of banning the Islamic veil in schools* [IZA DP No. 12645, pp. 1–42]. Institute of Labor Economics, Deutsche Post Foundation.
Mavelli, L. (2012). *Europe's encounter with Islam: The secular and the postsecular*. Routledge.
Maxwell, J. A. (1992). Understanding and validity in qualitative research. *Harvard Educational Review, 62*(3), 279–300.
Mayer, A. E. (2016). Islamic law and human rights: Conundrums and equivocations. In C. Gutafson & P. Juviler (Eds.), *Religion and human rights: Competing claims?* (pp. 180–202). Routledge.
Mayer, J. (2005). Outsourcing Torture: The secret history of America's "extraordinary rendition" program. *The New Yorker*. Retrieved January 24, 2019, from https://www.newyorker.com/magazine/2005/02/14/outsourcing-torture
Mazumdar, S., & Mazumdar, S. (2001). Rethinking public and private space: Religion and women in Muslim society. *Journal of Architectural and Planning Research, 18*(4), 302–324.
Mbembe, A. (2001). *On the postcolony*. University of California Press.
McAdam, D. (2010). *Political process and the development of black insurgency, 1930–1970*. University of Chicago Press.
McClintock, A. (1995). *Imperial leather: Race, gender and sexuality in the colonial conquest*. Routledge.
McCoy, T. (2014). Egypt's sexual harassment pandemic – and the powerlessness of hashtags. *The Washington Post*. https://www.washingtonpost.com/news/morning-mix/wp/2014/06/18/egypts-sexual-harassment-pandemic-and-the-powerlessness-of-hashtags/
McFadden, P. (2001). Cultural practice as gendered exclusion: Experiences from Southern Africa. In N. Kabeer (Ed.), *Discussing women's empowerment: Theory and practice* (pp. 58–70). The Swedish International Development Cooperation Agency.
McGhee, D. (2003). Moving to "our" common ground – A critical examination of community cohesion discourse in twenty-first century Britain. *The Sociological Review, 51*(3), 376–404.
McGreal, C., & Shenker, J. (2011). Hosni Mubarak resigns – And Egypt celebrates a new dawn. *The Guardian*. https://www.theguardian.com/world/2011/feb/11/hosni-mubarak-resigns-egypt-cairo
McKenna, A. (2018). *Muhammed Naguib: President of Egypt*. Encyclopedia Britannica. https://www.britannica.com/biography/Muhammad-Naguib
McKinley, A. (2007). Performativity and the politics of identity: Putting Butler to work. *Critical Perspectives on Accounting, 21*, 232–242.
McKinley, N. M. (1999). Women and objectified body consciousness: Mothers' and daughters' body experience in cultural, developmental and familial context. *Developmental Psychology, 35*, 760–769.

McNay, L. (2003). Agency, anticipation and indeterminacy in feminist theory. *Feminist Theory*, 4(2), 139–148.
McNeill, J. J. (1993). *The church and the homosexual*. Beacon Press.
McRobbie, A. (Ed.). (1997). *Back to reality? Social experience and cultural studies*. Manchester University Press.
Mead, G. H. (1934). *Mind, self, and society from the standpoint of a social behaviorist*. University of Chicago Press.
Mead, G. H. (1982). *The individual and the social self: Unpublished essays by G. H. Mead* (D. L. Miller, Ed., p. 5). University of Chicago Press.
Megahed, N., Ginsburg, M., Abdellah, A., & Zohry, A. (2012). The quest for educational quality in Egypt: Active-learning pedagogies as a reform initiative. In *Quality and qualities: Tensions in educational reforms* (pp. 41–67). Sense Publishers.
Memmi, A. (1965). *The colonizer and the colonized* (pp. 79–89). Souvenir Press.
Mendelsohn, O., & Vicziany, M. (1998). *The untouchables: Subordination, poverty and the state in modern India*. Cambridge University Press.
Méndez, M. (2013). Autoethnography as a research method: Advantages, limitations and criticisms. *Colombian Applied Linguistics Journal*, 15(2), 279–287.
Menon, R. (2012). *Machiavelli, meet Egypt's military brass*. The Huffington Post. Retrieved January 24, 2019, from https://www.huffingtonpost.com/rajan-menon/scaf-egypt_b_1598280.html
Mensch, B. S., Ibrahim, B. L., Lee, S. M., & El-Gibaly, O. (2000). *Socialization to gender roles and marriage among Egyptian adolescents* [Policy Research Division Working Paper No. 140]. Population Council.
Mensch, B. S., Ibrahim, B. L., Lee, S. M., & El-Gibaly, O. (2003). Gender attitudes among Egyptian adolescents. *Studies in Family Planning*, 34(1), 8–18.
Mernissi, F. (1982). Virginity and patriarchy. *Women's Studies International Forum*, 5(2), 183–191.
Mernissi, F. (1987). *Beyond the veil: Male–female dynamics in modern Muslim society*. Indiana University Press.
Mernissi, F. (1988a). Democracy as moral disintegration: The contradiction between religious belief and citizenship as a manifestation of the historicity of the Ara identity. In N. Toubia (Ed.), *Women of the Arab world* (pp. 36–43). Zed Publishing.
Mernissi, F. (1988b). Women and fundamentalism. *Middle East Report* (July–August), 8–11.
Mernissi, F. (1991a). *The veil and the male elite: A feminist interpretation of women's rights in Islam*. Addison-Wesley.
Mernissi, F. (1991b). *Women and Islam: An historical and theological enquiry* (M. J. Lakeland, Trans.). Blackwell.
Mernissi, F. (1996). *Women's rebellion and Islamic memory*. Zed Books.
Meyer-Resende, M. (2014). *Egypt: In-depth analysis of the main elements of the new constitution*. (*Directorate-General for External Policies of the Union: Policy Department*, pp. 5–15). The European Parliament's Committee on Foreign Affairs.
Mhajne, A. (2020). Women's rights and Islamic feminism in Egypt. *Georgetown Journal of International Affairs*. https://gjia.georgetown.edu/2022/06/08/womens-rights-and-islamic-feminism-in-egypt/
Michaelson, J. (2008). Chaos, law and god: The religious meanings of homosexuality. *Michigan Journal of Gender and Law*, 15(41), 41–118.
Michaelson, R., & Tondo, L. (2019). Egypt frustrates Giulio Regeni investigation three years on. *The Guardian*. https://www.theguardian.com/world/2019/jan/25/egypt-frustrates-giulio-regeni-investigation-three-years-on
Michaelson, R., & Tondo, L. (2020). Italy alarmed after Egyptian studying in Bologna arrested in Cairo. *The Guardian*. https://www.theguardian.com/world/2020/feb/09/italy-alarmed-after-egyptian-studying-in-bologna-arrested-in-cairo

Michelson, R. (2017). LGBTQ people in Egypt targeted in wave of arrests and violence. *The Guardian.* https://www.theguardian.com/world/2017/oct/08/lgbt-people-egypt-targeted-wave-arrests-violence

Middle East Monitor. (2014). *Political scientist: Al-Sisi is unfit to lead Egypt.* Middle East Monitor. https://www.middleeastmonitor.com/20140506-political-scientist-al-sisi-is-unfit-to-lead-egypt/

Milanovic, B. (2016). *Global inequality: A new approach for the age of globalization.* Harvard University Press.

Miller, S. (2009). Moral injury and relational harm: Analyzing rape in Darfur. *Journal of Social Philosophy, 40*(4), 504–523.

Mills, C. (1997). *The racial contract.* Cornell University Press.

Mills, S. (1995). *Feminist stylistics.* Routledge.

Ministry of Health and Population [Egypt], El-Zanaty and Associates [Egypt], & ICF International. (2014). *Egypt demographic and health survey.* Ministry of Health and Population and ICF International. https://dhsprogram.com/pubs/pdf/fr302/fr302.pdf.

Ministry of Waqfs and Information. (1994). *Islam's attitude toward family planning* (pp. 27–34). Egypt Ministries of Waqfs and Information.

Mir-Hosseini, Z. (1999). *Islam and gender: The religious debate in contemporary Iran.* Princeton University Press.

Mir-Hosseini, Z. (2000). *Marriage on trial: Islamic family law in Iran and Morocco.* I. B. Tauris.

Mirshak, N. (2020). Authoritarianism, education and the limits of political socialisation in Egypt. *Power and Education, 12*(1), 39–54.

Mishler, E. G. (1995). Models of narrative analysis: A typology. *Journal of Narrative and Life History, 5*(2), 87–123. https://doi.org/10.1075/jnlh.5.2.01mod

Mishori, R., Ferdowsian, H., Naimer, K., Volpellier, M., & McHale, T. (2019). The little tissue that couldn't – Dispelling myths about the Hymen's role in determining sexual history and assault. *Reproductive Health, 16*(1), 74.

Mitchell, T. (1969). *Colonising Egypt.* University of California Press.

Moghadam, V. M. (1988). *Women, work, and economic reform in the Middle East and North Africa.* Lynne Rienner.

Moghadam, V. M. (1993). *Modernizing women, gender and social change in the Middle East.* Lynne Rienner Publishers.

Moghadam, V. M. (1999). *Modernizing women: Gender and social change in the Middle East.* Lynne Rienner Publishers.

Moghadam, V. M. (2003). Patriarchy and the changing family. In *Modernizing women: Gender and social change in the Middle East* (2nd ed., pp. 70–112). Lynne Rienner.

Moghadam, V. M. (2004). *Towards gender equality in the Arab/Middle East region* [United Nations Development Programme. Background Paper for HDR]. Human Development Report Office.

Moghadam, V. M. (2020). Gender regimes in the Middle East and North Africa: The power of feminist movements. *Social Politics: International Studies in Gender, State & Society, 27*(3), 467–485.

Moghazy, N. H., & Kaluarachchi, J. J. (2020). Sustainable agriculture development in the western desert of Egypt: A case study on crop production, profit, and uncertainty in the Siwa Region. *Sustainability, 12*, 1–23.

Mohamad, M. Z., Salleh, A. Z., Hasan, A. F., Yusof, S., Deris, M. F. H. M., & Jamsari, E. A. (2020). Personal identity from an Islamic perspective. *International Journal of Academic Research in Business and Social Sciences, 10*(10), 199–207.

Mojab, S. (2001). Theorizing the politics of 'Islamic feminism'. *Feminist Review, 69*, 124–146.

Molek, F. (1975). *The admission and academic placement of students from selected Arab states – Egypt, Jordan, Saudi Arabia and Kuwait* [A Workshop Report, pp. 1–26]. American Association of Collegiate Registrars and Admissions Officers, Association for Foreign Student Affairs.
Molyneux, M. (1985). Mobilization without emancipation? Women's interests, the state and revolution in Nicaragua. *Feminist Studies, 11*(2), 227–254.
Monagan, S. L. (2010). Patriarchy: Perpetuating the practice of female genital mutilation. *Journal of Alternative Perspectives in the Social Sciences, 2*(1), 160–181.
Moneim, A. (2007). Towards the understanding of societal cultures and leadership in non-western countries: An exploratory study on Egypt. *Academic Leadership: The Online Journal, 5*(3), Article 19.
Monshipouri, M. (1995). *Democratization, liberalization, and human rights in the third world* (pp. 1–14). Lynne Rienner Publishing.
Moon, T. D., Audet, C. M, & Blevins, M. (2017). Understanding intra-vaginal and labia minora elongation practices among women heads-of-households in Zambézia Province, Mozambique. *Culture, Health and Sexuality, 19*(5), 616–629.
Moor, A. (2010). She dresses to attract, he perceives seduction: A gender gap in attribution of intent to women's revealing style of dress and its relation to blaming the victims of sexual violence. *Journal of International Women's Studies, 11*(4), 115–127.
Moore, C. H. (1974). Authoritarian politics in unincorporated society: The case of Nasser's Egypt. *Comparative Politics, 6*(2), 193–218.
Moore, W., & Scarritt, J. (1990). IMF conditionality and polity characteristics in Black Africa an exploratory analysis. *Africa Today, 37*(4), 39–60.
Moors, A. (2013). Discover the beauty of modesty. In L. Reina (Ed.), *Modest fashion: Styling bodies, mediating faith* (pp. 17–40). I. B. Tauris.
Moosa, E. (1997). Prospects for Muslim law in South Africa: A history and recent developments. In E. Cotrane & C. Mallet (Eds.), *Yearbook of Islamic and Middle Eastern law* (pp. 130–155). Kluwer Law International.
Morris, A. G. (2008). Searching for 'real' Hottentots: The Khoekhoe in the history of South African physical anthropology. *South African Humanities, 20*, 221–233.
Morrison, T. (1981). *Tar baby*. Vintage.
Morsy, A. (2011). *An independent voice for Egypt's al-Ahzar?* Carnegie Endowment for International Peace. https://carnegieendowment.org/sada/45052
Morsy, L. (1984). The military clauses of the Anglo–Egyptian treaty of friendship and alliance, 1936. *International Journal of Middle East Studies, 16*(1), 67–97.
Moser, C. (1993). *Gender planning and development: Theory, practice and training*. Routledge.
Moussalli, A. (1999). The fundamentalist discourses on politics: From pluralistic democracy to majoritarian tyranny. In *Moderate and radical Islamic fundamentalism: The quest for modernity, legitimacy, and the Islamic state* (pp. 68–106). University of Florida Press.
Moustafa, T. (2000). Conflict and cooperation between the state and religious institutions in contemporary Egypt. *International Journal of Middle East Studies, 32*(1), 3–22.
Mqotsi, L. (2002). Science, magic and religion as trajectories of the psychology of projection. In C. O. Hoppers (Ed.), *Indigenous knowledge and the integration of knowledge systems* (pp. 158–172). New Africa Books.
Mubarak, H. (2004). *Women's rights in the Middle East and North Africa: Progress amid resistance*. Rowman & Littlefield.
Mudimbe, V. Y. (1988). *The invention of Africa: Gnosis, philosophy and the order of knowledge*. James Currey.
Muhaiyadeen, M. R. B. (2008). *Islam and world peace: Explanations of a Sufi* (pp. 7–36). The Fellowship Press.
Mulcahy, K. (2000). Cultural imperialism and cultural sovereignty: US–Canadian cultural relations. *American Review of Canadian Studies, 30*(2), 181–206.

Mullet, D. R. (2018). A general critical discourse analysis framework for educational research. *Journal of Advanced Academics*, *29*(2), 116–142.
Muncey, T. (2005). Doing autoethnography. *International Journal of Qualitative Methods*, *4*(1), Article 5. https://sites.ualberta.ca/~iiqm/backissues/4_1/html/muncey.htm
Musallam, B. (1983). *Sex and society in Islam* (pp. 28–60). Cambridge University Press.
Musharraf, M. N., & Nabeel, F. B. (2015). Schooling options for Muslim children living in Muslim-majority countries – A thematic literature review. *International Journal of Social Science and Humanities Research*, *3*(4), 29–62.
Mustafa, O. (2021). *Ahmed Bassem Zaki sentenced to 8 years in prison for sexual assault*. Egyptian Streets. https://egyptianstreets.com/2021/04/11/ahmed-bassem-zaki-sentenced-to-8-years-in-prison-for-sexual-assault/
Nader, A. (2019). *Egypt's new NGO law: Better or 'repackaged' tyranny?* Al-Monitor. https://www.al-monitor.com/originals/2019/08/egypt-ngos-law-sisi-ratification-freedoms.html
Nalty, K. (2016). Strategies for confronting unconscious bias. *The Colorado Lawyer*, *45*(5), 45–52.
Nash, K. (1994). Feminist production of knowledge: Is deconstruction a practice for women? *Feminist Review*, *47*, 65–77.
Nasif, M. D. (1962). Ta'thir (Heritage). In M. D. Nasif (Ed.), *Ta'thir Bahithat Al Badiya Malak Hifni Nasif 1886–1918* [*Thee legacy of the searcher of the desert Malak Hifni Nasif*] (pp. 318–320). Al-Maaref Press.
Nasser, D. (2016). Gendered voices of youth and Tahrir in Ahdaf Soueif's Cairo: My city, our revolution. *Kohl: A Journal for Body and Gender Research*, *2*(2), 228–244.
Nawar, L., Lloyd, C. B., & Ibrahim, B. (1995). Women's autonomy and gender roles in Egyptian families. In C. Makhlouf-Obermeyer (Ed.), *Family, gender, and population in the Middle East, policies in context* (pp. 147–178). The American University in Cairo Press.
Nazir, S., & Ramadan, A. (2018). *Women's rights in the Middle East and North Africa: Progress amid resistance*. Rowman & Littlefield.
Nelissen, R., & Meijers, M. (2010). Social dominance orientation and economic ideologies. *Journal of Economic Psychology*, *31*(4), 593–605.
Nelissen, R., & Meijers, H. C. (2011). Social benefits of luxury brands as costly signals of wealth and status. *Evolution of Human Behavior*, *32*(5), 343–355.
Nelson, C. (1996). *Doria Shafik, Egyptian feminist: A woman apart* (p. 234). University Press of Florida.
New York Times (NYT). (1952). Cairo mufti bars votes for women: Condemns suffrage agitation in Egypt and rebukes leader who won beauty contest. *New York Times*. https://www.nytimes.com/1952/05/03/archives/cairo-mufti-bars-votes-for-women-condemns-suffrage-agitation-in.html
New York Times (NYT). (2020). The 22-year old force behind Egypt's growing #MeToo movement. *New York Times*. https://www.nytimes.com/2020/10/02/world/middleeast/egypt-metoo-sexual-harassment-ashraf.html
Nielsen, J. R., & Neubert, S. (2009). The Egyptian organization for human rights. In C. Hulsman (Ed.), *The Arab-West report, paper 15*. The Arab-West Foundation. Retrieved September 19, 2019, from http://hrlibrary.umn.edu/research/Egypt/Human%20Rights%20Organizations.pdf
Nietzsche, F. (1996). *On the genealogy of morals* [*Zur Genealogie der Moral*] (D. Smith, Trans.). Oxford University Press. (Original work published 1887)
Nietzsche, F. (2012). *Human, all-too-human: Parts one and two*. Courier Corporation.
Nirala, S., & Ray, M. (2008). *Amr Khaled: Egyptian televangelist*. Encyclopedia Britannica. https://www.britannica.com/biography/Amr-Khaled
Nnaemeka, O. (2005). *Female circumcision and the politics of knowledge: African women in imperialist discourses*. Praeger Publishers.

Noakes, G. (1995). *Cairo population conference still controversial* [Washington Report on Middle East Affairs]. Retrieved December 6, 2018, from https://www.wrmea.org/1995-april-may/cairo-population-conference-still-controversial.html

Noble, H., & Smith, J. (2015). Issues of validity and reliability in qualitative research. *Evidence-based Nursing, 18*(2), 34–35.

Nochlin, L. (1989). The imaginary orient. In *The politics of vision*. Routledge.

Nomani, A. (2007). The 2007 Time 100 – Heroes and pioneers: Amr Khaled. *Time*. http://content.time.com/time/specials/2007/time100/article/0,28804,1595326_1615754_1616173,00.html

Nomani, A. (2016). Wearing the Hijab in solidarity perpetuates oppression. *New York Times*. https://www.nytimes.com/roomfordebate/2016/01/06/do-non-muslims-help-or-hurt-women-by-wearing-hijabs/wearing-the-hijab-in-solidarity-perpetuates-oppression

Noonan, H. (Ed.). (1993). *Personal identity*. Dartmouth.

Northern Ireland Human Rights Commission (NIHRC). (2016). *Female genital mutilation in the United Kingdom*. NIHRC. https://nihrc.org/uploads/publications/FGMinUK-15.08.2016.pdf

Norton, A. R. (1995). Civil society and prospects for democratization. In *Civil society in the Middle East* (Vol. 1, pp. 1–27). E. J Brill.

Noshokaty, A. (2016). Women and the Press 2: The right to a voice. *Al Ahram English*. Retrieved January 30, 2019, from http://english.ahram.org.eg/NewsContent/32/1168/193604/Folk/Inspiring-Women/Women-and-the-press-The-right-to-a-voice.aspx

Nosseir, M. (2019). International Women's Day: An Egyptian perspective – How is it that young Egyptian men are often proud of their sexual virility? *Egyptian Streets*. Retrieved from https://egyptianstreets.com/2019/03/08/international-womens-day-an-egyptian-perspective-how-is-it-that-young-egyptian-men-are-often-proud-of-their-sexual-virility/

Nouh, Y. (2016). *The beautiful reasons why these women love wearing the Hijab*. The Huffington Post. Retrieved June 3, 2019, from https://www.huffingtonpost.co.uk/entry/the-beautiful-reasons-why-these-women-love-wearing-a-hijab_n_57320575e4b0bc9cb0482225

Nour, N. M., Michels, K. B., & Bryant, A. E. (2006). Defibulation to treat female genital cutting: Effect on symptoms and sexual function. *Obstetrics and Gynecology, 108*(1), 55–60.

Nussbaum, M. C. (1999). *Sex and social justice*. Oxford University Press.

O'Brien, G. V. (2003). People with cognitive disabilities: The argument from marginal cases and social work ethics. *Social Work, 48*, 331–337.

Ochs, E., & Taylor, C. (1992). Family narrative as political activity. *Discourse & Society, 3*(3), 301–340.

OECD. (2018). *Women's political participation in Egypt: Barriers, opportunities and gender sensitivity of select political institutions*. Organization for Economic Co-Operation and Development. https://www.oecd.org/mena/governance/womens-political-participation-in-egypt.pdf

Offenhauer, P. (2005). *Women in Islamic Societies: A Selected Review of Social Scientific Literature*. Library of Congress, Federal Research Division.

Oinas, E., & Arnfred, S. (2009). Introduction: Sex and politics – Case Africa. *Nordic Journal of Feminist and Gender Research, 17*(4), 691–731.

Olenick, I. (1998). Female circumcision is nearly universal in Egypt, Eritrea, Mali and Sudan. *International Family Planning Perspectives, 24*, 47–49.

Olmsted, J. C. (2005). Is paid work the (only) answer? Neoliberalism, Arab women's well-being, and the social contract. *Journal of Middle East Women's Studies, 1*(2), 112–141.

Olukoshi, A., & Nyamnjoh, F. B. (2004). Rethinking African development: Editorial. *CODESRIA Bulletin, 3&4*, 1–4.

Omran, A. R. (1992). *Family planning in the legacy of Islam* (pp. 145–182). Routledge.

O'Neil, T., Domingo, P., & Alters, C. (2014). *Progress on women's empowerment: From technical fixes to political action* [Working Paper 6]. Development Progress. https://cdn.odi.org/media/documents/9282.pdf

Onion, A., Sullivan, M., & Mullen, M. (2009). *United States withdraws offer of aid for Aswan Dam*. History. https://www.history.com/this-day-in-history/united-states-withdraws-offer-of-aid-for-aswan-dam

Onley, J. (2005). Britain's informal empire in the Gulf, 1820–1971. *Journal of Social Affairs, 22*(87), 29–45.

Onwuegbuzie, A. J., & Johnson, R. B. (2006). The validity issue in mixed research. *Research in the Schools, 13*(1), 48–63.

Orb, A., Eisenhauer, L., & Wynaden, D. (2000). Ethics in qualitative research. *Journal of Nursing Scholarship, 33*(1), 93–96.

Osha, S. (2004). *A postcolonial scene: On girls' sexuality* [Paper presentation]. 2nd Understanding Human Sexuality Seminar Series. Africa Sexuality Resource Centre.

Osman, A. Z. (2012). Women's movement: A stop at Egypt's socialist era. *Egypt Independent*. https://egyptindependent.com/womens-movement-stop-egypts-socialist-era/

Ostrove, J. M., & Cole, E. R. (2003). Privileging class: Toward a critical psychology of social class in the context of education. *Journal of Social Issues, 59*, 677–692.

Over, H. (2016). The origins of belonging: Social motivation in infants and young children. *Philosophical Transactions of the Royal Society of London Series B, 19*, 371–379.

Owen, R. (1989). Economic consequences of Suez for Egypt. In W. R. Louis & R. Owen (Eds.), *Suez 1956*. Clarendon Press.

Owen, R. (1994). Socio-economic change and political mobilization: The case of Egypt. In G. Salame (Ed.), *Democracy without democrats: The renewal of politics in the Muslim world* (pp. 183–199). I. B. Tauris.

Oyserman, D., & Lee, S. W. S. (2008). Priming "culture": Culture as situated in cognition. In S. Kitayama & D. Cohen (Eds.), *Handbook of cultural psychology* (pp. 255–279). Guilford Press.

Paciello, M. C. (2011). Behind the veil of stability of Hosni Mubarak's regime (1981–February 2011). In *Egypt: Changes and challenges of political transition* (pp. 1–23). The MEDPRO Project.

Palma, J. G. (2009). The revenge of the market on the rentiers: Why neo-liberal reports of the end of history turned out to be premature. *Cambridge Journal of Economics, 33*(4), 1–81.

Palomino, R. (2017). *The importance of religion in the development of societies today and tomorrow*. Universidad Complutense (Madrid, Spain). https://eprints.ucm.es/id/eprint/46057/1/Presentation%20Rafael%20Palomino%20%28sin%20v%C3%ADnculos%20notas%29.pdf

Panel Survey of Young People in Egypt. (2014). In R. Roushdy & M. Sieverding (Eds.), *Generating evidence for policy, programs, and research*. Central Agency for Public Mobilization and Statistics – Population Council. https://www.popcouncil.org/uploads/pdfs/2015PGY_SYPE-PanelSurvey.pdf

Parham, J. B., Lewis, C. C., Fretwell, C. E., Irwin, J. G., & Schrimscher, M. R. (2015). Influences on assertiveness: Gender, national culture, and ethnicity. *Journal of Management Development, 34*(4), 421–439.

Parikh, S. (2005). From auntie to disco: The bifurcation of risk and pleasure in sex education in Uganda. In V. Adams & S. L. Pigg (Eds.), *Sex in development*. Duke University Press.

Park, C. (2004). Chapter 17: Religion and geography. In J. Hinnells (Ed.), *Routledge companion to the study of religion*. Routledge.

Park, S. (2011). Defence of cultural relativism. *Cultura: International Journal of Philosophy of Culture and Axiology, 8*(1), 159–170.

Parolin, G. P. (2015). Shall we ask Al-Azhar? Maybe not. *Middle East Law and Governance, 7*(2), 212–235.

Patai, R. (1967). *Women in the modern world.* Free Press.
Pateman, C. (1997). Contract, the individual and slavery. In *The sexual contract* (pp. 39–76). Stanford University Press.
Paul, C., Clarke, C., Grill, B., & Dunigan, M. (2013). Algerian independence, 1954–1962: Case outcome: COIN loss. In *Paths to victory: Detailed insurgency case studies* (pp. 75–93). RAND Corporation.
Perry, J. (1985). Language reform in Turkey and Iran. *International Journal of Middle East Studies, 17*(3), 295–311.
Peters, M. A. (2001). Poststructuralist Marxism. In *Poststructuralism, Marxism, and neoliberalism: Between theory and politics* (pp. 3–40). Rowman and Littlefield Publishers.
Petras, J. (1993). Cultural imperialism in the late 20th century. *Journal of Contemporary Asia, 23*(2), 139–148.
Philipp, T. (1978). Feminism and nationalist politics in Egypt. In L. Beck & N. Keddie, N. (Eds.), *Women in the Muslim world* (pp. 277–294). Harvard University Press.
Phillips, T. M., & Pittman, J. F. (2003). Identity processes in poor adolescents: Exploring the linkages between economic disadvantage and the primary task of adolescence. *Identity: An International Journal of Theory and Research, 3*, 115–129.
Pines, J. (2006). Profiles in patient safety: Confirmation bias in emergency medicine. *Society for Academic Emergency Medicine, 13*(1), 90–94.
Pinnegar, S., & Daynes, J. G. (2007). Locating narrative inquiry historically. In D. J. Clandinin (Ed.), *Handbook of narrative inquiry: Mapping a methodology.* SAGE Publications.
Pitkin, H. (1967). *The concept of representation.* University of California Press.
Pitt-Rivers, J. (1977). *The fate of Shechem or the politics of sex: Essays in the anthropology of the Mediterranean.* Cambridge University Press.
Poggenpoel, M., & Myburgh, S. (2003). The researcher as research instrument in educational research: A possible threat to trust-worthiness? *Education, 124*(2), 418–421.
Polimeno, M. (2015). The 2014 Egyptian constitution: Balancing leadership with civil rights (al-madaniyya). *Electronic Journal of Islamic and Middle Eastern Law, 3*, 1–67.
Polkinghorne, D. E. (1988). *Narrative knowing and the human sciences.* State University of New York Press.
Polkinghorne, D. E. (1995). Narrative configuration in qualitative analysis. *Qualitative Studies in Education, 8*(1), 5–23.
Presley, C. A. (1998). The Mau Mau rebellion, Kikuyu women and social change. *Canadian Journal of African Studies, 22*, 502–527.
Prezworski, A. (1986). Some problems in the study of transition to democracy. In G. O'Donnell, L. Whitehead, & P. C. Schmitter (Eds.), *Transition from authoritarian rule: Comparative perspectives* (pp. 47–63). John Hopkins University Press.
Prodger, M. (2010). *Superstar Muslim preacher Amr Khaled battles Al Qaeda.* BBC News. http://news.bbc.co.uk/1/hi/programmes/newsnight/9264357.stm
Qur'an (2005). *The Qur'an: A new translation.* Oxford University Press. (Qur'an 2:30).
Raai, M. (2017). *Egypt shuts El Nadeem Centre for torture victims.* Al-Jazeera Media Network. Retrieved January 25, 2019, from https://www.aljazeera.com/news/2017/02/egypt-shuts-el-nadeem-centre-torture-victims-170209143119775.html
Radwan, S. (1977). Income distribution in Egypt. *Journal of Development Studies, 13*(3), 198–208.
Radwan, Z. (1982). *Bahth zahirat al hijab bain al jam'iyyat* [*A study of the phenomenon of the veil among university women*]. National Centre for Sociological and Criminological Research.
Rafter, N. (2004). Criminalization of mental retardation. In S. Noll & J. W. Trent (Eds.), *Mental retardation in America: A historical reader* (pp. 232–257). New York University Press.
Rahman, A. A. (2017). *Considering converting to another religion in Egypt? Think again.* Raseef 22. https://raseef22.net/article/1069506-thinking-converting-another-religion-egypt-think

Rahman, F. (1980). Chapter 2: Man as individual. In *Major themes in the Qur'an* (pp. 12–24). Bibliotheca Islamica.
Rahman, F. (1982). The status of women in Islam: A modernist interpretation. In H. Papanek & G. Munault (Eds.), *Separate worlds of purdah in South Asia* (pp. 285–310). South Asia books.
Rama, S. (2013). Remembering their roles: Keeping women involved post-Arab awakening. *Journal of Women and Human Rights in the Middle East, 1*, 31–48.
Ramazani, N. (1983). The veil – Piety or protest? *Journal of South-Asian and Middle Eastern Studies, 7*(2), 20–36.
Ramdani, N. (2013). Sexual violence in Egypt: 'The target is a woman'. *The Guardian.* https://www.theguardian.com/world/2013/jul/09/sexual-violence-egypt-target-woman
Ramdani, N. (2016). Women in the 1919 Egyptian Revolution: From feminist awakening to nationalist political activism. *Journal of International Women's Studies, 14*(2), 39–52.
Ranko, A. (2015). The state and the brotherhood under Nasser and Sadat (1954–1981): State-discourse and Islamist counter-discourse. In *The Muslim Brotherhood and its quest for hegemony in Egypt* (pp. 43–52). Springer.
Rapoport, Y. (2005). *Marriage, money and divorce in medieval Islamic society.* Cambridge Studies in Islamic Civilization.
Rappaport, R. (1999). *Ritual and religion in the making of humanity.* Cambridge University Press.
Rashid, F. M. (1937). *Muqaraa bain al mar'a al Misriyya wa al mar'a al Turkiyya [A comparison between the Egyptian and the Turkish woman].* Al Misriyya.
Read, J. G., & Bartkowski, J. P. (2000). To veil or not to veil? A case study of identity negotiation among Muslim women in Austin, Texas. *Gender & Society, 14*(3), 395–417.
Reed-Danahay, D. E. (1997). Auto/ethnography: Rewriting the self and the social. *American Ethnologist, 27*(2), 551–553.
Reed-Danahay, D. E. (2017). Bourdieu and critical anthropology: Implications of research, writing and teaching. *International Journal of Multicultural Education, 19*(1), 144–154.
Reid, D. (1990). The private university, 1908–1919. In *Cairo University and the making of modern Egypt* (pp. 9–68). Cambridge University Press.
Reinach, J. (1982). The Egyptian question and the French alliance. *Nineteenth Century, 12*, 821–838.
Rena, R. (2013). Is foreign aid panacea for African problems? The case of Namibia. *Managing Global Transitions, 11*(3), 223–241.
Retta, J. (2013). Consequences of the Arab spring for women's political participation. *Journal of Women and Human Rights in the Middle East, 1*, 3–20.
Reuters. (2010). Nasr Abu Zayd, who stirred debate on Koran, dies at 66. *The New York Times.* https://www.nytimes.com/2010/07/06/world/middleeast/06zayd.html
Richards, A. C. (1956). *A girl's initiation ceremony among the Bemba of Zambia.* Oxford University Press.
Richards, H. M., & Schwartz, L. J. (2002). Ethics of qualitative research: Are there special issues for health services research? *Family Practice, 19*, 135–139.
Richie, C. (2010). An argument against the use of the word 'homosexual' in English translations of the Bible. *The Heythrop Journal, 51*(5), 723–729.
Riessman, C. K. (1993). *Narrative analysis.* SAGE Publications.
Robinson, B. A. (2008). *Text of Corinthians 6:9-11 from the Christian scriptures.* Religious Tolerance. http://www.religioustolerance.org/chr_sav1.htm
Robinson, J., & Yeh, E. (2011). Transactional sex as a response to risk in western Kenya. *American Economic Journal, 3*, 35–64.
Rodney, W. (2004). *How Europe underdeveloped Africa* (New ed.). Bogle-L'Ouverture Publications.
Rogers, J. (2009). A child is being mutilated. *Australian Feminist Studies, 24*(60), 181–194.

Roskin, M. G. (2014). The new cold war. *Parameters, 44*(1), 5–9.
Roth, K. (2020). *Egypt: Events of 2020*. Human Rights Watch. Retrieved April 29, 2022, from https://www.hrw.org/world-report/2021/country-chapters/egypt
Rousseau, J. J. (1972). *Emile or, education, everyman's library* (pp. 326–328). Biblio Distribution Center.
Roya News. (2018). Young Egyptian man arrested for raping his mothers. *Roya News*. https://en.royanews.tv/news/14219/Young-Egyptian-man-arrested-for-raping-his-mother
Ruark, J. (2001). A second look at the big squeeze. *The Chronicle of Higher Education*. https://www.chronicle.com/article/a-second-look-at-the-big-squeeze/
Rubin, G. (1975). The traffic in women: Notes on a political economy of sex. In R. Rapp (Ed.), *Toward an anthropology of women* (pp. 157–210). Monthly Review.
Rubio-Marin, R. (2014a). The achievement of female suffrage in Europe. *European Constitutional Law Review, 10*(2), 221–248.
Rubio-Marin, R. (2014b). Women in Europe: How the different conceptions of citizenship reveal the gendered nature of the welfare state. *Social Politics, 21*(2), 287–315.
Ruby, T. (2006). Listening to the voices of hijab. *Women's Studies International Forum, 29*(1), 54–66.
Ruggi, S. (1998). Commodifying honor in female sexuality: Honor killings in Palestine. *Middle East Report, 206*, 12–15.
Ruggie, J. G. (1998). *Constructing the world polity: Essays on international institutionalization*. Routledge.
Runciman, W. G. (1983). *A treatise on social theory: The methodology of social theory*. Cambridge University Press.
Russel, S. (2004). The political economy of women's employment. *Development and Change, 35*(3), 457–472.
Russell, S. (2004). Globalization and its discontents: The rise of Islamism in the Middle East. *Middle East Policy, 11*(4), 120–133.
Ruxton, S. (2020). *What is the role of men in feminism*. Coopération Internationale pour le Développement et la Solidarité [International Cooperation for Development and Solidarity]. https://www.cidse.org/2020/03/04/what-is-the-role-of-men-in-feminism/
Ryan, C. R. (2001). Political strategies and regime survival in Egypt. *Journal of Third World Studies, 18*(2), 25–46.
Ryan, R. M., & Deci, E. L. (2006). Self-regulation and the problem of human autonomy: Does psychology need choice, self-determination, and will? *Journal of Personality, 74*, 1557–1585.
Ryrie, W. (1995). Success or failure? In *First world, third world* (pp. 33–51). Palgrave Macmillan.
Saadawi, N. (1977). *Woman at point zero*. Zed Books.
Sachs, J. D. (2005). China: Catching up after half a millennium. In *The end of poverty: Economic possibilities for our time* (pp. 148–169). The Penguin Press.
Saeed, A. (2011). Islam: Hadith and apostasy. *Public Discourse – Journal of the Witherspoon Institute*. https://www.thepublicdiscourse.com/2011/04/3082/
Sahih Al Bukhari. (2018). Al Kufr – Disbelief and its various manifestations. In *Sahih Al Bukhari Arabic-English* (M. Hassan Khan, Trans., pp. 1073–1079). Islamic University, Al Madina Al-Munawara.
Sa'id, A. (1972a). Awada illi hadith al ziyy hadhihi al dajja al mufti;ana ma ma'naha [Back to the issue of dress, this show of fuss, what does it mean?]. *Hawa*. Dar Al Hilal Archives.
Sa'id, A. (1972b). Hadhihi ithahira ma ma'naha [This phenomenon, what does it mean?]. *Hawa*. Dar Al Hilal Archives.
Sa'id, A. (1973). Id al sufur 'id al nahda [Feast of unveiling, feast of renaissance]. *Hawa*. Dar Al Hilal Archives.
Said, E. (1978). *Orientalism*. Pantheon Books.

Bibliography

Sakr, R. (2014). Why did the Muslim Brotherhood fail? The double-faced discourse of Ikhwan and political response to Islamist-secular diversity in Egypt. *Danubius, 32*, 76.

Salamé, G. (Ed.). (1994). *Democracy without democrats? The renewal of politics in the Muslim world*. I. B. Tauris.

Saleh, M. (2010). Historical origins of inter-religion differences: Evidence from 19th and 20th century Egypt. *Topics in Middle Eastern and African Economies, 12*, 2–22.

Salem, P. (2016). *Egypt's importance in times of troubles*. Middle East Institute. Retrieved January 8, 2019, from https://www.mei.edu/publications/egypts-importance-time-troubles

Salem, S. M. I. (2017). Four women of Egypt: Memory, geopolitics and the Egyptian women's movement during the Nasser and Sadat eras. *Hypatia, 32*(3), 593–608.

Salmoni, B. A. (2005). The limits of pedagogical revolution. In E. T. Ewing (Eds.), *Revolution and pedagogy* (pp. 61–85). Palgrave Macmillan.

Samir, R. (2021). The role of social media in Egyptian women's movements. *Arab Media & Society, 34*(2), 45–61.

Samra, Y. (2018). Egypt's GDP could jump to 32% by achieving gender equality: IFC. *Egypt Today*. https://www.egypttoday.com/Article/3/44750/Egypt's-GDP-could-jump-32-by-achieving-gender-equality-IFC

Sánchez Jankowski, M. (1991). *Islands in the street: Gangs in American urban society*. University of California Press.

Sarda, D. (2013). Women's rights in the post-revolutionary Middle East. *Middle East Policy, 20*(1), 72–89.

Schiller, H. (1976). *Communication and cultural domination*. ME Sharpe.

Schimmel, A. (1982). Women in mystical Islam. *Women's Studies International Forum, 5*(2), 145–151.

Schimmel, A. (1992). *Islam: An introduction*. State University of New York Press.

Schirrmacher, T. (2020). *Human rights and the separation of religion and state*. Wipf and Stock Publishers.

Schmidt, E. (2013). From the cold war to the war on terror, 1991–2010. In *Foreign intervention in Africa: From the cold war to the war on terror* (pp. 193–226). Cambridge University Press.

Scholars at Risk. (2018). *University of Washington PhD student detained in Egypt*. Scholars at Risk. https://www.scholarsatrisk.org/2018/06/university-of-washington-phd-student-detained-in-egypt/

Schuessler, A. A. (2000). Expressive voting. *Rationality and Society, 4*(2–3), 91–144.

Schulhofer, S. (1998). *Unwanted sex: The culture of intimidation and the failure of law*. Harvard University Press.

Schultz, K. A. (2001). Looking for audience costs. *Journal of Conflict Resolution, 45*, 32–60.

Schwartz, S. J., Luyckx, K., & Vignoles, V. L. (Eds.). (2011). Conceptions and measurement. In *Handbook of identity theory and research* (pp. 249–266). Springer.

Segal, L. (2010). Genders: Deconstructed, reconstructed, still on the move. In M. Wetherell & C. T. Mohanty (Eds.), *The SAGE handbook of identities* (pp. 321–338). SAGE Publications.

Sehlikoglu, S. (2018). Revisited: Muslim Women's agency and feminist anthropology of the Middle East. *Contemporary Islam, 12*, 73–92.

Selim, G. M. (2015). Egypt under SCAF and the Muslim Brotherhood: The triangle of counter-revolution. *Arab Studies Quarterly, 37*(2), 177–199.

Sen, A. (1974). *Resources, values, and development*. Harvard University Press.

Sen, A. (1979a). *Development as freedom*. Oxford University Press.

Sen, A. (1979b). *Poverty and famines: An essay on entitlement and deprivation*. Oxford University Press.

Sen, A. K. (1979). Informational analysis of moral principles. In R. Harrison (Ed.), *Rational action* (pp. 115–132). Cambridge University Press.

Sen, A. K. (1982). Liberty as control: An appraisal. *Midwest Studies in Philosophy, 7*, 207–221.

Sen, A. K. (1985a). Well-being agency and freedom: The Dewey lectures 1984. *Journal of Philosophy, 82*(4), 169–221.
Sen, A. K. (1985b). *Commodities and capabilities*. Elsevier.
Sen, A. K. (1987). The standard of living. In A. Sen, J. Muellbauer, R. Kanbur, K. Hart, & B. Williams (Eds.), *The standard of living: The tanner lectures on human values*. Cambridge University Press.
Sen, A. K. (1988). The concept of development. In H. Chenery & T. N. Srinivasen (Eds.), *The handbook of development economics* (Vol. 1). Elsevier Publishers.
Sen, A. K. (1990). Justice: Means versus freedoms. *Philosophy and Public Affairs, 19*, 107–121.
Sen, A. K. (1992). *Inequality reexamined*. Harvard University Press.
Sen, A. K. (1993). Capability and well-being. In A. Sen & M. Nussbaum (Eds.), *The quality of life* (pp. 30–53). Clarendon Press.
Sen, A. K. (1995). Gender inequality and theories of justice. In M. Nussbaum & J. Glover (Eds.), *Women, culture and development: A study of human capabilities* (pp. 259–273). Clarendon Press.
Sen, A. K. (1997). Maximization and the act of choice. *Econometrica, 65*(4), 745–779.
Sen, A. K. (1999). *Development as freedom*. Knopf Press.
Sen, A. K. (2000). Consequential evaluation and practical reasons. *The Journal of Philosophy, XCVII*(9), 477–502.
Sesardic, N. (2010). Race: A social destruction of a biological concept. *Biology and Philosophy, 25*, 143–162.
Shaarawi, H. (1986). *The Harem years: The memoirs of an Egyptian feminist* (Translated and introduced by M. Badran). The Feminist Press.
Shafik, D. (1945). *Tatawur al-Nahda al-nissai'iya fi Misr* [The development of the renaissance of women in Egypt] (A. Ibrahim, Trans.). Maktabat al-Tawakul.
Shafik, D. (1953). *al-Kitab al-Abiyad li huquq al-mar'ah al-siyasiyah* [The white book on the political rights of women]. Maktabat al-Tawakul.
Shafiq, N. (1953a). *Women and politics in the Middle East*. Al-Ahram Press.
Shafiq, N. (1953b). Women's rights in the Arab World. *Middle East Journal, 7*(1), 45–58.
Shafiq, D. [1956] (2004). Islam and the constitutional rights of woman. In M. Badran & M. Cooke (Eds.), *Opening the gates* (pp. 352–357). Indiana University Press.
Shaikh, S. (2009). In search of "Al-Insān": Sufism, Islamic law, and gender. *Journal of the American Academy of Religion, 77*(4), 781–822.
Shaikh, S. (2011). Morality, justice and gender: Reading Muslim tradition on reproductive choices. In Tamale, S. (Ed.), *African sexualities: A reader* (pp. 340–358). Pambazuka Press.
Shamsy, A., & Coulson, N. J. (2022). Sharīah. Encyclopedia Britannica. https://www.britannica.com/topic/Shariah/Development-of-different-schools-of-law
Shapiro, G. K. (2014). Abortion law in Muslim-majority countries: An overview of the Islamic discourse with policy implications. *Health, Policy and Planning, 29*, 483–494.
Sharabi, H. (1988). *Neopatriarchy: A theory of distorted change in Arab society*. Oxford University Press.
Sharawi-Lanfranchi, S. (2015a). A Wafdist ministry. In *Casting off the veil: The life of Huda Shaarawi, Egypt's first feminist* (pp. 106–122). I. B. Tauris.
Sharawi-Lanfranchi, S. (2015b). International feminism and the EFU. In *Casting off the veil: The life of Huda Shaarawi, Egypt's first feminist* (pp. 59–78). I. B. Tauris.
Shariati, A. (1981). *Capitalism wakes up* (M. Mohseni, Trans.). Ministry of Islamic Guidance.
Shariati, A. (1986). What is to be done? In F. Rajaee (Ed.), *The enlightenment thinkers and an Islamic renaissance*. Institute for Research and Islamic Studies.
Shenker, J. (2011). Egyptian vote on constitution reveals deep divisions. *The Guardian*. Retrieved December 11, 2018, from https://www.theguardian.com/world/2011/mar/18/egypt-constitution-vote-divisons

Shirrmacher, C. (2020). Leaving Islam. In D. Enstedt, G. Larsson, & T. Mantsinen, (Eds.), *Handbook of leaving religion* (pp. 81–98). Brill.

Shklar, J. N. (1991). *American citizenship: The quest for inclusion*. Harvard University Press.

Siddiqui, D. (2020). Egypt jails women for two years over TikTok videos – Court sentences Haneen Hossam, Mowada al-Adham and three others for 'violating public morals'. *The Guardian*. https://www.theguardian.com/world/2020/jul/27/egypt-jails-women-for-two-years-over-tiktok-videos

Siddiqui, K. (2012). Developing countries' experience with neoliberalism and globalization. *Research in Applied Economics*, *4*(4), 12–37.

Sigler, J. (2010). Engaging the Middle East: Napoleon's invasion of Egypt. *History: Reviews of New Books*, *38*(2), 40–44.

Sika, N. (2012). On step forward, two steps back? Egyptian women within the confines of authoritarianism. *Arab Women Arab Spring*, *13*(5), 91–100.

Simbrunner, P., & Schlegelmilch, B. B. (2017). Moral licensing: A culture-moderated meta-analysis. *Management Review Quarterly*, *67*, 201–225.

Singh, K. R. (1981). Egyptian non-alignment. *International Studies*, *20*(1–2), 315–336.

Siraj, A. (2011). Meanings of modesty and the hijab amongst Muslim women in Glasgow, Scotland. *Gender, Place and Culture*, *18*, 716–731.

Siraj, A. (2012). 'I don't want to taint the name of Islam': The influence of religion on the lives of Muslim lesbians. *Journal of Lesbian Studies*, *16*(4), 449–467.

Siwa Live. (2018). *Traditional costumes of the women in Siwa* [Blog]. Siwa Live. https://siwalive.blogspot.com/2018/11/traditional-costumes-of-women-in-siwa.html

Skeggs, B. (Ed.). (1995). *Feminist cultural theory: Process and production*. Manchester University Press.

Slininger, S. (2013). *Veiled women: Hijab, religion, and cultural practice* (pp. 69–78). Economics Intelligence Unit, EUI. https://www.eiu.edu/historia/Slininger2014.pdf

Sloan, L. (2011). Women's oppression or choice? On American's views on wearing the Hijab. *Affilia: Journal of Women and Social Work*, *26*(2), 218–221.

Smart, C. (1996). Desperately seeking post-heterosexual woman. In J. Holland & L. Adkins (Eds.), *Sex, sensibility and the gendered body*. Macmillan.

Smith, A. (1759) [1982]. *The theory of moral sentiments*. Liberty.

Smith, E. R. (1999). Affective and cognitive implications of a group becoming part of the self: New models of prejudice and of the self-concept. In D. Abams & M. A. Hogg (Eds.), *Social identity and social cognition* (pp. 183–196). Blackwell.

Smith, J. (1979). Women in Islam: Equity, equality, and the search for the natural order. *Journal of the American Academy of Religion*, *47*(4), 517–537.

Smith, L. T. (1999). *Decolonizing methodologies: Research and indigenous people*. Zed Books Ltd.

Smith, P. B. (2011). Cross-cultural perspectives on identity: The role of context and culture in shaping our understanding of self. In S. J. Schwartz, K. Luyckx, & V. L. Vignoles (Eds.), *Handbook of identity theory and research* (pp. 249–276). Springer.

Sobki, A. (1978a). *Islamic family law*. Brill.

Sobki, S. (1978b). Women and social change in Egypt. *Middle East Journal*, *32*(2), 201–211.

Sobki, A. (1986). *Al-haraka al-nisaa'iya fi misr ma bayna al-thawratayn 1919–1952* [*The women's movement in Egypt between the two revolutions 1919–1952*]. General Egyptian Book Organisation.

Soliman, S. (2012). Is politics in Egypt merely a struggle for power? The revolution showed that there can be more to politics than Machiavellian self-interest. *Al-Ahram Online*. https://english.ahram.org.eg/NewsContentP/4/56740/Opinion/Is-politics-in-Egypt-merely-a-struggle-for-power-.aspx

Soltan, M. (2018). The world has forgotten Egypt's Rabaa Massacre. I haven't. *The Washington Post*. https://www.washingtonpost.com/news/democracy-post/wp/2018/08/14/the-world-has-forgotten-egypts-rabaa-massacre-i-cant/

Somers, M. R. (1994). The narrative constitution of identity: A relational and network approach. *Theory and Society, 23*(5), 605–649.
Sookhdeo, P. (2006). Issues of interpreting the Koran and Hadith. *Connections, 5*(3), 57-82.
Sovacool, B. J., Axsen, J., & Sorrell, S. (2018). Promoting novelty, rigor, and style in energy social science: Towards codes of practice for appropriate methods and research design. *Energy Research and Social Science, 45*, 12–42.
Spark, C., & Cox, R. (2019). Mothering and the everyday work of organising the work of the home: Reflections on time, economy and value. *Australian Feminist Studies, 34*(101), 117–131.
Spark, C., & Cox, J. (2020). Gender, political representation and symbolic capital: How some women politicians succeed. *Third World Quarterly, 40*(7), 1227–1245.
Sparkes, A. C. (1996). The fatal flaw: A narrative of the fragile body-self. *Qualitative Inquiry, 2*(4), 463–494.
Sparkes, A. C. (2000). Autoethnography and narratives of self: Reflections on criteria in action. *Sociology of Sport Journal, 17*, 21–43.
Spears, R. (2011). Group identities: The social identity perspective. In S. J. Schwartz, K. Luyckx, & V. L. Vignoles (Eds.), *Handbook of identity theory and research* (pp. 201–224). Springer.
Specia, M. (2017). Who are Sufi Muslims and why do some extremists hate them? *The New York Times*. https://www.nytimes.com/2017/11/24/world/middleeast/sufi-muslim-explainer.html
Specia, M. (2018). Egypt sentences Lebanese tourist to 8 years in prison for Facebook video. *The New York Times*. Retrieved January 25, 2018, from https://www.nytimes.com/2018/07/07/world/africa/egypt-sentences-lebanese-tourist.html
Spencer, H. (1851). *Social statistics*. Chapman.
Spencer, H. (1963). *Education: Intellectual, moral, and physical*. Littlefield, Adams.
Speak, G. C. (1994). Can the subaltern speak? In P. Williams & L. Chrisman (Eds.), *Colonial discourse and post-colonial theory: A reader*. Harvester Wheatsheaf.
Spradley, J. P. (1979a). Ethnography and culture. In *The ethnographic interview* (pp. 3–16). Waveland Press Inc.
Spradley, J. P. (1979b). Part I: Ethnographic research. In *The ethonographic interview* (pp. 3–40). Holt, Rinehart and Winston.
Springborg, R. (1989a). *Mubarak's Egypt: Fragmentation of the political order*. Westview Press.
Springborg, R. (1989b). Mubarak, the political elite, and the changing political economy. In *Mubarak's Egypt: Fragmentation of the political order* (pp. 19–41). Westview Press.
Springborg, R. (2003). An evaluation of the political system at the end of the millennium. In R. El-Ghonemy (Ed.), *Egypt in the twenty-first century. Challenges for development* (pp. 183–198). Routledge.
Sreberny-Mohammadi, A. (1997). The many faces of cultural imperialism. In P. Golding & P. Harris (Eds.), *Beyond cultural imperialism: Globalization, communication & the new international order* (pp. 49–68). SAGE Publications.
Steding, W. (2014). Jimmy Carter's just peace in the Middle East. In *Presidential faith and foreign policy. Palgrave studies in religion, politics, and policy* (pp. 77–85). Palgrave Macmillan.
Stephens, W. (1972). A cross-cultural study of modesty. *Behavior Science Notes, 7*, 1–28.
Stewart, A. J., & Ostrove, J. M. (1993). Social class, social change, and gender. *Psychology of Women Quarterly, 17*, 475–497.
Stillman, Y. K. (2003). Arab dress: A short history form the dawn of Islam to modern times. In N. A. Stillman (Ed.), *Themes in Islamic studies* (2nd ed.). Brill Publishers.
Stokke, O. (2013). Core issues and state of the art. In *Aid and political conditionality* (pp. 1–87). Routledge.
Stowasser, B. (1996). *Women in the Qur'an, traditions, and interpretation*. Oxford University Press.

Stowasser, B. (1998). Gender issues in contemporary Qur'anic interpretation. In Y. Y. Haddad & J. L. Esposito (Eds.), *Islam, gender, and social change* (pp. 30–44). Oxford University Press.
Stryker, S. (1980). *Symbolic interactionism: A social structural vision*. Benjamin/Cummings.
Stryker, S., & Burke, P. J. (2000). The past, present, and future of an identity theory. *Social Psychology Quarterly, 63*(4), 284–297.
Sullivan, D. J., & Abdel-Kotob, S. (1999). The Muslim brotherhood. In *Islam in contemporary Egypt: Civil society vs. the state* (pp. 41–70). Lynne Rienner Publishers.
Sullivan, M. L. (1989). *Getting paid: Youth crime and work in the inner city*. Cornell University Press.
Susilastuti, D. H. (2003). *Women's education, work and autonomy: The Egyptian case*. [PhD dissertation, Florida State University Libraries].
Swaroop, V. (2016). *World Bank's experience with structural reforms for growth and development* [MFM Discussion Paper No. 11]. World Bank Group. https://documents1.worldbank.org/curated/en/826251468185377264/pdf/105822-NWP-ADD-SERIES-MFM-Discussion-Paper-11-PUBLIC.pdf
Tabassum, N., & Nayak, B. S. (2021). Gender stereotypes and their impact on women's career progressions from a managerial perspective. *IIM Kozhikode Society & Management Review, 10*(2), 192–208.
Tadros, M. (2014). *What does women dancing in public tell us about the pulse of the citizenry during Egypt's constitutional referendum?* [Blog Post]. Institute of Development Studies: Participation, Power and Social Change. Retrieved December 11, 2018, from https://participationpower.wordpress.com/2014/01/20/what-does-women-dancing-in-public-tell-us-about-the-pulse-of-the-citizenry-during-egypts-constitutional-referendum/
Taha, S. M. (1986). *Ahmed Orabi and his role in Egyptian political life*. General Egyptian Book Organization.
Tajfel, H. (1978). *Differentiation between social groups: Studies in intergroup relations*. Academic Press.
Tajfel, H. (1981). *Human groups and social categories: Studies in social psychology*. Cambridge University Press.
Tajfel, H., & Turner, J. (1979). An integrative theory of intergroup conflict. In W. G. Austin & S. Worchel (Eds.), *The social psychology of intergroup relations* (pp. 33–47). Brooks/Cole.
Talhami, G. (1996). *The mobilization of Muslim women in Egypt*. University Press of Florida.
Tamale, S. (2005). Eroticism, sexuality, and "women's secrets" among the Baganda: A critical analysis. *Feminist Africa, 5*, 9–36.
Tamale, S. (2011). Researching and theorizing sexualities in Africa. In *African sexualities: A reader* (pp. 11–36). Pambazuka Press.
Tandon, Y. (2008). *Ending aid dependence* (pp. 16–38). Fahamu Books.
Taraki, L. (1996). Jordanian Islamists and the agenda for women: Between discourse and practice. *Middle Eastern Studies, 32*(1), 140–158.
TARGET. (2006). *Scholars conference at Al Azhar, Cairo – The breakthrough*. http://w3i.targetnehberg.de/HP02_target/u12_alAzha_kairo/index.php?p=gelehrtenkonferenz
Tarlo, E., & Moors, A. (Eds.). (2013). *Islamic fashion and anti-fashion: New perspectives from Europe and North America*. A&C Black.
Taylor, C. (1985). Language and human nature. In C. Taylor (Ed.), *Human agency and language philosophical papers*. Cambridge University Press.
Temples, P. (1959). *Bantu philosophy*. Présence Africaine.
Terebessy, L. (2021). *Muhammad Abduh and the reform of Muslim education*. Independently Published.
The Civil Code. (2020). *The civil code of the Arab Republic of Egypt – In case of any discrepancy, the Arabic version of this law shall prevail*. Human Rights Library University of Minnesota. http://hrlibrary.umn.edu/research/Egypt/Civil%20Law.pdf

The Holy Bible, King James Version. (1769). Cambridge edition. *King James Bible Online*. Retrieved January 8, 2019, from www.kingjamesbibleonline.org
The Qur'an. (2005). M. A. S. Abdel Haleem (Trans.). Oxford University Press.
The Threshold Society. (2022). *Women and Sufism*. Sufism. https://sufism.org/sufism/writings-on-sufism/women-and-sufism-by-camille-adams-helminski-2
The Week. (2019). What is salafism. *The Week*. https://www.theweek.co.uk/world-news/6073/what-is-salafism-and-should-we-be-worried-by-it
Thomas, G. (2017a). Methodology Part 2: The design frame. In *How to do your research project: A guide for students* (3rd ed., pp. 137–198). SAGE Publications.
Thomas, G. (2017b). The right tools for the job: Data gathering. In *How to do your research project: A guide for students* (3rd ed., pp. 199–242). SAGE Publications.
Thomas, L. M. (1996). 'Ngaitana (I will circumcise myself)': The gender and generational politics of the 1956 ban on clitoridectomy in Meru, Kenya. *Gender and History*, *8*(3), 338–363.
Thompson, S. C. (1981). Will it hurt less if I can control it? A complex answer to a simple question. *Psychological Bulletin*, *90*, 89–101.
Thomson, M., Kentikelenis, A., & Stubbs, T. (2017). Structural adjustment programmes adversely affect vulnerable populations: A systematic-narrative review of their effect on child and maternal health. *Public Health Review*, *38*, 13.
Thussu, D. (Ed.). (1998). *Electronic empires: Global media and local resistance*. Arnold Publishing.
Tignor, R. L. (1966). Chapter X: Administrative change: Education and public health. In *Modernization and British colonial rule in Egypt, 1882–1914* (pp. 319–357). Princeton University Press.
Tignor, R. L. (1996). *Colonial modernization and British rule in Egypt, 1882–1914*. Princeton University Press.
Tikkanen, A. (2014). Fu'ād I. Encyclopedia Britannica. https://www.britannica.com/biography/Fuad-I.
Time. (1960). United Arab Republic: The house of obedience. *Time Magazine*. http://content.time.com/time/subscriber/article/0,33009,894721,00.html
Tingley, D. (2010). Donors and domestic politics: Political influences on foreign aid effort. *The Quarterly Review of Economics and Finance*, *50*(1), 40–49.
Tipler, C., & Ruscher, J. B. (2014). Agency's role in dehumanization: Non-human metaphors of out-groups. *Social and Personality Psychology Compass*, *8*(5), 214–228.
Tolino, S. (2018). Gender equality in the Egyptian constitution: From 1923 to 2014. *Oriente Moderno*, *98*(2), 140–165.
Tomilson, J. (2011). Globalization and cultural identity. In S. J. Schwartz, K. Luyckx, & V. L. Vignoles (Eds.), *Handbook of identity theory and research* (pp. 269–277). Springer Science+Business Media.
Torungolu, G. (2016). Feminism in Egypt: New alliances, old debates. In *Origins: Current events in historical perspective*. Ohio State University.
Torunoglu, S. (2016). *The politics of gender and the modern Egyptian state*. Palgrave Macmillan.
Toubia, N. (1994). Female circumcision as a public health issue. *The New England Journal of Medicine*, *331*(11), 712–716.
Trager, E. (2010). The Cairo agenda. *The New Republic*. https://newrepublic.com/article/79430/mubarak-steady-egypt-elections
Tran, M. (2006). Australian Muslim leader compares uncovered women to exposed meat. *The Guardian*. https://www.theguardian.com/world/2006/oct/26/australia.marktran
Triandis, H. C. (1993). The contingency model in cross-cultural perspective. In S. A. Wright & L. H. Rosenfeld (Eds.), *Organizational behavior in international context* (pp. 123–139). Westview Press.

Triandis, H. C. (1994). Theoretical and methodological approaches to the study of collectivisim and individualism. In U. Kim, H. C. Triandis, C. Kagitcibasi, S. C. Choi, & G. Yoon (Eds.), *Individualism and collectivism: Theory, method, and application* (pp. 41–51). SAGE Publications.

Triandis, H. C. (2001). Individualism–collectivism and personality. *Journal of Personality, 69*, 907–924.

Triandis, H. C., Bontempo, R., Betancourt, H., Bond, M., Leung, K., & Brenes, A. (1986). The measurement of ethnic aspects of individualism and collectivism across cultures. *Australian Journal of Psychology, 38*, 257–267.

Trueblood, L. A. (2000). Female genital mutilation: A discussion of international human rights instruments, cultural sovereignty and dominance theory. *Denver Journal of International Law and Policy, 28*(4), 437–442.

Tucker, J. (1985). Private and public life: Women and the growth of the state. In *Women in nineteenth-century Egypt* (pp. 102–130). Cambridge University Press.

Turner, J. C. (1982). Towards a cognitive redefinition. In H. Tajfel (Ed.), *Social identity and intergroup relations* (pp. 15–40). Cambridge University Press.

UN News. (2011). *Egypt's 'key role' in Middle East peace must be preserved in any transition – Ban Ki-Moon*. UN News. Retrieved January 8, 2019, from https://news.un.org/en/story/2011/02/366322-egypts-key-role-middle-east-peace-must-be-preserved-any-transition-ban

UN Women. (2018). *Ending violence against women (EVAW): Country profile – Egypt*. UN Women – Egypt Country Office. http://egypt.unwomen.org/en/digital-library/publications/2018/05/ending-violence-against-women-gender-profile-egypt-may-2018

UNDP. (2018a). *Egypt gender justice and the law: Assessment of laws affecting gender equality and protection against gender-based violence*. United Nations Development Report and UN Women. Retrieved April 29, 2022, from https://arabstates.unwomen.org/sites/default/files/Field%20Office%20Arab%20States/Attachments/Publications/2018/Gender%20Justices%20and%20The%20Law%20in%20the%20Arab%20Region/Country%20Assessments/Egypt%20Country%20Assessment%20-%20English.pdf

UNDP. (2018b). Protection from domestic violence and sexual violence. In *Egypt gender justice: Assessment of laws affecting gender equality and protection against gender-based violence* (pp. 13–23). United Nations Development Program. https://www.eg.undp.org/content/egypt/en/home/library/democratic_governance/egypt-gender-justice.html

UNESCO. (2018). *Education and literacy*. UNESCO. http://uis.unesco.org/en/country/eg?theme=education-and-literacy

UNFPA. (2018). *Gender-based violence in Egypt*. United Nations Population Fund. https://egypt.unfpa.org/en/node/22540

UNGA. (1960). *Declaration on the granting of independence to colonial countries and peoples, Resolution 1514 (XV)*. http://www.un.org/en/decolonization/declaration.shtml

UNHCR. (2011). *Driven by desperation: Transactional sex as a survival strategy in Port-au-Prince IDP camps*. United Nations High Commissioner for Refugees. https://www.urd.org/IMG/pdf/SGBV-UNHCR-report2_FINAL.pdf

UNICEF. (2015). *Female genital mutilation: A statistical overview and exploration of the dynamics of change*. https://data.unicef.org/wpcontent/uploads/2015/12/FGMC_Lo_res_Final_26.pdf

UNICEF. (2016). *Female genital mutilation/cutting: A global concern*. https://www.unicef.org/media/files/FGMC_2016_brochure_final_UNICEF_SPREAD.pdf

UNICEF. (2017). *UNICEF's data work on FGM/C*. https://data.unicef.org/resources/dataset/fgm/

UNICEF. (2018). *Female genital mutilation. UNICEF DATA: Monitoring the situation of children and women*. Retrieved December 15, 2018, from https://data.unicef.org/topic/child-protection/female-genital-mutilation/

UNICEF. (2020). *Female genital mutilation in Egypt: Recent trends and projections.* UNICEF. https://data.unicef.org/resources/female-genital-mutilation-in-egypt-recent-trends-and-projections/

UniPage. (2020). *Cairo University.* UniPage.net. https://www.unipage.net/en/84/cairo_university

United Nations. (1995). *Report of the fourth world conference on women, Beijing* [Sales No. E.96.IV.13; chap. I, resolution 1, annex I]. United Nations Publication. https://www.un.org/womenwatch/daw/beijing/pdf/Beijing%20full%20report%20E.pdf

United Nations. (2005). *Violence against women in Egypt.* United Nations in partnership with the Egyptian Center for Women's Rights. Retrieved January 25, 2019, from http://www.un.org/womenwatch/daw/vaw/ngocontribute/Egyptian%20Center%20for%20Women_s%20Rights.pdf

United Nations: Women Watch. (2008). *Ending female genital mutilation* [Sales No. E/CN.6/2008/L.2/Rev/1]. United Nations Publications. http://www.un.org/womenwatch/daw/csw/csw52/AC_resolutions/Final%20L2%20ending%20female%20genital%20mutilation%20-%20advance%20unedited.pdf

Universal Declaration of Human Rights. (2015). *Articles 2 and 5.* http://www.un.org/en/udhrbook/pdf/udhr_booklet_en_web.pdf

University Center for International Studies. (2021). *The grand mufti.* University Center for International Studies, University of Pittsburgh. https://www.ucis.pitt.edu/global/sites/default/files/curriculum_materials/contributed/TheGrandMufti.pdf

UNPO. (2018). *Amazigh.* Unrepresented Nations and Peoples Organization. https://unpo.org/members/20883

UNSCR. (1973). *Resolution 344: Peace conference in the Middle East.* United Nations Security Council Resolution. http://unscr.com/en/resolutions/doc/344

Uthman, I. O. (2011). A re-reading of the Egyptian Zaynab al-Ghazzali, the Muslim Brotherhood and the Islamic feminist movement in contemporary society. *International Journal of Sociology and Anthropology, 3*(11), 407–415.

Utych, S. M. (2018). How dehumanization influences attitudes toward immigrants. *Research Quarterly, 71*(2), 440–452.

Valassopoulos, A. (2010). Arab feminisms: Review article. *Feminist Theory, 11*(2), 215–221.

Valentine, G. (2007). Theorizing and researching intersectionality: A challenge for feminist geography. *The Professional Geographer, 59*(1), 10–21.

van Dijk, T. A. (1993). Principles of critical discourse analysis. *Discourse & Society, 4*, 249–283.

van Nieuwkerk, K. (2021). 'Uncovering the self': Religious doubts, spirituality and unveiling in Egypt. *Religions, 12*, 1–20.

van Teijlingen, E. R., & Hundley, V. (2001). The importance of pilot studies. *Social Research Update, 35*, ISSN: 1360-7898.

Vasileiou, K., Barnett, J., & Thorpe, S. (2018). Characterising and justifying sample size sufficiency in interview-based studies: Systematic analysis of qualitative health research over a 15-year period. *BMC Medical Research Methodology, 18*(148), 1–18.

Vatikiotis, P. J. (1991). Egypt for the Egyptians, 1952–1981: Nasser and Sadat. In *The history of modern Egypt: From Muhammad Ali to Mubarak* (pp. 256–281). Johns Hopkins University Press.

Vattimo, G. (1988) [1985]. *The end of modernity: Nihilism and hermeneutics in postmodern culture* (J. R. Snyder, Trans.). Johns Hopkins University Press.

Verme, P., Milanovic, B., Al-Shawarby, S., El Tawila, S., Gadallah, M., & El-Majeed, A. A. (2014). *Inside inequality in the Arab Republic of Egypt: Facts and perceptions across people, time and space.* International Bank for Reconstruction and Development/The World Bank.

Vignoles, V. (2017). Identity: Personal and social. In K. Deaux & M. Snyder (Eds.), *Oxford handbook of personality and social psychology* (2nd ed., pp. 289–316). Oxford University Press.

Vignoles, V. L., Chryssochoou, X., & Breakwell, G. M. (2001). Narratives of identity in social representations of history: Content and structure. *British Journal of Social Psychology*, *40*(4), 479–498.

Voll, J. O., & Sonn, T. (2009). *Political Islam*. Oxford Bibliographies. https://www.oxfordbibliographies.com/view/document/obo-9780195390155/obo-9780195390155-0063.xml

wa Thiong'o, N. (1988). *Decolonizing the mind: The politics of language in African literature*. Heinemann.

Waded, A. (1999). *Qu'ran and women: Rereading the sacred text from a woman's perspective* (pp. 94–104). Oxford University Press.

Wagdy, W. (2014). Palestinian liberation is ingrained into the Egyptian revolution. The Socialist Worker. https://socialistworker.co.uk/art/38576/Palestinian+liberation+is+ingrained+into+the+Egyptian+revolution

Wagner, W., Sen, R., Permanadeli, R., & Howarth, C. S. (2012). The veil and Muslim women's identity: Cultural pressures and resistance to stereotyping. *Culture & Psychology*, *18*(4), 521–541.

Walby, S. (1990). *Theorizing patriarchy*. Basil Blackwell.

Walby, S. (1996). *Gender transformations*. Routledge.

Walby, S. (2020). Varieties of gender regimes. *Social Politics: International Studies in Gender, State & Society*, *27*(3), 414–431.

Walsh, D. (2020). The 22-year-old force behind Egypt's growing #MeToo movement. *The New York Times*. https://www.nytimes.com/2020/10/02/world/middleeast/egypt-metoo-sexual-harassment-ashraf.html

Waterbury, J. (1983). *The Egypt of Nasser and Sadat: The political economy of two regimes*. Princeton University Press.

Weaver, J. D., & McCarthy, P. (2013). *Gender and society in contemporary Egypt*. University of Texas Press.

Weber, C. (2008). Between nationalism and feminism: The eastern women's congresses of 1930 and 1932. *Journal of Middle East Women's Studies*, *4*(1), 83–106.

Weinbaum, M. (1985). Egypt's "Infitah" and the politics of US economic assistance. *Middle Eastern Studies*, *21*(2), 206–222.

Wentworth, P. A., & Peterson, B. E. (2001). Crossing the line: Case studies of identity development in first-generation college women. *Journal of Adult Development*, *8*, 9–21.

Whisnant, R. (2007). A woman's body is like a foreign country: Thinking about national and bodily sovereignty. In P. DesAutels & R. Whisnant (Eds.), *Global feminist ethics* (pp. 155–176). Rowman and Littlefield.

WHO. (2018). *Female genital mutilation* [Fact sheet]. http://www.who.int/news-room/factsheets/detail/female-genital-mutilation

Wilkinson, S., & Kitzinger, C. (Eds.). (1993). *Heterosexuality: A feminism and psychology reader*. SAGE Publications.

Williams, J. A. (1979). A return to the veil in Egypt. *Middle East Review*, *11*(3), 49–54.

Williams, T., & Kornblum, W. (1985). *Growing up poor*. Lexington Books.

Wilson, E. K. (2017). The socio-political dynamics of secularism and epistemological injustice in global justice theory and practice. *European Societies*, *19*(5), 529–550.

Witcher, R. S. (2005). *The effects of western feminist ideology on Muslim feminists* (pp. 26–43). The NPS Institutional Archive.

Withcher, D. (2005a). *Gender and power in the third world*. Cambridge University Press.

Withcher, T. (2005b). The political economy of women's rights in Egypt. *Journal of Women's History*, *17*(4), 45–70.

Wong, D. B. (1984). *Moral relativity*. University of California Press.

Wong, D. B. (1986). On moral realism without foundations. *The Southern Journal of Philosophy*, *24*, 95–113.

Wong, D. B. (1996). Pluralistic relativism. *Midwest Studies in Philosophy: Moral Concepts*, *20*, 378–399.

Wong, D. B. (2006). *Natural moralities: A defense of pluralistic relativism*. Oxford University Press.
Wood, E. M. (1988). Capitalism and human emancipation. *New Left Review, 167*(January–February), 1–21.
Woodward, K. (2002). *Understanding identity*. Arnold.
World Bank. *Unemployment, total (% of total labor force) (modeled ILO estimate) – Egypt, Arab Republic*. World Bank. https://data.worldbank.org/indicator/SL.UEM.TOTL.ZS?locations=EG
World Bank. (2018). *Egypt's economic outlook – October 2018*. World Bank. https://www.worldbank.org/en/country/egypt/publication/economic-outlook-october-2018
World Bank. (2019a). *Labor force participation rate, female (% of female population ages 15–64) – Egypt, Arab Republic*. World Bank Data. https://data.worldbank.org/indicator/SL.TLF.ACTI.FE.ZS?end=2019&locations=EG&start=1990&view=chart
World Bank. (2019b). *World Bank group to extend current strategy in Egypt to maintain momentum on reforms*. World Bank. https://www.worldbank.org/en/news/press-release/2019/04/30/world-bank-group-to-extend-current-strategy-in-egypt-to-maintain-momentum-on-reforms
World Bank. (2020). *GDP per capita (current US$) Egypt, Arab Republic*. World Bank. https://data.worldbank.org/indicator/NY.GDP.PCAP.CD?locations=EG
World Population Review. (2020). *Gini coefficient by country 2020*. World Population Review. https://worldpopulationreview.com/country-rankings/gini-coefficient-by-country
Wynn, L. L., & Hassanein, S. (2017). Hymenoplasty, virginity testing and the simulacrum of female respectability. *Signs: Journal of Women in Culture and Society, 42*, 893–917.
Yanow, D. (2007). Interpretation in policy analysis: On methods and practice. *Critical Policy Analysis, 1*(1), 110–122.
Yaqin, A. (2007). Islamic Barbie: The politics of gender and performativity. *Fashion Theory: The Journal of Dress, Body & Culture, 11*(2–3), 2–3.
Yeğenoğlu, M. (2003). Veiled fantasies: Cultural and sexual difference in the discourse of orientalism. In R. Lewis & S. Mills (Eds.), *Feminist postcolonial theory: A reader* (pp. 542–566). Routledge.
Yin, R. K. (1989). *Case study research*. SAGE Publications.
Yoon, B., Simpson, A., & Haag, C. (2010). Assimilation ideology: Critically examining underlying messages in multicultural literature. *Journal of Adolescent and Adult Literacy, 54*(2), 109–118.
Younes, R. (2020). *Egypt's denial of sexual orientations and gender identities: Ignoring LBT rights endangers people in time of COVID-19*. Human Rights Watch. https://www.hrw.org/news/2020/03/20/egypts-denial-sexual-orientation-and-gender-identity
Younis, M. (2007). Daughters of the nil: Evolution of feminism in Egypt. *Washington and Lee Journal of Civil and Social Justice, 13*(2), 463–490.
Yousef, H. (2011). Malak Hifni Nasif: Negotiations of a feminist agenda between the European and the colonial. *Journal of Middle East Women's Studies, 7*(1), 70–89.
Zaytoun, S. (1982). The role of women in rural development: The case of Egypt. *Development and Change, 13*(1), 43–58.
Zeghal, M. (1999). Religion and politics in Egypt: The Ulema of Al-Azhar, radical Islam, and the state (1952–94). *International Journal of Middle East Studies, 31*(3), 371–399.
Zeidan, A. (2018). *Aminah al-Sai'd*. Encyclopedia Britannica. https://www.britannica.com/biography/Aminah-al-Said#ref794928
Zeiger, D. (2008). That (Afghan) girl! Ideology unveiled in National Geographic. In J. Heath (Ed.), *The veil: Women writers on its history, lore, and politics* (pp. 266–280). University of California Press.
Zubaida, S. (1989). *Islam, the people and the state: Political ideas and movements in the Middle East*. I.B. Tauris.
Zubair, M. (2019). *Opinion: If the hijab is such an 'oppressive tool', why do I feel so empowered?* The Bristol Cable. https://thebristolcable.org/2019/03/opinion-my-scarf-my-choice/

Printed in the USA
CPSIA information can be obtained
at www.ICGtesting.com
JSHW011759031224
74704JS00004B/108